SISTERS TO THE KING

SISTERS TO THE KING

The Tumultuous Lives of Henry VIII's
Sisters – Margaret of Scotland
and Mary of France

MARIA PERRY

André Deutsch

First published in Great Britain 1998
This paperback edition published 2002
Reprinted 2004 by

André Deutsch
an imprint of the
Carlton Publishing Group
20 Mortimer Street
London W1T 3JW

A catalogue record for this book is available from the British Library

ISBN 0-233-05090-6

Typeset by Derek Doyle & Associates
Printed in Great Britain by Mackays

Contents

For my friend John Pine
and in memory of
Haydn Davies and Kay Clayton

Acknowledgements

My thanks are due to the late Sir Geoffrey Elton for suggesting the topic and for sponsoring an application to the British Academy, which kindly provided some of the research funding; to Dr David Starkey for adding his sponsorship and for reading the manuscript; and to Dr Steven Gunn of Merton College, Oxford, Professor David Loades, Dr Michael Jones and especially Dr Nigel Ramsay, formerly Curator of the Cotton Manuscript, who edited the footnotes.

All the staff of the British Library deserve heartfelt thanks for their help throughout the difficult time during which they moved premises. Miss Janet Backhouse, Curator of Illuminated Manuscripts, and Mrs Patricia Basing, Curator of Manuscripts, gave unstintingly both of their time and of their expertise. I also thank the staff of the Kensington Library, the London Library, the Bodleian Library, Exeter University Library and Plymouth Central Library, and colleagues at the Institute of Historical Research, in particular Miss Frances Devereux, Dr Roger Metham, Dr George Bernard and Mr Donald Munro. Thank you too to Mrs Louise MacKenzie, who serves the North Library, although she is technically British Museum.

In Scotland Dr Rosalind Marshall, the Director of the Scottish National Portrait Gallery, was a tower of strength, while the staff of the National Library of Scotland, the Palace of Holyroodhouse, Edinburgh Castle and Stirling Castle could not have been kinder or more helpful. Mrs Wendy Morlcas, Head of the Classics Department at Manchester High School for Girls, checked my Latin. I could not have carried the project to completion without the personal encouragement of my agent, James Hale, and of Fiona MacDonald, Michael Kennedy, Bill Shepherd, Mr Philip Lawton, QC, Sister Wendy Beckett and the late Father Michael Hollings. Tom Rosenthal kick-started the project and the staff at André Deutsch took over valiantly when he retired. Mr C T Vance, formerly of the Queen's University, Belfast, arranged most interesting expeditions to Stirling, Flodden and Alnwick Castle.

THE HOUSE OF TUDOR

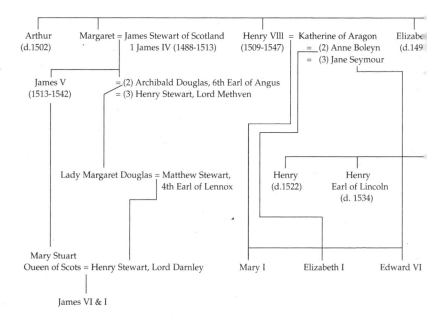

Arthur (d.1502)

Margaret = James Stewart of Scotland
1 James IV (1488-1513)

Henry Vlll = Katherine of Aragon
(1509-1547) = (2) Anne Boleyn
= (3) Jane Seymour

Elizabe
(d.149

James V (1513-1542)

= (2) Archibald Douglas, 6th Earl of Angus
= (3) Henry Stewart, Lord Methven

Lady Margaret Douglas = Matthew Stewart,
4th Earl of Lennox

Henry (d.1522)

Henry
Earl of Lincoln
(d. 1534)

Mary Stuart
Oueen of Scots = Henry Stewart, Lord Darnley

Mary I

Elizabeth I

Edward VI

James VI & I

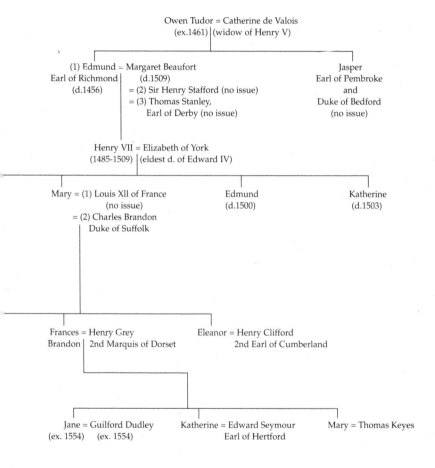

Owen Tudor = Catherine de Valois
(ex.1461) (widow of Henry V)

(1) Edmund = Margaret Beaufort
Earl of Richmond   (d.1509)
(d.1456)   = (2) Sir Henry Stafford (no issue)
                 = (3) Thomas Stanley,
                      Earl of Derby (no issue)

Jasper
Earl of Pembroke
and
Duke of Bedford
(no issue)

Henry VII = Elizabeth of York
(1485-1509) (eldest d. of Edward IV)

Mary = (1) Louis XII of France
              (no issue)
     = (2) Charles Brandon
            Duke of Suffolk

Edmund
(d.1500)

Katherine
(d.1503)

Frances = Henry Grey
Brandon   2nd Marquis of Dorset

Eleanor = Henry Clifford
           2nd Earl of Cumberland

Jane = Guilford Dudley
(ex. 1554)   (ex. 1554)

Katherine = Edward Seymour
            Earl of Hertford

Mary = Thomas Keyes

Introduction

Everyone knows Henry VIII had six wives. Few people realize he had two sisters – flesh and blood English princesses, who grew up to be the Queens of Scotland and France. They scandalized their brother and most of Europe in the process. While writing this book I have derived great pleasure from watching people's faces as they take in the unexpected information. The learned look superior; they know to whom one refers. The unlearned are amazed, though often deeply interested. They had thought of Henry VIII as an awesome Bluebeard, the fat man on the posters for Hampton Court Palace, devoted to feasting and wenching. The modest frown anxiously, trying to recall the Wars of the Roses and Henry VII's family tree, forgotten since the third form, and wasn't there something about a thornbush? It is to them, as well as to esoteric Tudor historians, that this narrative is addressed.

Elizabeth of York, Henry VIII's mother, was the oldest daughter of Edward IV. Henry VII married her after the Battle of Bosworth, when he is said to have retrieved the Crown of England from a thornbush, after defeating Richard III, Elizabeth's wicked uncle. Richard had murdered the Princes in the Tower, usurped the throne and after his wife, Queen Anne, died he contemplated marrying his niece, an act too horrible for the people of England to stomach. By contrast Henry Tudor, England's new King, had led an austere life, mostly in exile in France, where he had been brought up by his soldier uncle, Jasper Tudor, Earl of Pembroke. Henry married Elizabeth to strengthen his own claim to the throne. The marriage was approved, some say arranged, by the contracting parties' mothers, Edward IV's widow, Elizabeth Woodville, and Lady Margaret Beaufort, the redoubtable Countess of Richmond. Such marriages do not always turn into idylls of domestic happiness, but this one did.

Elizabeth of York was a glamorous creature. As a symbol of their union Henry VII commissioned the collar of the Order of the Garter, in which her emblem, the white rose, nestles peacefully at the centre of his own badge, the red rose of Lancaster, forming the heraldic device the Tudor rose. In 1488 at the Garter Feast on St George's Day, Elizabeth appeared at Windsor in a litter draped with cloth of gold and drawn by six white horses. Beside her was the King's mother. Both wore the robes of Ladies of the Garter. The Order's motto, '*Honi soit qui mal y pense*', summarized their moral values. The code of chivalry required them to praise and pray for their menfolk, turning a blind eye to indiscretions committed by their immediate kin.

Elizabeth was gentle, kind and a wonderful mother to the seven children she bore the King. Prince Arthur, their oldest son, died at fifteen, leaving the ten-year-old Henry heir to the throne. The couple's fourth child, Elizabeth, died at three, while Edmund, a babe in arms when our story begins, lived only a year. Katherine, the last Princess, survived a few weeks, but Margaret, Henry's older sister, was a sturdy, healthy child and Mary, his younger sister, was (judging from the number of pairs of shoes she wore out) lively and physically active from an early age. She was later to become an accomplished dancer, playing a leading part in court masques. A lock of her hair, preserved in the museum at Bury St Edmunds, is truly golden and not, as sometimes suggested in portraits or by fanciful biographers, the red-gold associated with other members of her family. In later life she may have helped it keep its colour with lye, an organic cosmetic much favoured by her niece, Elizabeth I.

The King paid for the children's upkeep from the Great Wardrobe, but the Queen also made contributions. Her Privy Purse Expenses show she had a clear understanding of her family's differing needs. As future Queen of Scotland, Margaret was encouraged in her passion for fine clothes. Henry, moody and mercurial, had his own fool, Goose, to coax him into a better humour if he sulked. Prince Arthur, as Prince of Wales, had a separate household and Council, but he often came to court. At Woodstock in 1497 the Milanese ambassador taken to meet Henry VII wrote, 'There also was the King's eldest son, Arthur Prince of

Wales, about eleven years of age, but taller than his years would warrant, of remarkable beauty and grace and very ready in speaking Latin.' On another occasion the ambassador visited the Queen and again found Prince Arthur present. At such audiences the King and Queen were always richly enthroned and robed in velvet or cloth of gold. Their children were brought up to observe full court ceremonial.

The younger children shared a household which was mainly based at Eltham Palace. In the account book it is 'My lord Prince's household', for Henry as a boy was its most important member. John Skelton taught Henry to read and write. The girls shared their brother's tutors, although they had separate attendants. Mary, being at a different educational level from Margaret and Henry, had her own schoolmaster. She wrote a better hand than her sister and may have learned to speak French early, as she was given a French companion, Jane Poppincourt, from the age of five. I suspect, however, that she never really got to grips with the grammar, even though John Palsgrave, who later taught her French, wrote a textbook so excellent that Henry VIII had it placed in all the schools in England.

It is called *L'Eclaircissment de la langue Francoyse*. If learned readers care to seek it out in the British Library, they can spend a wonderful afternoon practising Palsgrave's phonetics *sotto voce*. They will find French pronunciation has changed less since 1530 than English. Some of the useful phrases have a contemporary ring, '*Gardez-vous que cette gueppe ne vous picque*', for example, though sadly, 'I fumigate a place with sweet fumigation' and 'Strew your chamber with carpets against the King coming' are a little out of date.

I have read a great many more of Mary's holograph letters than are cited in the notes to this book. When she was in a panic, her handwriting deteriorated, but she obviously wrote as she spoke. The phrase 'I marvel much', which she may have picked up from her grandmother, indicates that she is standing on her dignity and some gem of sarcastic observation usually follows. Margaret's letters are querulous. Her spelling shows that, sent to Scotland at thirteen, she quickly adopted the accent. After her husband's death she was continuously involved in legal disputes as she battled to obtain the rightful income from her dower lands. Henry understood only that she owned substantial estates. He did not appreciate the difficulties of Scottish rent collection in a land infested with brigands and poachers, when dues were sometimes paid as a catch of salmon, or '400 brace of rabbits'. As Queen Dowager, Margaret had to read state documents. Faced with interminable paperwork, she frequently lapses into lawyers' jargon. Her concept of queenly honour was perhaps instilled into her by her grandmother and her father, shortly before she left Margaret Beaufort's palace at Collyweston on her epic journey to marry James IV. After she was widowed, Henry began to find Margaret's honour expensive. References to it generally prefaced a request for money to pay armies, hire bodyguards or purchase cloth of gold. Homesick for England for the greater part of her grown-up life, Margaret poured out her wounded feelings to Henry, to Wolsey, to Lord Dacre, Warden of the Marches, or to any compatriot who would sympathize, but she was a woman and none of them really trusted her. They read her letters for information, then pursued their own policies regardless of her advice. Henry underestimated her intelligence and her shrewd understanding of Scottish affairs, preferring to listen to her second husband, the Earl of Angus, even when she was estranged from him. This caused James V, who hated his stepfather, to resent interference by his uncle, the King of England, which wrecked Margaret's plans for her son, who by the logic of primogeniture had a legitimate place in the English line of succession.

When I began this book, I believed that by studying Henry's sisters chronologically, rather than separately, I might shed new light on their brother's complex and colourful personality. I had no idea how much material existed, nor how strongly the theme of the male succession would emerge. Procreative sex within marriage to assure the continuance of his dynasty seemed to Henry a royal and holy duty. He made a pilgrimage to Walsingham to achieve it, walking the last mile to the shrine barefoot. To this day Walsingham is associated with the Annunciation and childless couples go there to pray. Henry would have been amazed to think posterity considered him lustful or immoral.

That he died a cruel tyrant is true, but he had clear ideas about feminine virtue. His sister Margaret, who lived openly with her lover Henry Stewart, did not conform to them; his sister Mary did. Towards the end of his reign, Henry closed the London brothels, and penalties exacted from prostitutes who followed his armies were always severe. As a Renaissance ruler and a Christian prince the King saw nothing incongruous about executing the two women he believed had committed adultery. That Anne Boleyn had probably not was a tragedy, but her punishment served as a moral lesson to his court and to his people. Poor Anne Boleyn, who believed so fervently in the reformed religion and who tried so hard not to go the way of her sister Mary by becoming a royal wife instead of a royal mistress. Mistresses were the prerogative of kings. Henry behaved decently to both his known ones. Mary Boleyn and Elizabeth Blount were both married off into good families and the King salved his conscience with confession to Dr John Longland.

Contrary to popular belief, Henry did not have syphilis. Tudor historians have shown again and again that his doctor's prescriptions included none of the contemporary remedies for that disease. Anyone who still gives credence to the myth should study the medical history of his rival Francis I, the priapic King of France. Henry saw himself as unlucky in marriage, but he believed deeply in the institution. Katherine of Aragon's miscarriages, Anne's supposed adultery and Catherine Howard's sluttish behaviour did not stop him from marrying Katherine Parr *hilarii vultu*, with a smile on his face. His sixth wife, like his third, Jane Seymour, the mother of his heir Edward VI, brought happiness. She cared for his children, establishing a peaceful orderly household, similar to those at Richmond and Eltham, where he had been brought up.

It was Sir Geoffrey Elton's idea that I should write this book. He thought the sisters 'a rattling good story'. After Elton's death I worked mostly under the guidance of Dr David Starkey, who shared some of his own distinguished research on Henry's childhood, and for acknowledging my own when he gave a paper on 'The Youth of Henry VIII' at the Institute of Historical Research. We tried not to poach on each other's preserves, so I refrained from citing the many warrants in the Public Record Office which prove conclusively that the household at Eltham did exist and that Henry was encouraged there to assert himself over his sisters in a way which would now be thought incorrect but which was then considered manly.

The PRO warrants were David's find, so I referred only to one which struck me forcibly several years ago as Henry's earliest encounter with the full solemnity of death. He was nine when Prince Edmund died. The warrant shows the household at Eltham plunged into mourning. Black clothes were ordered even for Jane Poppincourt and 'the Lady Mary's scolemaster'. Twelve months later the whole gloomy procedure was repeated at Arthur's death, but Elizabeth of York was there to comfort and pray with her remaining children.* What Henry never forgot was his mother's death. Four years after the event, on a January day in 1507, the adolescent Prince was replying to a letter telling him the Holy Roman Emperor's son, Philip of Castile, had died. Henry explained that he had already, 'heard with great unhappiness the report about the death of the King of Castile, my deeply, deeply regretted brother . . . no less welcome news has ever come here since the death of my very dear mother'. He wrote from Richmond Palace, where the previous year Elizabeth's apartments, closed since her death, had been opened up for the visit of Philip and his wife, Queen Joanna. Briefly Henry VII's court, dreary since Elizabeth's passing, had sprung to life again. Prince Henry's mind slipped back to the dreadful scenes when his mother had died in childbirth and his father's grief was unrestrained. 'I was less enchanted with this part of your letter,' he wrote tersely, 'it seemed to open a wound which time had healed.' Then the schoolboy Prince remembered he was addressing the great Erasmus, mended his manners and praised his correspondent's elegant Latin.

Maria Perry, Kensington, 1998

---

* Since this book was first published, a complete reconstruction of Prince Arthur's funeral was staged at Worcester Cathedral to mark the 500th anniversary of the event. Dr Julian Litton estimates the cost, including livery and costumes for 144 officers, heralds and mourners plus the training and stabling of horses was £200,000.

Chapter 1

Dramatis Personae

It was an autumn morning in 1499. Perhaps a mist hung damply over the Thames, or perhaps it was one of those crisp, clear mornings when sunlight sparkles on the water and the trees along the river bank turn gloriously to russet and gold. Desiderius Erasmus, a notable scholar in his early thirties, was staying at Greenwich with his pupil and patron William Blount, Lord Mountjoy. Erasmus had not yet achieved that dazzling reputation which was to make him the most respected Humanist in all Europe, but he was a rising star. He was enjoying a long sabbatical, granted by the superiors of his Augustinian monastery at Steyn in the Netherlands, ostensibly to perfect his Greek and to take a degree in theology. He had been living in Paris, where Mountjoy and other young English gentlemen had been sent to finish their education. His brilliance as a teacher had made him 'a name to conjure with' and the radical young clustered eagerly about him.[1] Some, like Mountjoy, came from wealthy families. Anticipating further patronage, Erasmus cherished dreams of a visit to Italy, but at the end of May Mountjoy was summoned back to England to consummate his nuptials with Elizabeth Say, the heiress to whom he had been betrothed before he left for Paris.[2]

Mountjoy had studied twice under Erasmus, who thought him an elegant Latinist, but he was not free to travel.[3] He had been invited to be a companion in studies to Henry VII's second son, Henry, Duke of York.[4] Erasmus gave up his dreams of Italy and accepted the young nobleman's invitation to visit London and

Oxford. He was not disappointed. He discovered that English ladies had a delightful way of greeting their guests. As he wrote enthusiastically to his friend the poet Fausto Andrelini:

> When you arrive anywhere you are received with kisses on all sides, and when you take your leave, they speed you on your way with kisses. The kisses are renewed when you come back. When the guests come to your house, their arrival is pledged with kisses; and when they leave, kisses are shared once again. If you should happen to meet, then kisses are given profusely. In a word, wherever you turn, the world is full of kisses.[5]

To Erasmus, whose most sophisticated patrons to date were the Bishop of Cambrai and a kindly Dutch lady, Anna van Borssele, England seemed irresistible. At Oxford he enhanced his reputation as a theologian by debating with John Colet, a dynamic scholar who was upsetting the authorities of the day with a provocative series of lectures on the Epistles of St Paul. Colet had heard of Erasmus when visiting Paris. They had not previously met, but he was delighted to welcome such a fashionable personality to the Oxford scene, and gratified that he should fuel the controversy. Another new acquaintance was Thomas More, a twenty-two-year-old lawyer at Lincoln's Inn with impressive connections at court. On the autumn morning in question, More had arranged for Erasmus and another friend, Edward Arnold, to visit Eltham, the moated palace in Kent, where Henry VII's four youngest children were in residence.

Arthur, Prince of Wales, Henry VII's oldest son, was not at Eltham. His father had sent him to the Welsh Marches, where he had his own household and council at Ludlow Castle. His tutor, the blind poet Bernard André, thought him an outstanding classical scholar, but he was being prepared for the arduous duties of kingship which lay ahead. Henry was negotiating a marriage for him with the King of Spain's youngest daughter, Katherine of Aragon. Two of the Prince's love letters to her survive. They were written from Ludlow in October and November 1499, and are warm and affectionate.[6] A third, a rough draft of the November letter and full of crossings out, indicates the care he bestowed upon these romantic efforts.[7]

With the heir to the throne absent, Erasmus was not expecting a formal reception at Eltham. More had told him they were to visit the schoolroom. Instead, when he led Erasmus into the great hall with its magnificent hammer-beam roof, the Dutch scholar beheld a sight he was to remember for more than twenty years.[8] The King's younger children had assembled with all their attendants. In the middle stood the eight-year-old Prince Henry, probably under a canopy of estate, for as second in line to the throne he had a very clear idea of his own importance. Recently discovered records and warrants show that in the nursery at Eltham he was accustomed to ruling the roost. In an age when the male succession was considered vital no one would have put Prince Henry down for precocious behaviour, or for lording it over his sisters. On the contrary, his parents were delighted by the massive self-confidence which he displayed on public occasions. His older sister, Princess Margaret, had taken up her position to the right of Henry. Soon she was to be betrothed to the King of Scotland, and at ten was already being schooled in the grave demeanour fitting for a queen. The four-year-old Princess Mary, a child with beautiful golden hair, was playing on Henry's left and the King's youngest son, Prince Edmund, was in the arms of a courtier.[9]

Members of Mountjoy's household were also present. Something about the carefully arranged tableau suggests that the visitors were expected. More and Arnold courteously stepped forward, each putting some papers into Prince Henry's hand. Erasmus was embarrassed. He had not realized they would be received with so much ceremony. He had nothing to give to the young prince, whom he described as having 'a most regal air'. He felt More had played a shabby trick in not warning him to come better prepared. Later, at dinner, Henry sent him a note, challenging him to write some verses. Thoroughly discomforted, the scholar begged for time. He returned to Mountjoy's house and within three days composed a Latin poem in praise of Henry VII, his children and the whole kingdom of England. Dedicated to Prince Henry, but aimed at catching the attention of his father, the title was imposing: *Personification of Great Britain, once called Albion, now called Anglia, congratulating herself on the valour of her invincible King Henry and on the exceptional character of his son.* The poem, calculated to flatter and delight the little boy, was also skilfully phrased to stretch the young mind. Erasmus was clearly pleased by the piece, which he had printed in Paris the following year.[10] The choice of metre, a mixture of hexameter and iambics, although a commonplace of elegiac verse at that time, gave him a schoolmasterly thrill, and he was very proud to have devised further teaching materials for this royal child.[11]

Everything we know about Prince Henry at this time indicates that he was lively, intelligent and completely extrovert. He had been trained in elementary Latin by the poet John Skelton, but in the brief encounter at Eltham Erasmus sensed the boy had a precocious understanding of classical models. It must have given the scholar real pleasure to meet such a bright pupil. To a modern reader, however, the accompanying preface is much more amusing than the ode.[12] It reminds the eight-year-old child that the praises of poets are worth more than the gifts of wealthy men.[13] Regardless of how brave and splendid a prince might be, Erasmus argued, no one could respect his great deeds unless these were given some *publicity.* It was a lesson the young Duke of York, unaware that he would one day reign as King Henry VIII, was to take profoundly to heart.

The ceremony creating Henry Duke of York took place in 1494, when he was three years old. For political reasons there was maximum publicity. It was an even grander affair than Arthur's investiture as Prince of Wales, four years earlier, and was followed by a magnificent tournament, staged on three separate days, at which Princess Margaret, a month before her fifth birthday, played her first public role, giving out the prizes.[14] The court was at Woodstock, but the King intended to spend Hallowe'en in London that year and to celebrate in style the old Christian feast of All Saints' Day, followed, as it still is in the Roman Catholic calendar, by All Souls', the day of the dead. By medieval tradition All Saints' was a crown-wearing day, so the King would be in full regalia. On 27 October he came by river with his queen, Elizabeth

of York, and his mother, Lady Margaret Beaufort, Countess of
Richmond, from the old palace of Sheen to Westminster. Prince
Henry was summoned from Eltham, arriving with a great procession to be received by the Mayor of London, his aldermen and all
the leading craftsmen. Princess Margaret may have been with
Henry, or she may have come with her mother and father. The
chronicler does not mention her that day, but she probably
watched the procession and she was to play a leading role in the
next fortnight. Various lords and ladies of the court had
persuaded Henry to let them arrange the kind of old-fashioned
spectacle which had not been seen since the days of Edward IV. It
was to be the sporting event of the decade. Heralds and trumpeters went from Woodstock Fair to the heart of the City of
London proclaiming the worth of the prizes – a gold ring with a
huge ruby for the jousting and a gold ring with a diamond for the
hand-to-hand fighting, and all for the pleasure, they shouted, of
'the redoubted lady, and fairest young princess, the eldest daughter to our sovereign lord the King'.[15]

The ceremonies began when Henry VII dined in his Presence
Chamber at the Palace of Westminster. Lord Clifford and Lord
Fitzwarren held the basin and ewer, while the King washed his
hands. Then tiny Prince Henry stepped forward before the assembled courtiers to offer his father the towel. The details were
immensely important to the chronicler, who was a herald, because
during the bloodshed and chaos of the Wars of the Roses much of
the old court etiquette had become confused and it was an obses-
sive preoccupation of the new dynasty to get things right. It was a
widely held opinion that the doyenne in such matters was the
Countess of Richmond.[16] Thrice-married and a veteran of three
reigns, the King's mother was descended from John of Gaunt, the
illustrious Duke of Lancaster, whom Shakespeare later immortalized as 'time-honoured'.

Even though Lady Margaret was descended from the illegitimate Beaufort line, her ancestry went back to Edward III. She had
survived the Yorkist regime and was the best friend of Edward
IV's daughter Cecily of York, whom she later sheltered at her own
palace of Collyweston in Northamptonshire. The Countess was
ruthlessly practical, extremely devout and impeccably aristo-

cratic, and for as long as she survived, she was determined that no one should accuse the Tudors of being upstarts.[17] A regal figure in a rich gold coronet, she was present on most state occasions, walking proudly, despite appalling rheumatism, just behind the Queen, whom she frequently overshadowed by the sheer force of her personality. She was devoted to all her grandchildren, but Princess Margaret, who was also her godchild, was her favourite and scattered references amid the Countess's papers suggest she took an active part in the little girl's upbringing.

Twenty gentlemen were to be made Knights of the Bath with Prince Henry. In the fifteenth century the rites included full immersion, followed by a night of prayer and vigil. The little boy was bathed in his father's private apartment. The other gentlemen had their baths prepared for them in the Parliament Chamber. It had been adorned since the time of Henry III with a painted throng of saints and seraphs, but on this occasion it was transformed into a dormitory with twenty beds under separate canopies.[18] The King visited each knight in his bath to hear his professions of loyalty and chivalry. The following day they reassembled in the Presence Chamber, Sir William Sandys holding Prince Henry in his arms while the Duke of Buckingham, the grandest peer in the land, fastened a spur to the child's right heel and the Marquis of Dorset put one on his left heel. Then Henry VII took his sword, dubbed his son knight and lifted him on to the table for all to see. This impressive moment must have been one of the little boy's earliest memories of public life. Sir William carried him into St Stephen's Chapel to offer his sword at the high altar, and, having pledged himself before God and the King to perform feats of chivalry, the new Knight of the Bath was returned to the nursery, while the older members of the order feasted in style.[19]

On 1 November, All Saints' Day, flanked by Cardinal Morton, his Archbishop of Canterbury, the King sat in Parliament, surrounded by his nobles, bishops, judges and the Master of the Rolls, so that a sea of scarlet cloth must have confronted the child as once again he was brought before his father, who this time was robed in ermine with the golden circlet he had won at Bosworth Field gleaming above his brow. The Earl of Shrewsbury, the

King's trusted companion in arms, held the prince, while the Bishop of Exeter read aloud a patent creating him Duke of York, Lieutenant General of Ireland, Marshal of England and Warden of the Cinque Ports, with an income of £1,000 a year.[20]

The King rose to go. The nobles in their velvet and ermine formed a procession, but there was a hitch. No one could remember whether the Earl of Suffolk should have precedence over the Earl of Kent, or whether Lord Clifford should walk before Lord Grey. 'The King's mother was as yet in her closet,' commented the chronicler, perhaps implying that if *she* had been up and about, there would have been no such muddle. Nine days later, Lady Margaret was at the tournament, supervising her granddaughter as she presented the prizes to roars of applause from the excited crowd. Everyone enjoyed themselves enormously. The chronicler excelled himself, describing how the King and Queen took their places beneath twin canopies of estate on a stage hung with blue tapestries 'enramplished' with golden fleurs-de-lis, a reminder that England had not given up her hereditary claim to lands in France.

The challengers rode out of Westminster Hall, which was apparently used as a tiring room, into the lists, their horses trapped with the King's colours of green and white, their harnesses decorated with silver bells. 'You should have seen the good riders, the well-doing horses, the jangling bells, the glistening spangles,' enthused the chronicler, and above all he singled out Lord Abergavenny on a small black horse which 'did marvels', jumping high off the ground, again and again, to the delight of the spectators, who included the two royal children, Margaret and Henry, sitting beside their parents on cushions of cloth of gold.[21] Henry was too small to be present all the time, but Margaret attended each day, giving out the golden rings to the victorious challengers, who were led up to her by high-ranking court ladies. To the assembled crowd, this fair child, daughter of Lancaster and York, was a living symbol that the bloody conflict between the red and white roses was over.

On the last day of the tournament, 13 November, the jousts were held in her honour. The day began with a comedy. One of the challengers mislaid his helmet and an interlude followed during which he searched for it. Two knights on horses decked in paper entered the lists. Their accoutrements were painted to look real, one with red and white lozenges, the other with a curious device of two men playing at dice. The spectators were completely fooled, until the contestants ripped off each other's apparel with their lances, 'All to make the King laugh,' wrote the chronicler. Then four ladies, dramatically gowned in white damask and crimson velvet with jewelled circlets in their hair, rode out on four snow-white palfreys, leading the serious challengers. The fighting began afresh until the heralds called a halt and Margaret gave the last prizes to the victors of the day, Sir Edward à Borough and the Earl of Essex.

There was a sound political purpose behind the fortnight of extravagant pageantry. By making Prince Henry the Duke of York, the King of England was affirming to his courtiers, to his people and to the whole of Europe that he and his family were there to stay. Although Henry VII was the undisputed victor of Bosworth, his right to reign confirmed by the Pope and the machinations of his enemies cursed by the bishops with bell, book and candle, the peace of the realm was far from assured.[22] The story of the Princes in the Tower, Edward IV's murdered sons, had taken a strong hold on the popular imagination. Rumours that the boys might still be alive were to plague Henry Tudor for many years. There were other Yorkist claimants too, distant relations of Edward IV in whose veins flowed the dangerous blood royal, and this could always provide an excuse for disaffected nobles to rally round some powerful troublemaker. In 1487 Lambert Simnel had tried to pass himself off as the Earl of Warwick, son of Edward IV's brother the Duke of Clarence. Henry had dealt with the matter by temporarily releasing the real Warwick from the Tower and parading him through the streets of London.

Simnel was made a scullion in the royal kitchens, but Perkin Warbeck posed a more serious threat. The son of a Flemish boatman, he had been working as a haberdasher's model, gorgeously arrayed in silks and laces, when someone noticed that his features resembled those of the late king. Warbeck convinced a number of European princes that he really was Edward IV's younger son, among them Henry's hostile neighbours James IV of Scotland

and Charles VIII of France, with whom Henry was at war during 1492. Ferdinand of Aragon, the King of Spain, kept a more open mind, although he and Queen Isabella had received a letter calculated to plant unpleasant doubts in the minds of a couple planning to marry their daughter into England's ruling house.[23]

It had come from Edward IV's sister Margaret, Duchess of Burgundy. Nicknamed 'the Duchess Juno' by Henry's early biographers, who saw her as a warmongering she-devil, Margaret was to prove a powerful adversary. Her real quarrel with England was personal. Her brother had neglected to pay part of her dowry of 81,666 *écus d'or*. She also wanted rents which she considered due to her from the Manor of Hunsdon. Henry offered no reparation. 'The diabolical Duchess', as the chronicler Edward Hall called her, publicly recognized the pretender as her nephew, referring to him as 'the White Rose', a name certain to rouse popular sentiment.[24]

When England and France made peace at the end of 1492, Charles VIII expelled Warbeck. Margaret promptly sheltered him at her own court. This so incensed Henry VII that he broke off commercial relations with the Low Countries, seriously disrupting the cloth trade. Meanwhile it was rumoured that Maximilian, King of the Romans, heir to the dying Emperor, planned to invade England and put Warbeck on the throne. Henry genuinely feared attack. He mustered armies through the summer of 1493, even though he had by then made enough inquiries into Warbeck's background to refer to him contemptuously as 'the garçon'.[25] Margaret's intervention created a crisis at the English court, where many of the high officers of state were Yorkists. Men who had sworn fealty to Henry at Bosworth were prepared to renounce it if King Edward's son was really alive. One such was Sir William Stanley, brother of Lady Margaret Beaufort's third husband, the Earl of Derby. When he learned his stepfather's kinsman had been plotting, Henry ordered Stanley's execution for treason. The saga of bloodshed between Lancaster and York seemed set to continue. News of the grisly episode spread far beyond London. At Bruges the authorities, fearing riots, forbade merchants of the English nation to wear badges of the red and white roses.

Unabashed, the Duchess sent Warbeck to Vienna as her official representative at the Emperor's funeral. It was too much for Henry. English envoys arrived at the Burgundian court to challenge the pretender to his face. An ugly scene ensued. Maximilian, his son Philip and Margaret assembled to receive Henry VIII's herald. 'It seems,' said Margaret frostily, 'that you do not recognize my nephew, Richard, since you do not even bother to bow.'[26] The herald replied that 'Duke Richard' was an impostor. Warbeck called him 'a filthy, dirty liar'. The strained diplomatic relations between London and Brussels prompted Henry VII *to proclaim his own three-year-old son Duke of York forthwith.*

Throughout this turbulent period the King maintained his alliance with Spain. Two themes, however, dominate the correspondence between Henry and 'the Catholic Kings'. Ferdinand and Isabella made it clear that no daughter of theirs would set foot on English soil until Henry had made peace with Maximilian, while Henry was insistent that they must promise not to believe the lies of Margaret of Burgundy.

Amid such a climate of worry and suspicion, the birth of another daughter for Henry VII to barter in the European marriage market went almost unnoticed. Only her grandmother recorded in the margin of her beautiful Book of Hours on 18 March, *'Hodie nata Maria tertia filia Henricis VII, 1495'.*[27] There must have been a royal christening for Mary. Presumably it conformed to the age-old regulations to which Lady Margaret adhered for the baptism of all Henry's children. 'Ordnances as to what preparation is to be made against the deliverance of a Queen, as for the christening of the child of which she shall be delivered.'[28] So precise were these that the antiquary John Leland even believed the Countess of Richmond had drawn them up herself, although they simply followed earlier precedent. Certainly the King's mother wished her grandchildren to be baptized in accordance with the etiquette observed for the christening of Edward IV's ten children and there existed a set of rules which even specified the height of the stage upon which the silver-gilt font should be mounted and the type of scarlet covering to be used on the step upon which the officiating bishop should stand. A rich circular canopy surmounted by a golden ball was to be fixed above the stage, but there were to be no curtains. Royal children must be christened in full view of the congregation. If the child was a girl the Ordnances stated that a duchess should carry her, and that a second duchess should hold the richly embroidered chrisom cloth. A countess was to carry the cloth of gold train, furred with ermine, which was to hang from the infant's shoulders and custom demanded that the train should be so long that a gentleman usher was usually required to assist the said countess by holding up the middle section.[29]

At Prince Arthur's christening the congregation had included the remaining flower of the Yorkist nobility and their wives. The principal godmother had been the child's maternal grandmother, Edward IV's widow, Elizabeth Woodville. The ceremony had been held in Winchester Cathedral with its romantic echoes of an Arthurian past. It had rained horribly, delaying the Earl of Oxford, who was the Lord Chamberlain and one of the godfathers, so that the entire court had been obliged to hang about the nave, shivering for three hours, waiting for the moment when they would be served spiced wine and comfits. When the Earl finally arrived, offerings were made at the shrine of St Swithun, patron saint of the English weather, who lay handily buried beneath the high altar.[30]

Three years later everything had gone perfectly at Margaret's christening at Westminster Abbey. When Elizabeth of York withdrew for her confinement, Lady Margaret had attended her, so she had actually witnessed the birth of her grandchild on the night of 28 November 1489. This time there was ample opportunity to get the etiquette right, because the whole court was in London for the ceremony creating Arthur Prince of Wales. Cardinal Morton stood godfather to the infant Princess. The Queen's sister carried the chrisom. Lady Margaret was the principal godmother and the font was sent up from Canterbury, the old silver font in which the children of the kings of England had been baptized for as long as anyone could remember. Amid similar ceremonies Prince Henry was christened at Greenwich in the Church of the Observant Friars, but of Mary's baptism there is no record. Perhaps the panic caused by Perkin Warbeck's attempted invasion obscured the important event.[31]

The Pretender landed at Deal shortly before Mary was born.

Then he fled to Ireland, unsuccessfully besieged Waterford and eventually took refuge with James IV, the King of Scotland. He welcomed Warbeck warmly, giving him his kinswoman Lady Katherine Gordon as a bride – clear proof that James had been taken in. He backed Warbeck in two further abortive attacks, but, finding 'the White Rose' an expensive drain on Scottish funds, the King was relieved when the Pretender was routed in Cornwall, surrendering to Henry at Taunton in Somerset on 5 October 1497. He was put in the Tower, escaped briefly in 1498 and was finally hanged at Tyburn. As a result of a further attempt at Yorkist impersonation by one Ralph Wulfard, the Earl of Warwick was executed in 1499. He was twenty-five and had spent most of his life in the Tower, his only crime being that his surname was Plantagenet and that as the son of Edward IV's brother, the Duke of Clarence, he was an open target for ambitious pretenders.

Dr De Puebla, the Spanish ambassador charged with arranging the marriage between Arthur and Katherine, foresaw an end to his troubles as soon as he heard of Warbeck's defeat in the West Country. 'God be thanked,' he wrote to Queen Isabella, 'Perkin is already captured. The same hour that he was arrested, the King of England sent one of his gentlemen of the bedchamber to bring me the news.'[32] The Spanish sovereigns felt it was safe at last to proceed with their daughter's much-postponed marriage, but if Dr De Puebla hoped to enhance his own importance by boasting of his close relationship with Henry VII, he was misguided. Queen Isabella sent a new ambassador to Britain, ostensibly to Scotland, to further a peace between Henry and James IV. His main task would be to arrange the marriage between the Scottish King and Henry's elder daughter, which had been discussed since Margaret was six years old but was intermittently sabotaged by Warbeck's antics. If this marriage could be brought about, Ferdinand and Isabella fervently believed there might be perpetual peace between the island kingdoms.

The new ambassador, Don Pedro de Ayala, Bishop of the Canaries and a papal pronothary, was a colourful personality. His first exploit on arriving in Scotland was to accompany James IV on a border raid against England. This endeared him to the Scottish King, but it was scarcely in line with his brief as a peace-

maker. Don Pedro was a gentleman. In a long dispatch to their
Catholic Majesties he shrugged off the little skirmish.[33] It had,
after all, given him the opportunity to observe the King of
Scotland in the heat of battle. James was a passionate fighter. 'I
sometimes clung to his skirts and succeeded in keeping him
back,' explained Don Pedro. 'On such occasions he does not take
the least care of himself. He is not a good captain, because he
begins to fight before he has given his orders.' James, he added,
had the sort of charisma which caused his subjects to serve him
with blind loyalty; they fought with enthusiastic allegiance 'in
just and unjust quarrels'.

When the King of Scotland was not fighting, he was hunting in
the mountains. He was also a notable lover, although, continued
Don Pedro, piously recalling his own episcopal function, it was
believed that James had recently given up lovemaking, 'as well
from fear of God as from fear of scandal'. This was the man, aged
twenty-five at the time of Don Pedro's dispatch, to whom Henry
VII proposed to marry his eldest daughter. Margaret, however, was
only nine years old, and she was small and delicate for her age. The
Scots were keen to have her sent over the Border as soon as possible but Henry had his doubts, and, he confided to Don Pedro, there
were two formidable opponents to the match at the English court:
'The Queen and my mother are very much against the marriage.
They say if the marriage were concluded we should be obliged to
send the princess directly to Scotland, in which case they fear the
King of Scotland would not *wait*, but injure her and endanger her
health.'[34] Henry did not embarrass the ambassador by mentioning
something which was widely known in England, though perhaps
not often referred to in courtly circles. The King was Lady
Margaret's only child. In giving birth to him her womb had been
damaged; she was 'spoyled' and could have no more children.

The Countess's experience had been traumatic. Pregnant at
twelve, she had borne her only son during the Wars of the Roses,
three months after her husband, Edmund Tudor, had died of the
plague. He had been Henry VI's lieutenant in a particularly
dangerous part of Wales, and was captured and imprisoned by
Yorkist retainers. Although he was ransomed, his health never

recovered. Left alone at Carmarthen, Margaret had travelled through the winter storms to Pembroke Castle, where Edmund's brother Jasper Tudor had given her shelter. She was remarried before she was thirteen. After this experience, it is not surprising that the Queen and the King's mother would not hear of Princess Margaret being sent to Scotland until she was safely into puberty. Their opposition was also fuelled by current gossip about James IV's amorous adventures. He had two illegitimate children by Marion Boyd, with whom he had commenced a liaison shortly after his accession, and by the time De Ayala had arrived in Edinburgh the King was said to be simultaneously in love with two ladies, Janet Kennedy and Margaret Drummond. If the Queen and Lady Margaret had their way, Henry joked ruefully to Don Pedro, the King of Scotland might have to wait for Princess Margaret for 'another nine years'.[35]

The ambassador confirmed Margaret's immaturity. 'The daughter of Henry is, in fact, very young and very small for her years,' he wrote to Queen Isabella, but, he assured her, he had another plan up his sleeve to secure peace between England and Scotland. If Katherine married Arthur and James were to marry her sister, the Infanta Maria, there would surely be an end to the feuding between the island kingdoms. Preparations, meanwhile, were to go ahead for the Anglo–Spanish alliance, so Don Pedro forsook his post in Scotland to become a permanent resident at the English court. This greatly upset the resident ambassador, Dr De Puebla, although Queen Isabella continued to retain his services. On 19 May 1499 it was he who stood in for the bride when a proxy marriage at last took place between Arthur and Katherine at Bewdley in Worcestershire. Ferdinand and Henry then haggled over the terms of the payment of the dowry and it was another two years before the Princess set foot on English soil. Her ships were sighted off Plymouth Sound on 2 October 1501.[36] Her progress through the West Country was slow but joyful. The nobility and gentry flocked to meet her and there were festivities at every stopping place. At Exeter Lord Willoughby de Broke, the King's High Steward, welcomed her and at Amesbury the Duchess of Norfolk arrived with a great suite of ladies to escort her to London.[37]

Henry set out to meet her at Dogmersfield, about ten miles from London Bridge. At Elthamstead he was joined by Prince Arthur at the head of a long column of gorgeously dressed noblemen, but Don Pedro de Ayala intercepted them. The Archbishop of Santiago and the Princess's duenna, Doña Elvira Manuel, he explained, had decreed that the bride must not converse with the King or meet the bridegroom before her wedding day. It was an old Castilian custom. Without even dismounting from his horse, the King of England held a council in the field. It was decided that as Katherine was already betrothed to Prince Arthur, she was Henry's subject; the laws of Castile did not apply. The King rode on, demanding to see the Princess. When told that she was resting, Henry replied roundly that if she were in her bed he would still see and talk with her, that was why he had come. Doña Elvira was horrified, but she knew when to give in. Katherine also had a mind of her own, and soon the Princess was exchanging greetings with the King of England. Later, when the party had changed out of their riding clothes, she further shocked Doña Elvira by meeting Prince Arthur. Not only was she pretty, she was well mannered and obedient; but, as her letters to Arthur had already shown, she was no linguist. The Queen and Lady Margaret had advised her that she should learn French, but Katherine had made little progress. She conversed with the King and Prince in a mixture of Spanish and Latin, with an English bishop interpreting.

Henry and Arthur rode back to Richmond, where the Queen was waiting. The royal party then went by river to Baynard's Castle, a royal residence near Blackfriars, which was conveniently situated for St Paul's, while the bride rode on to Kingston-upon-Thames to be met by the Duke of Buckingham, grandly accompanied by 300 or 400 men in striking red and black livery. At St George's Fields she was welcomed by Prince Henry, now ten, and exuding that self-confidence Erasmus had noted two years earlier, as he rode about town with his own escort of 200 men in blue and tawny coats. Katherine was to stay at the Bishop of London's palace, which had been reglazed in her honour.[38] The whole city was *en fête*. Banners and flags festooned the streets. Triumphal arches were painted with the arms of England and the pomegranates of Spain. At Baynard's Castle excitement must have reached fever pitch as the two Princesses tried on their new clothes. Mary was to wear crimson velvet; Margaret, who would be shown off to the Scottish ambassadors, had a dress of cloth of gold.

On the morning of 14 November the bride appeared, in white satin, but dressed Spanish fashion. Her long hair flowed loose over her shoulders as a symbol of virginity. For the wedding ceremony she wore a long veil of white silk which reached to her waist. It was embroidered with pearls and gold thread. Her gown was pleated, and her ladies were similarly attired in Spanish styles, their petticoats stiffened by hoops, in marked contrast to the English ladies, whose gowns flowed smoothly over their hips. In St Paul's the court had assembled on two great platforms covered with scarlet cloth. Prince Arthur, also dressed in white satin, stood waiting at the high altar with the Archbishop of Canterbury, while Prince Henry proudly led the bride into the church. The King and Queen, anxious not to steal the couple's thunder, were in a small closet above the consistory, where they could watch the proceedings discreetly. The previous night they had gone to stay with Lord Abergavenny who had a house by St Paul's, so that there was no need for them to go in procession through the streets. This meant attention was focused on the bride and groom. The bishops celebrated the Nuptial Mass, the trumpets sounded and bells pealed through the city. Lady Margaret wept, and the conduits ran with red wine.[39] Enlivened by free drink, Londoners cheered the couple back to Baynard's Castle, where a huge wedding feast was followed by a formal bedding. The banquet went on until four or five in the afternoon. It included 'all the delicacies, dainties and curious meats that might be purveyed or got within the whole realm of England'. The Earl of Oxford led the way to the bedchamber. He tried the bed, first the side on which the Prince should lie and then the Princess's side. The Princess was then placed in the bed, beside the Prince and the bishops blessed both the bed and the anticipated union. Many years later the gentlemen in Arthur's suite were to swear that the next morning he emerged from his chamber, flushed with triumph, announcing, 'I have been this night in the midst of Spain.'

The celebrations went on for days. Lady Margaret gave a

banquet for the Spaniards at Coldharbour, serving superb food and 'abundant wines'. That evening her husband the Earl of Derby gave a supper party.[40] Stands had been erected at Westminster for a spectacular tournament. To cover some of the cost, seats were hired out to the common people at extortionate prices.[41] Katherine sat with the Queen, Lady Margaret and her new sisters-in-law, the Princesses Margaret and Mary. The Queen's ladies – 200 or 300, the chronicler estimated – took up all one side of the stands. Prince Arthur sat opposite with the King, Prince Henry, the Earl of Oxford and the Earl of Derby, who was Earl Marshall. The Duke of Buckingham was the King's Champion. During his minority he had been Lady Margaret's ward. He entered in a mobile pavilion striped in the Tudor colours of green and white.[42]

Sir Guillaume de la Rivière led the challengers. The tournament, like the various wedding processions, added to the pressures heaped upon Sir Thomas Brandon, the new Master of the Horse, who had a house at Southwark, situated conveniently opposite Baynard's Castle.[43] He had managed nevertheless to obtain a temporary position in Prince Arthur's household for his nephew, Charles Brandon, a young gentleman from Suffolk of good family, but without private means. Charles's father had died heroically at Bosworth, but the East Anglian estates of his grand-father Sir William Brandon went to his son Robert, leaving Charles and his sister no income. Watching his uncle's efforts to find stabling for all the extra horses in London that November must have provided Charles with an invaluable apprenticeship in the realities of court life.

No effort had been spared to entertain the Princess. On the Friday after the jousting a 'disguising' took place in Westminster Hall, that 'right craftye building', which, as the chronicler observed, could be transformed to suit any occasion. This time it was hung with rich tapestries and ornamented with gold plate, not just on the tables but also piled ostentatiously upon sideboards, for a plate cupboard was a significant means of displaying a Tudor nobleman's wealth and status. For the disguisings, new mobile stages of a type not previously used in England had been built. William Cornish, a gentleman of the Chapel Royal, had played a leading part in arranging the lavish spectacle. Pageant after pageant rolled in, bearing musicians and entertainers. The scene painters and carpenters had excelled in special effects. A castle filled with choristers was pulled by four heraldic beasts. At the front two lions, one silver, one gold, were made up of 'two men, one in the forepart, one in the hinder part', with their legs disguised. A ship in full sail glided effortlessly by on hidden wheels. Eight knights disembarked to dance with the ladies who descended from the castle. Then the court dances began. Ever chivalrous, Arthur led out his aunt, Lady Cecily of York. Katherine performed a Spanish dance with one of her ladies, but the climax of the merrymaking came when the young Duke of York, 'having with him the Lady Margaret, his sister in hand came down and danced two bass dances', but, 'perceiving himself encombered with his clothes, suddenly he cast off his gown and danced in his jacket'.[44] This extrovert feat delighted the King and Queen, but there is no record of how Margaret reacted.

The grand finale was still to come. At a banquet in the Parliament Chamber a great white lantern was brought in to the sound of trumpets. Its windows were covered with fine lawn and it was lit from inside by 100 tapers, so that twelve beautiful ladies were visible through the gauze. Even this spectacle was surpassed on the last day of the feasting. A pageant two storeys high appeared, drawn by three sea-horses. It was built to represent a chapel and was filled with children sweetly singing. Eight knights jumped down from the lower storey, setting free baby rabbits, which ran about among the guests, while from above eight ladies released a flock of white doves, which flew around the hall causing 'great laughter and disport'.[45]

At the end of November the court moved to Windsor. After some discussion among Henry's councillors, it was decided that the Prince and Princess should be sent to Wales. Katherine was saddened by saying goodbye to those members of her suite who had come only for the wedding. Although she was to take a fair number of Spaniards as part of her permanent household, the strain of parting with old friends and loyal retainers showed. Henry VII called the Princess to his library where he began to show her his books, some in English and some in Latin. Hidden in the library was a jeweller who suddenly appeared and offered her a selection of 'huge diamonds' and other jewels. The King told her to choose what she liked. When she had made her choice, he turned to her ladies and told them to take some too. This, wrote the chronicler, 'relieved her heaviness somewhat'.[46]

Arthur's modest manor house at Bewdley had been turned into a small palace to receive Katherine. Its windows were glazed, its roof repaired and every comfort installed. After a short stay there, the party moved on to Ludlow, where Arthur was to continue working with his council, under the guidance of its new Lord President, Dr William Smyth, Bishop of Lincoln. Sir Richard Pole, who was Arthur's Chamberlain and related by marriage to Lady Margaret, was also in attendance.

Immediately after the wedding festivities, the King resumed negotiations with the Scottish ambassadors. The Archbishop of Glasgow, the Earl of Bothwell and Andrew Forman, postulate Bishop of Moray, had all been sent to England in October for the joint purpose of representing James at Arthur's wedding, and discussing the finer points of Margaret's dowry in preparation for his own. As jointure, she was to have the castles and estates traditionally held by Queens of Scotland, including the beautiful Palace of Linlithgow, the mighty fortress, Stirling Castle, and the rents from Ettrick Forest. In Edinburgh James had also started to build the impressive new Palace of Holyrood. According to a false report started off by Don Pedro de Ayala, the Scottish King had installed his mistress Margaret Drummond at Stirling with her daughter, one of the five royal bastards to whose paternity James admitted. Henry had obtained a papal dispensation for his daughter's marriage the previous year because James IV and Margaret Tudor were distant cousins, but this was a formality.* In Scotland it was whispered that the real impediment to James's marriage was his love for Margaret Drummond, who had been his mistress since 1496. He was said to be passionately attached to her. Many people believed that her death by poisoning in 1501

---

* James I had married Joan Beaufort, whose brother John, Duke of Somerset, was Margaret's great-grandfather.

was deliberately contrived by courtiers, who feared their King would never marry and, more importantly, never conceive a legitimate heir while she lived. Her sisters Eupheme and Sybilla ate the same dish by which she was poisoned and died with her. Don Pedro, learning of the scandal, mixed her up with the King's aunt, Lady Margaret Stewart, which fuelled the rumour that James was maintaining and shamelessly visiting Margaret Drummond at the same time as he was officially wooing Margaret Tudor. An ambassador's task was not made any easier by the King of Scotland's habit of bestowing the name 'Stewart' on all his progeny. After siring his bastards, James, a faithful son of the Church, always did penance, devoutly shriving himself at the shrine of St Ninian.

Despite these ambivalent attitudes to love and procreation, James needed the English alliance. He rose splendidly to the occasion, explaining to Henry that as God had instituted the sacrament of matrimony in a state of innocence between our first parents 'for the propagation of the human race, causing Kings to rule and Princes to govern in happy succession', he now desired 'with a pure mind' to express the affection he felt for the King of England 'by the sacred bond of matrimonial alliance'.[47] More specifically, of course, he needed the dowry of 30,000 golden nobles (about £10,000) which Margaret would bring with her.

The marriage treaty was finally signed on 24 January, after some clauses had been inserted by Henry to ensure that Margaret should have enough English servants and that James would pay for the necessities of her wardrobe, residences, vehicles and stud. The proxy marriage took place at Richmond, Henry's sumptuous new palace by the Thames, on St Paul's Day, 25 January. The Earl of Bothwell stood in for King James and the 'fyancells' were preceded by a solemn High Mass attended by the King and Queen, Prince Henry, Princess Mary, the Pope's representative and Don Pedro, who considered himself responsible for the whole affair. Three archbishops and four bishops concelebrated.

Afterwards in the Queen's Great Chamber, the Archbishop of Glasgow asked if the King or Queen knew of any impediment to the match and if the Princess was acting 'without compulsion and of her own free will'. Margaret replied, 'if it please my Lord and Father the King and my Lady Mother the Queen', she was content. Then Bothwell took Margaret to be the wife and spouse of his sovereign, and in James's name promised 'for her all other to forsake'. The Princess spoke next:

> 'I, Margaret, the first begotten daughter of the right excellent, right high and mighty Prince and Princess, Henry by the grace of God, King of England and Elizabeth, Queen of the same, wittingly and of deliberate mind having twelve years complete in age in the month of November last past, contract matrimony with the right high and mighty Prince, James, King of Scotland unto and for my husband and spouse and all other for him forsake.'[48]

'That done,' recorded John Yonge, Somerset Herald, 'the trumpeters blew up and the minstrells played in the best and most joyfullest manner.' The Queen then took her daughter, the Queen of Scots, by the hand and they dined together at one table. There is a story that when Prince Henry realized that as a queen his sister would now take precedence over him, he wept with rage.

Chapter 2
The Thistle and the Rose

The celebrations for Margaret's betrothal were almost as spectacular as those for Arthur's wedding. The *Te deum* was sung at St Paul's and bells pealed joyfully from all the churches, while hogsheads of wine were distributed at bonfires throughout the city.[1] The royal family remained at Richmond, entertaining the Scottish ambassadors in the new palace, which, after fire had destroyed the old Yorkist palace at Sheen, had risen like a phoenix from the ashes. Rebuilding had begun on such a grand scale that contemporaries mockingly referred to the Tudors' new home as 'Riche mount', a pun on Henry's title as Earl of Richmond, and his conspicuous talent for heaping up wealth. The royal apartments were glazed, paved and sumptuously adorned with gold leaf.[2] Stone statues of heraldic beasts filled the gardens. For tournaments the latest hoisting harnesses had been installed to lift a fully armed knight on to his horse.

On the afternoon of the betrothal 'notable jousts' were held. Well wrapped in furs against the January cold, the ladies once more beheld the popinjay Duke of Buckingham enter the lists stunningly accoutred. His first horse was equipped with a short trapper emblazoned with his own arms, but later he changed mounts, reappearing on a charger gloriously decked in blue and crimson velvet and embroidered with the insignia of the Order of the Garter. As a show of manly strength at the end of the jousting, he shattered three spears into the ground.

The following day a new star of the tiltyard emerged in the person of Charles Brandon. The dashing young nephew of the

Master of the Horse took third prize amid a field of highly accomplished challengers.[3] Margaret, on the advice of all the ladies present, gave first prize to Lord William Courtenay, an established champion, son of the Earl of Devonshire and married to the Queen's sister, Lady Katherine. Dancing and feasting followed. Diligently chronicling the entertainments, John Yonge evidently did not realize that the props from Arthur's wedding had been shipped up the Thames from Westminster. The lantern pageant, which had been such a success in November, was used again, beautifully lit from inside as before but disgorging this time, instead of twelve elegant ladies, a troupe of Morris dancers, calculated to impress the Scots with their bucolic vigour.[4]

Before the ambassadors left, costly presents were exchanged. The King gave a golden goblet, six silver standing cups, twenty-four silver bowls and a basin and ewer to the Archbishop of Glasgow, and another set of equally magnificent plate to the Earl of Bothwell. He also rewarded the Scottish herald, Lyon King of Arms, with a satin gown and a purse containing 100 gold crowns. The Earl had given a similar purse to the English heralds and also the cloth of gold gown he had worn to represent James IV in the betrothal ceremony.

Scotland was a poor country. To cover the cost of sending three ambassadors to England, the King taxed the principal boroughs 1,000 marks and 100 crowns.[5] Margaret's dowry of £10,000 represented £30,000 in Scottish money, but this was only half the total sum Henry VII spent on rebuilding Richmond Palace.[6] After the earlier negotiations for a marriage between James and Margaret had been wrecked by the antics of Perkin Warbeck, border raids had continued as a matter of course. To the Scots this was lucrative sport. They had besieged Norham Castle on the Tweed, until heavily defeated by Henry's armies under the command of the Earl of Surrey. James had accused the English of breaking a truce, but at a meeting with the Bishop of Durham at Melrose Abbey, he had shown such an earnest desire for peace that the marriage negotiations had been resumed. At some point during the three-year discussions which followed, Henry VII is reputed to have said to councillors who were arguing against the match, 'Supposing, which God forbid, that all my male progeny should become extinct and the kingdom devolve by law to Margaret's heirs, will England be damaged thereby, or rather benefited? For since the less becomes subservient to the greater, the accession will be that of Scotland to England, not of England to Scotland', which, pointed out the King, was exactly what had happened in his ancestors' time in the case of Normandy, when that trifling portion of France had been added to his kingdom 'as a rivulet to a fountain'.[7]

This lofty observation later gained prophetic significance, particularly in the reign of Henry's granddaughter Elizabeth I, when it was becoming apparent that she would never marry and that the island kingdoms would indeed be united under Margaret's direct descendant James VI and I. In the winter of 1501–2, however, all England confidently awaited news from Ludlow that the Princess of Wales was pregnant and the King's remark about future genealogy seemed so fanciful that no one even bothered to note when or where he had made it.

A messenger did come from Ludlow that spring. On 4 April 1502 he arrived at Greenwich Palace after two days of hard riding. When he informed the privy councillors of his errand, they conferred among themselves and chose the King's confessor, a Friar Observant, to inform Henry of the news. The friar knocked on the door of the King's chamber and, on being admitted, asked everyone to leave the room. Then he told Henry VII that Prince Arthur had died on 2 April, it was thought of the sweating sickness. Stunned, the King sent for the Queen, saying that they should 'take the painful sorrow together'. When Elizabeth arrived and saw Henry's grief, she tried to comfort him, beseeching 'that he would, after God consider the weal of his own noble person, of his realm and of her', remembering that 'my lady your mother, had never no more children but you only, yet God by his grace has ever preserved you and brought you where you are now'. Over and above, the Queen pointed out, 'God has left you yet a fair Prince, two fair Princesses and God is where he was and we are both young enough.' Henry's prudence and wisdom were renowned through Christendom, she said, and now he should show proof of it by accepting their misfortune.[8]

The courageous woman had lost many of her friends and rela-

tives during the Wars of the Roses. She had borne Henry six children. Two, Elizabeth and Edmund, had died in infancy; now the
eleven-year-old Prince Henry was their only surviving son. The
King thanked the Queen and she returned to her own apartments. There she gave vent to her natural feelings and was soon
weeping so pitifully that her ladies sent for the King to comfort
her. He rushed to her side and 'with true gentle and faithful love'
soothed her, telling her what wise counsel she had given him
before and saying that he would thank God for his son and she
should do likewise.

Arthur's body was embalmed at Ludlow and placed in a
wooden coffin. The small provincial town was ill-equipped to
provide all the necessary trappings for a state funeral. Huge
quantities of black cloth were sent from London to Ludlow and
Worcester.[9] The coffin lay in state at Ludlow Castle until St
George's Day, 23 April. Then, covered with a rich pall of black
cloth of gold with a cross of white cloth of gold, it was borne to
the parish church by the Yeomen of the Prince's Chamber. It had
been decided that the Earl of Surrey should be the principal
mourner, closely followed by the Earls of Shrewsbury and Kent.

As the great procession moved out of the castle, two Spanish
noblemen representing the Princess were at its head. Next came
the Prince's standard bearer, Sir Griffith ap Rice, and then the
coffin, flanked by four gentlemen carrying a black velvet canopy.
Bishops, abbots and priors followed. The parson of Ludlow led a
contingent of secular priests. Eighty poor men in black mourning
habits carried torches. In the parish church Mass was celebrated,
with the Bishops of Lincoln, Salisbury and Chester reading the
lessons. The next day Our Lady's Mass was sung by children, and
the Mass of the Trinity was sung by the Bishop of Salisbury with
the choir. The third Mass was the Requiem.

The obsequies lasted for many days. The coffin was mounted
on a carriage drawn by four horses and covered in black velvet.
Luckily a waxed cloth had been provided to protect against the
rain, for on St Mark's Day, when the doleful procession set out for
Bewley, the chronicler recorded, 'It was the foulest cold, windy
and rainy day and the worst way that I have seen.'[10] The country
roads were so deep in mire that oxen had to be substituted for the

horses drawing the carriage. More masses were offered at Bewdley, until finally the cortège reached Worcester, where the weather changed and the gentlemen mourners were able to form a decent procession, riding in pairs to escort the corpse of their Prince to its final resting place in Worcester Cathedral.

The cathedral dignitaries were all assembled. The children of the choir wore white surplices. The bishops were dressed in rich copes. Torches and candles surrounded the coffin as it stood between the banners embroidered with the royal arms of Spain and England, of Wales, of Cornwall and, in honour of the Prince's Welsh descent, the ancient banner of Cadwallader. All Arthur's courtiers kept watch that night. Then, according to chivalric custom, the heralds delivered up his helm and shield, his sword and embroidered coat of arms. The Earl of Kildare's son, Lord Garrard, had been chosen as the Man of Arms. His task was to bear Arthur's harness. He entered the cathedral on a horse, its velvet trapper richly embroidered with the Prince's coat of arms, and he carried a pole axe, head downwards.

After these ceremonies were completed, the horse was offered to the Abbot of Tewkesbury, and the three earls, followed by many other lords and gentlemen, placed cloth of gold palls upon the coffin in the form of a great glittering cross. When the Mass was finished, the coffin was taken to the south end of the high altar, where a grave had been prepared.

Arthur had been loved by all who knew him. He had been coming to the Marches since he was four years old. Many must have remembered him performing his first ceremonial duties, when as a child of eight he had formally welcomed his father, his mother and his grandmother, who were making an official visit to the town of Shrewsbury.[11] Then there had been spiced wine and saffron bread. Now, as the coffin reached the graveside, the whole congregation were in tears. The Bishop of Lincoln wept openly as he threw earth into the grave and sprinkled it with holy water. Sir William Uvedale, Comptroller of the Prince's Household, broke his staff of office, holding it high above his head, and cast it into the grave. The other gentlemen followed suit. 'This was a piteous sight,' wrote the herald chronicler, 'to those who beheld it.'[12]

Arthur's death blighted the joyful atmosphere which had

prevailed since Margaret's engagement. The funeral bills for black cloth and trappings for the hearse run to twenty pages.[13] The total cost worked out at £892 2s ½d. Black clothes were ordered for the King's mother and for all the court. Even Princess Mary, who had just had her seventh birthday, went into mourning for her brother. The Earls of Shrewsbury and Kent, as official personnel, had their mourning cloaks paid for by the King.

As soon as the news of Arthur's death reached Spain, Queen Isabella wrote demanding that the Princess of Wales, who had fallen ill at the same time as her husband, 'be removed without loss of time from that unhealthy place where she now is'.[14] Queen Elizabeth ordered 'a litter of black velvet with black cloth, wherein the Princess was brought from Ludlow to London, fringed about with black valance and two head pieces of the same, bounden about with black ribbon'.[15] She paid from her own purse. For the rest of the year Elizabeth of York wore black, and so did the two Princesses. The Queen's account book is full of items such as the gown of black velvet, the bodice of which was relined for the Queen of Scots, and 'a black satin gown for my Lady Mary', both of which were paid for in June.[16]

Providing mourning apparel when she had expected to busy herself with her elder daughter's trousseau, drove the Queen to many small economies. She kept a running account with Henry Bryan, a London silk merchant, who presented his bill for £107 10s several times before it was finally paid off in instalments.[17]

As the summer wore on, Margaret's black gowns were relieved by sleeves of white sarcenet. She was also allowed a pair of orange sarcenet sleeves, which clearly became a favourite item in her wardrobe. There was a panic in July when they were left behind at Baynard's Castle. Richard Justice, the Queen's Page of the Robes, was paid extra for boat hire from Westminster to London to fetch them back.[18]

The Queen's account book gives lively and reliable glimpses of court life during Margaret's last year at home. Lord William Courtenay was implicated in a Yorkist plot involving Edward IV's grandsons, Edmund and Richard de la Pole, and was attainted for treason. The Queen paid the expenses of her nephews and niece, the children of Lady Katherine. Like their cousins the Princesses, they were dressed in black. The Queen herself remained in mourning for her firstborn, but just before the Feast of Corpus Christi she sent Richard Justice from Richmond to London for a cloth of gold gown, richly trimmed with expensive fur. True to her assertion 'We are both young enough', the Queen conceived again in May. It was her seventh pregnancy. Perhaps the many small payments she made at the shrines of efficacious saints, Our Lady at Northampton, St Frideswide at Oxford and St Edward the Confessor at Westminster, were accompanied by prayers for another boy.[19]

Henry, Duke of York, became *de facto* Prince of Wales, but he could not assume the title until it was established that the Princess of Wales was not carrying Arthur's child.[20] Margaret busied herself with her music. Mother and daughter shared this interest. On 5 July the Queen paid Giles the luter for strings for the Queen of Scots' lute. She also purchased a pair of clavicles,* though whether for her own or her children's use is unclear. The seasons changed and payments for flowers and cherries, chickens and larks gave way to payments for venison and fine cock pheasants. Christmas was spent at Richmond. The Queen's confinement approached serenely. Her needlewomen were constantly employed on a great state bed. Its hangings were a perpetual expense for silk and gold twist. In January Elizabeth paid 10s to Margaret's minstrels, who had evidently delighted her at Christmas or New Year. Towards the end of January, with Lady Katherine in attendance, she was rowed to the Tower, where she had decided to take her chamber.

On 2 February 1503 the Queen gave birth to a girl, who was named Katherine. Nine days later Elizabeth of York died. It was the day of her thirty-seventh birthday. The baby died some weeks later. Henry was devastated. A huge state funeral was arranged at Westminster Abbey. Lady Katherine Courtenay was chief mourner. The Queen's sisters all attended; even Lady Bridget, who had taken the veil, came from her convent for the occasion. All London mourned. At Cheapside groups of thirty-seven

---

* An early keyboard instrument.

virgins with chaplets of white and green were stationed bearing tapers. From Mark Lane to Temple Bar there were 3,000 torches, as well as candles burning in all the parish churches. 'Humble et reverente', the Queen's motto, was emblazoned on the hearse.

The spring of 1503 was a depressing time for the young Queen of Scots, who now had to face the preparations for her marriage without the guidance of her mother. Many details in Elizabeth's account book indicate that mother and daughter had been close during 1502.[21] When Elizabeth gave five shillings as a Mass offering, Margaret's donation of twelve pence (one shilling) immediately after implies they went to Mass together on feast days. Two queens at one court, the younger walking always a little behind the older, offered an excellent opportunity to assert the truth of Henry's remark that England was the greater of the two kingdoms. Elizabeth was also able to train her daughter at first hand in the finer points of courtly etiquette. One of her last presents to Margaret was to have a crimson velvet gown stunningly trimmed with pampilyon, a costly black fur resembling Persian lamb that was worn only by the very rich or royalty.[22]

Lady Margaret predictably came to the rescue. The practical Countess seems to have stepped in and taken charge of many of the arrangements for her granddaughter's journey to Scotland. On 27 June Henry VII set out from Richmond to accompany his daughter to Collyweston, Lady Margaret's palace in Northamptonshire. An entry in her Book of Hours records their arrival on 5 July: 'This day 1503 King Henry VII and the Queen of Scots his daughter with a great multitude of lords and other noble persons came to Collyweston unto my lady his mother.'[23] Collyweston was equipped to cope. Originally a simple country manor house four miles west of Stamford, it had been extensively renovated in 1502 and during the spring of 1503. A full-scale royal visit was expected from the moment of Margaret's betrothal and a large guest house had been built accordingly.

Everyone who knew Lady Margaret praised her talent for domestic organization. At her funeral Bishop Fisher remembered how four times a year her ordinances were read aloud to all her household. Henry Parker, her sewer, or domestic butler, for many years, left a memoir of the reception she had given for the arrival of Katherine of Aragon at her London house, Coldharbour, where rooms were refurbished, windows reglazed and ovens enlarged. The account book shows that an early conservatory was installed so that even in November there should be a supply of fresh herbs.[24] At Collyweston the park had been enlarged at the beginning of the reign and enclosed for the King's pleasure so that whenever he visited his mother he could hunt there. For the 1503 occasion four great bay windows were built. Stained glass depicting the Beaufort arms was specially commissioned, but William Hollmer, an unfortunate local craftsman, mistook the mythical beast the yale, one of the supporters of the arms, for an antelope. Seven shillings had to be given to John Delyon of Peterborough for 'changing of Antelope into an Yale'. As her biographers observe, 'one could almost sense the eruption', when Lady Margaret discovered the mistake.[25] The entire court was expected to accompany the Queen of Scots on the first stage of her progress, so the gardens were enlarged, summerhouses built and ponds cleared. The Countess even borrowed choristers from Cambridge and Westminster to augment her own small choir, which performed at the various entertainments and disguisings.

The royal party remained three weeks at Collyweston. Then on 8 July Margaret took leave of her father and grandmother to set out on the thirty-three-day journey to Edinburgh. The wedding progress was meant to be a display of power and magnificence. Henry entrusted his daughter to the care of the Earl of Surrey, under whose command his armies had suppressed border raids. Lady Surrey was also to accompany Margaret in a dual role as chaperone and mentor. John Yonge, Somerset Herald, who had recorded the 'fyancells' at Richmond was chosen as chronicler. He wrote, he explained, with the intent 'to comfort the hearts of age for to hear it and to give courage to the young'.[26]

The Scottish ambassador, the Bishop of Moray, accompanied the procession. The Bishop of Norwich went as far as York. Surrey rode first with a troop of armed men. Then came lords, knights, squires and yeomen in the proper order, the strictest precedence being at all times observed. Margaret herself, 'richly dressed and mounted on a fair palfrey', rode immediately behind her standard-bearer, Sir Davey Owen. She was followed by her Master of the Horse, Sir

Thomas Wortley, leading a spare palfrey. In case she should tire of riding, a superb litter was borne by two noble coursers. Her principal ladies, accompanied by their squires, rode behind the litter, all on beautiful palfreys. Four older ladies travelled in a carriage drawn by six fine horses. Their limbs must have been jolted black and blue, for the vehicle, though rich in appearance, would have had no springs and must have been about as comfortable as the meanest farm cart. A train of other gentlewomen, also splendidly mounted, followed the carriage. Every time Margaret entered a town, John English and his company of drummers began what Yonge called their 'ran-tan-tissing', while other minstrels and the trumpeters, their instruments decorated with banners, sounded a tremendous fanfare so that all the citizens should know who was arriving.[27] They were accompanied by heralds in tabards blazoned with the royal arms and by sergeants carrying heavy maces. The Master of the Horse bustled to the front on such occasions with a company of gentlemen whose office was to control the crowds as they thronged to see King Henry's daughter.

Sometimes she entered a town on her palfrey, its saddle-cloth richly embroidered with the red roses of Lancaster. At other times she used her litter, shining with its fringe of Venice gold, so that all the people should have a good view. Squires, pages, footmen and gentlemen of the household rode behind the ladies. Everyone was in the livery of his lord and master, with badges gaily displayed. Each morning the baggage wagons went ahead. Some carried Margaret's magnificent wardrobe. Others contained provisions and were accompanied by a retinue of cooks, carvers and cellarers. The Queen's personal belongings were stored in wagons covered with protective canvas, striped in the Tudor colours of white and green, and stamped with the royal arms of England and Scotland, with red roses and the Beaufort portcullis surmounted by a crown, which Henry had incorporated to emphasize his Lancastrian descent.[28] Other lords and ladies had their coats of arms painted on their baggage wagons, so that even the most mundane part of the mighty procession had a festive air.

From Collyweston Margaret went to Grantham in Lincolnshire, where she stayed quietly at the house of a Mr Hall on the first night of her journey.[29] She was greeted by the Sheriff of Lincoln, Sir Robert Dymock, with a company of thirty horsemen. A procession of friars sang anthems as she approached, and before entering the town the Bishop of Norwich got down from his horse and gave Margaret the cross to kiss. This mixture of administrative pomp and religious ritual occurred at every stopping place. If any were still in doubt that Henry Tudor ruled England, his daughter's incredible entourage served to thrust home the might of the Crown.

As a show of allegiance, the sheriff of one county would accompany the procession to the next. The Sheriff of Northampton went right through Lincolnshire into Yorkshire. There companies of local gentry rode out to meet the young Queen from every town and from every sizeable country seat. Sir William Scargill, the Sheriff of Yorkshire, had a company of sixty horsemen, their bridles all trimmed with silver and gold bells. Each small contingent wanted to show off their prancing steeds, so Margaret was treated to equestrian displays every few miles along the route. At times, despite the great dignity with which it assembled every morning, the procession must have had all the merriment of a travelling circus.

At Doncaster the mayor and burgesses were on foot. By Pontefract even John Yonge was exhausted from counting and re-counting the number of local grandees and simply wrote, 'many other noble squires and gentlemen of Yorkshire also came to her'. At Tadcaster Lord and Lady Latimer and the two Lords Scroop joined the throng. Then the great Earl of Northumberland, Harry Percy himself, arrived on a horse covered with crimson velvet and with gilded stirrups hanging from his saddle. Dressed in a crimson velvet mantle, his sleeves bordered with flashing jewels, he wore black velvet boots with gilded spurs.[30] Yonge, ever alert to a new fashion, described everything the Earl wore for the next ten days in the minutest detail, but what the herald, riding along with the lords and ladies, did not know was that the procession heading towards York had swelled so alarmingly that there were now too many people to get safely through the city gate. Having been informed of this fact by outriders, the mayor, Sir John Guillot, ordered a hole to be made in the city walls, and to this day a plaque marks the spot where Margaret made her entry.

Even the young Queen of Scots must have been impressed by
the show that the ancient city laid on. The bells pealed, the trumpeters sounded their fanfares and 'all the windows were so full of
nobles, ladies, gentlemen, damsels, burgesses and others in so
great multitude that it was a fair sight for to see', wrote John
Yonge.[31] It took two hours to reach the Minster, where Margaret
was received by the Archbishop of York and a full complement of
bishops. The next day was Sunday. Margaret wore a gown of
cloth of gold with a rich collar of precious stones and a golden
girdle sweeping to the ground. The Countess of Surrey, who
seems to have assumed a dominant role early on the journey, was
relegated to her proper place as train-bearer, with a gentleman
usher to assist her. Everyone wore their finest clothes. The Earl of
Northumberland dressed in cloth of gold and kept state like a
prince. Later that day, the Archbishop of York held open house
and the Countess of Northumberland was presented to Margaret.

The Queen left York on 17 July, travelling through various
small towns to Durham, where her arrival coincided with the
Bishop's installation. She stayed three days as his guest and was
'well cherished'. On 23 July he gave what Yonge called 'a double
dinner and double supper to all comers worthy to be there'.[32] At
Newcastle children were assembled at the city gates, singing
cheerful hymns. Once again Margaret made a state entry and on
the quayside people climbed into the rigging of the ships to get a
better view. On seeing the ships' masts, the herald rather hoped
they would fire a gun salute, but he was disappointed: 'they
made no sound of artillery and ordnance'.

At last the excitement died down and Margaret was able to get
a good night's rest at the Augustinian monastery. The following
day was 25 July, St James's Day, which the Earl of
Northumberland celebrated by giving a banquet in Newcastle
which lasted until midnight because of the 'games, dances, sports
and songs'. The company then rode to his mighty fortress,
Alnwick Castle, where Margaret was able to relax. She spent a
day hunting in the park and shot a fine buck. On 30 July the party
reached Berwick, where Somerset Herald at last heard the desired
gun salute. The border stronghold had many times been captured
or raided by the Scots, but it was now firmly in English hands. At

Berwick Lord Dacre, Henry's chief representative in the Borders, had joined the company with Lady Dacre and another train of ladies and gentlemen, so that the procession which finally assembled to cross the Border was estimated at between 1,800 and 2,000 persons.[33]

The Archbishop of Glasgow welcomed Margaret on behalf of the King at Lamberton Kirk. He was at the head of a huge company of Scottish lords and gentlemen. John Yonge was fascinated by their jackets of velvet and damask, some decorated with their arms and crests. The Bishop of Moray joined the Archbishop, while five of King James's trumpeters sounded a welcoming fanfare. Followed by the Earl of Surrey, the Archbishop of York and the Bishop of Durham, the Queen was led to a pavilion for a private reception attended only by the chief nobility. Somerset Herald glimpsed a Scottish lady inside dressed in scarlet and apparently at the head of a group of gentlewomen who were offering the Queen fresh fruit. Three other pavilions comprised a pantry, a buttery and a kitchen, where the whole company helped themselves to food and drink. Then the procession reassembled and many of the English lords took their leave and went back over the Border. The Earl of Northumberland and the elder Lord Scroop left in grand style, making their horses leap and prance in a farewell salute. Margaret stayed at Fast Castle with the Bishop of Moray's sister. About 1,000 Scots had come to welcome their Queen, of whom 500, Yonge estimated, were on horses. He reckoned that between 500 and 600 of her English escort remained with her for the journey to Edinburgh.

At Dalkeith she was received by the Earl and Countess of Morton. When Lady Morton went down on her knees as a sign of respect, Margaret quickly raised her up and kissed her. Then the King, who was officially scheduled to meet Margaret at Edinburgh, came clattering into the courtyard with sixty horsemen.[34] Custom demanded that he should appear to have been on a hunting expedition and to have decided, hearing his bride was near, to pay her a surprise visit. James was attired in a crimson velvet jacket edged with cloth of gold and instead of a crossbow he carried his lyre upon his back. Even Yonge was startled by the length of the King's beard. It was 3 August, five days before the wedding. Margaret curtsied deeply and James IV bowed low. They exchanged a kiss of greeting and then the King kissed each of Margaret's ladies and gave a hearty welcome to the Earl of Surrey. Bride and groom then drew aside to talk and take stock of each other. They sat together at supper. Later the minstrels struck up and Margaret performed a court dance with Lady Surrey. The King then rode back to Edinburgh, apparently in excellent spirits.

During the night there was a fire in the stables and Margaret lost some of her favourite horses. The King immediately rode over to comfort her and came upon her playing cards. She rose spontaneously to greet him and James, having welcomed the Archbishop of York and the Bishop of Durham, suggested more music. After a stately bass dance, the musicians played a round. Everybody joined in as Margaret and Lord Grey began the dancing. Soon the atmosphere was so relaxed that the King began to play the clavichord and later his lute, which pleased Margaret very much. Sir Edward Stanley sang a ballad and the King called on a Scottish gentleman to sing a duet. Having won Margaret's confidence, James began to show off a little. When he took leave of her that evening, he leapt on to his horse without touching the stirrup and galloped away.

On 5 August the King arrived for supper. Margaret was expecting him and they continued their musical flirtation. This time she showed off her skill on the clavichord and he knelt beside her while she played the lute. At supper Margaret had an uncomfortable chair. James immediately ceded the place of honour to her. That evening the Earl of Surrey gave James a horse which King Henry had sent as a wedding present. It was superbly harnessed and covered by a long trapper in green and white. Two days later James sent Margaret a string of horses to replace the palfreys she had lost in the fire, and also the traditional lover's gift of a hart.[35]

On the morning that Margaret was to enter Edinburgh, the King rode out to meet her. Margaret wore cloth of gold trimmed with black velvet. She sat in her litter, with one of the horses James had given her following behind. The King was also in cloth of gold, bordered with black fur. He leapt from his horse, doffing his hat, kissed her and then remounted to ride alongside her litter. Outside Edinburgh they came upon two knights fighting a symbolic combat in a field. It was an elaborate allegory of courtly love. After the King and Queen called a halt to the fighting, James arranged for the hart he had given Margaret to be loosed and chased by a greyhound. The hart escaped and was given protection. Just as Margaret's senses were quickened by this display, the King sent for the palfrey he had given her, vaulted into its saddle and had Margaret lifted up behind him.[36]

To deafening cheers they rode into the city on one horse, the Earl of Bothwell preceding them with the King's sword held aloft in a scabbard of purple velvet with 'God my Defender' embroidered upon it in pearls. Whether Margaret was disturbed by the sudden intimacy of sharing a saddle we shall never know. There is only one way a woman can ride pillion on a horse and that is by clasping her fellow rider firmly round the waist. If she objected, she did not show it. Yonge reports no change in her serene demeanour. Two hundred Scottish knights led by James's cousin, Lord Hamilton, escorted the pair through the city. There were many pageants. The royal procession passed through a wooden gate with painted turrets filled with choristers dressed as angels 'singing joyously for the coming of so noble a lady'. In the centre of the city a fountain ran with wine. On a scaffold, Paris was deliberating over the golden apple he was to award to the most beautiful of three goddesses. At Margaret's approach, he chose Venus. Further on, the angel Gabriel saluted Mary, and four Virtues sat enthroned, with Temperance trampling upon Epicurus and Prudence rather mysteriously subduing Sardanapalus. A unicorn and a greyhound supported a great shield upon which a thistle in full flower was intertwined with a red rose.[37]

These two emblems were famously embraced by the court poet, William Dunbar, who composed a wedding ode, urging the amorous James to be faithful to his bride.

> Nor hold no other flower in such dainty
> As the fresh rose of colour red and white
> For if thou dost, hurt is thine honesty
> Considering that no flower is so perfite
> So full of virtue pleasance and delight.[38]

On 8 August the whole court were dressed in their finest clothes by nine o'clock in the morning. 'The ladies,' wrote Yonge, 'came richly arrayed, some in gowns of cloth of gold, the others of crimson velvet and black. Others of satin and tinsel, of damask of many colours, hoods, chains and collars upon their necks.' The Earl of Surrey was in cloth of gold with the collar of the Order of the Garter. Most of the gentlemen had heavy gold chains round their necks. The Bishop of Moray led them to the King's presence chamber to listen to the wedding sermon.

The lords brought Margaret from her chamber to the church, which was the chapel of Holyroodhouse. She wore a golden crown studded with pearls and precious stones. The Archbishop of York and the Earl of Surrey led her down the aisle. Helped by a gentleman usher, the Countess of Surrey again bore her train. The Queen was followed by her English and Scottish ladies, walking four abreast in a processional order devised by the Earl of Surrey to give them equal precedence, thus preventing any unseemly squabbling over rank. Then the King, resplendent in white damask figured with gold and wearing a jacket with crimson satin sleeves, was led in by his brother, the Archbishop of St Andrews. Margaret's gown was also trimmed with crimson and her hair hung down her back beneath a long coif. The Archbishop of Glasgow and the Archbishop of York performed the marriage ceremony, reading aloud the special dispensation already granted by the Pope because of the parties' consanguinity. 'This done,' recorded Yonge, 'the trumpets blew for joy, and the King being bareheaded and holding her by the right hand was convayed through the said company to the High Altar, before which was a place for them to kneel upon rich cushions of cloth of gold.'[39] A short coronation followed the Nuptial Mass. Margaret was anointed and James himself put a sceptre in her hand. During a large part of the ceremony, his arm firmly encircled Margaret's waist.

The rest of the day passed in feasting. A gilded boar's head was served, followed by a piece of brawn, a great ham and then another twelve dishes. The King and Queen ate from gold plates and the second course consisted of forty or fifty different entrées. In the Great Chamber, where the Queen's ladies dined, the observant Yonge spotted new coats of arms in the windowpanes. Once again the arms of England and Scotland had a thistle entwined with a rose, surmounted by a crown added to them. After dinner there was dancing, then further feasting at supper. The young Queen must have been completely exhausted. She rested briefly while James attended Evensong, then night approached and, at last, 'the King had the Queen apart and they went together,' wrote the herald, adding, 'God by his grace will hold them in long prosperity.' That evening in Edinburgh there were bonfires throughout the city.[40]

The Earl of Surrey's brisk organization of the ladies in the wedding procession was characteristic. He was an outstanding military commander and he and his wife had been given the immense responsibility of seeing that their sovereign's daughter reached Edinburgh safely. Margaret viewed the matter differently. Her entourage included several persons who were trusted friends of her grandmother or who had been part of her mother's household. Sir Ralph Verney, her own chamberlain, was paid the enormous annual salary of £175 and his wife, Lady Verney, received a further £116 13s 4d. There was friction because Margaret would give one set of orders to her household and, ignoring them, Surrey would relay his own instructions directly to James's officers. At some point after her arrival in Scotland, either during the wedding celebrations, when she had no time to herself, or immediately afterwards, when various English courtiers were returning, Margaret wrote to her father. She dictated the first part of her letter to a secretary. It has been quoted to suggest that she showed little gratitude for all that had been done for her and that she sulked because of the Surreys' overbearing behaviour. This is because various printed versions of the letter have been abridged. The original manuscript begins:

My most dear lord and father, in the most humble wise that I can, I commend me unto your grace, beseeching you of your daily blessing and that it will please you to give hearty thanks to all your servants which by your commandment have given right good attendance.[41]

She asks Henry to thank especially 'all those ladies and gentle-women which hath accompanied me hither', adding that the bearer of the letter, a lady who is about to return to England, will explain a number of things which she does not wish to write down. She also asks Henry to take care of Thomas, 'which was footman to the Queen my mother', explaining, 'he hath been one of my footmen with so much diligence and labour to his great charge of his own goods and I am not able to prosper him except by favour of your grace'. There follows a complaint about Surrey, who, she says, has spent too much time with James, not allowing Sir Ralph Verney any autonomy.

The letter was printed in full by Sir Henry Ellis, Keeper of the Manuscripts in the British Museum in 1824.[42] In the later printed versions the letter usually begins: 'Sir, as for news I have none to send, but that my lord of Surrey is in great favour with the King here.'[43] This gives the letter a querulous tone which is absent from the gentle original. The last ten lines are in Margaret's own hand, scribbled untidily and with great haste. They are the *cri de coeur* of a thirteen-year-old adolescent, who has sustained a taxing role publicly, and brilliantly, for many weeks. Suddenly the proud little Queen of Scots, married to a man nearly twenty years older than herself, realizes she may never see her father again. The persona drops and she is a very homesick child indeed.

I would I were with your grace now and many times more, when I would answer. For this that I have written to your grace, it is very true, but I pray God I may find it well for myself. No more to your grace at this time, but our Lord have you in his keeping. Written with the hand of your humble daughter, Margaret.[44]

Chapter 3
Princess of Castile

When Elizabeth of York died, Mary was approaching her eighth birthday. The youngest princess was a pretty child, golden-haired like her mother, and usually dressed in rich fabrics and striking colours. At three she had been sought in marriage by Ludovico Sforza, the Duke of Milan, as a bride for his infant son, Massimiliano, Count of Pavia. The wars in Italy were to dominate European politics for the next two decades. Ludovico hoped Henry VII would support him against Louis XII of France, who was threatening to attack the rich city state of Milan, which the Sforzas had controlled since the middle of the fifteenth century.[1] Henry pointed out that the French and the English were at peace. The King of France was even a member of the Order of the Garter. He also claimed that his daughter was too young for such a match, adding that if the Duke would care to ask again in another four years the situation might have changed. In fact, by the time Mary was seven the marriage between Katherine and Arthur had so much enhanced England's status as a European power that Henry Tudor could afford to seek a far grander match for his daughter than the son of Ludovico, il Moro. At five she had been promised to the four-month-old Charles of Castile, the son of the Archduke of Austria and Katherine's sister Joanna. This betrothal was short-lived. By the time Charles was two, he was betrothed to Louis XII's daughter Claude.

Scattered references in the household accounts help us to build up an idea of Mary's early life. Her first governess was Elizabeth Denton, who was in charge of a suite of attendants, including a doctor, a school-master, a wardrobe keeper and several gentlewomen. Up to the time of Margaret's betrothal, Mary was usually in the same household as her sister. Oarsmen in the Tudor livery of green and white would row the Princesses in one of the state barges between the country palaces which were their main homes, Richmond, with its fairy-tale towers, and Greenwich, where they could watch tall-masted merchant ships putting out to sea. On summer days a consort of musicians would serenade the party as they floated gently down the Thames. In London they stayed mostly at Baynard's Castle or the Tower residences their mother preferred to the cramped Palace of Westminster.

This peripatetic life meant that the royal ladies and their gentle-women lived amid the constant uncertainties of packing, and when the weather changed, as in England it does, the account books record a flurry of small payments to pages who would be sent from Greenwich to London, or from Richmond to Windsor, to collect some vital accessory which had been left behind. Richard Justice, the Queen's Page of the Robes, was constantly ferried between Richmond and Baynard's Castle retrieving Margaret's sarcenet sleeves, or small parcels of haberdashery from Mistress Dent, the furrier.

Mary also lived at Eltham, where Erasmus remembered her at four, playing insouciantly beside Margaret and Henry, who were so gravely royal. It has been assumed she was educated there, perhaps under the surveillance of her brother's tutor, John Skelton, but sticking to a lighter curriculum, probably devised by her efficient grandmother, who was a vigorous patron of learning and an early champion of the printing press.[2] Lady Margaret's influence was strong at Eltham. She had finished building the chapel begun by Edward IV, and even the swans on the moat wore enamelled badges bearing the Beaufort insignia chained lightly about their necks. By 1503, when Mary was eight, the Countess was already founding the first of her two great Chairs of Divinity at Oxford and Cambridge. Men of learning frequently visited her household, but she interested herself in all branches of education, read French books after supper and would certainly have seen to it that her granddaughters received early training in conversational French. She had already advised Queen Isabella that Katherine should learn French in order to feel at ease at the English court.[3] When it was reported that the infanta was making progress, the entire English royal family sent encouraging messages to Toledo and asked Don Pedro de Ayala to signify their approval.[4] Latin was not so important for girls, music and needlework being considered more elegant accomplishments. After the Queen's death, Mary spent some time in her grandmother's house at Coldharbour, where she probably spoke French with Lady Margaret's trusted attendant Perrot Doryn. She also had a French maid of honour among her own gentlewomen, Jane Poppincourt, who was to scandalize the English court many years later by openly becoming the mistress of the Duc de Longueville. Jane seems to have been one of Mary's companions from earliest childhood, and the Queen's account book includes payments for mending her dresses.

Mary's own clothes were paid for by the Great Wardrobe, her mother adding to them from her privy purse when the need arose. In 1499, the year Erasmus met her, Mary wore a gown of green velvet edged with purple tinsel, and one of blue velvet over a kirtle of tawny-coloured damask. She had a kirtle of black satin and fourteen pairs of double-soled shoes. For Katherine's wedding she was given two new dresses, the crimson velvet she wore at St Paul's and another of russet velvet. Both were luxuriously furred against the November cold. She also received a new kirtle of green satin. In 1502 her mother paid 12s 8d for a black satin gown for her which must have been mourning for Prince Arthur. It was the Pope's Jubilee Year and a payment of 12d for a pardon for Mary suggests she was of age to have made her first confession, and so to have taken part in the joyful ceremonies which marked the occasion in all the courts of Europe. She attended Mass with her parents before Margaret's betrothal and must have watched the jousts at Richmond, when Charles Brandon fought so memorably. A year later his uncle, Sir Thomas, obtained him a small court post, sewer to the board's end.[5]

The impression gained is that Mary was often at court, although she did not receive as much of the limelight as her elder sister. There is no record of her performing official duties, as when Arthur welcomed his parents to Shrewsbury, Margaret gave out the tournament prizes and Prince Henry conducted Katherine's wedding procession to St Paul's. By thirteen, Mary was an accomplished musician, playing both the lute and the clavicles. When she was in the same household as Prince Henry, she must have enjoyed giggling at Goose, his fool, and when she visited her father, the King, she probably played with his pet monkey, which once caused an uproar at court by tearing up Henry VII's notebook, which was filled with private memoranda.[6] Although the King never fully recovered from his wife's death, we know court life had resumed an even tenor by the summer of 1504. The Princesses Mary and Katherine joined Henry for a hunting expedition at Windsor and in that year the cost of Mary's household was £100 a month, since the King referred to this sum in correspondence with Ferdinand and Isabella, who were complaining of his niggardly treatment of their daughter. This was a generous allowance for a nine-year-old child with no separate establishment and suggests that Mary was much cherished.[7]

The Princess Dowager, as Katherine was now styled, did not fare so happily. She had remained at Ludlow for several weeks after Arthur's death, suffering from the same sweating sickness that had killed her husband. Queen Isabella had written as soon as the news reached Spain, demanding that her daughter should be 'removed without loss of time from that unhealthy place, where she now is', but Katherine had been too sick to travel.[8] It had been left to Elizabeth of York to supervise her daughter-in-law's journey back from Wales in the beribboned black litter with its formidable fringing. While the Queen of England was alive, Isabella felt her daughter had protection. The Spanish Queen with her high Castilian breeding had always sensed that the daughter of Edward IV was a true gentlewoman, but a vague uneasiness about Henry Tudor, whom she persistently viewed as an opportunist and an upstart, surfaces in her correspondence with the various Spanish ambassadors.[9] Even before Katherine had set out for England, Isabella, though flattered, had been genuinely shocked by the ostentatious sums Henry seemed to be spending on the preparations for her daughter's wedding. She had written to De Puebla in the spring of 1501:

I am told that much money will be spent upon her reception and her wedding. Nevertheless it would be more in accordance with my feelings if the expenses were moderate. We do not wish that our daughter should be the cause of loss to England in money, nor in any other respect. On the contrary we desire that she should be the cause of all kinds of happiness.[10]

After Elizabeth's death these gracious sentiments gave way to fierce maternal anxiety. Isabella sensed cause for alarm. She was soon to demand that her daughter should be sent back to Spain to mourn in a manner fitting to a daughter of Castile.

It had taken five weeks for news of the Prince's death to reach Spain. As soon as the couriers arrived in Toledo, Ferdinand and Isabella had sent a special envoy, Hernan Duque de Estrada, to Henry's court. He set out for London on 12 May, carrying a letter of condolence and a document imperiously requesting the return of the 100,000 crowns of the Princess's dowry which had been paid out at the time of her marriage. The Catholic Kings further demanded that Henry should stick to the terms of the Treaty of Westminster, which stated that, if widowed, Katherine should receive one third of the revenues of Wales, Chester and Cornwall.[11]

This should have been ample income to support the Princess and her suite of some fifty or sixty persons, but with the royal household in shock and turmoil after Arthur's funeral, the money was not paid promptly. Tension mounted among the Spaniards. When the Infanta Joanna had gone to Flanders to be married to the Archduke Philip, they remembered, the Emperor had dismissed some of her attendants. Isabella wrote reassuringly to De Puebla on 29 May. It was not to be believed that King Henry could be capable of 'exposing the Princess in her time of grief to want and privation'.[12] The fact that she needed to write, however, suggests panic had already broken out among Katherine's staff. Fear that her household would be reduced is the key to much of what happened in the subsequent months.

Unseemly haggling over Katherine's dowry was to go on between the Kings of England and Spain for years to come. Probably Henry had earmarked part of the 100,000 crowns, which he felt Ferdinand still owed him, to put towards Margaret's dowry to James IV. He was determined to get his hands on the second

instalment, but it is doubtful that he would have gone to the fantas-
tic lengths suspected by the demoralized Spaniards to cheat their
Princess out of her jewels and treasure.[13] Ferdinand, who at this
point needed to pay armies in order to stem the French advance
into Italy, wanted to prevaricate as long as possible, while Isabella
considered Henry VII had a moral duty to return the 100,000
crowns already paid out. She felt the King of England was not
behaving like a gentleman towards her daughter.[14] Katherine
herself simply needed her rightful dower revenues, the rents of
Wales, Chester and Cornwall, to pay the huge retinue of Spaniards
who had loyally accompanied her. The Queen of England, meanwhile, sensing that this was not a good moment to approach the
King for petty cash, pawned plate to the value of £266 13s and
borrowed the sum of £320 from two gentlemen in the city.[15]

By the summer of 1502 Louis XII had already driven the Sforzas
out of Milan. It was a foregone conclusion that he would soon try
to annexe the Aragonese Kingdom of Naples. If he succeeded,
France would be the most powerful nation in Europe, a situation
Ferdinand wished at all costs to prevent. He could not afford,
therefore, to lose the English alliance, and Estrada had been
authorized to arrange a new marriage for Katherine with the
eleven-year-old Prince Henry, who would be heir to the English
throne, unless Katherine happened to be pregnant with Arthur's
child. In the first weeks of May 1502, it seemed that this might be
the case, but three months in an age of unsophisticated gynaecol-
ogy was the time traditionally required to prove the point.

When Estrada arrived in London, Katherine and her entourage
of fifty bickering Spaniards had been lodged at Durham House in
the Strand. Officially the London residence of the Bishops of
Durham, it was often requisitioned as a temporary home for visiting ambassadors. With its walled gardens and watergate, in the
early months of Katherine's widowhood it seemed a convenient
place for the Princess and her court, being within easy reach of both
Westminster and Baynard's Castle. In the seclusion of Durham
House a curious interlude was now played out which, thirty years
later, was to be of immense significance when Henry VIII wanted to
marry Anne Boleyn.

As permanent Spanish ambassador in London, De Puebla guessed even before Estrada arrived with his documents that Ferdinand and Isabella would try to arrange a marriage between Katherine and Prince Henry. A formal dispensation would be required from Rome on account of the text in Leviticus, Chapter 20, which forbade a man to marry his brother's wife. The Scriptures were quite clear on the point: 'If a man shall take his brother's wife, it is an unclean thing, he hath uncovered his brother's nakedness, they shall be childless.' De Puebla, a qualified practitioner of canon law, realized that the type of dispensation requested would depend on whether the first marriage had been successfully consummated. He consulted the person most likely to know, Don Alessandro Geraldini, for many years the Princess's tutor and now her chaplain and confessor. Don Alessandro had insisted that the marriage was a true one. Indeed, he confidently expected there to be issue, but just as De Puebla had written a short dispatch to Isabella, Katherine's duenna, Doña Elvira Manuel, intervened. She insisted that Katherine was a spotless virgin, denounced Don Alessandro as an unprincipled liar and told De Puebla he had no business to go spreading slanderous stories. Katherine's biographer, Garrett Mattingly, has pointed out that Doña Elvira had no motive to make this sensational statement unless she believed it to be true. Virginity was a state which could be proven. If Doña Elvira was lying, she would never be trusted by Queen Isabella again, and if Katherine and Arthur in five months of living together had not consummated their marriage, it would obviously have been easier to get a dispensation from Rome for a second match. The first union would be annulled, but Katherine would not then legally have been Princess of Wales. From the Spanish viewpoint, this would have been disastrous, since Henry could claim he was under no obligation to support her or her retinue. The King of England was not slow to take up this line of fire. The news that he had done so was received at Toledo on 16 June 1502. Katherine's parents were horrified. 'Be careful,' they wrote to Estrada, 'to get at the truth as regards the fact whether the Prince and Princess of Wales consummated the marriage, since nobody has told us about it.' They were even prepared to believe the English would lie simply to avoid paying Katherine's dower revenues. 'Use all the flattering persuasions you can,' Ferdinand advised, 'to prevent them from concealing it from you.'[16]

In short, it would have been much better for all concerned if Doña Elvira had kept her mouth shut. She was, after all, opening herself to criticism from the English, ridicule even, for after the holy and splendid marriage at St Paul's, one of the duenna's tasks should have been to see that her charge got on, gently and gracefully, with the first solemn duty of matrimony, the begetting of an heir. From a sixteenth-century perspective, there was no virtue in a bride, particularly a royal bride, who held back on her wedding night. Lawyers, statesmen, diplomats and the Kings of England and Spain had laboured unceasingly for thirteen years to produce a dynastic union and here was Doña Elvira claiming that the whole thing was a failure and a sham.

What induced her to such folly? Why was she so passionate, so adamant, and upon what evidence was her conclusion based? Contemporary tests for establishing virginity or ascertaining pregnancy ranged from a classic internal examination to a process whereby a chicken wing was waved over the abdomen. Sexual ignorance was also common. It was whispered that Katherine's brother, the handsome, dark-eyed Infante Juan, who had married Margaret of Austria, had worn himself out through carnal excess at an early age. Perhaps Doña Elvira felt that she had a duty to Isabella to restrain Katherine from her natural appetites even after marriage. Very young couples were sometimes separated by their parents so that the boy could complete his studies and the girl grow riper for childbirth. Neither Katherine nor Arthur would have been considered young by their contemporaries, however. He was fifteen and her sixteenth birthday came one month after the marriage. Twelve for a girl and fourteen for a boy were the official ages of maturity and separations on grounds of youth usually took place after betrothal, so that premarital temptation would be ruled out, or after consummation, when property transactions were considered intact and inviolable even in the eyes of the family lawyers. Doña Elvira had not thought matters through.

Was she driven by blind hatred of Don Alessandro? As Katherine's tutor, he still had influence over her. Did the duenna feel he was a challenge to her authority? Immediately after the marriage there had been talk of Katherine and her household remaining at Richmond for the Christmas celebrations in the luxurious new palace with the Queen and the Princesses Margaret and Mary. Don Alessandro had apparently overruled that suggestion. When he heard that Henry's council required the Prince to return to the Marches, the Chaplain had told the King that Ferdinand and Isabella would be deeply dissatisfied if Katherine did not go too.[17] Doña Elvira and her husband, Don Pedro Manrique, obviously thought otherwise. Some days later King Henry had suggested that Don Pedro should be demoted from head of Katherine's household to the rank of usher. Juan de Cuero, her chamberlain, should also be replaced. Probably Henry merely wished to avert clashes with the Welsh and thought indigenous retainers more suitable than Spanish grandees. Ferdinand, sensing trouble ahead, wrote on 6 January to De Puebla that he should 'entreat King Henry that such an affront should not be offered to Don Pedro'.[18]

Poor Doña Elvira. She had been in culture shock from the moment of landing in these barbarous isles. In complete violation of Castilian custom, the King had insisted on seeing the Princess unveiled before the wedding ceremony. Then her husband's salary was threatened and on 21 December, just as the court was about to begin feasting, she was forced to make the arduous journey to Wales. She had every reason to detest England, its ruler, its ways and its weather. She must have longed for Katherine and all her entourage to be recalled to Spain. Given such circumstances, it is not difficult to imagine the venom with which she must have spat out her claim that Katherine was a spotless virgin. With its inference that Arthur may have been impotent, it must have been deeply offensive information for Henry even to try to digest, when grief-stricken over the loss of his eldest son. Significantly, it must have been just after the duenna delivered her broadside that the gallant Queen began her seventh pregnancy.

Doña Elvira's information also flatly contradicted the Prince's memorable morning-after comment. 'Gentlemen, I have been this night in the midst of Spain.' He had called, his attendants remembered, for a drink, implying that his exertions had been heroic, manly, unstinting.[19] Was this youthful bravado? Had the daughter of Castile fought him off like a little hellcat? Or had the young Prince, exhausted from the madcap feasting, fallen meekly asleep in her arms a little the worse for drink? If the latter were the case, why in five months of marriage had the young couple not tried again? It had been suggested shortly after the wedding that perhaps they should be separated on account of the Prince's 'tender age'. This would mean not that he was thought incapable of consummation, but on the contrary that, being young and ardent, he might, like the Infante Juan, have a tendency to overdo things. Arthur's comment could, of course, have been fiction, 'half-remembered kitchen talk', as Professor Scarisbrick suggests, 'bandied about thirty years later by those who wished to remain in favour with Henry VIII'.[20] One thing is certain, however: the duenna's insistence upon non-consummation was considered astonishing by contemporaries. The King and his council loftily ignored it, requesting from Rome the type of dispensation which assumed the marriage had been valid. When the document was finally drawn up, the Holy See, not knowing which side to believe, tactfully included the Latin word *'forsan'*. The marriage had 'perhaps' not been consummated.[21]

Being pivotal to the whole argument upon which the English Reformation was eventually to be based, the 'perhaps' has been debated forcefully for over 400 years.[22] Prince Arthur's virility has not had a good press. Doña Elvira, as First Lady of the Bedchamber, was in a unique position to check with all her gentlewomen on each occasion that the royal couple slept together. Clearly the sheets were not bloodstained, as they should have been after a true Castilian consummation. Arthur was not in the same league as the Infante Juan. The duenna stuck fiercely to her testimony and Katherine, who was perhaps too naïve to know otherwise, supported her. All subsequent discussion has been from the premise that one side or the other must have been lying, although it is perfectly possible to argue that both sides were telling the truth in so far as they understood it. Arthur perhaps experienced happiness undreamed of, while Katherine may have escaped the pain Doña Elvira had warned her to expect. Two weeks after the wedding the Prince wrote to his father-in-law from Richmond to say that he had never felt so much joy in his life as when he beheld the 'sweet face' of his bride. 'No woman in the world could be more agreeable.'[23] He promised to make her a good husband. If there were problems of non-consummation, the Prince of Wales had been blissfully unaware of them.

Still in mourning, Katherine did not attend the Christmas celebrations of 1502, but the court recovered a little as plans went ahead for Margaret's wedding. This transient gaiety was eclipsed two months later when the Queen died. At forty-six, Henry was still a relatively young man. His bust by Pietro Torrigiano shows a lean, handsome face, careworn but full of intelligence. With only one son to succeed him, the King naturally thought of remarriage. His first choice was Katherine herself. She was by this time seventeen. Isabella thought the idea 'barbarous'.[24] At her suggestion, Henry transferred his interest to the young Queen of Naples, sending off a trio of ambassadors to gain a detailed inventory of her charms. They were to report on the clearness of her skin, the colour of her hair and eyebrows, the condition of her teeth and the size of her arms, her hands, her fingers, her neck, her breasts and her income. The last was deficient. Other plans followed, to marry the Duchess of Savoy or Marguerite d'Angoulême, but the King never remarried. On the last day of September 1503 the treaty for a marriage between Katherine and Prince Henry was ratified.

It took another year for the dispensation to reach England. Queen Isabella saw a copy a few days before she died, in the great fortress of Medina del Campo in the heart of the very oldest region of Castile. She had reigned there as 'King' in her own right; Ferdinand was her consort, just as she was his in Aragon. The succession of Castile went to her daughter Joanna. No figure could have been more tragic than Katherine's beautiful, highly strung elder sister, but as things turned out amid the tangled web of European dynastic politics, Joanna's fortunes were directly to influence the fate of Princess Mary. Isabella's daughter had married the Archduke Philip in 1496. As the son of the Emperor Maximilian, Philip had remained in Flanders, but he longed to control Castile. As Joanna was so far away at the time of Isabella's death, Ferdinand announced that he would act for his daughter as 'Governor and Administrator' of Castile. This idea was approved by the Cortes, the ancient council of the region. Philip was prepared to fight his father-in-law and rumours were spread that Queen Joanna was mentally unstable, so that her husband would rule as her proxy. In January 1506 Philip set sail for Spain with the avowed purpose of taking Castile by force of arms. When Ferdinand heard that Philip was approaching, he was so enraged that, according to his secretary of state, Miguel Perez de Almazan, he wanted to fly at Philip with '*capa y spada*', the cloak and sword of the bullfighter.[25]

Before any such thing could come to pass, Philip's ships were blown off course by a mighty tempest in the English Channel. For forty-eight hours the Armada transporting his soldiers to Spain was tossed in the storm and finally the ships were scattered. Landing at Melcombe Regis in Dorset on 13 January 1506, the Archduke sent formal notification of his plight to Henry VII. To the King of England it seemed an act of God. Sir Thomas Brandon appeared with an escort of horse and a train of palfreys, litters and baggage wagons to conduct the royal guests to Windsor. Queen Joanna, shaken by her ordeal, was not fit to travel by road and rested until Prince Henry, now Prince of Wales and in his fourteenth year, was dispatched to Winchester with a delegation of gorgeously dressed nobles to perform an official welcome.

Anglo–Spanish relations had deteriorated since Isabella's death. Castilian separatists hated Ferdinand, while trade treaties favourable to the English, which the Queen had established by royal proclamation, were held to have lapsed by the conservative faction in the Cortes. In August 1505 800 English merchants and entrepreneurs had returned to London from Seville 'lost and ruined'.[26] Ferdinand also made the Treaty of Blois with Louis XII, which prevented Philip from crossing Europe to reach Castile. Henry regarded the Archduke's arrival on his own shores as a chance to revive the old Anglo–Burgundian alliance and to side with the Habsburgs. He was determined to entertain his guest in a style fitting to the son of the Emperor and chose Windsor Castle, the home of the Order of the Garter, which he had made into Europe's most coveted order of chivalry, as the scene for three weeks of bargaining and diplomacy.

Philip was perhaps impatient to get his ships repaired and to continue on his way to Castile, but he succumbed to Henry's lavish hospitality. The King of England rode out to meet his guest on 31 January. There was much ceremony as they doffed their hats to each other. Then they rode back to the castle in a great procession, trumpeters and minstrels striking up as they entered the main gate side by side so that neither should take precedence. Henry showed Philip four chambers richly hung with tapestries and cloth of gold. Then he conducted him to a state bedroom decked in crimson velvet with many embroideries of the royal arms. Philip thought this must have been Henry's own chamber, but the King insisted it was for his guest. The Queen's lodgings, unused since Elizabeth of York's death, had been opened up and Henry moved into them.

By 1 February the Princesses Katherine and Mary arrived. Philip kissed the royal ladies and all their gentlewomen. Entertainments were held in the King's dining chamber. Katherine and one of her ladies showed off some Spanish dances. Then she asked her brother-in-law to partner her, but he excused himself on the grounds that he was a sailor, not a dancer, and continued his earnest talk with the King. Princess Mary then performed two or three English dances and later played the lute and the clavicles. She was not quite eleven years old, but she played excellently and was praised by everyone present. 'In everything,' wrote the herald chronicler, 'she behaved herself so very well.'[27]

Philip was said to be enchanted by the golden-haired child. As the royal quarters were filled to capacity, Lady Margaret had borrowed the Archbishop of Canterbury's palace at Croydon and she was lodging some of Philip's suite there, including his own lutenists. Her servants were sent to fetch Mary to Croydon to be serenaded by the Flemish musicians.[28] Her sweetness and poise won everyone's hearts. Although Mary was too young to realize it, the King of Castile's visit was to be the start of her long career in state diplomacy.

On the afternoon of the Feast of Candlemas the two sovereigns hunted in the park with crossbows. Later Philip played tennis, beating the Marquis of Dorset by fifteen points. On 9 February Henry made him a member of the Order of the Garter. Queen Joanna, having rested from her ordeal, arrived at Windsor the following week. Henry, Katherine and Mary welcomed her. It

was the first time Katherine had seen her sister in ten years. If
Joanna showed any signs of the insanity later ascribed to her, it
went unrecorded. Henry treated her with great deference, placing
the rich litter which had belonged to Elizabeth of York at her
disposal.

Windsor was the ancient seat of the Kings of England. Henry
wanted Philip and Joanna to see the modern one. Katherine and
Mary were sent ahead to Richmond to make preparations there.
At Richmond there was more hawking and hunting, more feasting and dancing. Philip, whose own palace of Beau Regard was
one of the show places of Europe, pronounced himself impressed.
On the Saturday before Philip left, Henry took him to Eton, where
the schoolboys lined the churchyard waving and cheering.[29]

Much bargaining took place at Windsor. By the treaty which
they signed on 9 February, Henry promised not to aid Philip's
enemies and Philip promised to hand over Edmund de la Pole,
the last 'White Rose' pretender of the reign, who had sought
refuge in the Netherlands. Self-styled 'Duke' of Suffolk, he was
the cousin to the Earl of Warwick, who had been executed to
make the realm safe before Katherine's arrival. Her status was not
improved by the meeting. Ferdinand had still not sent the second
instalment of her dowry. She was to go on pouring out letters to
her father for three years, describing her trials as a 'grace and
favour' guest of the King of England. Her Castilian pride suffered
as she watched her dresses grow shabbier and as she sold or
pledged her small store of plate to pay her daily expenses.

On 27 June 1505 Prince Henry had sworn before the Bishop of
Winchester that he considered his marriage contract with
Katherine null and void, because it had been made in the time of
his minority.[30] This was probably intended not so much as a slight
to the Princess as a spur to her father, but though Ferdinand
offered plentiful advice no dowry was forthcoming. The Treaty of
Blois with King Louis, signed four months after Prince Henry's
repudiation, set the final seal on hostilities between England and
Spain. In the private sessions at Windsor the groundwork was
laid between Philip and Henry for what the King of England was
to consider the dynastic masterplan of his reign. The King himself
would wed Philip's sister, the twice-widowed Margaret of

Savoy.* Mary would marry Philip's son Prince Charles of Castile, who was also heir to the Burgundian lands, and Prince Henry was loosely promised to Philip's daughter Eleanor. Unfortunately, the Duchess of Savoy had never been consulted and, when the news filtered through to her, she firmly and flatly refused to marry the King of England.

Philip's unexpected death in the autumn of 1506 meant that Henry had to win the co-operation of Charles's grandfather, the Emperor Maximilian. A judicious loan of 100,000 crowns helped to smooth the way, for the Emperor was chronically short of cash and the King of England's wealth was becoming ever more apparent. A treaty was signed at Calais in December 1507. Mary's betrothal was to take place the following Easter and her marriage would be solemnized forty days after Prince Charles's fourteenth birthday. On Christmas Day 1507 Henry ordered general rejoicing in London, and the citizens, glad that England's old trade options with the Low Countries were restored, were swift to comply. Bells pealed, bonfires burned and free hogsheads of wine were distributed through the city.

In December of the following year the Emperor's ambassadors arrived for Mary's betrothal. An embassy of eight dignitaries was led by the Sieur de Berghes, one of the great lords of Brabant. The Governor of Bresse came in person, as did the President of the Council of Flanders. The Emperor had sent his personal secretary and a herald called Toison d'Or, but Dr Pflug, who was to see to the legal side, caused great difficulty both to Henry's Latin secretary, Petrus Carmelianus, and the London printer Richard Pynson, because of his unpronounceable name. Pynson, who produced a souvenir of the event in two editions, rendered him 'Dr Splonke'.[31]

The King received the ambassadors at Greenwich, seated under a golden canopy of estate. He was flanked by the Archbishop of Canterbury and Prince Henry. The paperwork was dealt with the following day, huge bonds and penalty clauses being inserted to make the agreement more binding. Princess Mary was to have a dowry of 250,000 golden crowns. Her jointure

* As the Emperor's daughter, known also as Margaret of Austria.

would be all the lands which had once belonged to Margaret of Burgundy, the Yorkist duchess who had caused Henry so much embarrassment in the early part of his reign. The formalities completed, the ambassadors were taken to Richmond.

There, ten days later, Mary was betrothed to Charles, the Sieur de Berghes standing proxy for the eight-year-old Prince. They stood on a high dais beneath a glittering canopy. First Lord Berghes took Mary's hand and spoke the words of matrimony, then she, with a grave and dignified expression, took his hand and without any prompting recited her promises in perfect French. Her speech was extremely long. The witnesses were astonished by her composure and unfaltering delivery. A few courtiers were moved to tears. Then the trumpets sounded, the minstrels played and Mary, with Charles's golden ring upon her finger, went with her father to hear Mass said by the Bishop of London. Feasting and dancing were followed by three days of jousts. Carmelianus composed a Latin poem which was printed in Pynson's record of the occasion, which was probably written by a herald. The anonymous chronicler was quite overcome by the staggering amount of gold plate used: 'I shall not rehearse what delicate and sumptuous meats, what diversity of pleasant wines, what plate of gold and silver-gilted the King had,' he confided, 'no dish or saucer but it was gilded and as bright as gold.'

His account, illustrated with woodcuts of the royal arms and of the King enthroned, was circulated in Latin in 1508 and reprinted in English the following year.[32] It was also translated into Castilian Spanish, so that a copy reached Prince Charles's other grandfather, the King of Aragon. The Emperor sent Mary a gift of a huge ruby set with pearls and diamonds. Charles sent a pendant in the form of a 'K' for 'Karolus', all set with diamonds and pearls and inscribed, 'Mary has chosen the best part, no one shall take it from her'. As Princess of Castile, Mary now took precedence over her sister-in-law at the English court. Writing to her father to beg for money to pay her servants, the Dowager Princess of Wales cried tears of shame.

Chapter 4
God us Defend

It was the custom for the Kings of Scotland to give their brides a 'morrowing gift' and the morning after their wedding James gave Margaret Kilmarnock in the south of the kingdom.[1] That autumn he took her on a tour of her dower lands, a journey of some forty miles north-west of Edinburgh. On 18 September they set off for the beautiful palace of Linlithgow. Its foundations went back to the fourteenth century, when Margaret's ancestor Edward I had built a fortress there. In her grandmother's time Henry VI had taken refuge in the stronghold when driven from his own kingdom during the Wars of the Roses. Wildly romantic and situated by a loch which stretched as far as the eye could see, the palace had been sumptuously refurbished before Margaret's arrival. At thirteen she possibly took more delight in its tiled pavements decorated with the initials J and M, surrounded by chains of love knots, than in the palace's historic past, but its deer park was legendary and here she could relax, away from the pressures of Holyrood.

From Linlithgow the party moved to Stirling, the King paying out vast sums to the carters and servants, who transported Margaret's abundant 'gear'.* This consisted of not only her own dresses, jewels, tapestries and plate but also the baggage of all her ladies. At one point the gear filled eighteen wagons. Extra help was hired at Leith, where the King paid 36 shillings to professional carters and 4s in tips to porters for heaving the assorted trunks and coffers.[2] James was particularly liberal in rewarding his wife's musicians. The love of music which had

* sic in the *Treasurer's Accounts.*

71

drawn the couple together at their first meeting continued through a marriage which was not always harmonious. On 7 October eight of Margaret's minstrels, who had originally been employed by Henry VII as part of the wedding progress, were sent home to England, but James retained an unnamed performer known as 'the Queen's luter', Bountas her cornet player and four Italian musicians who, on account of their excellence, were taken permanently into the royal household.[3]

When she reached Stirling, the rugged fortress towering above the Forth, Margaret, who must have heard stories of her husband's 'past', was taken aback to find her dower castle was used as a nursery for the King's illegitimate children. There were seven in all. One had died ten days before the couple set out on their journey, causing a messenger to be sent to Edinburgh and a winding sheet to be procured for 'the said bairn' at a cost of 2s.[4] Stirling never became Margaret's favourite residence. As James was a most affectionate father, however, he failed to understand why his wife resented the presence of the royal bairns. Her own mother and father had been models of domestic propriety and the young Queen found the permissive standards of the Scottish court hard to accept. Sadly there are no accounts of the confrontation which must have taken place between husband and wife on this issue, so we shall never know whether Margaret threw a fine Tudor tantrum, astounding James by the force of her unleashed passions, or whether she resorted to cold disapproval.

In the best known picture of Margaret as a young woman, Daniel Mytens's full-length portrait, now hanging at Holyrood House, Margaret stands with her hands clasped demurely in front of her in a gesture almost of submissiveness. Perched on her right forearm a small marmoset emphasizes her childlike vulnerability. Her auburn hair is drawn back under a jewelled coif and her dark velvet gown falls regally about the robust little figure, but despite her bland features, Mytens has managed to capture an obdurate expression in the dark eyes and slightly pouting mouth, which reveals the other side of Margaret Tudor's nature. Whatever means of persuasion she used to have the bairns removed, she got her own way.

James Stewart, Earl of Moray, the son of Janet Kennedy, was sent to join his half-brother, Alexander Stewart, the son of Marion Boyd. Eventually they were shipped off to Padua to be educated by Erasmus. Lady Margaret Stewart, a girl of almost the same age as the Queen, and daughter of the murdered Margaret Drummond, was packed off to Edinburgh Castle to be brought up in an independent household as befitted a King's daughter.[5] As Margaret, when she stayed in Edinburgh, lived at Holyrood House, she could scarcely object to these arrangements, but since she did not bear children immediately, the King legitimized his son by Janet Kennedy.

If this scandalized the Queen there was little she could do about it. Had James IV lived in our own time, he would simply have been credited with a tragic excess of testosterone. His relationship with Janet Kennedy seems to have continued intermittently until 1510, when her other suitor, Archibald Douglas, fifth Earl of Angus and surnamed Bell-the-Cat, was released after seven years of confinement on the Isle of Bute.[6] Cynics hold that James banished him because of his constant political intriguing and a dispute over lands in Lanarkshire, but the gossips thought otherwise, and the tale is often told by Scottish historians, as a story of bitter sexual rivalry between the two men.[7] Janet was Angus's mistress before she was the King's. After his release from Bute the Earl settled lands on her, which meant that she was often referred to as 'the Lady of Bothwell', but as the mother of James Stewart, it was natural that the King loved her very much. Shortly before promising that for Margaret Tudor he would 'all others forsake', James provided for Janet with a life tenure of Darnaway Castle, which she was allowed to keep 'as long as she remains without a husband or other man along with the King's and her beloved son'.[8] This property was far away from Edinburgh in the north-east of Scotland and close to the shrine of St Duthac, whom the King venerated enthusiastically in the summer months. The little Earl of Moray was brought up there until he was old enough to be placed under the tuition of Erasmus, and Lady Margaret Stewart seems to have gone there for her summer holidays. The King stayed regularly at Darnaway, whenever he went to pray to St Duthac at Tain, and a glance at the wine bills and the payments for salmon from the Spey suggest that he enjoyed himself.[9]

By the standards of her time the Queen had little to complain about. James was a generous and attentive husband. He lavished beautiful dresses and elegant jewels on his young wife. Even before she set out for Scotland a complete winter wardrobe was ordered for her with gowns of tawny velvet to set off her red gold hair and mantles lined with ermine to protect her from the icy winds. If she required spending money in excess of the £2,000 a year from her dower lands, the Queen had only to ask for it. After the tour of her estates was finished, the court returned to Edinburgh in time for her fourteenth birthday, which was followed by the Christmas festivities. The King chose a French doctor, who was also an alchemist, as Master of the Revels. He put on a tremendous show for the young Queen's pleasure, assembling harpists and lute players, pipers and fiddlers to accompany the traditional Scottish dancers. James was at Margaret's card table every evening, laughingly handsome and scattering largesse. On one occasion, after doubling his stake, he gave all his winnings to the harpists.

As a New Year's gift he presented Margaret with a 'heavy ducat' weighing an ounce of gold. The next day she received two gold rings set with sapphires and two beautiful crosses studded with pearls.[10] James also gave costly gifts to her ladies, but the feasting was curtailed by the death of the King's brother, James, Duke of Ross, heir presumptive to the Scottish throne and incumbent of the wealthy Archbishopric of St Andrews. James immediately nominated his illegitimate son, the eleven-year-old Alexander Stewart to the see. It was imperative for Margaret to produce an heir. Whether she did not conceive, or whether the King chose patiently and deliberately to exercise some form of continence, surprising in a man of his appetites, we do not know, but Margaret Tudor's first child was not born until she was sixteen. The first three years of her marriage were filled with social pleasures. In her velvet dresses and flashing jewels, Margaret seems publicly to have played her role as Queen consort impeccably. When the court moved for the freshening of one of the castles, she would set out with her ladies and the great baggage train filled with clothes and accessories. Such progresses were enlivened by the Scottish people who turned out to welcome their sovereign and his bride. If it was known the Queen was coming to a town, pig sties and cattle were cleared from the streets, which were strewn with rushes and garlanded with flowers.

James travelled constantly about his kingdom, sometimes to quell rebellion, as he was forced to in 1504, when there were disturbances in the Western Isles, sometimes to preside at the ayres, local courts at which he dispensed summary justice, and sometimes to collect revenues. Assessing his reign at the end of the sixteenth century, Bishop Leslie wrote, 'For his political government and due administration of justice' the King was 'to be numbered amongst the best princes that ever reigned above that nation. All theft, rape, murder and robbery ceased in his days by such sharp execution of laws penal, as he caused to be exercised through all the bounds of Scotland.'[11] He was interested in every branch of learning, every craft and all forms of scientific discovery. In 1494 he had founded the University of Aberdeen and two years later the Scottish Parliament passed a decree stating that the sons of barons and free-holders must attend school. It was Europe's first compulsory education act. Later the King founded the Royal College of Surgeons. He was immensely proud of his own skills in carpentry, barbering and dentistry. His private accounts sometimes itemize unusual tools: 'Paid for a psalter, 3 compasses, a hammer, a turcase to take teeth out and two pair of beads to the King 7s 8d.'[12] When James himself operated, he compassionately paid the patients rather than demanding a fee: 'Item to ane fellow because the King pulit forth his tooth 14s. Item to Kynnard the barber for two teeth drawn of his head by the King 14s.'

When Margaret finally gave birth to a son on 21 February 1507, the court was at Edinburgh. The King was overjoyed. He presented the gentlewoman who brought him the news with a goblet filled with golden coins. Two days later in a magnificent ceremony at Holyrood the baby was baptized James. Swaddled in white silk and carried on a cloth of gold pillow trimmed with ermine, he was proclaimed Prince of Scotland and the Isles and Duke of Rothesay, titles which clearly distinguished the little

Prince of the blood from James Stewart, Janet Kennedy's child.
Messengers were sent to England to inform Henry VII that he was
a grandfather, but Margaret lay dangerously ill and her
husband's delight at having begotten a legitimate heir was short-
lived. He made a pilgrimage to the shrine of St Ninian at
Whithorn on the Galloway coast to pray for his wife's recovery,
walking for seven days to complete the 120-mile journey. The four
Italian musicians who also went to pray for the Queen's health
were so footsore that they had to be sent back to Tongland on
horses hired specially for the occasion.[13] Margaret's fever left her
at the exact moment that James knelt in supplication at St
Ninian's tomb. The miracle was marvelled at in Scotland and
reported widely throughout Christendom. Even the Queen must
have ceased to doubt the sincerity of the chivalrous, romantic,
though constitutionally unfaithful man she had married.

It was a part of James's nature to alternate between moods of
deep piety and wayward knight-errantry. In his darker moments
he believed he had been responsible for the death of his own
father at the battle of Sauchieburn. Aged fifteen the Prince had
fought against James III on the side of the rebels but under a
banner bearing the royal arms.[14] When the King was wounded he
took refuge in a cottage and called for a priest. A hooded figure
pretending to be a friar came to attend him and stabbed him
through the heart. James IV was not personally responsible for
the deed, but he bore the guilt throughout his life trusting
fervently for his salvation in the mercy of Christ and the sacrament of Penance, which he practised with great simplicity by
wearing a heavy iron chain about his waist next to his skin. He
believed that if only he could pray and atone enough, God would
forgive him, and he made regular retreats into monasteries in
Lent and on other fast days appointed by the Church.

James had frequently vowed that he would one day make a
crusade to the Holy Land, where the heart of his ancestor, James
I, lay buried in the Church of the Holy Sepulchre in Jerusalem.
This intention greatly increased his prestige at Rome. On Easter
Sunday, 4 April 1507, a special envoy from Julius II presented the
King of Scots with a purple cap encircled with golden leaves and
a jewelled sword of state. The sword and a replica of the cap can

still be seen in the Honours of Scotland room at Edinburgh Castle. Along with the sword and hat went the title 'Protector of the Christian Religion'. James was the first Scottish monarch to receive these honours since William the Lion in 1202. As James Beaton, the Abbot of Dunfermline, offered the coveted gifts to the King in the Abbey Church at Holyrood, drummers, harpists, heralds, trumpeters and thirty-seven minstrels blared forth their approval.[15] It must have been one of the most solemn moments of James's life, confirming outwardly that the stain of Sauchieburn had been washed away and greatly reinforcing his desire to go to the Holy Land. To those close to the King, the Queen's recovery must have seemed like a sign of divine forgiveness. To commemorate his gratitude, the King gave Antonio Inviziati, the papal emissary, a gift of 1,000 French crowns, and the carpenters of Leith redoubled their efforts to build up the Scottish fleet in preparation for the great pilgrimage which James proposed to make to Jerusalem. For the rest of his life, James visualized himself as the upholder of Christian values in Europe, although this was not always the view held by other monarchs seeking his military help or the loan of his great ships.

When their baby was six months old, Margaret also made a pilgrimage to Whithorn to give thanks to St Ninian for her miraculous recovery.

The Queen's devotions were less spectacular and less strenuous than those of her husband. She practised no austerities, but travelled in a litter, her baggage loaded upon seventeen packhorses. A confirmed believer in the efficacy of relics, when on progress her 'chapel gear', or personal altar plate, went with her. In the last week before setting off on her epic journey to Scotland, when staying with her father and grandmother at Collyweston, she had been given a finely illustrated Book of Hours.[16] It was probably intended for use on the journey. At the end of the calendar, which traditionally formed the first part of such works, there is an inscription in Henry VII's handwriting: 'Remember your kind and loving father in your good prayers, Henry R.' This was written on a blank page opposite a picture of Christ as ruler of the whole world. Eighteen pages further, at the end of the commemoration to St George, the patron of England, the King wrote, 'Pray for your loving father that gave you this book and gives you at all times God's blessing and mine. Henry R.' The reminder that as a Princess of England she must at all times put her country's interests first was obvious.

When she reached Scotland, Margaret was introduced to a more sophisticated devotional work. It was by a Flemish master, and is considered today to be one of the finest illuminated books in Europe. Usually known as the 'James IV Book of Hours', it is assumed that it was commissioned by the King as a present for Margaret, but as there are no records of payment for such a work it may have been sent as a wedding gift to both the King and the Queen, possibly from the Netherlands. After the Calendar and before the Sanctoral, the arms of Scotland, the lion rampant with two slender unicorns as supporters, are displayed, surrounded by a festive border of golden thistles and golden marguerites proclaiming the happy union. James's own motto 'In my Defence' is depicted in gold.[17]

There follow many gloriously illustrated pages with miniatures from the lives of the saints. The borders are decorated with a profusion of flowers and butterflies. Sometimes, as a compliment to Margaret, the red rose of England has its petals outlined in fine gold leaf, emphasizing her descent from the royal house of Lancaster. Sometimes white and tortoiseshell butterflies alight delicately on sweet peas, columbines, pansies and gentians. There are lillies of the valley, rosa alba, purple and white violets, thistles in bud and in flower, and on one page a Scottish harebell, painted as perfectly as a botanical specimen.

Many of the miniatures appear to be by the celebrated artist Gerard Horenbout who was a court painter to Margaret of Austria, Regent of the Netherlands, and who worked on the famously beautiful Isabella Breviary, which was given to the Spanish Queen at the time of her daughter Joanna's marriage to the Regent's brother, Philip of Burgundy. Some experts are so convinced that the miniatures in the James IV book are Horenbout's work that he is often referred to as 'the Master of James IV of Scotland', but such books were usually produced by teams of artists and the harebell painter may well have been a native Scot. Certainly the scribe who wrote out the text must have focused his mind on the royal couple for whom the book was destined, for when he reached the page where St Mary Magdalene, voluptuously robed in pink, holds up her alabaster box of ointment, he rather unsuitably wrote 'Saint *Margaret* Magdalene'.

On the twenty-fourth leaf of the book, a full page picture of James IV at prayer shows the King crowned and robed in ermine. Before him the royal arms of Scotland are displayed on an altar frontal of blue velvet and there appears again the motto 'In my Defence'. At the end of the book there is a picture of Margaret, crowned and wearing an elegant blue velvet jacket with an open-work collar of gold. She is in coronation robes and the artist seems to have depicted her in Holyrood Abbey. A cloth of gold skirt falls in graceful folds about her knees and a mantle of the same material, lined with ermine, hangs from her shoulders. The Queen kneels at a *prie dieu*, draped with blue damask, which stands before an altar, its scarlet frontal embroidered with the arms of Scotland and England impaled. Beside her the figure of a Bishop reminds her of the solemnity of her new role as she gazes at a vision of the Virgin and Child. Embroidered on the altar cloth above the arms of the two countries is the new motto for James and Margaret, 'God us Defend'.

The solemnity of the kneeling figure echoes an earlier picture in a Book of Hours, which Margaret might have been shown in her childhood. Now at Alnwick Castle in Northumberland, the book was believed to have been the property of Margaret herself until a close study of the heraldry proved it belonged to her grandmother. Lady Margaret, wearing a coronet and enveloped in a garment illuminated with the arms of England, kneels before a vision of the Virgin, who is surrounded by cherubim and seraphim. Whether Margaret was ever filled with such ecstatic patriotism or imbued with as high a sense of destiny as the Countess of Richmond, we cannot know.

After Margaret's pilgrimage to Whithorn, the King and Queen celebrated the birth of her firstborn by arranging a tournament at Edinburgh Castle. James, ever interested in the latest artillery, had just installed new bronze cannon on the walls. Lists were set up in the courtyard and 'Black Ellen', a Moorish girl who had been brought to Scotland by Robert Barton, one of the King's sea captains, was made Lady of Honour. She was something of a novelty among Margaret's attendants. Dunbar, who had never before seen anyone of African descent called her the 'lady with the muckle* lips'.

The dark-skinned beauty made her entrance in a golden chariot, wearing a damask gown trimmed with green and yellow taffeta. She was rescued from a terrible mêlée by a 'Wild Knight', accompanied by 'wild men' dressed in shaggy goat skins with antlers upon their helmets. When the Wild Knight removed his helmet after vanquishing all his opponents, he proved to be James himself. The spectators feigned complete astonishment and the spectacle was considered an unqualified success. According to Dunbar, the victors were allowed to claim a kiss from Ellen's desirable lips.

> Who for her sake with spear and shield
> Proves most mightily in the field
> Shall kiss and with her go in grips
> And from thenceforth her love shall wield
> My lady with the muckle lips.

Things grew more boisterous later in the day, and it seems the losers were required to kiss her backside.

> And who in field receiveth shame,
> And tarnish there his knightly name
> Shall come behind and kiss her hips
> And never to other comfort claim
> My lady with the muckle lips.[18]

On 27 February 1508, twelve months after he was born, the baby Prince died at Stirling Castle. The Queen was already pregnant with her second child when she received the news. On 15 July she gave birth to a daughter at Holyrood Palace, but the infant died the same day. Margaret was grievously ill during each confinement. By

* Full.

the spring of 1509 she was pregnant again. It was a difficult time for the young Queen of Scots. From the moment of her coronation she had been the living emblem of the alliance between England and Scotland, but throughout 1508 James received embassies and envoys from Louis XII, who had formed the League of Cambrai with the Emperor Maximilian, ostensibly to crush the power of Venice. Henry VII did not want to be involved in costly wars in Italy and did not join the League, even though by December it had the official blessing of the Pope. James at first held aloof, but Louis continued his friendly overtures. For reasons beyond the scope of her comprehension, Margaret was soon to find Anglo–Scottish friendship strained almost to breaking point.

Henry VII had managed to pay Margaret's dowry punctually. The first instalment had been handed over by Surrey, who was Lord Treasurer of England, on 10 August 1503, two days after the wedding; the second was paid at Coldingham on 28 July 1504 and the last on 13 August 1505. This meant that for the first three years of his marriage James IV's annual income was increased by more than £10,000 Scots.[19] The wedding had cost £6,125 4s 6d and James's expenditure had been increased by the cost of the war in the Isles, the renovation of royal castles and palaces, the expansion of his navy and the upkeep of Margaret and her entourage, to say nothing of the huge sums disbursed for royal entertainments. After 1505, when the dowry payments ceased, the King urgently needed to find new sources of revenue. He and his council began a policy of systematically raising rentals on crown lands and of reviewing feudal dues. Wherever possible the crown's income was increased by exercising tighter control over the Church offices. The shocking appointment of the boy archbishop, the King's illegitimate son by Marion Boyd, was a case in point. The King's fiscal policy worked two ways. By enriching the crown and keeping a firm control over appointments, James was able to retain the respect of his nobles, so that in times of war he was able to muster efficient forces quickly, but as he stayed consistently richer than his warlords, certain Scottish magnates began to hanker after the 'auld alliance' with France, which had traditionally been a source of useful pensions.

In general the Treaty of Perpetual Peace, signed at the time of

Margaret's marriage, had held firm. There were incidents of course. Raiding and sheep stealing had been a normal part of the economy in Border counties since Roman times, but James IV and Henry VII had both appointed remarkably efficient wardens for the Border strongholds. Regular courts or 'days of truce' were held when offenders were brought to trial. The system worked perfectly until Sir Robert Ker of Fernieside, the Warden of the Middle Marches, was killed by an English miscreant, John Heron, known as the Bastard, and his ruffianly companions Starkhed and Lilburn. James regarded the murder of a warden as a serious offence, punishable by hanging, but although Henry delivered up Lilburn and sent Heron's brother as a hostage, Bastard Heron escaped and stayed free for several years, committing every kind of atrocity.[20]

The King of England further infuriated his son-in-law by detaining a Scottish subject, the Earl of Arran. The Earl and his brother, Sir Patrick Hamilton, were James's cousins. Arran had sailed for France in 1507 aboard the royal ship *The Treasurer*, which was taking the fourteen-year-old Archbishop of St Andrews to study under Erasmus. Arran carried a letter of marque from James to cover his outward journey. The following year he returned from France through England without requesting a safe-conduct. It was a minor offence, but Henry chose to treat it as a breach of the Treaty of Perpetual Peace and arrested him. He knew perfectly well that the Earl had been negotiating with the French, for Louis XII had openly requested James to send him Scottish troops to help with the defence of Milan. James had refused, but very diplomatically and in such a way that the 'auld alliance' could always be renewed. He was incensed by his father-in-law's high-handed treatment of his kinsman. Henry sent one of his ablest diplomats to Scotland to sort the matter out, a young man who had recently become a royal chaplain and was soon to be made Dean of Lincoln and raised to the status of a royal almoner. His name was Thomas Wolsey.[21]

James was at Whithorn, so Wolsey had to wait five days at the Border before he was given a safe-conduct. The young diplomat sensed great hostility among the Scots, since everybody believed Henry VII had sent him specifically to prevent James from renewing the French alliance. Gossip travelled so fast in Scotland,

Wolsey reported, that even 'the wives in the market knoweth every cause of my coming'. He reached Edinburgh on 28 March and immediately had an audience with the Queen. Margaret suddenly found she was required to exercise diplomatic skills which she had not yet had occasion to develop. James grandly announced he was too 'busy in shooting guns and making gunpowder' to see the English ambassador.[22] Wolsey had to wait a further five days for a meeting. He then saw James every day for a week, during which he drafted a shrewd and brilliant dispatch which detailed the deteriorating position between England and Scotland.

Sir Patrick Hamilton then added to the furore by appearing at the Scottish court in person. Whether he had escaped or been sent on parole is not clear. He made a courteous and kindly effort to spare the Queen's feelings by telling her that her father had treated him well, but Wolsey observed that 'he reported the opposite to the King'.[23] Margaret made a clumsy effort to defend her father by contradicting everyone who asserted that Henry had treated Arran harshly. This caused considerable embarrassment at court.

Wolsey's letter makes fascinating reading. It is in his own hand-writing. The surviving copy is the original draft; a neater version must have been sent to Henry, but Wolsey's crossings-out (the whole of the third paragraph is deleted and rewritten) show that his brain reeled when he tried to recollect the twists and turns in James's rhetoric. The King of Scots was under tremendous pressure from his own nobility to renew the French alliance, but he fully grasped the wider implications of Henry's European policy. He thanked his father-in-law for the distinction which the Castile marriage brought to both of them, for Margaret still stood second in line of succession to the English throne. He was indebted to Henry, he said graciously, for enabling him to become the ally of the Emperor and Princes with whom he had not previously been associated, but certain matters still rankled. Henry had made no redress for the murder of Sir Robert Ker and Bastard Heron still roamed the Borders unpunished. The entire Scots nobility were incensed over Arran's arrest and 'attemptats', or raids, were continuing along the Border.[24]

At this juncture Wolsey himself intervened, pointing out that for every raid made by the English, the Scots made four in return. Lord Hume, who was Warden of the East March and whose responsibility it was to deal with such matters, 'looked somewhat abashed'. Wolsey stressed that the King, the Queen and Andrew Forman, the Bishop of Moray, who had helped negotiate the Treaty of Perpetual Peace, were eager for the English alliance to continue, but when Wolsey recited Henry's grievances, such as a mention of the large number of Scottish subjects, some of them great persons in disguise, who kept passing through England without safe-conducts, James became wary and wily. He shifted his opinions so fast that Wolsey could 'not conceive what report' to make to Henry. He suggested that the Earl of Arran might be sent back on parole, but James replied that if Arran made an oath to Henry 'he would hang him as soon as he entered Scotland'. The whole matter was reduced to a nit-picking piece of protocol as James argued that since Arran was his subject, he should not be returned on conditions set by Henry. Wolsey was certain that the only thing which would stop James from renewing the French amity was for Arran to be returned unconditionally: 'He would fain have him back, but he is too headstrong to ask for him openly,' he wrote.

In the end no formal renewal of the French alliance took place. With his customary suave diplomacy, Andrew Forman arranged for the release of Arran while Louis XII sent Bernard Stewart, the Seigneur d'Aubigny, to Scotland at the head of an embassy. Royal patronage of St Ninian had turned the shrine at Whithorn into a major tourist attraction. Officially d'Aubigny announced he was making a pilgrimage to pray to the saint. He arrived with the Lord President of the Parliament of Paris and an entourage of sixty persons. The French guests were lavishly entertained with a programme of feasts, jousts, and a repeat of the Wild Knight tournament. The total cost of the pious Seigneur's visit was £1,083 7s 7d.[25] Andrew Forman, however, was sent to London to reassure Henry VII with an open account of all that took place. The King of England could scarcely object, since d'Aubigny had fought beside him at Bosworth. As a goodwill present, Henry sent his son-in-law a fine string of horses.

On 21 April 1509 Henry VII died. It must have been a great blow to Margaret, who had just started her third pregnancy. She was now heiress to the English throne, and Anglo–Scottish relations were temporarily healed amid the general rejoicing which heralded the reign of Henry VIII. During the last weeks of the old King's life, Prince Henry had been at his bedside at Richmond. Perhaps both had reflected on the words Henry VII had spoken at the time of Margaret's betrothal. 'Supposing, which God forbid, that all my male progeny were to become extinct and the kingdom devolve by law upon Margaret's heirs, will England be damaged thereby or rather benefited? For since the less becomes subservient to the greater the accession will be that of Scotland to England, not of England to Scotland.' It was unthinkable that a woman should remain heiress to the throne, and Henry VIII was later to claim that his father's last urgent wish was for him to marry Katherine of Aragon and to beget male heirs for the succession. In the first week of the new reign, Don Gutierre Gomez de Fuensalida, Knight Commander of Membrilla and ambassador to the King of Spain, was preparing to rescue the Princess before the next regime began. He had already started to salvage what was left of her dowry, prior to sending it out of the country. She regarded him with contempt. She had told her father she would rather die in England than return disgraced to Spain. 'Your ambassador here is a traitor,' she wrote to Ferdinand. 'Recall him at once and punish him as he deserves.'[26]

Henry VII's funeral was at St Paul's and he was buried in the magnificent chapel where Elizabeth of York already lay entombed in Westminster Abbey. A few days later Fuensalida was summoned to be informed of the new arrangements for the Princess and by 11 June Henry married Katherine in the Church of the Friars Observant at Greenwich, where seventeen years earlier he had been christened. A fortnight after the marriage the King celebrated his eighteenth birthday. For a brief ten weeks Lady Margaret Beaufort acted as Regent of England.

Chapter 5
Ye Are to Fight a Mighty People

The new King was tall and well proportioned, with auburn hair cut straight in the French fashion. It was universally agreed that he was extremely handsome. After the wedding at Greenwich, he went, as custom demanded, to take up residence in the Tower of London. Midsummer Day, 24 June, was the day set for the coronation. The ceremonies started on 22 June, when twenty-six gentlemen were appointed 'to bear dishes that day in token that they shall never bear none after that day'.[1] All were made Knights of the Bath. These were the men who would serve Henry VIII in his Privy Chamber, the charmed inner circle who would be trusted with office, who would dance, masque, hunt, joust and join the King in 'pastime and good company', and who, gradually, would replace the grave, elderly councillors who had surrounded Henry VII. On 23 June the traditional procession through the streets of London took place. Princess Mary watched with her grandmother from the window of a house in Cheapside.[2] Overcome with pride and apprehension, the Countess of Richmond burst into tears.[3]

Dressed in white damask and cloth of gold, Henry left the Tower with his escort of knights, and Katherine followed after him in a litter on cushions of white damask under a canopy lined with white silk and decorated with golden ribbons. For a few moments perhaps, it evoked memories of that other litter with its black fringing in which she had travelled so dolefully from Ludlow to Richmond as Arthur's widow. Now she was dressed in a kirtle of white damask and cloth of gold, furred with miniver.* Her hair

---

* Fur made of fine squirrel pelts, worn only by the nobility.

hung down her back and she was bare-headed except for a small circlet of gold set with pearls and precious stones. She was followed by her henchmen in doublets of crimson satin and gowns of blue velvet. Her ladies, dressed in blue velvet edged with crimson, rode behind on identical palfreys.[4] Throughout May and June Sir Andrew Windsor, Master of the Great Wardrobe, and Sir Thomas Lovell, Keeper of the Great Wardrobe of the Household, had scoured London and Flanders with their staff for the 1,641 yards of scarlet cloth and 2,040 yards of red cloth required to clothe the court and hang the streets. When the 'silks and necessaries' for the Queen and her household, and the fourteen-year-old Princess of Castile and her ladies, were added to the bill, the total came to £4,748 6s 3d.[5] 'If I should declare what pain, labour and diligence the tailors, embroiderers and goldsmiths took both to make and devise garments for the lords, ladies, knights and esquires against this coronation,' wrote chronicler Hall, 'it were too long to rehearse.'[6]

On 24 June there was a second, shorter procession from the Palace of Westminster to the Abbey. All the lords and ladies were in scarlet robes trimmed with fur. As Henry entered the church, the crowds closed in behind him and the souvenir hunters cut the carpet he had walked on to pieces. In a long and dignified ceremony, Archbishop Warham blessed the crown of St Edward. The King prostrated himself before the high altar and the Queen did likewise. Then holy oil was brought forward and Henry and Katherine were crowned and anointed.[7] The choir sang Gloria in Excelsis, and after a solemn Mass the procession moved to the shrine of Edward the Confessor, where the two heavy state crowns were exchanged for lighter versions. The King and Queen then returned to Westminster Hall for a magnificent banquet at which the Duke of Buckingham and the Lord Steward entered on horseback and to fanfares to lead in the procession of dishes. When the company had feasted to 'repletion, a tournament was held which lasted until midnight.[8]

A full report of the glorious day probably reached Scotland some time in July. Apologizing for his bad handwriting, James IV wrote to congratulate Henry, coincidentally on 11 June, the very day the King of England had married Katherine.[9] Until the new Queen bore

children, the child Margaret was carrying was the putative successor to both kingdoms, Margaret herself being the heiress presumptive. On 29 June, James confirmed the Treaty of Perpetual Peace
with the Great Seal of Scotland. He commissioned Andrew Forman
as his plenipotentiary to organize a meeting between himself and
Henry to see if they could bring to a final 'redress and reformation
all the disturbances on both the borders'.[10] By 29 August Forman
gave Henry his solemn promise that the Scots would keep every
article of the treaty, which had been sworn at Margaret's betrothal,
and when her third child was born on 21 October he was christened
Arthur in memory of her brother. The name was also chosen to
herald a new age of chivalry and to promote altogether rosier relations between the two island kingdoms, but before he died Arthur,
Prince of Wales, had left his small personal fortune to Margaret to
be held in trust by Henry VII. After a decent interval of mourning,
the Queen of Scots asked her brother to send the legacy to her, and
there began the strange and bitter saga of Margaret's jewels.

On the same day that James confirmed the Treaty of Perpetual
Peace, Lady Margaret Beaufort died. After the coronation she had
been staying at Cheyney Gates, a house adjoining the Palace of
Westminster. Henry Parker, her cupbearer, recorded that she died
of eating a cygnet. She was buried amid great honours in
Westminster Abbey in the same chapel as her son and his Queen.
In her will she left many legacies, particularly to Christ's College,
her foundation at Cambridge and to Westminster Abbey, where
one of her fine Books of Hours was chained in the Lady Chapel.
Among personal bequests she left jewels to Katherine of Aragon
and to her granddaughters Margaret and Mary. To Henry she
bequeathed a number of valuable books, including a copy of
Froissart's *Chronicles*, describing glorious battles in which the
Kings of England had beaten the Kings of France.[11]

The young King had made no secret of his intention to reverse
his father's policy by reviving England's traditional claim to the
Angevin empire.[12] Clearly he saw himself in the heroic mould of
Henry V, but he was not initially able to make war on France,
partly because England's prospective allies were absorbed by the
power struggles in Italy and partly because of the opposition he
met within his own council. Archbishop Warham and the two

conservative bishops Fox and Fisher were totally opposed to the idea of fighting Louis XII. They had served under a King who felt he owed his throne to French intervention and had struggled at all times to remember his debts of obligation, but by 1510 the League of Cambrai between France and the Empire was showing signs of strain, and as Henry had established his own envoy, the francophobe Christopher Bainbridge, at Rome, change seemed imminent. At the time of these power shifts in Europe, the English succession seemed assured. Queen Katherine was pregnant. Her first child had been stillborn, but on New Year's Day 1511 she was delivered of a boy. Bells pealed joyfully, cannon boomed from the Tower and bonfires were lit in the streets of London in honour of the birth of Henry, Prince of Wales. At Richmond the King held a magnificent tournament in which he took the role of Sir Loyal Heart. Towards the end the crowd jostled through the barriers and started tearing strips from the cloth-of-gold hangings which decorated the boxes. The courtiers took it in good part, retreating cheerfully dishevelled, but the child survived only seven weeks. His father had no serious reason to believe that the Queen would not produce another, healthier boy. The Queen of Scots, however, remained first in line of succession to the English throne.

By October 1511 a Holy League against France was signed at Rome between Spain, the Empire and Venice. England joined in November. Having helped Julius II to regain Faenza, Rimini and Ravenna, the French had overreached themselves by calling for a General Council of the Church to meet at Pisa, ostensibly to reform some of the abuses of ecclesiastical power which had grown up in a system riddled with nepotism and simony. The warrior pontiff, who had himself fathered three illegitimate children, immediately placed France under an interdict. Following the defeat of Louis XII at Ravenna, he grandly opened the fifth Lateran Council to deal with Church reform himself.

Officially the armies of the Holy League were to invade and subdue France that spring. Included in the overall plan to protect the papacy was a private deal between the English and the Spanish, whereby Ferdinand would regain Navarre, helping Henry to reconquer Aquitaine. Both sovereigns would support

Julius II's bid to recapture papal territory in Bordeaux, which had been under French rule for half a century, and at the end of April 1512 Lancaster Herald arrived at the French court with England's declaration of war. Six thousand men set off under the command of Edward Howard, and by June a further 12,000 sailed from Southampton led by the Marquis of Dorset. The expedition was an ignominious disaster. Ferdinand seized Navarre and made a separate peace with France. Dorset's army waited in vain at Fuenterabbia for their rendezvous with the Spaniards, who did not turn up. Illness broke out and by the time the English army had marched back to Calais, half of them were mutinous. Ferdinand treacherously blamed the whole dismal failure on the King of England's youth and lack of experience.

James IV was horrified. On 2 March a papal messenger had arrived at Holyrood with the warlike brief the Pope had issued against Louis XII, exhorting the sovereigns of Europe to unite against the French. The King of Scots had never read anything so depressing. He spent several days composing a reply. Whoever was the victor in this conflict between Christian Princes would be the moral loser. 'Christendom is betrayed to be trodden under foot by the enemies of Christ,' he wrote passionately to Julius.[13] Quixotically, in view of the new turn of events, James still dreamed of uniting his brother sovereigns in a crusade against the infidel. He sent letters to all the Kings of Europe, entreating them to keep the peace. He made Margaret write too, believing that the marriage tie between Henry and Katherine had given his wife an affinity with Ferdinand of Aragon. Pregnant with the future James V, the Queen of Scots was probably less passionately interested in international affairs than was her husband. She was in the last three weeks of her confinement.

The birth of her son left Margaret ill again. James cherished her for a short while, but left her little time for recovery. She was pregnant again by May and at the end of November 1512 gave birth to a premature child, which died shortly after baptism.[14] This still left James and Margaret dynastically ahead of Henry and Katherine, though in the see-sawing matter of the English succession they did not realize Prince James was to be their sole surviving heir. Both Kings had excellent intelligence services, so that each had a shrewd idea of the other's long-term aspirations, which created a climate of mutual suspicion. Replying to a complaint from his uncle John of Denmark about Scottish pirates, James reported, 'The English force operating in the Pyrenees has returned. It could not face a winter camp far from home, after failing to pass the summer there without suffering loss and discomfort.'[15]

James tried to send Andrew Forman to France via Westminster to see if he could negotiate a peace, but Henry refused to grant the Bishop of Moray a safe-conduct. This was scarcely surprising, since Lord Dacre had written from Ford Castle in Northumberland on 10 December to say De la Motte, the French admiral, had anchored at Leith with a ship containing '30 tuns of wine, 8 lasts of gunpowder, 200 iron gunstones, 8 serpentines* of brass for the field', some plate and eight rolls of cloth of gold for Queen Margaret.[16] Dacre had got his figures wrong about the 'gunstones'. Louis XII had in fact placed an order with the Receiver General of Normandy to send James 800 cannon-balls.[17] It must have been difficult for Margaret to accept the cloth of gold with equanimity, since James's intelligence service had already reported that her brother had issued a proclamation to levy funds for continuing the war with France, and as she convalesced from her fifth pregnancy, she knew this meant that James would almost certainly go to the aid of Louis XII. Her postnatal illness became more serious and James made another pilgrimage to Tain to invoke the aid of St Duthac. Margaret's recovery was slow and the deteriorating relations between her husband and brother cannot have made for a cheerful Christmas. Henry had issued a proclamation announcing that he intended to resist 'the purposed malice and errors' of his adversary the French King in order to help the Holy Father chastise Louis 'for the health of his soul'.[18] For this pious exercise Henry was imposing a tax on the people of England which ranged from £6 13s 4d from a duke to 6d from a working man with an annual wage above 40s.

James reported to his uncle John of Denmark that as Henry was levying a greater tax than had ever been raised before in England, he was certain to attack Scotland as well as France. The

---

* Light artillery, the most accurate of its kind.

fickle English, he said, 'threatened to rise against the tax collectors', but they were arming their land and sea forces against him and he therefore had no choice but to renew his alliance with Louis. The Scots, he added virtuously, 'were thinking only of peace', and the Pope had specifically instructed James to act as a peacemaker between the King of England and the King of France. The King of France would accept his mediation, but Henry would not.[19] Both sides now claimed to be acting on the instructions of the Pope. Although Julius II died in February 1513, his successor, Leo X, did not lift the interdict on France. Louis XII's Queen, Anne of Brittany, affected by the general war fever, wrote to James asking him to be her champion. In a gesture of outdated chivalry she sent him her glove and a turquoise ring. James would receive 14,000 French crowns, she promised, in return for his knightly service against the evil triumvirate of Maximilian, Ferdinand of Aragon and Henry VIII. It was an offer which James found hard to refuse, but which drove Margaret to nervous hysteria. She is said to have dreamed James was hurled from a cliff to his death hundreds of feet below, and that she looked at her jewels, seeing diamonds turn strangely to pearls, the emblems of widowhood. She is said to have accused James of preferring Anne of Brittany to herself, the mother of his child. According to one version, the King of Scots told her to go back to sleep.[20]

By the spring of 1513 Henry was in a ferment of excitement as he prepared a huge invasion force against France. Thousands of suits of armour had been ordered from Italy and Spain. Twelve new cannon, nicknamed 'the twelve apostles', were coming from Germany. Transport ships were ready to carry an army of 40,000 men across the Channel. Henry went daily to the dockyards to inspect his ships. The pride of his navy, the 1,500-ton *Great Harry*, was nearly ready for launching. The only ship in Europe to match her was his brother-in-law's vessel, the *Great Michael*. In a last effort to secure a promise from James to refrain from aiding France, Henry sent Dr Nicholas West, the Dean of Windsor, to Scotland. He was cynically instructed to use Margaret's jewels as bargaining power.

West arrived in Lent, when James had withdrawn on a religious retreat to the monastery of the Friars Observant at Stirling. After sending Henry a preliminary report to say Scottish ships had come from France carrying wheat and more supplies of gunpowder and cannon-balls, West met the Queen on Good Friday. Margaret was overjoyed to receive her brother's letters. Despite the build-up of suspicion between the two Kings, family relations had remained cordial. When Margaret had been pregnant with Prince James, Henry and Katherine had sent one of the holiest relics in Europe, the girdle of Our Lady, through the Abbot of Westminster, who was its guardian. It rarely failed pregnant queens and had been placed in Margaret's bedchamber at Linlithgow during her confinement. When West brought her news of the English court, the Queen, remembering how ill she had been after the birth of the premature child in November, cried, 'If I were now in my great sickness again this were enough to make me whole.'[21]

Her euphoria was short-lived. Although he was to spend three weeks in Scotland and to meet the King and key members of his council, West was in no position to procure the promise Henry VIII desired. Louis XII had better incentives to offer. At first all seemed set for reconciliation. On Holy Saturday the Queen went to confession and the ambassador and his household also performed their Easter duties. The following day, Easter Sunday, after High Mass James told West that he would give him an audience on the Monday. Tactfully the King left Margaret to dine with her brother's ambassador that day. She asked him many questions, for she had last seen Henry when he was twelve years old, and, as West later told the King, she inquired 'specially of your stature and good personage'. She also plied him with queries about the English navy. In 1511, when the *Great Michael* had been under construction, Margaret had been aboard her with James in the shipyards of Leith. She may merely have wished to impress the ambassador with her knowledge of ships, but he clearly resented her probing and assumed she had been briefed by her husband to obtain naval secrets. He told her bluntly of her brother's design to pass with his army into France, at which, wrote West, 'she was right heavy'.[22]

Urbanely, the ambassador suggested that it was up to Margaret to preserve a good understanding between the two crowns. She promptly asked for her legacy, which now included not only the plate and jewels left to her by Prince Arthur but also the small bequest from her grandmother. For four years her brother had promised to send 'silverwork, goldenwork, rings, chains, precious stones and the other habillements pertaining to a prince'.[23] Then the Dean of Windsor shot his bolt. He was ready to hand it over, he said, if James would promise to keep the peace, but not otherwise.

The following day West met James. The talk was of Border raids and the depredations made by James's piratical seamen, who regularly terrorized international shipping, even when they were carrying the King's own letters of marque. The most recent incident concerned a Portuguese ship which had been attacked by James's captains while passing through English waters. The King retaliated by saying that there were atrocities on both sides. One of his magistrates, Mr Drury, was so weary of trying pirates he reckoned that no Scotch ship could 'go to sea without being taken'. West singled out Robert Barton, nephew of the late Sir Andrew Barton, who had tangled with Henry's admirals Edward and Thomas Howard, the sons of the Earl of Surrey. Rob Barton was already in the pay of Louis XII and James knew it. West asked outright if Henry could borrow the *Great Michael*. He offered James a bribe of 1,000 marks to keep the peace; at which the King broke out in scorn. 'He said he had no need of your money,' wrote West. The ambassador then pressed a little harder. Margaret's legacy would be paid if James kept the peace; if not, said West menacingly, the English would take from the Scots 'the best towns they had'. Mercifully, at that moment the Dean of Stirling came to say the Friar wanted to get on with the sermon and was waiting for the King.

By the Tuesday West was losing his self-confidence. He felt the Scots were mocking him, so the following day he called on James uninvited. The King spoke of his planned voyage to Jerusalem. He sent his secretary, Patrick Paniter, to fetch 'a little quire of four sheets of paper sewn together and signed at the end with the French King's hand'. This was a grant from Louis XII allowing James to make a levy which would enable him to set out on his cherished ideal – a pilgrimage to the Holy Land. James read some of the document aloud to West and then he said, 'Now you see wherefore I favour the French King and wherefore I am loth to lose him, for if I do I shall never be able to perform my journey.'[24]

The poignant words have the ring of truth. It is arguable that at this point James was appealing from his innermost being to the Dean of Windsor for a little understanding of his spiritual needs. If this was the case, his yearning went undetected. The ambassador cynically changed tack, saying that Louis would never honour his promises. In the end West put the onus on Margaret. He wanted to get out of Scotland as quickly as possible. He would rather have been sent to Turkey, he wrote, than be among people 'so miserly and ungracious'.[25] The tussle of allegiances in Margaret's heart must have been unbearable. She promised to do her best for the peace, but she could no longer conceal that she was deeply hurt by her brother's double-dealing. Shortly after the Easter ceremonies at Holyrood, Margaret had gone to Linlithgow with the baby Prince. James suggested that West should visit them before he departed. Margaret made absolutely no mention of the legacy. She was sad, but she gave the ambassador gifts for Henry, Katherine and Princess Mary. West admired Prince James. He wrote to Henry that his nephew was 'a right fair child and large for his age'.[26] He then rode as fast as his horses could carry him for Berwick with the King of Scots' sarcastic taunt that Henry had bitten off more than he could chew by enterprising 'so great a matter as to make war upon France' ringing in his ears.

Margaret kept her word. Her letter of 11 April written from Linlithgow was a masterpiece of diplomacy. Maybe James helped her compose it. It was written by a secretary, but sealed with a small personal seal which she kept for private communications. She tactfully suggested that Henry himself could not possibly have been responsible for her being 'so strangely dealt with' in the matter 'of our father's legacy'. She understood, she wrote with dignity, that this was a matter of state. It was because of her husband's policies that the jewels were withheld, but James, she assured Henry, would recompense her. He could give all she required. The longer she remained with him, the better he became. She wished to God the issue had not been raised, but Henry was making too much of the matter. However, as she dictated the last sentences, Margaret's anger rose up inside her:

We are ashamed therewith, and would God never word had been thereof. It is not worth such estimation as is in your diverse letters of the same. And we lack nothing: our husband is ever the longer the better to us, as knows God, who right high and mighty Prince our dearest and best beloved brother have you in his governance.

Given under our signet at our Palace of Linlithgow the 11th day of April. Your loving sister, Margaret.[27]

By the time West returned to London, all parties knew that the Treaty of Perpetual Peace was doomed. Henry, on hearing James had refused to give a written promise not to invade England, commented that if only his brother-in-law would have signed such a document, he would have been willing, with the consent of all his nobles, to have made him 'Duke of York and Governor of England. For the heirs of England,' said Henry, 'must come either of him or of me, *for I have none as yet lawful of my body*, but I hear say Margaret my eldest sister has an heir male of good expectation. I pray God to bless him and keep him from his enemies, and that I may see him in honour and estimation.'[28] By 8 May Louis was urging James not merely to join him in a defensive alliance but also to invade England. He sent Master James Ogilvy to Scotland with an offer of victuals, the loan of his best admiral and 50,000 golden *écus* if James would break openly with the King of England and 'invade by land as soon as the said King shall have embarked his army for France'. By invading England 'in great force', wrote Louis, James might attain the crown himself.[29]

On 30 June Henry and his huge entourage arrived at Calais. Three weeks later the English army began an eleven-day march to Thérouanne, a small town in Artois, which the English had taken in 1346 after the Battle of Crécy. This time the King was in command. There would be no indiscipline. Strict rules had been drawn up for the conduct of the English army on campaign. Every man was bound to obey the King on pain of 'drawing, hanging and quartering'.[30] There was to be no pillaging of churches or violation of nuns on pain of death; the giving in of bogus returns for musters, a time-honoured fraud, later to be hilariously treated by Shakespeare, was punishable by imprisonment for a first offence and death for a second. Captains were to pay their men promptly. Archers must carry full equipment, including a service-

Henry VII's mother, Lady Margaret Beaufort, at prayer. The three wedding rings indicate her dynastic marriages. Faced with a choice of suitors, she prayed, aged nine, to St Nicholas and was rewarded with a dream advising her to choose Edmund Tudor, Earl of Richmond, Henry VI's half brother. Lady Margaret was very proud of her royal connections. *(By permission of the Masters and Fellows of St John's College, Cambridge)*

Henry VII and Henry VIII. Holbein's cartoon was for a life-sized mural of father and son. It was commissioned in 1537, when Jane Seymour was expecting Prince Edward, Henry VIII's heir. *(By courtesy of the National Portrait Gallery, London)*

Henry VII's Queen, Elizabeth of York. The King created the collar of the Order of the Garter, uniting the White Rose of York with his own badge, the Red Rose of Lancaster. No contemporary portraits do her justice, but chroniclers assert that she was a great beauty. *(The Royal Collection © Her Majesty The Queen)*

The family of Henry VII with George and the Dragon. Elizabeth of York bore seven children: the Princesses Margaret, Elizabeth, Mary and Katherine are on the right; Princes Arthur, Henry and Edmund are on the left. In the background St George, patron of England and of the Order of the Garter, slays the dragon and rescues the mythical maiden. *(The Royal Collection © Her Majesty The Queen)*

Arthur Prince of Wales married Katherine of Aragon shortly after his fifteenth
birthday. Six months later, he died of the sweating sickness. Henry could not become
Prince of Wales until it was established that Katherine was not bearing Arthur's child.
(The Royal Collection © Her Majesty The Queen)

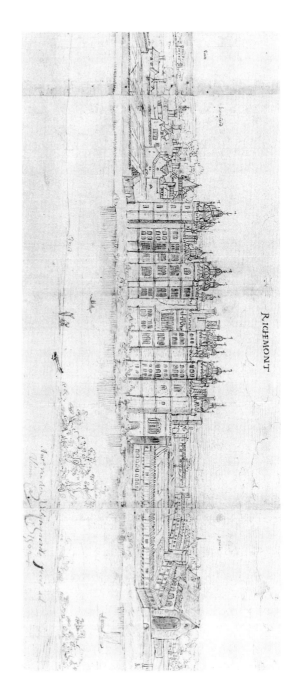

RICHMONT

After the old Yorkist Palace of Sheen was destroyed by fire, Henry VII built a luxurious new riverside home at Richmond, to emphasise the splendour of his dynasty. Contemporaries made a sly pun of his title as Earl of Richmond by hinting that the 'riche mont' was a little 'nouveau'. (*Ashmolean Museum, Oxford*)

James IV. Henry VII sought a dynastic alliance with the House of Stewart for his daughter Margaret to establish Perpetual Peace between England and Scotland. James, King of Scots, was a notable lover – and urgently needed Margaret's dowry. *(In a private Scottish Collection)*

Daniel Mytens's portrait shows Margaret around the time of her marriage to James IV. Later pictures suggest she had a weight problem in middle age. Monkeys were favourite royal pets. *(The Royal Collection © Her Majesty The Queen)*

Archibald Douglas, Sixth Earl of Angus, married Margaret after his father, George
Master of Douglas, and her husband, James IV, were killed at the Battle of Flodden.
When he tried to take control of Scotland and the young King, Margaret turned the
cannon of Holyrood House on him. (The Royal Collection © Her Majesty The Queen)

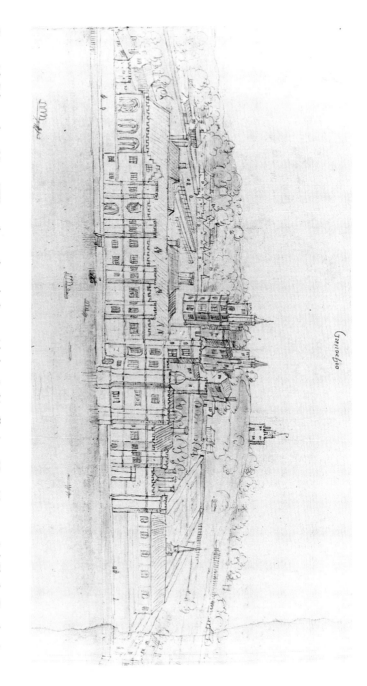

Greenwich Palace, where Henry VIII was born, always had a special place in his affections. Here, Mary married Charles Brandon in 1516, after the King forgave them for their whirlwind romance. (*Ashmolean Museum, Oxford*)

able bow and a sheaf with at least thirty arrows with sharpened metal tips. Night watches were to be kept strictly, 'upon pain of losing four days wages'. In camp after the watch began, there was a ban on rowdy behaviour; 'no shouting, blowing of horns, nor none other whistling or great noise' was allowed, the exception being trumpets used for reveille or alarm calls. When setting up camp any captain found using more than the correct quota of common soldiers for pitching tents or setting up pavilions could lose a month's wages. There was to be no dicing, card playing or other gambling likely to make the soldiers waste their money or fall into quarrels. Clearly such a rule was hard to enforce and second offenders were threatened with loss of a month's pay. No whoring was permitted either among men or officers, and prostitutes caught within a three-mile radius of the camp were to be branded on the cheek with a hot iron and imprisoned.[31]

By the second week of August Henry learned that his ally the Emperor was approaching. All the English nobles changed into their best apparel – cloth of gold and tissue of silver. The King strode through the camp glittering with jewels and in light armour. The Duke of Buckingham put on purple satin and decked his horse with a bridle full of 'spangles and little bells of gold'. His courser wore light plate armour engraved with antelopes and swans. The King, when he mounted, was followed by his Master of the Horse and nine henchmen dressed in white cloth of gold and crimson cloth of gold. Each of the henchmen carried a piece of the King's battle armour, his helmet, his spear and his axe. In the most foul weather imaginable, the glorious procession set out to meet the Emperor, whose second wife, Bianca Maria Sforza, had recently died, so that Maximilian and his men rode towards Henry's camp dramatically dressed in plain black cloth.[32] The huge genial figure who was so permanently short of cash to administer his vast domains was later to ride beside Henry in the uniform of an English soldier, his surcoat embroidered with the crimson cross of St George, as a sign that he was in Henry's pay. He was a veteran campaigner and the meeting was short on account of the weather.

A day or two later, by Hall's reckoning about 13 August, in the midst of all this pageantry James IV's herald, Lyon King of Arms, arrived with a declaration of war.[33] Henry read the letter and then, with withering contempt, accused the King of Scots of breaking his oath, pledged first at Richmond to Henry VII at the time of Margaret's marriage and renewed at the time of his own accession, when James had confirmed the Treaty of Perpetual Peace. 'Now we perceive the King of Scots, our brother in law and your master, to be the same person, whom we ever took him to be,' roared Henry at the terrified officer, 'for we never esteemed him to be of any truth, and so now we have found it. For notwithstanding his oath, his promise in the word of a King and his own hand and seal, yet now he hath broken his faith and promise to his great dishonour and infamy for ever and intendeth to invade our realm in our absence.' James, continued Henry, would never have dared such a thing if he himself had been back in England. The King of Scots was exhibiting the traditional faithlessness of his forefathers, whose oaths had never been trustworthy, and Henry vowed that he would make sure that James never joined any alliance of European Princes in which Henry took part. 'I, suspecting his truth,' boasted Henry, 'have left an Earl in my realm at home, which shall be able to defend* him and all his power, for we have provided so that he shall not find our land destitute of people as he thinketh to do.' Then, his mind stretching magnificently back to the time of Edward I, he bid the startled herald tell his master, 'I am the very *owner* of Scotland, he holdeth it of me by homage.' According to ancient law, Henry claimed, James was his vassal, and, 'contrary to his bounden duty', the King of Scots was a rebel. 'With God's help I shall at my return, expulse him his realm, and so tell him.'[34] Lyon protested that he could not give such a message to his sovereign. He asked the King of England to write it down. Henry chivalrously sent him off with Garter King of Arms to receive refreshment. The herald, reported chronicler Hall, 'was sore appalled'.

When the unfortunate man returned to Scotland, King James called a full council to deliberate Henry's letter and composed an immediate reply. It was full of reasonable arguments. The King of Scots pointed out that after Ferdinand, Henry's own father-in-law,

* To fend him off.

had made peace with Louis, Henry had allowed himself to be drawn into the Holy League to 'make actual war' against France, steadfastly refusing to discuss the matter with the Bishop of Moray, whom James had tried to send as a peacemaker. Henry had postponed the personal meeting at which James had hoped to discuss border affairs, and when raids continued from the English side, had allowed a particularly obnoxious practice of taking the Scots prisoner and chaining them by their necks. Henry had been hostile towards James's cousin the Duke of Gueldres and had failed to deal with a number of other grievances. Pirates, privateers and Bastard Heron ranked high on the list. The slaying of James's sea captain Andrew Barton had not been redressed. The King of England had shrugged it off, saying that such matters should be dealt with by lawyers. He had presumably not realized that Barton was a close friend of James's, and often joined court soirées, regularly playing cards with the King after supper. If in criminal actions no punishment should follow for murder, and those who murdered at sea should simply be represented by their attorneys instead of brought to trial, James argued, all murderers would get off free. It was against the law of God and mankind. Finally, there was the matter of Margaret's legacy, which Henry had 'promised in divers letters' to deliver. As it had never been sent, James considered the King of England had 'manifestly wronged his own sister' out of petty spite.

James's letter was dated 26 July and signed with the wish, 'Our dearest brother and cousin, the Trinity have you in keeping.'[35] It had taken Lyon approximately three weeks to travel from Edinburgh to Thérouanne. Given the distances involved, James could reasonably have waited until the beginning of September for a reply. In fact, he watched his own fleet depart for France and then summoned the Scottish armies to meet at Ellem in Berwickshire by the third week of August. The King of Scots went on pilgrimage to St Duthac at Tain and then went to bid farewell to Margaret at Linlithgow, but some of the clansmen were so eager to recommence hostilities against the English that Lord Hume rode into Northumberland with his Borderers, to be defeated in a heavy skirmish with Sir William Bulmer, who happened to be in the vicinity with a force of 1,000 men, including 200 expert archers. This episode was christened by Leslie 'the Ill Raid'.

By 22 August the Scottish armies reached the muster point. During the King's visit to Linlithgow, Margaret, pregnant with her sixth child, was tortured by prophetic dreams. She begged James not to go to war, but he dismissed her warnings as fantasies. 'It is no dream. Ye are to fight a mighty people,' she warned.[36]

The rest of the story has been told many times by chroniclers and historians through the ages. In the last week of August, with a mighty host, James forded the Tweed and advanced into Northumberland. His first target was Norham Castle, the stronghold of Thomas Ruthal, the Bishop of Durham. Surrey's army marched up from Pontefract. They were low on provisions and, worst of all, running out of ale.[37] The Earl sent a challenge for James to come and avenge the death of Andrew Barton. On 9 September the English advanced towards James, who had placed his cannon on Flodden Ridge. He moved to a superior position on Branxton Hill. Three hours after the encounter began, almost all the Scottish nobles lay dead. The Scots had superior artillery, but the English did better in the hand-to-hand mêlée. The young Archbishop of St Andrews fell fighting beside his father.

When the dead were counted the Scots were alleged to have lost between 9,000 and 10,000 men.[38] The English set their losses at 1,500. A body believed by Lord Dacre to be that of James IV was sent to England, though its identity was later queried as there was no iron chain about its waist. One of the most ghoulish details recorded is that Queen Katherine sent Henry a blood-covered surcoat, thought to be the garment in which her brother-in-law fell. Queen Margaret had been so certain of the outcome after her dream that she did not even send a party to search the battlefield.

Chapter 6
The Person of the King

At the ruined Palace of Linlithgow there is a turret room commanding a fine view of the surrounding countryside. Tradition has it that from here Margaret kept watch for the returning army, even though her dream had foretold that James himself would never come back. The room is called Queen Margaret's Bower. Tourists are also shown a window in the south transept of St Michael's Church, where the King was supposed to have seen a ghostly figure warning him not to go to war. In the nineteenth century one explanation was that Margaret had been so desperate to prevent her husband from setting out that she had paid an actor to stage a 'vision'.[1]

The Scottish people were loath to accept the death of their dashing and popular King. Stories abounded that he had escaped from Flodden and gone on a pilgrimage to the Holy Land. One rumour which persisted was that he had been sighted at Kelso the evening after the battle and that the body sent to England was that of Andrew, Lord Elphinstone, a dear friend of the King's who was of similar age and stature.

The fighting had begun between four and five in the afternoon. When night fell the English had retired. Pillage and plunder went on through the darkness, so that when Lord Dacre set out with a reconnaissance party the next day, many of the bodies had been stripped naked, their weapons and armour looted by the Borderers. Savage, ignorant men with little allegiance to either side, they had concentrated their efforts on the dead and the dying. Corpses were heaped about the field, but as first light broke over Branxton Hill the real spoils of war, James's magnificent cannon, stood stark and unmanned against the skyline. Surrey sent them to Etal Castle. Eventually Lord Dacre, who had known James well, identified the King's body, which had been stripped naked like the rest. It was wrapped in what remained of his banner and laid in Branxton Church, until Surrey sent it to Berwick upon Tweed for embalming. The Bishop of Durham, Thomas Ruthal, was convinced that victory was due to the intercession of St Cuthbert. His men brought home James's banner, sword and leg armour, which were placed in Durham Cathedral. Writing to Wolsey eleven days later he claimed, 'The Borderers are not to be trusted. They have done much harm.'[2] His property, Norham Castle, had been razed to the ground a few days before the battle, when the Scots advanced into England. Only the dungeon was left intact.

Another of the rumours which swept along the Borders was that James had indulged in romantic dalliance with Lady Heron, the chatelaine of Ford Castle. Her husband had at one point been sent to Scotland by Henry VII as a hostage for his brother, Bastard Heron, the outlawed ruffian who had murdered Sir Robert Ker of Fernieside.[3] After the six-day siege of Norham Castle, James had marched down the Tweed, swiftly subduing the garrisons at Wark Castle and Etal Castle. Bastard Heron was said to be acting as a guide to the English army, and Lady Heron wisely surrendered Ford on 4 September. James remained there a few days, probably to gain information and to await reinforcements, as illness had broken out among some of his troops. If the king found time to seduce Lady Heron, he did so with an uncharacteristic disregard for the rules of chivalry, since before taking leave of her he burned her home to the ground. The story of his amours took root, however, drawing upon him some colourful invective from Lindsay of Pitscottie. Writing at the end of the sixteenth century, the Scots chronicler viewed Lady Heron as a veritable Delilah who ensnared her prey, then sent secret information to Surrey encamped at York concerning the state of the Scots army and armaments. 'Being ane beautiful woman, the King melled with her,' wrote Pitscottie, while his son, the young Archbishop of St Andrews, committed fornication with her daughter, 'which was against the order of all good captains of war, to begin at whoredom and harlotry before any good success of battle or victory'.[4]

There is no record that the story reached Margaret, who was in the third month of pregnancy. Separated from Flodden by 140 miles of wild, mountainous countryside, all she could do was to wait and pray. News of the defeat must have been brought to Linlithgow three or four days after the battle. The Queen moved with speed and resolution, taking the seventeen-month-old King to the impregnable fortress of Stirling. He was crowned there by James Beaton, the Archbishop of Glasgow, on 21 September, twelve days after his father's death.[5] The event went down in Scottish history as 'the Mourning Coronation', for as the Archbishop held the massive crown over the infant King's head, the Scots lords wept afresh for their dead. Margaret was left with a handful of advisers, the Bishops of Glasgow, Aberdeen, Galloway, Dunblane, Caithness, Argyll and Orkney, and the Earls of Angus, Huntly, Morton, Argyll, Crawford, Lennox, Eglinton, Glencairn and Atholl. There were about fifteen lords temporal left in the land.[6]

A council was called immediately, at which James IV's will appointing Margaret as Regent was read and approved, although it was later to be argued that a woman ruler was contrary to the ancient laws and customs of the realm. Margaret and her son were officially styled 'James by the Grace of God, King of Scots and Margaret Queen of Scotland and testamentary tutrix of the same'. James Beaton was appointed Chancellor, and the Earls of Angus, Huntly and Home were delegated to assist the Queen. At Flodden Angus had lost two sons and 200 clansmen. Old Archibald, Bell-the-Cat, the fiery fifth Earl who had loved Janet Kennedy and made her Lady Bothwell, was suddenly an elder statesman, pitied but respected. His third son, Gavin Douglas, poet, scholar and cleric, was all he had left. The Bishop of Aberdeen, William Elphinstone, continued as tutor to the King, and it was arranged that a rota of noblemen should attend the council to advise the Queen on day-to-day affairs. It was firmly understood that she would not act without consulting a quorum of three lords spiritual and three lords temporal.[7]

Stirling was to be the main royal residence, with Lord Borthwick as its Captain. Louis XII had sent James IV a huge shipment of arms as soon as he heard his ally intended to invade England. One of the council's first acts was to transport these from Dumbarton to Stirling, so that the mighty fortress on the rock was more grimly impregnable than ever before.[8] There was such a shortage of military personnel that the Bishops of Caithness and Paisley and their men were put in charge of this operation. Patrick Crichton, the Captain of Edinburgh Castle, declared it was 'desolate of artillery'. He would prefer to see its outworks 'stuffed' with men and munitions.[9] The last pages of the old Treasurer's Accounts written up before the battle show Margaret at twenty-three, a cosseted young wife, ordering gowns of crimson velvet, trimmed with her favourite pampillion, or fashions from France to show off the dusky beauty of Black Ellen.[10] When her husband was alive the Queen had thought nothing of asking the Exchequer for £60 to spend on haberdashery. Now suddenly she was called upon to pay armies and budget for artillery. James had left her the 18,000 crowns which Louis had offered as a bribe to win Scotland's support. She was also to keep Stirling, her dower castle, until James V came of age, but as guardian of the King's person, Margaret was Queen of Scotland *de facto* and on 2 December she sent out writs for a Parliament to meet the following spring.[11]

Overtures of peace came quickly from the English side. Katherine of Aragon professed to feel nothing but compassion for her sister-in-law. She sent Friar Bonaventure Langley, Provincial of the Friars Observant, to Stirling to comfort Margaret and see what could be done about arranging a truce. He arrived early in November. Lord Dacre, however, acting on Henry's instructions, had continued to raid the Borders throughout October, burning corn and destroying villages to teach the Scots a lesson.[12] Appointed Regent while the King was in France, Katherine had revelled in her role as warrior Queen. In imitation of her mother, the warlike Isabella, she had harangued the English army before they set out on their march north.[13] After Flodden, when the King of Scots' bloodstained surcoat was brought to her, she wrote to Henry, sending him a piece as a battle trophy. She would have dispatched James's corpse too, had the idea not sickened the English captains. 'Your Grace shall see how I can keep my promise, sending you for your banners a King's coat,' she boasted. 'I thought to send himself unto you, but our Englishmen's hearts would not suffer it.'[14] She wrote from Woburn, while on a pilgrimage to the shrine of Our Lady of Walsingham, but despite her efforts and her prayers no truce was signed with the Scots.

Henry himself was by no means as heartless as has sometimes been supposed. A tradition exists that Christian burial was denied to James IV because Leo X upheld the excommunication decreed by Julius II when the King invaded England, breaking his solemn oath given at the signing of the Treaty of Perpetual Peace.[15] In fact, Henry wrote from France as early as 12 October requesting Leo's permission to bury his brother-in-law and the Pope wrote back on 29 November, freely granting the King of England the right to bury James at St Paul's with full funeral honours and trusting the whole matter to the Bishop of London. The Pope said he 'presumed the King gave some signs of repentance in his extremities'.[16]

The mopping-up operation which faced Margaret and her council was formidable, but the factions which later divided her government have so fascinated historians that little attention has been paid to what happened in Scotland as news of the defeat spread through the land. Margaret was queen of a country full of despairing widows and fatherless young men. Everywhere feelings of shame and hopelessness gave rise to bursts of violent disorder. On 26 September a royal proclamation was issued to prevent the looting of houses and the molesting of women and children.[17] A week later a second one was published in the name of James V but echoing the words of a proclamation James IV had made before he marched into England. 'Diverse true subjects being with our father at the last field in Northumberland were slain and their wives are widows and desolate, and their daughters maidens being heirs to them,' it ran.[18] The second proclamation forbade the deflowering of maidens and widows, the robbing of premises and the taking of goods 'on pain of treason'. It was as though Margaret and her council were trying to evoke the spirit of the dead King to come to their aid. The plight of

Scottish women was desperate. In a chauvinistic society, some of them had no legal title to their own homes. Cases came before the council like that of Isobel Dunbar, the mother of a four-year-old son who had inherited all his father possessed. She petitioned to have 'the profits of my bairn's lands and goods' for the sustenance of her son and his 'five fatherless brethren'.[19] The council promised to redress such matters, but there was a great deal of lying and thieving. If a woman went to live with a neighbour for protection, she ran the risk of being branded a harlot, or of having her actions misunderstood. There was the celebrated case of the Abbot of Kilwinning's procurator, who was publicly accused at the Market Cross in Edinburgh of having done violence to 'one Sybel Galloway, who was neither maiden, man's wife nor widow, but a single gentlewoman' who had gone to him for shelter.[20] Tragedy after tragedy came before the council. There were not enough responsible persons left in the land to maintain law and order. By January 1514 the lords were still debating how to strengthen the fortresses of Dunbar and Fastcastle with insufficient personnel to garrison them.[21] The manhood of a nation had been wiped out.

Several bishoprics were vacant because their incumbents had fallen at Flodden. Margaret knew that James had kept careful control over Church offices because of the revenues involved. A Scottish bishop in the sixteenth century also had power over the bailies, or chief stewards. Since the bailies ensured that taxes were collected and also had the right to apprehend criminals, whom they could turn over to the sheriffs, it was vital that the sees should be filled. Otherwise the whole system of justice and taxation would break down.[22] Margaret wrote to the Pope to suggest her own candidates. Her husband had always done so, but she failed to consult the nobles and many thought this was an abuse of her prerogative. By now the council had divided into two groups, the hawks and the doves. There was no question of disloyalty to the Queen and the divisions were not yet deep enough to be labelled faction, but several lords felt they could scarcely trust the mediations of Friar Langley, while Lord Dacre continued to terrorize the Borders.

Fired by the desire to avenge their fathers' deaths, the young men wanted to prolong the war with England. They found it natural to turn to the French King for further help, particularly since the heir to the Scottish throne, John Stuart, Duke of Albany, had lived in exile in France for the whole of his life. The son of James III's younger brother Alexander, Duke of Albany, he had been brought up at the French court since his father had left Scotland after an unsuccessful attempt to seize the throne in Edward IV's reign. It seemed to many of the young lords in Margaret's council that a strong military leader was needed, both to oppose Lord Dacre on the Borders and to restore law and order in Scotland. They decided Albany should be recalled at once, but Louis XII anticipated their request. Letters of condolence that he wrote to Margaret from Amiens on 4 and 5 October show that the Scottish ships which James had lent him were still in France.[23] While the council debated whether to send for Albany, Louis wrote courteously to Margaret to say he would not send the Duke until he knew her wishes, nor would he make peace with her brother, unless he had permission from the Queen and her council to do so. Before sending Albany, he would send Monsieur La Bastie, a trusted diplomat widely known as Le Chevalier Blanc. As James IV's cousin the Earl of Arran and Lord John Fleming were still in France, the King also asked whether he should send them to command a naval expedition against England. He assured Margaret that he would do 'everything befitting an ally'. One reason for Louis's caution was that the rumour about James IV being still alive had reached him. The French King was taking no chances until he knew whether it was true.

A full session of the Scottish council met at Perth on 26 November. This was a far more imposing assembly than the ad-hoc regency council which had gathered around the Queen. It included the Earl of Arran and Lord Fleming, who had returned with the Scottish fleet.[24] They laid concrete plans, outlined in a letter from Louis, before the assembled lords. There was no intention to challenge the Queen's power as Regent. 'The person of the young King of Scotland' was to be 'kept as devised in the late King's will', but there was a confirmation of the long alliance between France and Scotland and a firm letter was sent to Louis hoping that as many Scottish subjects had laid down their lives in the quarrel between England and France, 'it would please the most Christian King to send the Duke of Albany to Scotland for its defence'.[25] Significantly, the old Earl of Angus, who supported the English alliance, was absent from the assembly. He was sick and, grieving for the loss of his two sons, had gone home to his great fortress of Tantallon to die.

Henry VIII was horrified when he learned what the Scottish nobles proposed. As James V's uncle, he saw himself as the child's natural protector. He advised Margaret that she should do everything within her power to prevent Albany from coming to Scotland, for he guessed immediately that if the Scots had a strong male leader in their midst, who was also heir to the throne, it would be all too easy for that leader to usurp Margaret's powers of regency and to abduct the precious person of the King. In an undated letter to Lord Dacre he warned his sister to be on her guard against any plans to spirit the little boy to the Outer Isles.[26] The memory of what had happened to the Princes in the Tower remained sharply in Englishmen's minds. Throughout the autumn of 1513, rumours that Albany would soon set out for Scotland were circulating in Europe. Even before the council wrote from Perth to invite the Duke, Thomas Spinelly, the English agent in the Netherlands, had sent Henry information gained from the crews of two Scottish ships that had put into Zeeland. The Scots lords, he reported, were 'not pleased that the Queen should have rule, as they fear she will comply too much with England'.[27] Henry was concerned. He even sent a herald to Louis asking him to delay Albany from setting out until peace had officially been made between England and France. For Margaret, the strain of divided loyalties must have been intolerable. If she leaned too much on her brother, her own council would distrust her. Henry sent a rather guarded message to Dacre that he was to assure the Queen of Scots that her sister-in-law sent love.

On the surface the French campaign had been a glittering success and there were no indications that the King of England would seek a permanent peace. Indeed, in the autumn of 1513 he had every intention of returning to France the following spring to add to his conquests. During the siege of Thérouanne, a detachment of French cavalry had arrived, apparently to relieve the town. On seeing the combined might of the allied forces encamped about its walls, however, they had retreated so fast, with the English and Burgundians in hot pursuit, that the encounter was known ever afterwards as the Battle of the Spurs. It was England's first victory in France since 1453. When Thérouanne finally surrendered, Henry and Maximilian were able to make a triumphal entry into the town to the sounds of the Te Deum sung in the local church by the King's choir. Maximilian, whose men were in Henry's pay, had insisted that the young man should precede him, so Henry had the singular glory of being a king riding before an emperor. He and his entourage then made a forty-mile detour to Lille, where they were lavishly entertained by Maximilian's daughter, Margaret of Austria, Regent of the Netherlands.

After three days of masques and balls, during which Charles Brandon, egged on shamelessly by Henry, began a courtly flirtation with the widowed Regent, the English returned to besiege Tournai, which the King entered on 25 September. He was given the keys of the city and a great quantity of *vin de Beaune*.[28] Tournai became his headquarters throughout October, and while he and his nobles were celebrating their success, Charles of Castile arrived in the camp in person to discuss his forthcoming marriage with Princess Mary. Henry was 'much delighted with his conversation'.[29] By 15 October it was confirmed that Charles and Mary were to be married before 15 May 1514. The King of England was therefore anxious to get home. His Parliament was due to meet on 1 November, and as the campaigning season drew to a close it was imperative for him to conclude matters in France and to consolidate his alliance with the Emperor. With the prospect of the grand and glorious wedding he intended to arrange for his younger sister, and the enhanced prestige it would bring him in Europe, Henry had a full programme ahead.

When the army reached Calais, England's most enduring posession on French soil, there was a shortage of hay for the horses and Henry noted that more must be supplied by next spring, when Charles and Mary were to meet there. With his mind full of elaborate details for the festivities, he had little appetite for Scottish affairs. He was inclined to leave such tedious matters to Wolsey, Dacre and the Bishop of Durham. Mary herself had already begun to correspond eagerly with Margaret of Austria. She wanted to know exactly how the Flemish ladies dressed, and by the end of November 1513 she was ordering copious quantities of red velvet from the Great Wardrobe.[30]

Margaret finally procured an uneasy truce with England in February 1514. Lord Dacre's men still patrolled the Borders and this did not appease those lords in the council 'whose heat,' as Bishop Leslie put it, 'was hotter than the rest'. Instead of seeing the Queen as the tragic widow of their lost leader, they tended to think of her as the sister of the hated English King. It was a significant change of perspective. Anne of Brittany had died at the end of January, leaving Louis XII an elderly but eligible widower once more, and it was obvious to many that the Queen of Scots would be a most suitable bride for him, although etiquette forbade that he should propose to her while she was still carrying James IV's child. The Venetians were also speculating on the possibility that 'the Queen widow of Scotland would make a good match for the Emperor'.[31]

By the time the Scottish Parliament assembled on 13 March, Margaret was already in the eighth month of her pregnancy. The people of Edinburgh cheered enthusiastically as she rode through the streets of the capital. This must have improved her morale, as well as greatly enhancing her prestige in the eyes of the lords of the council, for the affair of the bishoprics and Margaret's use of the 18,000 crowns James had left in the Treasury had set off further opposition to the idea of a woman ruler, but her opening speech to Parliament, dictated from Stirling, was gracious and gentle. She thanked them for the great diligence and labours they took 'for the common good of our realm, our son and us', and then left the main business of the session to the Lord Treasurer.[32] Margaret won many hearts, but the assembly she had imagined would back her to the hilt managed to curtail her powers of regency even further by taking control of all the main fortresses in the country. By 8 April Lord Dacre, who had spies everywhere, wrote to Henry from Carlisle, 'the Queen of Scotland has taken her chamber in the Castle of Stirling and by sundry reports that are made unto me, I am informed that if the French King be disposed to marry her upon knowledge thereof had, he shall have her at his pleasure'.[33]

For once Lord Dacre was wrong. The old Earl of Angus who had died at Tantallon had left as his heir his nineteen-year-old grandson, who was also called Archibald. This young man took his place in the council introduced by his other grandfather, Lord Drummond, the Chief Justiciary of Scotland. Ironically, since Bell-the-Cat had been the lover of Janet Kennedy, Lord Drummond was the father of Lady Margaret Drummond, who had been James IV's mistress, until she was murdered just before his betrothal to Margaret Tudor. Whether the Queen knew of this interesting pedigree we shall never know. On 30 April she gave birth to a son. He was christened Alexander and proclaimed Duke of Ross, the traditional title of the second in line to the Scottish throne. No child was ever received more rapturously by the people than this little Prince, the posthumous son of their beloved King. As Henry and Katherine had still not produced a child which survived infancy, Margaret remained heiress to the English throne and her two sons followed her in the succession.[34] It was assumed the widowed Queen of Scots would remarry after a decent interval of mourning, and it was naturally expected that she would be guided by her brother in making a second choice.

In the fifteenth and sixteenth centuries, tradition decreed that a noblewoman should marry the first time according to the wishes of her father and for the good of her family, but in a second marriage she might follow her heart and marry for love. This tradition, however, seldom applied to widowed queens. In the months after the birth of the little Duke of Ross, Margaret must have been particularly vulnerable. The precise moment at which she began to notice the young Earl of Angus has not been recorded. He took his seat in the council in March 1514 and, according to Pitscottie, 'he haunted the court and was very lusty in the sight of the Queen', who loved him, 'and thought him most able'.[35] He had been married at an early age to Margaret Hepburn, who had died in childbirth. When he succeeded to his grandfather's title he was already betrothed to Lady Jane Stuart of Traquair and he was said to be deeply in love with her, until old Lord Drummond began to fire his ambition by pushing him

towards the Queen. That summer, despite the uproar over the
vacant bishoprics, the nobles were still willing to sign a unani-
mous statement in support of her regency, which was tantamount
to a promise not to divide into the factions which had been the
bane of Scottish history in the past. 'Madame,' they wrote, 'we are
content to stand in one mind and will to concur with all the lords
of the realm to the pleasure of our master the King's grace, your
grace and for the common weal, and to use none other bands now
or in time to come.'[36] All those present in the council chamber that
day, 12 July, signed the document at eleven in the morning.

By 26 August the council tried to force Margaret to call the
Duke of Albany from France to become 'Governor of Scotland'.
The majority of the nobles requested she should deliver up the
Great Seal and demanded that their Queen should issue no more
proclamations.[37] By 17 September at Dunfermline the Bishops of
Glasgow, Aberdeen and Galloway and the Earls of Arran, Huntly
and Home were debating whether she still had the right to be
testamentary tutrix to the King. The following day they wrote for
Albany and all the ships that had been sent to France to come
back for the defence of the realm.[38] The reason for this volte-face
was that on 14 August, in a secret ceremony at Kinnoul Church,
where the parson, the Dean of Dunblane, was a nephew of Lord
Drummond, the Queen had married the Earl of Angus. In one
moment of womanly weakness and romantic folly, Margaret
Tudor had effectively destroyed her own powerbase.

The Queen was twenty-four. She had shown courage, dignity
and resourcefulness. At a time when women usually retired from
public life to prepare for gestation, she had dealt daily with
national emergencies and listened to the policies of her volatile
nobles when her own common sense dictated she should make
peace with her brother. She was recently bereaved. She must have
felt bullied and bewildered. Apart from overwhelming sexual
attraction, she must have believed that marriage to Angus would
give her the protection of one of the most powerful families in the
country. To understand the ferocity of the opposition she now
unleashed against herself, we must glance briefly at the events of
James II's reign.

Throughout the fifteenth century, the house of Douglas had

rivalled the crown in wealth, power and prestige. James II made it his life's work to crush them. He came to the throne aged six and under the guardianship of his mother, Queen Jane, widow of James I and daughter of John, Duke of Somerset. For the very reasons rehearsed to Margaret, that the ancient laws of Scotland forbade a woman ruler, Archibald, fifth Earl of Douglas, became Regent. In 1439 Jane remarried, taking as her husband Sir James Stewart, Knight of Lorne. The guardianship of the King went immediately to Sir William Crichton and Sir Alexander Livingstone. The Crichtons and the Douglases feuded to a point where civil war broke out. When he was eighteen, James II took over the government of Scotland himself. The Douglases continued to intrigue and in 1452 the King invited William, the eighth Earl, to Stirling, stabbed him and then stood by while his attendants finished the job. Visitors to Stirling Castle are still shown the window from which the mutilated body of the Douglas was hurled into the moat. The ninth Earl made his submission to the crown, but feuding broke out again and all the Douglas lands were forfeited by attainder. Despite this, the family had returned to power by the end of the century.

Margaret Tudor could not have been Queen of Scotland for ten years and remained ignorant of these facts. She must also have known of the deep antagonism other families felt towards the Douglases. Gavin Douglas, Angus's uncle and the third son of Bell-the-Cat, was a poet and a scholar. He had completed a Master's degree at St Andrews in 1494 and had received rapid ecclesiastical preferment from James IV, who recognized his abilities. He was the first person to translate the *Aeneid* into English and had dedicated a long allegorical poem, 'The Palace of Honour', to James at the time of his betrothal, but he could never gain the office he coveted most, the Deanery of Dunkeld, because of opposition from the Hepburns.[39] Gavin Douglas also loathed James IV's most trusted diplomat, Andrew Forman, whom he referred to as 'yon evil-minded Bishop of Moray', and Forman was the Pope's nominee for the most important of the vacant sees, the wealthy Archbishopric of St Andrews.

It had been empty since Alexander Stewart, the King's son, had died at Flodden. Apart from being the primacy of Scotland, it had the richest revenues in the country. On receiving a series of letters from Margaret and her council, written in the winter of 1513, Leo X appointed Cardinal Cibo as its administrator. At one point he considered sending Cibo himself to fill the vacancy. This prompted a storm of violent protest from the Scots. The kings of their realm held ancient and inviolable privileges to nominate their own candidates to episcopal sees. Traditionally, when their king was a minor, the Archbishop of St Andrews was his guardian. The post could not go to a foreigner. The nobles and people of Scotland would defend their ancient privileges with the sword.[40] In short, the Pope was out of order. He gave in gracefully and Margaret tactfully offered the see to the venerable William Elphinstone, the Bishop of Aberdeen, whom James IV had appointed his son's tutor. Elphinstone was so deeply respected that no one contested the choice, but as he was nearly eighty he refused the preferment. Margaret was by then experiencing many difficulties with her council. She clearly had her eye on the urbane and witty Gavin Douglas, who was postulant of Arbroath, a post which gave him less influence in her government than the Douglases considered his due.

Leo X had little interest in Scottish affairs, but when Elphinstone died, as the young men eager for preferment hoped he would, the Pope chose Andrew Forman, pointing out that this internationally distinguished diplomat was one 'who can do much for Scotland at the Roman court'.[41] Gavin Douglas's party were so incensed, they believed the Pope had been bribed. Since England and Scotland were now at peace, Margaret managed to drag Henry VIII into the squabble, getting him to write to Leo on behalf of Patrick Paniter, James IV's secretary, whom the Queen also wished to bind to her party. Paniter, who had retained the secretaryship under James V, was the ablest of the lot. He understood more about the administration of Scotland and its financial systems than most of the lords who surrounded the Queen. Henry wrote him a glowing testimonial.[42] The Pope listened to the King on the matter of Paniter, but was obdurate about the see of St Andrews. His final word on the matter was sent on 8 December 1514, when he exhorted Margaret and her council 'in virtue of that obedience which opens Heaven to believers' to

agree to Forman, thus 'doing what is acceptable to God and grat-
ifying to the Pope'.[43]

Some of the correspondence with the papacy predates
Margaret's marriage to Angus. It sheds an interesting sidelight,
showing that she had a far clearer understanding of government
than has sometimes been supposed. She may have been prepared
to listen to the opinions of her troublesome nobles in council, but
underneath there was a steely determination to preserve the
powers of the crown both for herself and for her sons. The council, however, were utterly determined to depose her from the
regency on the grounds that she had forfeited it by marrying
Angus. 'We have shown heretofore our willingness to honour the
Queen contrary to the ancient law and custom of this kingdom,'
said Lord Home. 'We suffered and obeyed her authority the
whiles she herself kept her right by keeping her widowhood.
Now she has quit it by marrying, why should we not choose
another to succeed in the place she has voluntarily left?'[44]

Solemnly and formally, all the lords present voted to depose
the Queen from the regency. The unfortunate Sir William Comyn,
that same Lyon Herald who had faced Henry VIII with James IV's
declaration of war, was sent to inform her of their decision. He
was also to summon Angus to answer before his peers for his
boldness in marrying the Queen without their assent. The lot of a
herald is not a happy one in times of trouble. When Sir William
entered Margaret's Presence Chamber, he is supposed to have
addressed Margaret by the new title decided by the council. She
was no longer 'the Queen's Grace' but was to be called 'My Lady
the King's mother'. It was more than old Lord Drummond could
stomach. He rose from his chair, faced Lyon Herald fair and
square and boxed his ears. Scotland was on the brink of civil war.

Chapter 7
A Nymph from Heaven

Shortly after the Christmas celebrations of 1513, Henry VIII fell ill
with smallpox. This naturally brought the issue of the succession
to the fore, but nothing, it seemed, could deflate the buoyant spirits of the victor of Thérouanne. By February a fretful convalescent,
staying at Lambeth Palace because fire had damaged Westminster,
the King was energetically dictating memoranda planning the
next season's campaign and sending out streams of messages to
Margaret of Austria, Regent of the Netherlands, in preparation for
Mary's marriage to her nephew, the Prince of Castile. Hay for the
horses was uppermost in Henry's mind. He had not forgotten the
shock of returning from Thérouanne with his superbly disciplined
troops only to find a shortage of fodder. According to one memorandum taken down by the Bishop of Winchester:

> When the King was at Calais with his army, not only the
> corn and hay, but the grass on the ground was consumed
> and destroyed so that at the King's returning thither there
> was no provision of hay for the horses; and though oats can
> be brought out of England, hay cannot be had in any plenty;
> and though hay be had in those parts sufficient for those
> resorting to the solemnization of the marriage, as the King
> must land there at the same time with his army, much hay
> will be required.[1]

Henry clearly visualized a magnificent double event. His sister's
wedding procession was to arrive at Calais escorted by an entire

English expeditionary force. Envoys were sent to the Netherlands to discover the exact size of the three cavalcades which would accompany the Emperor, Prince Charles and the Regent. The King was particularly anxious to know whether he was supposed to provide hangings and furniture for the Burgundian contingent, and whether the marriage was to be celebrated in a private chapel or a parish church. He assumed that, after the custom of the time, the principal royal visitors, the Emperor, the Prince and Margaret of Austria, would bring their own beds, but he needed a guest list, and since he proposed to march off to war immediately after the wedding, he wanted to find out what great personages would be staying on in Calais, so that he could provide suitable accommodation for them.

Wedding fever broke out at the English court. Henry took great delight in supervising Mary's trousseau. He was proud of his sister's beauty, which was famous throughout Europe. Erasmus told the Abbot of St Berthin that Prince Charles was 'thrice blessed to acquire such a bride. Nature never formed anything more beautiful and she exceeds no less in goodness and wisdom.'[2] Peter Martyr was more specific: 'Her deportment in dancing and conversation is as pleasing as you would desire,' he wrote, adding that her legendary complexion was achieved without the help of cosmetics. Queen Katherine, although she was still young and pretty, did not have Mary's vivacity and stamina, so that brother and sister often led the dancing and the masques together. Strict precedence was observed, with the Queen in the place of honour, but as soon as the music struck up for dancing it was Mary who was the star of Henry's court. At eighteen she shared her brother's love of dressing up and disguising, and as the London cloth merchants competed to show her their finest wares, the King, who was used to choosing costumes which suited her, took control. During his visit to Lille the previous autumn he had been deeply impressed by the splendours of the Regent's entourage. The Archduchess Margaret was a woman of taste. Henry sent her relays of fabric samples by royal courier with requests that she should decide how they should be made up and advise him what styles would be most appropriate for the Princess to wear as Charles's bride. The King wanted his sister to be dressed in the Burgundian fashion, but as he knew her preference and colouring, he wished to select the materials himself. The Regent was to 'devise all things so that Mary's apparel would be queenly and honourable'.[3]

Her wedding dress was practically a state secret, with Henry's most confidential secretary, Dr William Knight, sworn not to divulge details. A list of ladies, officers and household servants who would accompany Mary from England was drawn up for Margaret's approval. There were 101 persons in all. The Queen had provisionally chosen Lady Oxford as chief Lady of the Bedchamber, and the search was on for a sober, reliable person to act as the Princess's Treasurer. Sir Edward Jernyngham was to be her Master of the Horse, and an inventory had already been made of the plate and jewels she was to take with her. It is eleven pages long and still perfectly preserved. Nothing that money could buy had been omitted. The bridal bed was surmounted by a canopy of cloth of gold with matching curtains. Mary's plate filled four coffers; there were dishes, standing cups and salt cellars of solid gold. Everything had been chosen with love and everything was of the finest quality, from the feather bed and bolster for the marriage chamber down to a tiny pair of silver-plated weighing scales for spices and 'a little pot for ginger with a fork'.[4] Nevertheless, Henry asked Margaret to scrutinize the list and say if anything was wanting. Interspersed with the wedding plans and pattern books came a request for 6,000 Flemish cavalry men, 6,000 of the Emperor's German foot soldiers, and the services of the Count Palatine, the Prince of Nassau and several other noblemen, who were to be in Henry's pay during the next phase of the war. The King also needed Margaret to requisition a number of hoys, small boats to carry his army to France.[5]

There is no record of Mary's feelings at this time, towards either her future husband or her energetic brother. Charles had written to her as 'my good wife', inquiring after her health and wishing her happiness: 'Something I most desire, as knows the blessed Son of God, to whom I pray to give you by his grace all that you desire.' The sentiment might have been sincere, but the note was written by a secretary and signed 'Votre bon mari, Charles' in a surprisingly childish hand.[6] Mary already referred to the Regent as 'Ma bonne tante' and presumably looked forward to meeting her since Henry had returned with such glowing accounts of her court. She was also alleged to carry a miniature of Charles about with her, 'sighing dutifully' as the occasion required.[7] It seems more probable that she spent most of her time pirouetting at dress fittings or making desultory efforts to improve her French conversation. If Maximilian stuck to his bargain, there would be a rush to get the Princess's clothes ready in time, since the wedding was scheduled to take place not later than 15 May. Lodgings had already been arranged at Calais. The Emperor was to have the Deputy's House, the Prince the Staple House and the Archduchess the Treasurer's House, while Henry would entertain them at the Castle.[8] He had spent a small fortune on cloth-of-gold hangings for the Emperor's bedchamber, but before the army could embark or the seamstresses finish the hems of Mary's gowns, a swift volte-face occurred in international affairs. Having first plotted with Maximilian to make a separate attack on France, Ferdinand deserted the Holy League to make peace with Louis XII. The Emperor followed suit, leaving Henry fuming at their duplicity.

At first he declared he would attack France, backed only by the Swiss, but Leo X now urged peace and by mid-May sent an emissary to England with the coveted cap and sword, which were the mark of the Holy See's special esteem for secular rulers, and the combined efforts of Fox and Wolsey, who declared themselves to be of one mind in such a 'very holy cause', persuaded Henry to make peace with France.[9] Continental warfare had proved spectacularly expensive. Between Henry's accession and June 1513 over a million pounds had flowed out of the Treasurer of the Chamber's department, two-thirds of it on the war with France.[10] Ten years later, Wolsey's protégé Thomas Cromwell was to remark that the 'winning of Thérouanne cost his Highness more than twenty such ungracious dogholes could be worth to him'.[11]

The true hero of Thérouanne had been Thomas Wolsey. He had been an advocate of war with France at the start of the new reign and he took much of the blame for the failure of the 1512 campaign, but as secretary to Sir Richard Nanfan (the post he held immediately before becoming a royal chaplain), Wolsey had been resident in Calais. It was through his working knowledge of northern France that he had achieved the superb planning which enabled the smooth running of the 1513 expedition. Wolsey's rise to power had been meteoric. Shortly after he returned from his embassy to

Scotland in 1508, Henry VII sent him on a mission to Flanders. The story told by George Cavendish, Wolsey's gentleman usher and his earliest biographer, is that the young diplomat left Richmond at noon, took a barge from London to Gravesend, travelled by post horse to Dover, sailed to Calais within three hours and reached the Emperor's court to dispatch his business the next day. He returned to Richmond by the same route and, on his way to early Mass, Henry VII found him in his Presence Chamber only three days after he had sent him on his errand. The King chided him for not having set out. When he learned Wolsey had already achieved his objective, he made him Dean of Lincoln. Some months later the Ipswich butcher's son who had risen to royal service after a stint as Junior Bursar at Magdalen College, Oxford, was promoted from King's Chaplain to Royal Almoner, the position he held at the beginning of Henry VIII's reign. His efficient grasp of administrative matters brought him to the notice of the new King and, Cavendish believed, Wolsey became a favourite because he was 'most earnest and readiest among all the council to advance the King's mere will and pleasure'. The King, said Cavendish, was 'young and lusty, disposed to all mirth and pleasure . . . not caring to toil in the busy affairs of this realm. The which the Almoner perceived very well and took upon him therefore to disburden the King of so weighty a charge and troublesome business', so that Henry 'should not need to spare any time from his pleasure'.[12]

Wolsey acquired many honours. Bishop of Lincoln in the spring of 1514, he was Archbishop of York by August, and the University of Oxford, never slow to recognize a prospective patron, accommodatingly granted him an honorary Doctorate of Divinity, enabling him to hold sees in plurality. In the hearts of the English royal family, however, Wolsey remained 'Mr Almoner', the one with power to smooth their paths and ease their worries in times of difficulty or distress, and this 'Mr Fix It' role, combined with a certain urbanity, greatly endeared 'My lord of York' to both the King's sisters, who never hesitated to approach him with their problems. To Mary, who had been barely fourteen when Henry VII died, he was a much trusted father figure. She instinctively preferred him to the Earl of Surrey, who in recognition of his services at Flodden had been restored to his father's title. The ceremony creating him Duke of Norfolk was deferred to Candlemas on account of Henry's smallpox. On the same day Charles Brandon, by this time Viscount Lisle, was made Duke of Suffolk, while Lord Herbert became the Earl of Worcester. Buckingham, who since 1502 had been the only duke in England, absented himself from court in a fit of pique.

There was immediate speculation in Europe about Brandon's elevation to a dukedom. A rumour had spread by March 1514 that he was to marry the Archduchess Margaret and that Henry had raised his friend's status to make this possible. Suffolk had begun his after-dinner flirtation with the Regent during one of the excursions Henry had made to her court from Tournai. For some reason, the appearance of the King and the Duke at the May Day tournament of 1514, fancifully disguised as hermits, fuelled the rumours. Brandon was dressed in black velvet, Henry in white with a mantle made of overlapping pieces of leather and a hat of cloth of silver. The jousting was fast and furious, with a total of 114 broken lances, but before it began Henry and Suffolk rode about the tiltyard and then took off their disguises, which they threw to the Queen and her ladies as a largesse. This revealed the King in black and Suffolk in white, both bearing pennants with the motto 'Who can hold that will away'. According to Hall, 'this poesy' was an allusion to the romance between the Duke and Margaret.[13] Betting on a marriage opened in London and the rumours filtered back to the Low Countries. What had started off as the high-spirited behaviour of two young men on campaign suddenly turned into a great scandal, damaging to Margaret's honour and not in keeping with the massive dignity of the House of Habsburg.

Suffolk was Marshal of the Army. In England he had the added glamour of being a tournament star, but that hardly made him an equal match for the Emperor's daughter. In European eyes Brandon was no more than a jumped-up East Anglian squire. Erasmus, who had spent the winter in Cambridge and had intended going to London to visit Wolsey, wrote to his friend Gonnell, 'Gossip has it that Maximilian's daughter Margaret is to marry that new duke, whom the King has recently turned from a stableboy into a nobleman.'[14] 'Stableboy' alluded to Brandon's previous office as Master of the Horse, but the comment was considered so damaging that it was expurgated from the edition of Erasmus's *Letters* printed at Basel five years later.[15] In addition, the 'new duke's' marital status was a little dubious. He had been in love with Anne Browne, the daughter of Sir Anthony Browne, but had jilted her for her aunt, Dame Margaret Mortimer, who was considerably better off. Shortly after marrying Dame Margaret, Brandon had the contract annulled on grounds of consanguinity, claiming that his grandmother had been related to his first wife's husband.[16] Charles and his friends then virtually kidnapped Anne Browne, whom he married in 1508. There were two daughters by the marriage, but Anne had died a fortnight after the birth of the second child, in the summer of 1510. This left Brandon a free man until he acquired the wardship of Lady Elizabeth Grey, Viscountess Lisle in her own right, to whom he was tentatively betrothed in order that he could use her title, which Henry granted to him during the Christmas celebrations of 1512. Lady Elizabeth was ten at the time of Charles's flirtation with the Regent.

At Tournai an exchange of rings had taken place. Margaret claimed she had regarded it as a joke, a meaningless piece of courtly lovemaking. She reminded Henry that Brandon had knelt before her, drawn a ring from her finger, tried it on his own and generally been so droll that she had burst out laughing. Henry had then urged her to take Brandon as a husband, for it was well known that the twice-widowed Regent had sworn she would never remarry. Everyone had probably had a good deal to drink and the two young men, flushed with the excitement of military conquest, were in a mood of high hilarity. Things quickly went too far, however, and the rumour reached Maximilian that his daughter was seriously contemplating such a match. The Emperor had been deeply shocked. Margaret had to explain that the wild stories flying about were base lies and that she would 'rather have died a thousand times than have them taken for true'.[17]

Henry was embarrassed. He wrote disingenuous letters of apology to both Margaret and Maximilian, wondering how such stories could have originated, but he took the episode seriously enough to cancel Brandon's projected trip to Flanders to levy troops.[18] By this time the Emperor and Ferdinand were trying to postpone the date of Mary's marriage. In May it was claimed that the plague had broken out in Calais. In June Prince Charles was said to be suffering from a fever. Henry felt Maximilian was trying to make a fool of him. Dr William Knight, who had been sent as English ambassador to Flanders, wrote to say that there was a faction in the Prince's council who would gladly 'hinder his marriage with the Lady Mary, saying he is a child and she a woman full grown'.[19]

Mary was just past her nineteenth birthday. She was generally acclaimed as the fairest Princess in Europe. Her beautiful gowns and magnificent jewels were all ready for the journey which was now apparently not to take place. Again we have no record of her reactions, but she must have shared Henry's feelings of humiliation and disappointment. She had been betrothed to Charles since she was thirteen years old. The Regent Margaret wrote anxiously to Maximilian, reminding him how important the marriage was for the safety of the Low Countries. She pointed out that the treaty signed the previous year had included 'great penalties' to be 'exacted from towns, nobles and burgesses', if the nuptials were not solemnized before the end of May.[20] She also begged her father to remember that the English were due to pay 100,000 crowns of Mary's dowry at Bruges. According to Hall, Henry

sent again to Flanders for the performance of the marriage of the young Prince of Castile and the fair lady Mary, but the Council of Flanders answered that they would not receive her that year, with many subtle arguements by reason whereof the perfect love between England and the Low Countries was much slaked.[21]

Peace with France was now a serious prospect. Henry demanded Thérouanne, Boulogne and St Quentin and one and a half million gold crowns, which included arrears of the pension the Kings of France had been supposed to pay to the Kings of England since the fifteenth century. He also offered Mary as a bride to the ageing and sickly Louis XII, though if the French King was willing to accept the Queen of Scotland instead, Henry was prepared to lower his sights and settle for an annual payment of 100,000 crowns.

News of his elder sister's impending liaison with the Earl of Angus had not yet reached the English court, but although Louis sent polite condolences to the Queen of Scots and although Lord Dacre considered such a match a real possibility, the King of France was not seriously interested in Margaret as a wife. Tempted by the stories of Mary's beauty and her entrancing personality, he held out for the King of England's younger sister. It is doubtful whether the Princess herself was ever consulted, but on 30 July 1514, in a formal ceremony at Wanstead in Essex, she repudiated her contract to marry the Prince of Castile, meekly swearing before Wolsey, Norfolk and Suffolk that she was acting of her own volition and that 'in all things she was ever ready to obey the King's good pleasure'.[22] If Mary Tudor entertained any dangerous longings to marry a man of her own choice, they were not apparent. One week later England and France were officially at peace. On 12 August Henry wrote to the Pope to inform him of the new arrangements. His sister had been betrothed to Charles for six years, he explained to Leo. Last summer at Lille the Emperor had renewed promises made originally to Henry VII and the marriage date had been set for 15 May, but nothing had happened. Maximilian had prevaricated once too often; the Princess would marry the King of France.[23]

Although the negotiations were supposed to be secret, news of Mary's betrothal spread swiftly round Europe. The Regent could not believe it. She sent envoys to London to find out if the rumour was true. When it was affirmed, she broke down and sobbed, while Prince Charles, told by his councillors that he was no longer to marry Mary, bitterly accused them of breaking their promises. 'You are young,' they replied soothingly, 'but the King of France is the first King in Christendom and having no wife, it rests with him to take for his wife any woman he pleases.' The Prince looked out of the window, where he saw a man with a hawk. He ordered one of his courtiers to buy the bird. The councillor told him that the hawk was not fully trained, not a fit sporting bird for a prince to own. Charles stormed out, purchased the hawk himself and, returning to the council chamber with it on his fist, he began to pluck out its feathers one by one before the eyes of his startled advisers. When they asked him what he was doing, he replied, 'You ask me why I plucked this hawk; he is young, you see, and because he is young he is held in small account, and because I am young, you have plucked me at your good pleasure; and because I was young, I knew not how to complain, but,' he added contemptuously, 'bear in mind for the future I shall pluck you.'[24]

Nicolo di Favri, a diplomat sent to London with the Venetian ambassador, told the story with feeling to his friend Francesco Gradenigo. The King of Spain and the Emperor had played false, he wrote. Maximilian had received 'many thousands of pounds from King Henry on condition he was to be at Calais in the month of May, but the Emperor pocketed the money and never came. King Henry was deceived in every direction.'[25] Di Favri had arrived in London at an exciting moment. 'Great events,' he noted, 'were passing in England.' The capital was full of ambassadors, one from the Emperor, one from the Pope, one from the Duke of Milan. In general, however, the peace with France was unpopular. After the formal signing of the treaty on 7 August, the news had been proclaimed in the streets of London on 11 August. 'Neither trumpet nor any other instrument was sounded,' wrote the Venetian, 'and but a few persons heard the proclamations; neither were bonfires burnt, nor any other demonstration made.'[26]

This was scarcely surprising. The English people were not ready for peace. In May Prior John, the freebooting French admiral from Rhodes, who had intermittently attacked English shipping ever since it had been discovered that his Levantine galleys were more manoeuvrable than any other vessel in the Mediterranean, had landed one night at an obscure small town on the Sussex coast called Brighton. Before the watch spied him, he set fire to the town 'and took such poor goods as he found'. When the alarm was sounded, six intrepid English archers, well drilled for the wars, chased the Frenchmen back to the sea. They beat back an armed rowing boat and wounded several sailors, shooting so fast and accurately that they even grazed Prior John's face.[27] When Edward Howard, the commander of Henry's fleet, heard this news, he sent Sir John Wallop to Normandy, where the English burned twenty-one small towns and villages in reprisal. Sir Nicholas Vaux, the garrison commander at Guisnes, also feared the French would attack. Henry sent Sir Thomas Lovell to strengthen the defences at Calais. It followed that the whole idea of peace with France was anathema to the English and Londoners were in no mood to celebrate with bonfires; but, as Hall observed, 'the voice of the people has seldom caused princes to change their purpose'.

As soon as the formalities were completed, King Louis lost no time in securing his bride. On Sunday 13 August a gentleman arrived by barge very early in the morning at the house of the Venetian ambassador. Nicolo di Favri was among those bidden to come to court immediately for the proxy wedding of 'King Henry's sister as Queen of France'. When they reached Greenwich, the Venetians were ushered into a large chamber, its walls covered with cloth-of-gold hangings richly embroidered with the royal coat of arms. Many lords were present, magnificent in cloth of gold and fine silks, with heavy gold chains about their necks.

Everyone waited courteously, passing the time in pleasant conversation until Mary, followed by her ladies, arrived with the King and Queen. Louis XII was represented by the Duc de Longueville, who had been in England since he had been taken prisoner at the Battle of the Spurs the previous year. As a high-ranking captive he had been treated as an honoured guest and had become thoroughly popular at court, indulging in a long-lasting romance with one of Mary's ladies, Jane Poppincourt. A prince of the House of Orléans, he was the ideal person to act as proxy for the French King. The Archbishop of Canterbury began the marriage with a Latin sermon. Then the French ambassador made a speech and De Longueville put a ring on Mary's finger. By this time it was nearly midday, so the King went to High Mass, preceded by a long procession of peers of the realm. The Spanish ambassador, Di Favri noted, was not present, but the Venetian ambassador, who was one of the witnesses, had the honour of walking nearest to Henry, paired with the Archbishop.

The King wore cloth of gold chequered with silver-grey satin and the Duke, dressed in cloth of gold chequered with purple satin, walked beside him, though out of politeness not quite abreast. Queen Katherine, joyfully pregnant, wore silver-grey satin with a little gold cap perched on her head Venetian fashion. The bride, who had kept everyone waiting for three hours while she completed her toilette, was predictably radiant. She was dressed to match the Duke in a kirtle of silver-grey satin under a purple and gold chequered gown, since it was the custom of the French court that a king and queen should appear in public together as a pair. If Mary felt any revulsion at the thought of marrying the decrepit Louis, it was successfully concealed from the guests at Greenwich that day. She was covered in brilliant jewels, attended by a great many ladies, and Di Favri thought she looked so young and beautiful that he guessed her age as sixteen.[28] After the Mass there was a banquet, followed by dancing which went on for nearly two hours. Henry and the Duke of Buckingham threw off their long gowns and danced energetically in their doublets, and the other gentlemen did the same until even the elderly Venetian ambassador, Andrea Badoer, confessed that he would have liked to join them but felt he had to abstain on account of his age.

The ceremony had included a symbolic bedding. Mary lay down fully clothed in a great bed which had been set up in the marriage chamber. Before the assembled company, De Longueville drew off his red hose, suggestively exposing a naked leg with which he touched the bride, while Archbishop Warham blessed the union.[29] Since the Prince d'Orléans, '*un jeune homme tres honnete*', was regarded as thoroughly personable, there is no reason to suppose Mary found the experience unpleasant. One biographer has suggested that she may well have thought the prospect of becoming Queen of France preferable to the idea of marrying the lantern-jawed Charles, who, even in adolescence, showed signs of inheriting the Habsburg bone structure which no official portrait could ever quite conceal.[30] What puzzled the Venetian ambassador, however, was Mary's apparent euphoria. When Badoer made his official report to the Signory two weeks after the proxy wedding, the bride's happiness had evidently impressed him. Although she was 'a young maiden', he commented, she did not seem to 'care for the French King's being an old man and gouty . . . so pleased was she to be the Queen of France'.[31] As one of the chief witnesses of the marriage, and particularly since he had refrained from dancing, Badoer had been in a unique position to sit and observe Mary closely throughout the evening. What he did not know was that at some point between her repudiation of Charles on 30 July and the drawing up of the carefully worded French marriage treaty, which was signed in its final form on 14 September, Henry had struck a bargain with his sister. She was later to remind him that she had 'consented to his request, and for the peace of Christendom, to marry Lewis of France, though he was very aged and sickly on condition that if she survived him she should marry whom she liked'.[32]

This was the expectation which must have buoyed up Mary's spirits throughout the last five months of 1514 and helped her to approach her new role with such zest. There was, of course, a certain amount of public outrage. Bitterly resentful that the Princess was not to come to the Netherlands, the Dutch 'spake shamefully of this marriage, that a feeble, old and pocky man should marry so fair a lady'.[33] From Valladolid Peter Martyr reflected the Spanish view, that 'an old valetudinarian' should not consort with 'a handsome girl of eighteen'. She would be the death of him.[34] The Spanish ambassador, who had been noticeably absent from the wedding celebrations, disconsolately left London, which must have been an added cause of anxiety to the pregnant Katherine.

With hindsight, historians have suggested that Mary at nineteen was wily, calculating and manipulative, but as there is no contemporary record of the scenes which took place between the Princess, her brother and Wolsey, we can only guess how she behaved when informed of their decision. Either she wheedled a promise from Henry, allowing her to make her own choice when Louis died, or they sweetened the pill with a bribe, understanding perhaps better than she did herself the sacrifice she was about to make. Marriage to Louis was a matter of state. As a Tudor princess Mary had no real choice in the matter. Her own motto, 'To do God's will is enough for me', was an ironic summary of her position, but Henry had obviously taken a heroic stance, appealing to her sense of patriotism and duty. 'The peace of Christendom' had been mentioned and that phrase stuck in her head. Against the titanic background of Habsburg–Valois power struggles, Mary had been asked, more literally than any bride in history, to shut her eyes and think of England, for the French King had no son and if she managed to bear him a male child, ousting his heir, Francis of Angoulême, from the succession, she would place herself and her brother at the apex of an alliance which would be one of the strongest in Europe.

What she had not bargained for was that the pill was relatively sweet in the first place. From the moment she became Queen of France, Mary Tudor's life began to take on the improbable glamour of a fairy tale. The day after the ceremony at Greenwich, his ransom paid, De Longueville set out for Paris. By 16 August he reached Canterbury, where messengers from Louis awaited him. He wrote to Mary at once to say that the official meeting and the solemnization of the marriage would be held at Abbeville. His sovereign was impatient to see her.[35] It was all very different from the chilling formal notes she had received from Charles. Her new spouse pestered her with letters and showered her with gifts. The Sieur de Marigny was sent to London, accompanied by the French artist Jean Perréal, who was not only to paint the bride's portrait but also to help design her wardrobe, according to the very latest canons of Parisian taste. Their arrival at the English court was sensational. Marigny brought two coffers of jewels so heavy that they had to be borne into the Presence Chamber on a white horse. The courtiers must have gasped as he presented Mary with the legendary 'Mirror of Naples', a pearl and diamond pendant which had belonged to Anne of Brittany's father. It was so precious that Henry sent it to be valued by the 'jewellers of the Row'.[36] Lorenzo Pasqualigo, an Italian merchant resident in London, described the stones in awestruck detail: a diamond as big as a person's finger, with a pearl beneath it 'the size of a pigeon's egg'. He estimated their worth at 60,000 crowns.[37]

Throughout September the French and English courts were in a frenzy of diplomatic activity. Henry sent the Earl of Worcester, the Dean of Windsor and Sir Thomas Docwra, Prior of the Order of St John, to France to finalize the paperwork of both the peace treaty and the marriage. They reached Boulogne on 3 September and Abbeville on 7 September. Worcester, a name the French found so impossible to pronounce that they spelled it 'Nonshere', wrote immediately: 'The King's furriers have arrived here to prepare the royal lodgings. The King waits for them in Paris. The match is very popular with all classes.'[38] He wished to know what retinue Mary would bring. Her dowry had finally been settled at 400,000 gold crowns. This was to include her jewels and plate, but since the English knew of the French King's poor health, there was a clause ensuring the return of her personal belongings if Louis should die. Her jointure was to be the lands and revenues traditional for a queen of France. Like Anne of Brittany, she was to have the town of La Rochelle and the county of Saintonge, Chinon with its magical castle and the revenues from Rochefort, Pezenas, Montigny, Cessenon and Cabrières. She would receive dues from Montpellier and rents and taxes from other estates scattered through France to the value of over 10,000 'livres Tournois'.[39] According to the Venetians, Henry also wanted her to have the Duchy of Milan. In addition, Louis was to pay the King of England the million crowns stipulated in the peace treaty.

When the agreements were signed and sealed, the French King also went through a formal betrothal ceremony in Paris with the Earl of Worcester acting as Mary's proxy, though mercifully there was no symbolic bedding. For the second time that year, Henry laid out money for his sister's trousseau. According to most accounts, he equipped her with sixteen gowns of cloth of gold and cloth of silver in the French fashion, as well as a great many sapphires, rubies and diamonds, set in the form of Tudor roses and fleurs-de-lis. The documents tell a slightly different story. A carefully written inventory signed by Thomas Bohier, the reliable receiver general whom Louis had appointed to take care of such matters at this hectic time, records eighteen dresses in 'the English style' and five in the Milanese style with matching hats.[40] Everything was made in silk, cloth of gold, rich brocade or crimson velvet, exquisitely packed and loaded on to elegant *charettes* or closed carts, emblazoned with Mary's coat of arms and with the fleur-de-lis, which was now her rightful emblem, painted on the side.

Her saddle cloths, chapel hangings and bed curtains were embroidered with goldsmith's work. Elaborate designs of lilies and Tudor roses were painted on the coaches her ladies were to use on the journey and, more mundanely, she was provided, at a cost of £10 13s 4d, with a great quantity of the best English stockings from the London hosier John Barker, even though, as Queen of France, it would soon be her patriotic duty to get through hundreds of pairs of the finest silk stockings in the civilized world. Indeed one of her perquisites was a tax of five sous from every hosier in her new realm. When it was collected it amounted to a total of 20,000 francs.

Instead of the Countess of Oxford, Lady Guildford had been selected as Mary's chief attendant. She was expected to combine the roles of Lady of the Bedchamber with those of chaperon and mentor. Jane Guildford had known the Princess since her childhood. She was considered an eminently suitable person by Henry, Katherine and Wolsey to guide and advise Mary and the younger, giddier ladies in her entourage upon matters of etiquette and behaviour. She spoke French but came of impeccably English stock, and despite Jean Perréal's interference she liberally patronized the London milliners. By 12 September over £76 had been spent on hats alone.[41] Many of the gowns that had been ordered for the Flemish trousseau must have been remodelled, however, and a flurry of last-minute bills from silkwomen, embroiderers, saddlers, robe makers and gold-wire drawers suggests the insignia of Castile had been speedily unpicked from the more expensive items ordered earlier in the year. It must have been a mammoth undertaking. Henry, perhaps with a touch of wry humour, added a magnificent set of seven tapestries depicting the Labours of Hercules.[42]

Mary had been such a generous patron of the London cloth merchants in the five hectic weeks after her proxy marriage that a few days before her departure all the drapers, mercers and haberdashers in London assembled to bid her farewell. 'Merchants of every nation,' reported Lorenzo Pasqualigo with professional interest, 'went to the Court. The Queen of France desired to see them all and gave her hand to each of them. She wore a gown in the French fashion, of wove gold, very costly.' The Mirror of Naples glittered against her fair skin. She was so beautiful and affable that Pasqualigo thought her 'a nymph from Heaven'.[43] After the merchants had kissed her hand she delighted everyone by speaking a few words of thanks in French.

The heavenly nymph had been practising the language with her tutor, John Palsgrave. In the fervent hope of securing a place in her entourage, so had everyone else. 'The whole court now speaks both French and English as in the time of the late King,' wrote Pasqualigo. Mary had probably lisped her first French words at her mother's knee. Certainly between Elizabeth of York's death in 1503

and Lady Margaret Beaufort's in the summer of 1509, she would
have learned French in the schoolroom at Eltham. It would also
have been used in her grandmother's establishment at
Coldharbour, for Lady Margaret had translated, and caused Caxton
to print, a popular devotional work, *The Mirror of Gold for the Sinful
Soul*, from French into English. She was also an avid reader of
French romances, but obviously during the hostilities of 1512–13
conversational French had dropped out of use at court. It was now
considered an essential requirement for any gentlewoman who
wanted to accompany Mary. Lists were compiled and vetted for
Louis's approval. Some were sent to Abbeville with the marriage
papers on 23 September. The King of France had learned of De
Longueville's affair with Jane Poppincourt. Since the Duke was
already married and his Duchess, as a Princess of the Blood, would
be among the wedding guests, Louis indignantly struck Mary's
friend off the list. The Earl of Worcester was generally blamed for
telling of Jane's indiscretion. Apparently the King said he would
rather see her burned alive than have such an immoral woman
about his new wife. This decision was not popular with the bride.
Jane Poppincourt had been in Mary's household since the Princess
was five years old.[44]

In the last week of September Henry and Katherine accompanied Mary to Dover, where a whole squadron of ships was waiting
to convey her across the Channel. The King intended to escort her
ten miles out to sea aboard the *Henry Grace à Dieu*, but blustery
weather caused him to abandon the plan, and the party had to wait
in Dover Castle until the storms abated. On the progress from
London to Dover Henry had ridden beside Mary, with Katherine
following in a litter because of her pregnancy. The entire court,
with all their retainers and personal servants, joined the procession, as did many merchants and their wives and country gentle-
folk, who flocked to see the splendid sight. Because of the spon-
taneity of the event, no official count was ever made, but
Pasqualigo reckoned 400 knights and barons and 200 gentlemen
and squires with their horses rode behind the main court party.
'The lords, knights and barons were all accompanied by their
wives, attended by their damsels. There would be about 1,000
palfreys and one hundred women's carriages.'[45]

Everyone wore their best clothes. Some of the noblemen, Pasqualigo estimated, had spent as much as 200,000 crowns on their costumes and accoutrements. There were 'so many gowns of wove gold and with gold grounds, housings for the horses and palfreys of the same materials and chains and jewels' that he thought they were 'worth a vast amount of treasure'.[46] At the centre of this glittering cavalcade, winding through the autumnal glories of the Kent countryside, Mary seemed radiant and serene. Her motto, *'La volonte de Dieu me suffit'*, emblazoned beneath her arms on the carriages and hangings, seemed to signify her complete acceptance of a situation she could do nothing to change.

After a few days, during which the company were forced to amuse themselves amid the limited facilities offered by Dover Castle, the winds dropped and it was judged safe for Mary to sail. At four o'clock in the morning on 2 October she left the Castle with her brother to catch the morning tide. They walked to the wharf together and there, as she was later to remind him, 'at the water-side', he renewed the promise he had made to her earlier. If King Louis should die, she could marry again according to the dictates of her own heart. Brother and sister embraced affectionately. Henry kissed her, giving her his blessing: 'I betoken you to God and to the fortunes of the sea and the government of the King your husband.'[47] Then, supervised by the Duke of Norfolk, Mary and her ladies, with their attendants, baggage and palfreys, embarked for France. The wind did not stand fair. After the ships had completed a quarter of the voyage, more gales swept the Channel and separated the ships, so that some were blown towards Calais and others went right off course to Flanders. Mary's ship, 'with great difficulty was brought to Boulogne and with great jeopardy,' wrote Hall, entered the harbour, 'for the master ran the ship hard on shore'.[48] The landing craft went out to meet her, but as they approached the shore there was another hitch since the sea was too choppy for them to reach the jetty. Sir Christopher Garnyshe, one of Mary's gentlemen, leapt gallantly into the water in all his finery and, lifting the Queen of France in his arms, with the waves lapping at her salt-splashed petticoats, carried her safely ashore.

Chapter 8
La Reine Blanche

News of Margaret's marriage to the Earl of Angus had reached the English court in September. The loss of a potential alliance was painful to Henry. As the Queen of Scotland's brother, he had assumed it would be his natural right to choose her next husband, but his irritation was short-lived, since preparations for Mary's departure took precedence over all other affairs. Her elder sister's example must have put fresh heart into the 'nymph from Heaven'. If Margaret, deprived of her first husband in the prime of his life, could find new happiness, Mary's hopes that God would deliver her speedily from the 'aged and sickly' Louis XII were not unrealistic. As Henry rode back from Dover, his mind turned to the succession. On the journey to London the royal party stayed for a few days at Otford, a manor in Kent belonging to Archbishop Warham. Katherine's fourth pregnancy was by then well advanced. In September 1513 she had suffered a miscarriage, deeply disappointing Henry, who began a flirtation with Bessie Blount during the New Year revels of 1514. It was swiftly interrupted by his attack of smallpox and Katherine became pregnant again almost as soon as he was up and about. At Otford the child had obviously stirred in her womb. Messengers were sent ahead with orders for the Great Wardrobe to deliver blue saye for the Queen's bed curtains, but a pathetic scrap of paper in the exchequer records tells the private hopes and fears of the twenty-three-year-old King of England. On 4 October he signed a warrant for William Lambert to collect 'a cradle covered with scarlet cloth – for the use of our nursery, God willing'.[1]

Louis XII also longed for a son. Anne of Brittany had borne him four children. Two daughters, Claude and René, survived, but by French law a woman could not inherit the throne, so his heir was his cousin, the twenty-one-year-old Francis of Angoulême, who had married Claude. The Dauphin had been brought up by his ambitious mother, the widowed Louise of Savoy, at her château at Amboise, some ninety miles south-west of Paris. Louise lived for her son, and the King's marriage filled her with dread, lest the beautiful English Princess should produce an heir. On 22 September, the day before Mary was due to embark, Louis left Paris for Abbeville and the Duchess wrote scornfully in her journal that the King, 'very antique and feeble', had gone to meet his 'young bride'.[2]

The official plan had been for De Longueville to welcome Mary at Boulogne with an entourage of 200 French ladies, but the foul weather continued and there was minimal ceremony.[3] When Sir Christopher Garnyshe set the pale, dishevelled bundle that was the new Queen of France on her feet, her kirtle soaked with sea water, she was met by the Duke of Vendôme and the Cardinal of Amboise. She arrived on 4 October, ten days behind schedule and with one of her ships wrecked off the Kent coast. She travelled to Montreuil, a village ten miles from Abbeville, and stopped there to rest and to unpack the costume in which she was to meet the King. The French had devised an efficient communications system. Messengers and post horses sped continuously between Louis's headquarters and Mary's entourage, so that at precisely two in the afternoon on 8 October the King, 'understanding that his consort was about to mount on horseback and come to Abbeville', sent the Dauphin ahead with an escort of royal dukes to guide her procession.[4]

Francis detained Mary's party at a prearranged rendezvous about two miles from Abbeville, until Louis himself arrived, elaborately dressed for hawking, as Renaissance custom demanded, in order that he should appear to have come upon the Queen quite by accident. He was accompanied by the Cardinals of Auch and Bayeux, by Monseigneur de Vendôme and the Duke of Albany, the heir to Mary's infant nephew, James V of Scotland, and the cause of so much anxiety to her sister, Margaret. Two hundred other gentlemen had joined the King's hawking expedition, as well as his

guard of mounted archers and the Swiss foot guard.[5] Louis rode
his beautiful Spanish horse, Bayart, caparisoned with cloth of gold
chequered with black satin, 'He himself being clad in a short riding
dress of cloth of gold on crimson.'[6] Great crowds had assembled to
watch the royal couple meet, despite the rain which fell steadily all
day. Among those able to get a good view was the Dauphin's best
friend, Robert de la Marck, the young Sieur de Fleuranges, who
swore the King made Bayart caracole, no mean feat for a man who
was supposed to be 'antique, feeble' and riddled with gout.[7]

There followed a little pantomime when Mary blew Louis a
kiss English fashion, 'a ceremonious proceeding,' reported one of
the Venetians, 'which he did not understand'. Unabashed, the
King gallantly blew a kiss back, then he rode up to Mary, brought
Bayart close to her palfrey and kissed her without dismounting,
once again a fairly athletic manoeuvre for one allegedly senile
and in the last throes of physical decline. According to the
Venetian, the King 'kissed her as kindly as if he had been five and
twenty and came in this dress and on horseback the more to
prove his vigour'.[8] Artlessly attired in a gown of cloth of gold on
crimson to match Louis's riding coat, Mary feigned complete
surprise at their meeting so unexpectedly.

After exchanging a few words with her, the King greeted
Norfolk and all the English lords. He then went on his way to
continue hawking, leaving Mary to make her grand entry into
Abbeville accompanied by the princes of the blood and 'an infin-
ity of gentlemen'. No one had ever seen anything so spectacular.
The Swiss guard marched first, followed by the French gentlemen, and then, in a brilliant piece of pairing devised by the
Master of the Horse, the French princes and the English lords in
their sumptuous brocades and heavy gold chains. The Papal,
Venetian and Florentine ambassadors followed. Fleuranges later
insisted that Mary was escorted that day by 2,000 chevaliers.[9]

Many accounts survive, varying a little according to the different vantage points the writers procured along the route. The
French ambassador to Venice, the Bishop of Asti, was kept
informed by a particularly observant Italian, who had a gift for
slipping to the centre of every mêlée. Mary herself rode a white
palfrey over which four footmen held a canopy of white satin,

lavishly embroidered with the roses of England and two bristling porcupines, the heraldic beasts which traditionally supported the arms of France. Her hair was dressed in the English fashion with gold and pearl ornaments, and her gown had tight-fitting sleeves, which was also considered *'style anglais'*. How she managed to change again is not reported, but by the time she reached Abbeville to be welcomed by all the dignitaries of the town and a deafening salute from the artillery, she was wearing a gown of white and gold brocade, embroidered with jewels, instead of the cloth of gold and crimson outfit in which she had met the King earlier in the afternoon. Throughout the procession she kept on her crimson silk hat, which she wore jauntily cocked over her left eye.[10] Francis rode beside her in a surcoat of silver and gold, but he remained outside the canopy, so that the Queen should be the central figure in the great pageant. She was preceded by her squires, dressed in silk with heavy gold collars. After her came her litter, embroidered with golden fleurs-de-lis. Two running foot-men in velvet caps and black and gold chequered doublets kept pace with the palfrey and were much admired by the Venetians.

Three carriages had been shipped from England. The first two were covered in cloth of gold and drawn by horses with magnif-icent golden bridles. Each carriage was occupied by four ladies 'very well dressed', which suggests the Duchess of Norfolk, her daughter the Countess of Oxford and Lady Guildford took prece-dence. Then came six gentlewomen on palfreys trapped in cloth of gold and purple velvet. They were followed by a carriage covered in crimson velvet with another four fine ladies. More ladies rode after the carriages, their horses caparisoned in mulberry-coloured velvet, edged with silk fringing in white and light blue. Somewhere in this flashing parade of wealth and beauty rode Mary Boleyn, the elder daughter of Sir Thomas Boleyn, Henry's semi-permanent ambassador in the Low Countries.[11] His younger daughter, the thirteen-year-old Anne, had been sent the previous year to Margaret of Austria's court, which was regarded as one of the finest finishing schools in Europe. She was said to be making excellent progress with her French, and Mary Tudor, perhaps after the disappointment of learning she could not take Jane Poppincourt to Paris, had specifically requested Anne as one of her *demoiselles d'honneur*. Sir Thomas had written with some embarrassment asking Margaret to send his daughter back, for having been involved in the previous marriage negotiations, he knew how bitterly the Regent felt over the repudiation of her nephew. In her first weeks at Malines, Anne had copied out her letters home, giving the impression of perfect French. Later she wrote from the Regent's summer palace of La Vure, where Maître Semmonet instructed the young ladies in dictation. Her letter apologizing for her erratic grasp of French spelling is a gem in the annals of orthography.[12] However, she had obviously mastered conversational French and, reluctantly, Margaret parted with her, though she did not join Mary's retinue in time for the entry into Abbeville.

After the ladies 200 English archers marched in pairs, the front row dressed in the Tudor livery of green and white. Fleuranges, who had started his military career at an early age and was affectionately known to King Louis as 'the Young Adventurer', was deeply impressed by their precision. When the procession reached Abbeville, it was swelled by the clergy and magistrates of the town and also the local guard in coats of red and yellow. All the Venetian observers commented on the gold chains worn by the Englishmen, doubled, tripled and sometimes looped six times about their necks and shoulders, until one wag described the milords as dressed 'prisoner fashion', so shackled were they by their wealth.[13]

The Venetians had their own reasons for reporting the marriage in such detail. They wanted to know whether Louis planned to recapture Milan. The French had retreated from the city in 1512, after the death of their brilliant general, Gaston de Foix, at the Battle of Ravenna. This ignominious defeat had left the Sforzas once again in power, and the Signory was avid for news of the French King's intentions. Some days after Mary's arrival, Marco Dandolo, the Venetian ambassador, managed to broach the subject during one of the wedding banquets. At the beginning of 1514, when Anne of Brittany died, the French King had been so depressed he said they should leave space for his coffin beside her, as he would not last another year. Now he assured the ambassador not only that he intended to undertake another Italian expedition but also that Mary had begged him to take her to Venice.

The Duke of Bourbon, the King said, would see to the recapturing of Milan, and, 'Mr Ambassador,' he added grandly, 'with regard to coming to Venice, we wish her to go and see that town, so write to the most illustrious Signory that she will assuredly come.'[14]

When the procession reached the centre of Abbeville, Mary attended a Mass of thanksgiving at the Church of St Vulfran before rejoining the King for a state reception. His eldest daughter, the plain Madame Claude, welcomed Mary in the main square and conducted her to the palace, the ancient Hôtel de Gruthuse, where her apartments were separated from those of the King by a pleasant garden. That evening Francis and Claude gave a ball in Mary's honour. The Dauphin excelled in organizing lavish spectacles and the Bishop of Asti's correspondent ran out of adjectives. 'Your Right Reverend Lordship must not be surprised at my representing well nigh everything in the superlative degree,' he wrote, 'for the reality exceeds my description to the great glory of this Queen.' After supper he reported that there had been 'dancing and music resounding to the skies'. He had learned from the English visitors that Mary loved 'dancing and listening to singing and instrumental music more than anything in the world'.[15] On the same evening as the Dauphin's ball, he explained, a fire had broken out in the area of the town where many of the Venetians were lodging. Four houses burned down, but the Italians were unharmed because the river 'flowed between; yet the wind was very high and carried the flames towards the neighbouring houses, especially in the direction of the Venetian ambassador's house. I believe our prayers saved us,' wrote the Italian piously, adding that 'the fire made greater progress than it would have done had it been permitted to ring the bells, but this was forbidden to avoid disturbing the King at his amusements; and his people not knowing anything of the fire, could not give assistance'.[16]

The following morning the Bishop's correspondent was up early enough to report that Mary, accompanied by Norfolk, the Marquis of Dorset, the Bishop of Durham and all the other lords in her entourage, had risen an hour and a half before daybreak. The wedding procession formed up inside the Queen's apartments and the Italian seems to have gained admittance to the garden which separated these from the main part of the palace.

He saw 'knights and lords well-arrayed, some in velvet, damasks and satins, though the greater part of them were clad in cloth of gold'. It must have been cold in the October dawn and he noted enviously that the Englishmen wore gowns lined 'with the most beautiful sables'. As Mary made her way across the garden, she was preceded by twenty-six knights, two heralds and the royal mace-bearers. Norfolk, as her brother's representative, was at her side and her ladies followed, each walking between two gentlemen carrying their caps in their hands. According to the Italian, there was a great crush inside the palace. He understood the Cardinals of Auch and Bayeux, who were to perform the marriage, were joined by 'a few bishops, barons captains and some of the house stewards', but for once the Bishop's informant could not push through the throng. 'I am unable to write details of what took place in the hall,' he wrote despondently.[17]

As a member of the Dauphin's inner circle, Fleuranges had a better view. He described the ceremony as taking place *'dans une belle grande salle'* entirely hung with cloth of gold.[18] Mary entered to a fanfare of trumpets. Her magnificent fair hair flowed loose over her shoulders, held in place by a coronet of precious stones. She was dressed in gold brocade, richly trimmed with ermine, and her gown, blazing with diamond clasps, was received with a chorus of approval from the Venetians, who thought the French fashion suited her better than the English costume she had worn the previous day. Louis also wore gold brocade, edged with ermine. He swept off his hat and bowed ceremoniously. Mary curtsied to the ground. The King raised her to her feet, kissed her and then turned to his treasurer, Robertet, who was holding a wonderful necklace of rubies and pearls, which Louis clasped round Mary's neck. After this the bishops celebrated the Nuptial Mass, the Dauphin and the Dauphine assisting. Francis handed the offertory money to the King, while Claude held it for the Queen. Fleuranges thought the Dauphine must have felt quite upset, as she was used to performing the same duty for her mother and only ten months had passed since Anne of Brittany's death. The Bishop divided the consecrated wafer. He gave one half to Louis and one half to Mary, who kissed it as a sign of respect and then swallowed it. After this solemn moment she curtsied gracefully and returned to her own apartments to dine with her ladies.[19]

That evening the King and Queen gave a ball at the Hôtel de Gruthuse. They held open house to all comers, with feasting which lasted for three days. At eight o'clock Madame Claude came to take Mary to sleep with the King, the bishops having already blessed the bridal bed. Claude herself was pregnant with Francis's child and although the Dauphin and his circle affected insouciance, the company were agog to know what would happen. Could Mary succeed where Anne of Brittany and Louis's first wife, Jeanne de France, had failed by giving the King a male heir? To his intimates, Francis admitted that Louis's marriage had 'pierced his heart', though to Fleuranges he insisted the King was incapable of begetting a son.[20] Whether Mary emerged from the marriage bed glowing with submission or pale with shock has not been recorded, but the Bishop of Asti's correspondent heard next day that the King had triumphantly assured the Venetian ambassador that he had 'crossed the river three times that night and would have done more had he chosen'.[21] This information sped round the court and was discussed with varying degrees of hilarity and disbelief. Fleuranges did not doubt it. 'In the morning the King said he had performed marvels,' he wrote, adding candidly, 'I certainly believe this was true for he was most uncomfortable.'[22]

Louise of Savoy viewed her sovereign as a lecherous old dotard. 'On 9 October took place the amorous marriage of Louis XII, King of France and Mary of England,' she wrote in her journal. 'They were married at 10 in the morning and in the evening they went to bed together.'[23] For some days Louis appeared much rejuvenated and the French, delighted by Mary's beauty, threw themselves wholeheartedly into welcoming her as their Queen. As the Venetian ambassador grumbled:

> Everything is held up, politics like the rest. No one speaks of anything but fêtes. There you have the French. They always believe that what they wish for will be successful. This marriage has been a success; they see themselves already installed in Milan. They feared only England; this phantom has vanished. The King says everywhere that he

will take Milan or die . . . no one thinks of an obstacle, which
terrifies me. To amuse himself with a wife of eighteen is
very dangerous in his state of health.[24]

Louis's health was to become a matter of daily speculation.
Shortly after the wedding he suffered from a bad attack of gout.*
The state entry into Paris was postponed and the court remained
at Abbeville, while Francis planned and replanned the magnificent jousts he was organizing in honour of Mary's coronation.

Between the signing of the peace treaty and the Queen's departure for France, detailed lists had been drawn up naming the
attendants who would be retained in her household when her
main escort, including the Norfolks, returned to England.[25] These
lists had been sent to Paris on 22 September with a specific
request from Henry for Louis to approve them and send back
signed copies to London. The King's only objection had been to
Jane Poppincourt on account of her light morals, but two days
after the wedding he suddenly created a great upheaval by
announcing the dismissal of a number of his wife's retainers and
gentlewomen, including her chief lady of honour, Lady
Guildford. Mary was shocked and frightened. On 12 October she
wrote to Henry:

My Good Brother,
As heartily as I can I recommend me to your Grace. I marvel
much that I have [not] heard from you since my departing,
so often as I have sent and written to you. Now am I left
post alone, in effect, for on the morn next after my marriage
my Chamberlain and all other menservants were
discharged and in likewise my mother Guildford, with
other my women and maidens except such as never had
experience nor knowledge how to advise or give me counsel in any time of need, which is to be feared more shortly
than your Grace thought at the time of my departing, as my
mother Guildford can more plainly show your Grace than I
can write, to whom I beseech you give credence, and if it

* In the sixteenth century a generic term for every kind of muscular or
arthritic pain.

may be by any means possible, I humbly request you to cause my mother Guildford to repair hither to me again. For if any chance happen other than well, I shall not know where nor of whom to ask my good counsel to your pleasure nor yet to my own desert.

I marvel much that my good Lord of Norfolk would at all times so lightly grant everything at their requests here. I am well assured that when ye know the truth of anything as my mother Guildford can show you, ye would full little have thought I should have been thus treated. Would God my Lord of York had come with me in the room [i.e. place] of my Lord of Norfolk. For I am sure I should have been left much more at my heartsease than I am now, and thus I bid your Grace farewell.

She had managed to dictate the letter, although she was not even allowed to retain her secretary, John Palsgrave, her former French tutor, but she signed with an urgent entreaty in her own hand:

Give credence to my mother Guildford
By your loving sister, Mary Queen of France.[26]

The letter was addressed to 'The King's Grace my kind and loving brother' and a more urgently worded copy was sent to Wolsey on the same day, pointing out that Mary had been carefully briefed not to do anything without first consulting Lady Guildford, and begging the Archbishop to find some way to have her sent back. Bearing in mind the Venetian ambassador's report that on the morning of 1 October the King, to judge by his countenance, was 'very jovial gay and in love', it seems probable that the wedding night proved more strenuous than the nymph from Heaven expected.[27] If so, Lady Guildford, who had been a lady-in-waiting to both Elizabeth of York and Lady Margaret Beaufort, would have had a wealth of experience in dealing with such matters. The widow of Sir Richard Guildford, Controller of the Household to Henry VII, she had known Mary since her childhood and must have been adept in the art of soothing ruffled royal nerves. Evidently she had been a tower of strength the

morning after the wedding, since Mary wailed to Wolsey, 'I have
not yet seen in France any lady or gentlewoman so necessary for
me as she is', rising to a sorrowful crescendo with, 'I had as lief
lose all the winning I shall have in France, as lose her counsel',
and, in case anyone thought she was exaggerating, she added the
same desperate postscript in her own hand that she had written
to Henry: 'Pray give credence to my mother Guildford.'[28]
Whatever indignities Mary had suffered, they were too delicate to
be set down on paper, but Jane Guildford knew all and in plain
language she would tell both the King of England and the
Archbishop of York exactly what had gone on.

Wolsey did his best. He wrote tactfully to Louis from Eltham
on 23 October, explaining that Lady Guildford had been chosen
for her wisdom, discretion and honour, but the King refused to
reinstate her. Mary was obliged to submit to the ministrations of
Madame d'Aumont, an experienced Frenchwoman, as her principal Lady of the Bedchamber. As Queen of France, she was also
attended by Claude, Mary of Luxembourg and the Dauphin's
brilliant sister, Marguerite d'Angoulême. Six of the younger
English ladies stayed on: Lady Elizabeth Grey, the Marquis of
Dorset's sister, Lady Grey of Wilton, Anne Jernyngham, Mary
Fiennes, Lady Jane Bourchier and Anne Boleyn, who seems to
have caught up with the household just before Mary's coronation.

The cause of Louis's antipathy to Lady Guildford later
emerged in a conversation between the King and Worcester, who
continued as English ambassador. She had taken it upon herself
to chaperon Mary in a way the King considered quite unneces-
sary. 'In nowise,' said the King, would he have her about his wife,
for he was 'a sickly body' and Lady Guildford's interference was
quite out of keeping with his own ideas of what was allowable
between a married couple. He did not want 'when he would be
merry with his wife to have any strange woman with her, but one
that he is well-acquainted withal, afore whom he durst be merry,'
wrote Worcester.[29] This explanation was regarded as perfectly
satisfactory, and Lady Guildford was pensioned off by Henry VIII
with an annuity of £20, which was later raised to £60 as a reward
for her dedicated service.

Louis's gout delayed the court's progress to Paris. It took two weeks for the royal party to travel to St Denis, where Mary was to be crowned, since by ancient custom no queen of France could enter Paris until after her coronation. The Dauphin's jousts were to be held immediately after her state entry into the capital. They were the talk of all Europe, and the English nobles who had attended the wedding took a proclamation back to London, inviting challengers and detailing the rules of the tournament.[30] Henry sent a formidable team, the Duke of Suffolk, the Marquis of Dorset and his four brothers, Lord Clinton, Sir Edward Neville, Sir Giles Capell and Thomas Cheyney. All were champions in their own right. Suffolk and Dorset were also charged with a diplomatic mission. They were to arrange a meeting between Henry and Louis, which was to take place the following spring. It had been discussed for many weeks, but neither the French nor the English could agree where it should take place. Dover, Calais and Picardy had all been considered, but one of the chief obstacles was Louis's eagerness to get on with his Italian expedition. He wanted to travel towards Lyons, but the chief purpose of the summit would be to discuss expelling the Spanish from Navarre.

In the last week of October Suffolk, Neville and Sir William Sidney crossed the Channel, travelling in disguise.[31] Brandon caught up with the royal party at Beauvais on 25 October. He suspected, from intelligence which had reached him at Canterbury, that the dismissal of Mary's attendants had been part of a malicious attempt by Norfolk to interfere with Wolsey's policies, and had advised the Archbishop to do all he could to reinstate Lady Guildford.[32] From Beauvais he wrote directly to Henry. He had found King Louis lying in bed with the Queen sitting nearby, 'and so I did my reverence and knelt down by his bedside,' he wrote. Louis embraced Suffolk, holding him firmly in his arms as an expression of the sincere brotherly love he felt for Henry, who, he reckoned, had given him 'the greatest jewel ever one prince had of another'. Brandon was to assure his King that 'never Queen behaved herself more wisely and honourably' and, he added, 'so say all the noblemen in France and no man ever set his mind more upon a woman on account of her loving manner'.[33]

The rest of the letter is devoted to sport. Brandon was in France principally for the tournament. There is no evidence that he entertained any feelings for Mary apart from loyal approbation for the way in which she was fulfilling her role and pleasure that he could report back to Henry that the French marriage was working out well. With unaffected good humour, he told how the King had introduced him to the Dauphin, suggesting he and Dorset should be aides at the tournament, and how Francis had entertained the English lords to dinner, saying they should not be his aides but his brethren. Suffolk repeated a lewd joke Louis had made. The King promised to send Henry a harness and a courser, 'For he says your Grace has mounted him so well, he will seek all Christendom.'[34] Louis made no secret of his physical passion for his new wife and took pleasure in hinting at its rejuvenating effect whenever the Dauphin was present. The day before Mary arrived in France, he had shown Worcester the jewels he intended to give her. The Earl noted at least fifty-six superb pieces, but the King understood the psychology of young women: 'My wife shall not have all at once, but at diverse times,' he said, adding that, 'he would have many kisses and thanks for them'.[35] Once he had set eyes upon Mary, he could deny her nothing and the courtiers watched with bated breath as he showered her with gifts. After the marriage he presented her with 'a marvellous great pointed diamond with a ruby about two inches long'. The following day Worcester noted 'a ruby two and a half inches long, valued at 10,000 marks'. On the third day 'the King gave the Queen a great diamond with a great round pearl hanging by it'.[36] Madame d'Aumont divulged nothing, but it was presumed by all that the kisses had been duly paid.

After inviting Suffolk and Dorset to join a wild boar hunt, Francis had enlisted them to help him organize the tournament. Brandon, who had brought his harness but apparently not all his horses, declared they needed more time to equip themselves and managed to get the date postponed by another week. An arch had been set up in front of the Bastille with four shields fixed to its walls, upon which contestants were invited to register their names. Challengers who wished to perform according to the ordinary rules of European jousting, by 'running at the tilt', were invited to register their names on a silver shield, but tournament stars of the calibre of Suffolk and Dorset were expected to inscribe the gold shield which bore the names of those who would 'run with the sharp spears and fight with the sharp swords'. Gentlemen who wished to fight on foot or in the mêlée signed up on the black and tawny shields.[37]

While these preparations were in progress, Mary was crowned on Sunday 5 November in the Abbey of St Denis. Once again the Bishop of Bayeux officiated. After she had received the ring, the sceptre and the rod of justice, the crown was placed briefly on her head. It was so heavy that the Dauphin later relieved her of the weight by holding it symbol-ically above her, while she sat enthroned in the sanctuary to hear High Mass. The Queen and the Dauphin then joined the King for dinner, which he had now started to take at noon, having completely broken the strict regime which the doctors had prescribed for his health. The Duchess of Savoy had ridden to Paris two days earlier. She had been advised to go and greet the Queen at St Denis. Louise left the capital at three o'clock in the afternoon with a large retinue of gentlemen. She welcomed Mary politely and remained at court long enough to watch the beautiful young woman take Paris by storm the next day, recording laconically in her journal that the Queen entered the city at four in the afternoon.[38]

Despite the November weather the Parisians had excelled themselves. The whole town was decorated with lilies and roses. Some were silk, some were painted upon arras, others were represented on the giant scaffolds which stood at intervals along the processional route. A series of tableaux vivants had been devised to welcome Mary with a wonderful mixture of heraldry, allegory and pantomime verse. The first was at St Denis, which at that time was still the main gate of the walled medieval town. A gigantic ship, complete with real sailors climbing the rigging, bore figures of Ceres, Bacchus and, at the helm, Paris herself, symbolizing the corn, wine and commerce of the city. The four winds puffed energetically into the sails, while a choir sang songs of welcome. As most of these had been composed by the court poet, Pierre Gringoire, he presented Mary with a handwritten souvenir programme of the event with beautiful pictures, lavishly illuminated with gold leaf.[39]

In a gown of gold brocade and a diadem of magnificent pearls, her jewels flashing at her throat, the youngest Tudor sat in an open carriage, draped with white cloth of gold. She was preceded by yet another mighty procession. The Dauphin and the Dukes of Alençon, Bourbon, Vendôme and De Longueville rode at its head, but this time instead of the unsympathetic Duke of Norfolk she had the comfort of knowing Suffolk and Dorset, and the other English lords who had come to fight in the tournament, were close at hand. At St Denis she was met by officials of the town and, according to Hall, a daunting assembly of 3,000 members of the French clergy.[40]

Passing through the gate, she came to the second tableau, in which a marble fountain played against a background of celestial blue, while three Graces danced in a garden. Lilies and roses grew in the fountain bowl and a poem celebrated the miraculous entwining of the two flowers.[41] The third pageant showed Solomon and the Queen of Sheba, a flattering allusion to Louis's wisdom and his title 'Father of the people'. At the fourth stop a two-tier scaffold had been erected in front of the Church of the Holy Innocents. God the Father, dressed in the best traditions of the medieval Mysteries, held a huge pasteboard heart and a bouquet of red roses over the figures of a king and queen, robed in gold and ermine, but to the romantic Parisians steeped in the love stories of Guillaume de Loris, familiar even to the illiterate from the lyrics of popular ballads, it was surely the fifth pageant which had most significance. By an ingenious feat of scene-painting, a walled city had been created, enclosing a garden with a rose bush growing centre stage. Out of the bush sprouted an enormous rosebud, which ascended by means of concealed machinery towards a balcony where a lily grew before a golden throne, sheltered by a rich pavilion. Four Virtues, clad in the fashions of the day, gazed out across golden trelliswork, while outside the city walls Peace vanquished a villainous figure of Discord. When the rose had completed its ascent, the petals opened before the astonished spectators to disclose a live maiden, who recited the most complimentary of Gringoire's verses.[42] He likened Mary to the fragrant 'rose vermeille', the symbol of peace, the fabled blossom which had grown in the gardens of Jericho and which bloomed in the margins of a thousand romances. To the Parisians their King's beautiful bride was love incarnate.

The procession moved on to the Chastellet de Paris, where Justice and Truth sat enthroned beneath a vast replica of the

French crown, amid a pageant of worthies. Phoebus, Diana, Minerva, Stella Maris and Concord posed in a meadow listening to an orator speaking a long ode comparing Louis to the Sun and Mary to the Moon. The Queen, whose public duties had begun at nine in the morning, must have been exhausted when, at about five-thirty, she reached the Palais Royale. There on another double stage the Angel of the Annunciation addressed the Virgin Mary beneath the arms of France, supported by a porcupine and a lion hung above yet another representation of a king and a queen. At the bottom of the stage rustically clad shepherds and shepherdesses sang an anthem, celebrating Mary in Heaven and Mary on Earth, and still the long day went on, for the dignitaries of the Sorbonne wished to greet her, so that it was six o'clock before the earthly Mary finally escaped into the quiet of Notre-Dame.

The jousts began on 13 November and continued for three days. The Dauphin and his aides rode into the field to salute the King and Queen. Louis watched from a couch, being again enfeebled with gout. Mary stood to receive the adulation of the crowds. Everyone was captivated by her radiance. Three hundred and five challengers entered the lists and every knight ran five courses. The English fought fiercely; it was only six months since the peace treaty and, although technically the tournament was a sporting event, old rivalries died hard. Suffolk and Dorset both wounded opponents, but the most dramatic casualty was Francis himself, who was hurt on his hand, so that he had to put in one of his seconds. Suffolk and Dorset were the undoubted champions in the jousting and Francis, whose self-esteem had clearly suffered, became bitterly jealous. He chose a German, a man of superhuman height and strength, to bring Suffolk down. Brandon unhorsed him and struck him in the fighting on the ground with the butt end of his spear, until he staggered and seemed about to fall, but the judges let the contestants go on and many hard blows were delivered before they dropped the rail that signified the end of a course. Suffolk and the German raised their visors to take air. Then they set to again with blunt-edged swords. The German was a formidable opponent. In the end Suffolk took him by the neck and pummelled his head until his nose began to bleed. The Dauphin then withdrew the German, whose identity was never revealed. Dorset withdrew after losing his spear, but his younger brother, the nineteen-year-old Lord Edward Grey, fought with great skill and strategy, disarming another of the French 'giants'.

The Frenchmen were gloriously accoutred. The Dauphin wore different armour and different colours each day, appearing first in silver and gold, next in crimson and yellow velvet and on the third day, as a compliment to the new Queen, in the Tudor colours of green and white. The Duke of Bourbon and the Earl of St Polle were also magnificently dressed, the Earl in stunning purple velvet and the Duke in tawny velvet and cloth of silver. The Englishmen did not apparently try to outdo the French in costume, but all wore the red cross of St George on some part of their apparel. There was the usual quota of stunt riders, in particular a gentleman called Anthony Bownarme, who came on to the field armed like a French porcupine with spears in his hand, spears under his arm, spears stuck in his stirrup. He rode before the Queen and shattered ten spears into the ground.[43] This was wildly applauded. Suffolk's own account of the tournament was understatement to say the least. He wrote to Wolsey on 18 November, 'the jousts are done and, blessed be God, all our Englishmen sped well as I am sure ye shall hear by others'.[44]

Dorset wrote in more detail. He and Suffolk had fought on three days and put themselves forward even for the fighting on foot, but when it came to the general mêlée, they found no French noblemen participated, so they put in their seconds. 'Many were hurt on both sides,' explained the Marquis, 'but no great hurt and of our Englishmen, none overthrown.' He described Suffolk's encounter without actually blaming the Dauphin: 'they brought a German and put him to my Lord of Suffolk to have put us to shame, but advantage they got none of us, but rather the contrary. I ended without any manner hurt. My Lord of Suffolk is a little hurt in the hand.

'The Queen continues her goodness and wisdom and increases in the favour of her husband and the Privy Council. She has said to my Lord of Suffolk and me that the King her husband said to her that my Lord of Suffolk and I did shame all France and that we should carry the prize into England.'[45]

Their mission concluded, the English lords went home for Christmas. If at any point Mary Tudor permitted herself romantic reveries, it was surely in the weeks immediately after the tournament. Technically Suffolk was fighting for her. The jousts were in her honour and the contrast between Brandon's vigorous, athletic body and her husband's frailty must have been hard for a young woman of eighteen to ignore, particularly at the French court, where the daily parlance was of love. The Dauphin had become embarrassingly attracted to his young stepmother. It was public knowledge, unflattering for Claude, and indeed Louise at one point lost her temper, reprimanding Francis and warning him to control his priapic urges, for which he seemed prepared to risk a throne. The King, meanwhile, continued in high spirits and full of hope. On 22 December, when Marco Dandolo was asking him to name the date he would set out for Italy, he replied:

> Ambassador, urge me no more, and heat not yourself, for I am warmer than you and the expedition shall soon be undertaken. This gout rather troubles me. We shall soon have 24,000 landsknechts, 6,000 English, 2,000 spears and 800 light horse, and on the day of the Epiphany everything will be arranged. By Candlemas I shall be at Lyons, send troops into Italy and have with me my guard of 8,000 foot and 1,000 men at arms.[46]

Louis was not to see another Candlemas. He did not even celebrate the Feast of the Epiphany on 6 January, for which elaborate preparations were being made, since in France the feast was known then, as now, as the 'jour des Rois'. He wrote to Henry VIII on 28 December to say how entirely satisfied he was with his lovely wife, then on New Year's Day 1515, wasted by illness, he died.

The future of the French monarchy hung in the balance. No one seriously expected that Mary would be pregnant. Louise, as soon as they brought her the news of Louis's death, rode triumphantly to Paris to be with her son, but Francis could not formally be crowned until it was certain that Mary had not conceived a male child. By ancient custom she was required to wear the white robes which were the traditional mourning for

Queens of France and to go into seclusion at the Hôtel de Cluny, the royal palace on the left bank of the Seine, which had once been a Benedictine abbey. Wolsey, anticipating Louis's death by some sixth sense, had already written warning Mary to be careful in everything she said or did, 'and if any motions of marriage be made unto you, in no wise give hearing unto them'.[47] She received his letter only a few days after her widowhood and wrote back on 10 January, thanking him for his advice and promising to do nothing but what was ordered by 'the King my brother and his Council'. She was even a little indignant that Wolsey had felt the need to warn her; she was no longer a child, she reminded him. Every inch a Queen Dowager, Mary dictated her letter to a secretary, but she evidently spoke very fast for towards the end of the page, as her indignation mounted, she began to repeat herself:

> I trust the King my brother and you will not reckon in me such childhood. I trust I have so ordered myself, so since that I came hither, that I trust it hath been to the honour of the King my brother and me since I came hither and if there is anything that I may do [for] you, I would be glad for to do it. And no more to you at this time.
> Written at Paris the 10th day of January 1515.[48]

Henry sent Suffolk to comfort her. He reached Paris on 4 February and visited her in company with the other ambassadors, Nicholas West and Sir Richard Wingfield. They made a formal report to Henry as soon as they arrived. Mary thanked her brother for sending 'in her heaviness my Lord of Suffolk and others as well to comfort her as for obtaining her dower'. Difficulties were to be expected, because although Louis's councillors had so recently set their hands to documents confirming that in the event of her widowhood she would be at liberty to return 'with her servants, jewels and effects into England', part of her dowry had been offset against the French debt of 1 million crowns. There was also the question of whether she would be allowed to keep the jewels which Louis had showered so liberally upon her, or whether these rightfully belonged to the French crown. Francis was also anxious to have back Tournai, which Henry had captured the previous year, and Wolsey had set his heart on the bishopric of the town, which had been promised him throughout all the negotiations between Henry and Louis XII, despite the minor complication that the Pope purposed otherwise. The ambassadors, therefore, had set out fully expecting to haggle, and as the astronomical bill for conveying Mary and her stuff to France in September had been settled at Greenwich on 28 January, as well as compensation paid out to the survivors of the *Great Elizabeth*, the ship which had been wrecked off Sandwich, the King expected his envoys to drive a hard bargain.[49]

As soon as Mary had physical proof that she was not pregnant, she reassured Francis that she was not carrying Louis's heir. He cut short the traditional period of court mourning and was crowned at Reims at the end of January, so that the English ambassadors arrived too late for the ceremony, although fortuitously in time to attend the coronation jousts.[50] It was still thought proper, however, for Mary to remain in seclusion at Cluny for the traditional forty days of mourning. She was allowed to have some of her English ladies to keep her company, but was confined to the gloomy *'chambre de la reine blanche'*, its windows covered, so that she lived day and night by candlelight, dressed in the terrible white garments which made her look more like an abbess than a queen. What happened next is the stuff of French romances or Italian *novelle*, but the story is well substantiated by the many letters which flew back and forth between Mary and Henry, Suffolk and Wolsey over the next three months. The correspondence runs to approximately ninety pages, all of which are well preserved in the Cotton manuscript and the Public Record Office.[51] The letters from Mary and Suffolk have been interpreted in many ways, but pieced together in as accurate a chronological order as possible, this was the sequence of events.

Before she left Dover, Henry promised Mary 'at the waterside' that if she married the 'aged and sickly' Louis, on his death she would be free to choose whomsoever she pleased as a second husband. Henry knew that she was fond of Charles Brandon, but there was no clear agreement between the couple and it seems reasonable to assume that Mary had been too shy and too loyally bred to admit her feelings to Charles, while he had never dared to aspire to the hand of his sovereign's sister.[52] Henry, when he sent Brandon back to France in January, guessed that Mary, who was homesick for England, might throw herself upon Suffolk, coming as he would in the role of a knightly rescuer. The King, therefore, extracted a promise from his handsome friend not to propose to Mary.[53] From letters written by Wolsey after the event, it seems clear that Henry was prepared to keep his word to Mary and allow a marriage between her and Brandon, but as King of England he wished to keep his options open, for Henry guessed, rightly, that as soon as Mary was back on the marriage market, there would be a flood of offers from other European Princes, whose friendship might be valuable. Backed by Wolsey, he wished to preserve the French alliance. Affairs in Scotland had taken a disastrous turn and Brandon was to avoid antagonizing Francis at all costs, lest he renege on Louis's promise to restrain the Duke of Albany from going to the aid of what Margaret called the 'contrary party'.

Immediately after Louis's death, two friars had been sent from the English court to console Mary at Cluny. They reached her before Suffolk, West and Wingfield. One of them was that same Friar Bonaventure Langley who had taken Katherine's condolences to Margaret after Flodden. Although Mary never specifically stated so, it is usually assumed that Henry sent the friars, but it is at least plausible to suppose that they may have been dispatched on the initiative of the Queen of England to facilitate an Anglo–Spanish or Anglo–Habsburg rapprochement. The friars succeeded in terrifying Mary into believing that Henry did not mean to keep his 'waterside' promise. They also tried to plant a suspicion in her mind that Suffolk had been sent to entice her back to England only so that Henry could marry her to Charles of Castile.[54] Suffolk was convinced that Norfolk and his supporters in the council wished to bring down Wolsey and himself and to reverse the French alliance. 'I know their drifts [devious ways],' he had written to Wolsey, in an earlier letter sent after the dismissal of Lady Guildford. Katherine herself was certainly very depressed in the spring of 1515, because in November, supported by the prayers of a nation and the good wishes of all the court, she had been delivered of a stillborn boy. Louis XII and Margaret of Austria had promised to stand as godparents.

Many rumours were flying about the French court, including one which Suffolk reported in his first letter to England, that Mary might marry the Duke of Lorraine. There are also grounds for believing that Francis himself paid unwelcome attentions to Mary, hinting that he would even be prepared to divorce Claude and marry her himself. Such a course of action was not unknown in French history. Within living memory of many at Francis's court, King Charles VIII of France had repudiated Margaret of Austria, who had been betrothed to him, raised in France and then cruelly sent back to her father, Maximilian. Louis himself had also divorced Jeanne de France to marry Anne of Brittany. The only possible grounds for such an action would have been if Claude had proved barren. Brandon had been asked to convey Henry's congratulations because Claude was thought to be pregnant, although his first dispatch from Paris records that she had told him this was not yet so.[55]

To complicate things further, the story of Francis's infatuation was wildly exaggerated by the French historian Brantôme, who presented Mary as a conniving minx who bewitched Francis because she wished to remain Queen of France. Anyone who has read Mary's plaintive series of letters to Henry and Wolsey knows the reverse to be true. According to Brantôme, however, she married Brandon only *after* Francis came to his senses and rejected her. Unable to resist embroidering his tale, Brantôme added various extraneous details, including that Mary stuffed her clothes with pillows at Cluny to make Louise of Savoy and Marguerite d'Angoulême think she was pregnant. Mary's own letters, as they exist in the Cotton Manuscript, show that she had worked herself to a pitch of nervous hysteria by the time Suffolk arrived. She wrote in her own hand, and it may be that only drafts are preserved. Perhaps fair copies reached Henry, judiciously corrected and adjusted by Wolsey, but the originals, scribbled unevenly and filled with crossings-out and repetitions, indicate her desperate frame of mind. When Brandon finally saw her alone, she blurted out her fears and feelings, giving him a straight choice. Either he must marry her at once or she would retire into a convent. What transpired between them was so unexpected that Brandon made a clean breast of it to Henry at the earliest possible opportunity.

'She showed me she had verily understood by Friar Langley,' wrote the Duke, 'that if ever she came in England she should never have me'; the best in France had said so. If she went to England, they had told her, she would be sent straight to Flanders. 'To the which she said she had rather to be torn in pieces than ever she should come there, and with that wept.' He continued, 'Sir, I never saw woman so weep.' It was the incontrovertible truth. Henry knew as well as Brandon what a torrent Mary could shed, when she wanted her own way. Charles explained that he had protested: 'I showed unto her Grace that there was none such thing, upon my faith, with the best words I could, but in none ways I could make her believe it.' He had suggested gently that Mary should write to her brother to obtain his goodwill. Then Brandon should have felt easy about the matter. He had also explained to her that he had made 'a promise' to Henry not to propose without the King's consent, but Mary would not be satisfied. In conclusion she had said, 'If the King my brother is content and the French King both, the one by his letters and the other by his words, that I should have you, I will have the time after my desire.' Otherwise, she went on, she would believe that what she had heard was true and that Suffolk had simply been sent to entice her back. She had therefore, or so she claimed, already told Francis her feelings, and if Charles Brandon did not marry her forthwith he should 'never after this day look to have the proffer again'. Pleading with a naïve certainty that Henry would realize he had taken the only course open to him, Suffolk informed Henry, 'and so she and I was married'. Only ten witnesses had been present and these had not included Wingfield or West, since Mary was sure they would have argued against the plan. 'Therefore they know not of it, nor the writing of this letter on my faith and truth.'[56]

Suffolk's explanation is undated, but Mary obviously told Francis her feelings in January, before he left for his coronation at Reims, because on 3 February, after the English ambassadors brought Henry's congratulations, the French King sent for the

Duke. In a private audience in his bed-chamber, Francis told Suffolk that he understood he had come to marry 'the Queen his master's sister'. Suffolk denied this, pointing out that it would be a strange thing to marry the queen dowager of a country without requesting the permission of that country's king. After the interview he wrote immediately to Wolsey, who praised his discretion. The following day was completely taken up with Francis's triumphal entry into Paris.

By 15 February, after her meeting with Brandon, Mary wrote boldly to Henry to say she had confessed 'the good mind I bear towards my Lord of Suffolk' to Francis, to prevent his unpleasant advances. This implies Suffolk wrote to Henry on or around that day, preferring the King to hear his own version rather than anything Francis might have to say. Worse was to come. Rejoicing in the passionate embraces of her virile new husband, Mary, who had previously known only Louis's lovemaking, assumed she had conceived. It was a premature and overwrought conclusion, but Suffolk, aghast, wrote to Wolsey on 5 March, less than three weeks after the secret marriage. 'The Queen would never let me rest until I had granted her to be married,' he wrote bluntly, 'and so to be plain with you, I have married her, heartily, and have lain with her insomuch I fear me she may be with child.'[57]

Wolsey was thunderstruck. Not only was marriage without royal permission to a blood relation of the sovereign a capital offence, there was also the matter of the Duke's nebulous betrothal to his thirteen-year-old ward Lady Lisle, whose income he enjoyed. The tone of the Archbishop's letters changed immediately. His attitude to Mary had previously been one of fatherly concern. He wrote now with the full weight of priestly authority. Suffolk's account of the secret marriage made it sound like a contract *per verba de praesenti*, a technical term which meant it could still be dissolved.[58] Letters flew between England and France, discussing whether a second, more public marriage could take place in Lent, which had then begun. By English custom it could not; by French usage, Suffolk learned, it could by episcopal dispensation. On 9 March Mary signed a document agreeing to give up her dowry to Henry. When Wolsey's letter describing her brother's rage arrived, she also smuggled the most precious jewel

Louis had given her out of the country as a peace offering. She sent Henry the Mirror of Naples, which may have been why Francis, many years later, scrawled across her portrait *'plus sale que royne'* – more dirty than queenly.[59] Suffolk forewarned Wolsey that 'a diamond with a great pearl' should soon be delivered to the King. Mary herself could not write, he explained, because she had toothache, 'My Lord, she and I remit these matters wholly to your discretion,' he wrote optimistically.[60]

The Archbishop of York replied immediately. He had shown Suffolk's earlier letter, stating he had 'secretly married the King's sister and they have lived together as man and wife', to Henry; he had not been able to do otherwise. The King was furious. 'He could not believe it but took the same grievously and displeasantly,' wrote Wolsey, not merely for Suffolk's presumption but *'for breaking his promise made to the King at Eltham'*. Oath-breaking was a serious business. It hit at the very core of the chivalric code. Wolsey himself had been present when Brandon had given his word. Neither he nor Henry could credit it. They thought that rather than have broken a promise, Charles would have preferred to be 'torn with wild horses . . . Cursed be the blind affection and counsel that hath brought ye hereunto,' thundered the Archbishop. Suffolk, he advised, must now make sure that Francis wrote very favourably to Henry on his behalf. The Duke's diplomatic efforts must be shown to be as successful as they had been in Louis XII's time. He was also to pay Henry the vast sum of £4,000 a year during Mary's lifetime, leaving her £36,000 a year to live on. Charles was also to bring back all the gold, plate and jewels she had taken with her into France, and he was to extract a legally binding promise from Francis to pay 200,000 crowns of the dowry money back to England. For the present, Wolsey thought it best for the Duke to do nothing about Tournai. He would have enough to do looking after his own affairs.[61]

Brandon was heartbroken. 'Punish me rather with prison, Sir, rather than you should have me in mistrust in your heart,' he wrote to Henry. 'Strike off my head and let me not live.'[62] Wolsey had written that his enemies in the council, by which he meant the Howards, suspected him of being in league with France – in short, a traitor.

By now there was also uproar in Paris. Everyone knew that by marrying without Henry's permission, Mary and Suffolk had technically put their lives in jeopardy. Inwardly gloating that he had scored politically, as his *'belle mère'* could not now be dangerously remarried to a Habsburg, Francis wrote to Henry. Mary wrote too, begging for mercy and saying she was entirely to blame. Even Claude, whose genuine affection for Mary had survived Francis's indiscreet attentions, wrote to Henry. A second, more public wedding took place in Paris on Saturday 31 March. 'The Duke of Suffolk, *homme de bonne condition*, whom Henry VIII had sent as Ambassador to the King, married Mary, sister of the aforesaid Henry, widow of Louis XII,' noted Louise in her journal.[63] Sixteen days later she wrote, 'Marie d'Angleterre, widow of Louis XII, left Paris with her husband, the Duke of Suffolk, to return to England.'

Suffolk and Mary reached Dover on 2 May. Henry's anger was short-lived. Wolsey met them and escorted them to Lord Abergavenny's house at Birling, where the King awaited them with a great retinue. He accepted the explanation that she was completely to blame for the secret marriage.[64] Financial agreement was completed by 11 May: instead of £4,000 a year, Mary was required to pay Henry £2,000 a year for the next twelve years, or until the sum of £24,000 had been paid off. Suffolk also had to forfeit the wardship of Lady Lisle and Mary was bound against a penalty of £100,000 to give up all the plate and jewels she had received.[65] When these legal formalities were completed, the couple married publicly and joyously at Greenwich on 13 May 1515, in the presence of the King and Queen and all the nobles then at court. Sir William Sidney, who had been one of the ten witnesses at the ceremony in Paris, signed a document binding him to absolute secrecy.[66] West, who remained in Paris, had the delicate task of reminding Francis that the French pension, due on 1 May, had not been paid. Francis mentioned the equally delicate matter of the Mirror of Naples.[67] Its 'theft' by Mary continued to rankle for some years, and it was said that during the Field of the Cloth of Gold Henry VIII was seen wearing it on his cap.

Chapter 9

One of the Lowest-brought Ladies

For as long as Louis XII lived, enchanted by the pretty wife to whom he could deny nothing, the Duke of Albany was destined to remain in France. The show of emotion with which the French King had greeted Suffolk when he had arrived at Beauvais for Mary's coronation jousts had impressed Brandon deeply. He believed Louis's protestations of brotherly love towards Henry were completely sincere and had taken pains to impress this on his sovereign. It seems unlikely that the French King would have granted Albany, who was a French subject, permission to interfere in Scotland's internal affairs, when his own relations with his brother-in-law of England had reached such a point of euphoria. By the birth of Alexander, Duke of Ross, the child Margaret had conceived before James IV's death at Flodden, Albany stood second in line to the Scottish throne, but to the lords who formed what Margaret called the 'party adversary', he was the obvious leader to help them check the power of the hated Douglases.

The series of events which began when Angus's grandfather Old Lord Drummond, the chief Justiciary, had struck Lyon King of Arms with his glove soon escalated to a situation where Scotland was on the brink of civil war. Henry had signed a cursory peace in August 1514, but pre-occupied with the French alliance, which Mary with her tact and sweetness had turned into such a glittering triumph, he had little time to devote to the affairs of his elder sister. Margaret made light of the glove incident. In a memorandum dictated at a later date for the benefit of her brother's lawyers, she denied Lord Drummond had boxed Sir William's ears, remembering only that the irate peer had come to the defence of her honour. 'The said Lord Drummond wafted his sleeve at an herald and gave him upon the breast with his hand for because the said herald behaved offensively.' Instead of addressing Margaret as the Queen's grace, Lyon had said he 'came in message from the lords to my lady the King's mother'.[1] The Privy Council instantly sent Lyon to France with an official announcement that they were electing Albany Regent of Scotland and Governor in James V's minority on grounds of the Queen having forfeited her powers of office. Margaret, in the first ecstasy of romantic love, had rashly nominated Angus as her co-Regent. The hot-headed youth promptly provoked the council further by attacking Lord Chancellor Beaton at Perth and snatching the Great Seal of Scotland from him.

As Archbishop of Glasgow, Beaton had publicly expressed his disapproval of the marriage. In reprisal, the nobility took up arms against Angus's family, the Red Douglases, and the all-powerful council stopped payment of Margaret's dower rents. The Archbishop himself was in such a great fury that he and his party rode to Edinburgh, occupied the town and surrounded it with all his followers.[2] Margaret and Angus had prudently retreated to Stirling Castle, the most impregnable stronghold in the country, taking with them the infant King and his brother, the Duke of Ross. Margaret's opponents were led by James Hamilton, Earl of Arran, who fiercely resented the domination of the Douglases. He had royal blood. The son of James II's daughter Mary, he had married Elizabeth Home, whom he divorced in 1504 but with whom he continued to live. He was backed, therefore, by Lord Home and the powerful Bothwells, who controlled the Scottish Parliament, which met first in Edinburgh and later in Dunfermline. Margaret regarded both assemblies as unlawful. 'My party adversary continues in their malice and proceeds in their Parliament usurping the King's authority as [though] I and my lords were of no reputation, reputing us as rebels,' she wrote to Henry.[3]

The council offered to let her keep the guardianship of her sons, provided she relinquished the title of regent. She, meanwhile, clung fiercely to the crown's right to nominate bishops and continued her suit at Rome for Gavin Douglas, her husband's uncle, to have the wealthy see of St Andrews in preference to the chapter's candidate, James Hepburn, and the Pope's own nominee, the internationally renowned diplomat Andrew Forman, Bishop of Moray. Traditionally the Archbishop of St Andrews was guardian of the king, so the election became a violent political issue. Margaret begged Henry to send armies both by land and by sea to relieve the Castle of St Andrews, where Gavin Douglas was besieged by Hepburn's men and a combined force put together by Lord Fleming and the Bothwells. 'I have sent my husband, Lord Angus, to break the siege if he may,' she informed Henry. Angus had grasped the rudiments of siege warfare, but had no inkling of its cost. Every day, Margaret told her brother, she was paying out 'a thousand in wages and my money is nigh hand wasted. If you send not soon succours in men and money, I shall be super extended, which were to my dishonour, for I can get no answer to my rents, as I showed you before.' She had complete faith in her brother to overthrow the rebels, and entire confidence that God would be on her side, since she was an anointed queen. 'All the hope that my party-adversaries have,' she assured Henry contemptuously, 'is in the Duke of Albany's coming, which I beseech you to hinder in any way.'[4]

On the date she wrote, 23 November 1514, Louis XII still reigned, her sister Mary was Queen of France, and Margaret regarded herself as indisputably Regent of Scotland, both by James IV's will, and by the fact that she and Angus held the person of the King. The arrival of Albany seemed a remote possibility. She was, however, fully aware of the harm an English army could do to her own popularity with the Scottish people. She feared some of the lords who remained loyal to her might desert to the other side if they encountered, and were beaten by, the English soldiery. The memory of Flodden would be too powerful. She begged Henry to make a proclamation that he would be sending a peace-keeping force. His heralds must tell the Scots that 'their lands and goods shall not be hurt and they shall be recompensed double and treble'. She reassured Henry about her children, who had apparently revelled in the excitement of galloping about Scotland in midwinter. The King and his brother were well and 'right life-like', God be thanked, but Margaret feared 'that the lord adversaries are purposed to [be]siege me in this Castle of Stirling'. She thought she could hold out until the arrival of an English army and suggested Henry's ships should put in at Berwick upon Tweed, before advancing to St Andrews. In the meantime, the adversary party had regained possession of the Great Seal of Scotland and were forging her signature, 'Margaret R', which was easy to copy from official documents. Henry should take as genuine only letters signed 'your loving sister, Margaret R'. Her courage was high, but she still ended with the urgent plea, 'Brother all the welfare of me and my children rests in your hands, which I pray Jesu to help and keep eternally to his pleasure.'[5] The letter from Stirling describing the thriving condition of his nephews must have reached Henry shortly after Katherine was delivered of her stillborn male child. James V remained heir to the English throne and Henry VIII must have been near to despair.

Correspondence between Margaret and Henry now passed exclusively through Lord Dacre, who still controlled the Border castles. Margaret's confidential secretary, Sir James English, and a trusted royal servant, Adam Williamson, acted as couriers. The Scottish council had split into several factions. Some lords wanted complete independence from England, viewing Margaret, backed by the Douglases and the large force they feared Henry would send over the Border, as a dangerous adversary, they began to oppose her more strenuously. Arran, Argyll, Lennox and Home, four of the most powerful lords in the land, all wanted their own supremacy. Spies were everywhere and anyone caught carrying a letter from either party was liable to be attacked and robbed on the spot.

By January Margaret had moved to Perth. On 21 January she received instructions from Henry, brought to her by Sir James English, outlining a scheme for her to flee to the Border. She replied immediately, consenting to the plan, and sent her letter by the first messenger available to Lord Dacre.[6] Later the same day she wrote a second letter explaining that neither she, Angus nor Gavin Douglas could see how to put the plan into action. She was surrounded by spies and trusted no one. 'God send I were such a woman that might go with my bairns in my arms,' she wrote, 'I should not be long from you.'[7] Adam Williamson, meanwhile, hastening back from London, had been set upon by outlaws who stripped him of all his possessions. Communications were a nightmare. Dacre sent his brother, Sir Christopher Dacre, to punish the attackers. Five days later the English commander wrote again to Margaret, explaining Henry's dilemma now that the King of France was dead. There was no longer any certainty that the English diplomats her brother was sending to Paris would be able to detain Albany. If Henry invaded Scotland before the formalities which were proper at the beginning of a new reign were completed, he might antagonize Francis. This would endanger the safety of Mary, who at this point was in seclusion at Cluny, where she could virtually be held prisoner if hostilities broke out between England and France. Henry believed it was vital for Margaret to flee to England. If Albany were to arrive suddenly in Scotland, Dacre pointed out, Margaret would be in danger, and if he did not, considering the anarchy into which the country had fallen, she would still be in danger, as the lords adversary would almost certainly try to kidnap the King. If she would trust in Dacre, he would convey her safely to England. She should try, therefore, to escape under cover of darkness and reach either the Douglas stronghold of Tantallon or some other rendezvous ten miles south of her present position. If she delayed, 'till the days are long and the nights short', he warned, the attempt would be too dangerous. She must have faith in Henry. The lords of Scotland would not be 'so true to her as her brother'.[8]

By the end of January, acutely aware of the perils that threatened both the King's sisters, Henry and Wolsey ordered Suffolk to redouble activities in Paris to preserve the agreement which had been made with Louis XII. France was to lend England 200,000 gold crowns to further the cherished invasion of Milan; Henry must not make a separate peace with Ferdinand of Aragon, and England and Scotland should abstain from hostilities. To ensure this last condition, France's envoy in Scotland, the Sieur de la Bastie, was supposed to act as mediator.[9]

Lord Dacre was puzzled by Margaret's prevarication. He wrote to the council to say that more letters had arrived from the Queen and he didn't entirely trust Gavin Douglas, who appeared to be very keen to have the see of St Andrews 'for his own advancement'. Although Henry had sent warships in response to Margaret's earlier request, these had not been heard of for the past three weeks, when they were known to have been revictualling at Hull. As Margaret had been expected to flee to the Border, Dacre wasn't sure whether the warships should still be sent to St Andrews or more usefully deployed in the North Sea. Just as he was finishing his letter, a messenger arrived to say that the warships had been sighted and were proceeding to the Firth of Forth.[10] On the same day Adam Williamson, fresh from the English court, wrote to Margaret urging her to follow Henry's advice. He was in a high state of excitement after his escape from the outlaws. If Margaret obeyed her brother, Williamson pointed out, her son would become 'the greatest Scotchman that ever was'.[11] From the moment the news had come in that Margaret felt she could not 'resort to Marches of England with her children and her husband', Dacre had suspected manipulation. Williamson therefore wrote a long, persuasive letter directly to Gavin Douglas.

He pointed out that although the Queen had 'no sure friends in Scotland' except the Douglases, she was still a figure to be respected. Henry, he said, meant his sister to be obeyed in Scotland till his nephew came of age. 'For God's sake, my lord, do after the King's counsel and ye cannot do amiss,' he exhorted. To encourage Douglas further, he promised him that he had spread the most damaging stories in England against the Bishop of Moray, for Dacre had picked up a rumour that Leo X had actually elected Forman to the see. (He had been buying up benefices ever since James IV's death and was referred to by Margaret as 'Yon wicked Bishop of Moray'.) The Queen, said Williamson, had placed herself and her children in Gavin Douglas's hands. If he followed Henry's counsel his family would be 'made for ever', but if he did not, then Margaret might 'curse the time that ever she melled with your blood'. He repeated that if the Queen came to England her sons 'by great possibility will be the greatest Scotchmen that ever were'. He knew more than he dared write. The course proposed by Henry would be for the perpetual good of both realms. 'Otherwise,' he forecast darkly, 'there will be no justice in Scotland; it will be a land of robbery and come to final destruction.' In England there were 'wisdom, strength, honour and riches' to protect Margaret and her sons. Henry had also written to the Pope by the fastest courier possible to further Gavin Douglas's claim to the see of St Andrews.[12]

It was obviously being whispered at the English court that Katherine of Aragon could not bear live children, and it certainly appeared to Adam Williamson that Henry proposed to take control of his nephews' welfare and education, perhaps establishing Margaret at the head of a regency council of English composition. The King was making strenuous efforts to protect his elder sister. On 28 January, only two days after Williamson arrived back at the Border, Henry wrote to Leo X in the strongest terms a Renaissance monarch could use even to a Medici Pope. He fully supported the promotion urged by his sister, the Queen of Scots, whose letters had surely by now reached Rome, for Gavin Douglas, Postulate of Arbroath, to be elected Archbishop of St Andrews. Douglas was of noble birth and a man of learning, Henry pointed out, and as King of England he had absolute knowledge that Andrew Forman would not be acceptable to the Queen, his sister, or to the chapter as a candidate for that see.[13]

In Paris Suffolk redoubled his efforts to prevent Albany leaving France. Preparations for his voyage were already under way. On 3 March a sea captain who said he had piloted James IV's ship the *Great Michael* between Scotland and France came to Suffolk. He claimed he knew what route Albany would take and he offered his services to the English, on the natural assumption that Henry would send out his navy to intercept the Duke.[14] On 2 April Suffolk had an audience with Francis, where he played Henry's highest card. The King of England would renew the treaty made with Louis only 'if the French King would promise not to send the Duke of Albany into Scotland'. Francis simply replied that such a peace should be renewed without any conditions. 'They had remonstrated about the Duke of Albany's going for two hours,' wrote Suffolk. Francis's final answer had been 'that he had promised the Scots to send him and could not now stop him with honour'. Suffolk and Wingfield used the most persuasive arguments they knew. Albany was a 'suspect person' who 'pretended title to the crown of Scotland'; he had been sent for 'by the young King's adversaries'; he would put the safety of the Queen and the two princes in jeopardy. Francis replied implacably that it was not so, Albany was going purely to arrange a peace between Margaret and the lords of the council, and if he did not bring one about in three or four months, Francis would recall him. 'Nor,' continued Suffolk in a long dispatch to Wolsey, 'would he consent to delay Albany's departure, saying if he were not there within 15 days he should do little good', so at five o'clock on the afternoon of 2 April, Albany had set out for Orléans. He would travel through Brittany and then sail for Scotland. As a final piece of double-dealing, Francis had laid the blame on his predecessor, claiming it was Louis who had promised the Scots he would send the Duke and that, as his heir, Francis had a duty to fulfil the dead King's wishes. Otherwise, he said blandly, he would have done no such thing.[15]

Wingfield confirmed the news:

This day we have had a great day with the King for keeping [back] the Duke of Albany, but as far as we can perceive there is no remedy, but that he shall keep his voyage, in so much as he is departed yesterday towards Orléans and from thence to St Malo. I pray God that the said unhappy Duke be not occasion of too great evil and inconvenience.[16]

On 5 April Francis and Henry formally renewed the peace between France and England. It was not immediately obvious, but in the matter of becoming his nephew's protector, Henry VIII had been outmanoeuvred.

The arrival of the Duke of Albany in Scotland on 18 May 1515 was in some ways a pleasant surprise for Margaret. He was courteous and kind, chivalrous and well educated, a great contrast to the wild Scots lords who had tried to overturn her authority, but he did not appreciate the volatile nature of the people he had come to rule. His first *faux pas* was to insult Lord Home by making a Latin joke which the Earl did not understand. The Duke landed at Dumbarton with eight ships full of French stores and a small contingent of men at arms. Lord Home went to greet him at the head of 10,000 horsemen. He was dressed in green velvet as befitted a great feudal chieftain. La Bastie had inferred to Albany that Home had been partly responsible for James IV's defeat at Flodden. It was the old slander which the Home family have been contesting for the past 400 years. Albany, surprised by the size of Home's escort, muttered something in diplomatic Latin, which caused the Scot to think he was belittling him. He was so offended that he changed sides and, from being Margaret's sworn enemy, vowed to affirm her as Regent. His wife, Lady Home, was related to the powerful Bothwells, so Albany had unconsciously made a grave mistake. The Queen, meanwhile, rode out from Edinburgh Castle in full state. Her vanity had been much appeased as she had been told that Albany had wanted to marry her and had heard of his disappointment on learning that she had already married Angus. At their first meeting, she discovered the Duke had been happily married for ten years to a great French heiress, Anne de la Tour Auvergne, from whom he derived all his wealth and vast estates in France. As the son of James III's brother, Alexander, Duke of Albany, who had spent most of his life in exile, John Stuart had been educated at the French court. He spelled his name the French way, 'Jehan', and did not even bother to anglicize it when signing official documents.[17] He was Admiral of France and understood French methods of government and European law, as opposed to the ancient law of precedent used in the two island kingdoms. He spoke little English and he never grasped the intricacies of Scottish dialect, unlike Margaret, who had adapted to Scottish expressions and, from the spelling of her letters, to Scottish pronunciation, since the age of thirteen.

Parliament officially declared the Duke Regent of Scotland on 12 July. He was invested with the sword and sceptre of state and promptly set about disciplining the unruly lords. The Pope had been so confused by the stream of conflicting letters and reports pouring out of Scotland that he had made Gavin Douglas Bishop of Dunkeld and had sent Andrew Forman back without appointing him to the see of St Andrews. Albany placed Forman under strict surveillance at the Priory of Pettenween.[18] Lord Drummond was reprimanded for striking Lyon Herald and sent to Blackness Castle. Gavin Douglas was also imprisoned. Margaret was horrified. In an account set down long after the event, she recollected how she had begged Albany to be merciful to her husband's relations: 'I came from Holyroodhouse to solicit the said Duke, sore weeping for the said Lord Drummond and Postulate, being my counsellors, but grace got I none.'[19]

Albany understood little of clan feuding and still less of the fierce loyalties which both divided and united Scotland. Having tried to punish the Douglases and administer justice in what he saw as an impartial manner, he was taken aback when the entire Parliament supported Margaret's appeal to free Lord Drummond, whom he was obliged to pardon. The custody of the King then came under discussion. Eight peers were chosen from whose number Albany was to appoint four as the little boy's guardians. Margaret was then allowed to vet his selection. The people of Edinburgh flocked to the castle to watch the new guardians meet their sovereign. The gates opened to reveal Margaret standing in the forecourt holding James V by the hand. Angus stood near her and a nurse holding the Duke of Ross in her arms stood a little behind them. The royal household formed a respectful semicircle in the background. The people shouted themselves hoarse. When the cheering died down, the delegates from the council approached the castle. With great dignity, Margaret cried, 'Stand, declare the cause of your coming.' The lords said they had come for the King, whereupon Margaret gave the signal for the portcullis to be dropped. She then addressed the people through its bars, reminding the lords that Edinburgh Castle belonged to her, 'By the late King my husband, I was made sole Governess of it,' she said proudly. She requested six days to consider Parliament's decision and then led her train back into the safety of the castle's inner walls.[20] It was a superb *coup de théâtre*, calculated to impress the crowds thronging the castle approach, for most of them would have recognized the portcullis as a device forming part of the Beaufort arms, which, through Lady Margaret, was incorporated into the magnificent royal arms of England.[21]

According to Lord Dacre, Margaret was now bitterly sorry that she had not fled to England in January before Albany had arrived. She was pregnant with Angus's child and making 'great lamentation and weeping daily'.[22] Her husband tried to persuade her to give the children up peaceably to the Regent, for he had been badly frightened by the imprisoning of his grandfather and uncle. Margaret, however, slipped away from Edinburgh, taking the King and the Duke of Ross to the greater safety of Stirling Castle. Albany chased after her, prepared for a siege if need be. His concept of his legal authority was as stern and unshakeable as her own of her sovereignty. The Duke even endeavoured to get Angus to help him cut her supply lines, but the young Earl retreated to his own estates.

Lord Home had now sided firmly with the English. He was still Chamberlain of Scotland, with rights of access to the King and his brother. Albany had not fully comprehended Home's defection. The Chamberlain rode to Stirling with Angus and a small force of his famous outriders, planning to rescue the Princes, but when the relief party reached the castle, they found Albany had already sent the Earls of Lennox and Cassilis to surround it. There was skirmishing in which about sixteen lives were lost, but Angus's brother, Sir George Douglas, was left behind to protect the Queen, while the Chamberlain went for reinforcements. Albany himself had not yet arrived, but Margaret had arranged with Angus, and with the approval of Lord Dacre, that if the Regent tried to storm the castle, she was to appear on the battlements and to 'set the young King upon the walls in the sight of all persons, crowned, and the sceptre in his hand', so that it should be 'manifestly known to every person that the war shall be made against the King's own person'.[23]

On 6 August, with a force of 7,000 men, the Duke reached the castle, grimly determined to starve Margaret out. In Lord Dacre's opinion, the garrison could have held the position until the end of September, but George Douglas fled, hearing that Albany had brought James IV's heavy artillery with him, including Mons Meg, the greatest cannon in all Scotland.[24] Margaret was terrified. She surrendered, but again with a great show of queenly dignity, for she made the infant King hand over the keys of Stirling Castle to the Regent in person. She begged mercy for herself, her sons and Angus, and the Duke is said to have treated her with great clemency, but her own recollection was only of violence. 'John

Duke of Albany took upon him to put and remove me from my throne; he came into my Castle of Stirling accompanied by great processions of people having with him also great guns,' she said.[25]

Declaring that he would dally with no traitors, the Regent then set off in pursuit of the Douglases, leaving Lord Fleming and Lord Borthwick in charge of Margaret, with a vigilant guard of 140 men at arms. Dacre had a low opinion of Angus after this débâcle, but wrote to London to say he still had faith in Lord Home, who was provisioning Fast Castle for a siege. He had been joined by his wife's uncle, the Earl of Bothwell. Albany had also arrested James IV's faithful secretary, Patrick Painter, who had remained loyal to the Queen, and imprisoned him in a sea-girt tower at the end of a promontory near Queensferry. Against her will, Margaret went back to Edinburgh, where the Regent formally took charge of her children with the full consent of the Scottish Parliament. On 20 August she signed a statement declaring that she wished him 'to have charge and keeping of the King and his brother'. It purported to be 'written under my signet and subscribed with my hand', but the signature, although not forged, has none of Margaret's usual boldness. Even to this day it looks wan, small and coerced.[26] She was later to remember this episode with burning indignation:

> [Albany] by reason of his might and power did take from me the King and Duke my said tender children. He removed and put me from out of my said castle [of Stirling] being my enfeoffment paid for by the King my father of most blessed memory . . . and by his crafty and subtle ways made me signify in writing to the Pope's Holiness and to my dearest brother the King of England and the King of France that I of my own mooting and free will did renounce my said office of tutrix and governess.

Later, when she was told she would have access to her children, she said this proviso 'was colourably refuted by the said Duke', who addressed her 'with many haughty and high words'.[27]

Dacre was horrified. Henry's worst fears had been confirmed.

Once again the Warden of the Marches suggested Margaret should flee. With infinite patience, he pointed out to her what destruction she had brought upon herself, her children, her husband and her husband's grandfather. 'And therefore, Madame,' he entreated, 'finally and without further delay think of the high mind and plea-sure of the King, my master, your brother. With all the politic ways and wisdom you can use and with all haste possible withdraw yourself from Edinburgh,' he wrote.[28] If she would only get to the Border, she need have no fears; she could place herself under his protection and everything she needed would be provided.

Dacre wrote on 1 September. A few days earlier Margaret had announced to the Regent that she would retire to Linlithgow with her women in preparation for her confinement. Albany could scarcely object to a royal lady wishing to take to her chamber. Using the secret passwords which had been agreed earlier, the Queen did her best to let Henry, and more specifically Dacre, know that she was ready to comply with their schemes. As early as 20 August, the day Albany had made her sign the declaration that she was content for him to have care of the children, she had notified Henry that she expected to set out for Linlithgow on 31 August. Her letter, she guessed, would be scrutinized by the Regent and, as a sign that it was not a forgery, she ended with the special signature 'your loving sister, Margaret R'.[29] Four days later Lord Home scribbled a hasty note in his own hand to Dacre, explaining that Margaret was very far from content. She had been forced to write any letter Henry might receive saying she was willing to give up her children. He ended with a cryptic PS, 'Now or never', presumably meaning it was high time for Henry to send an army.[30]

Margaret, meanwhile, reached Linlithgow, where a lying-in chamber had been prepared. She immediately feigned sickness so that Albany would give permission for Angus to visit her. As soon as he arrived, they planned their escape. Under cover of darkness, with four or five trusted servants, they stole out of the palace and rode to a spot three miles outside the town of Linlithgow, where they were met by Lord Home with an escort of horsemen. Margaret was in the eighth month of her pregnancy, but the party kept up a breakneck speed and before dawn they reached the Douglas stronghold, Tantallon Castle, which was within easy reach of the Border.

A situation of great complexity now arose. England and France were at peace; Dacre and Albany were merely the representatives acting on behalf of Henry VIII and Francis I, who wished to maintain that peace. 'Beware lest the affairs of Scotland should damage our friendship,' wrote Henry to Francis in one of many communications professing brotherly esteem. Dacre, therefore, throughout all the period of Margaret's misfortunes had kept up the ordinary procedures established between Henry VII and James IV to promote law and order. That is, days of truce were still regularly held along the Borders, when grievances could be aired and redress made for the petty crimes of robbery, arson and murder which continued to be part of the normal lifestyle in that turbulent region.

Albany understood from the moment he arrived in Scotland the importance of the truce days and knew that on no account was he to let the affairs of England and Scotland escalate into open war. He kept up regular communications with Dacre and the two leaders had been trying for some weeks to organize a meeting at Coldstream for 31 August at which grievances over border-raiding could be discussed. This was part of the routine policy of government, but Albany's representative, Lord Patrick Lindsay, failed to turn up. He was delayed by waiting for some papers from the Duke, who in turn had been distracted by having just got wind of Home's plan to kidnap the Princes and take them to England. The Regent immediately issued a proclamation for the Scottish armies to meet him in the Marches. Dacre warned him that this was a bad idea and that Home was a chieftain of considerable influence. 'No man in Scotland,' he wrote to Albany, 'is so able to rule misguided folks.'[31] Dacre had already notified the council that if it should come to war, Home would fight on the English side at the head of the light troops from Tynedale, Redesdale, Bewcastle and Gilsland. In the Marches he was something of a folk hero and had a considerable following. Technically Home was still Chamberlain of Scotland, but Albany now declared him an outlaw, causing Lord Dacre to joke grimly to the English council that perhaps his own brother, Sir Christopher

Dacre, should also be made an outlaw and join forces with the Chamberlain, 'to waste Scotland', until Albany had no choice but to give up custody of the King.[32] The Regent had already confiscated premises belonging to Home and his brothers in Edinburgh, while Lord Fleming seized and occupied Home Castle. On Dacre's advice, the Earl promptly laid waste his own property, unroofed all the houses 'until no thatch was left', and was proposing to set the place on fire to flush out Fleming and his men, who had taken refuge in a cellar.[33]

At Tantallon, meanwhile, Margaret and Angus learned that Albany was preparing to pursue them. They took flight so swiftly that Margaret's wardrobe and jewel coffers were left behind. Blackadder Castle, which belonged to Lord Home, was their next refuge, but a report came in that the Regent had assembled an army of 40,000 men to storm its walls.[34] This led the fugitives to gallop towards England. As they reached the Border and Berwick Castle came into view, Margaret Tudor, her womb heavy and her nerves strained to breaking point, must have felt her spirits rise, but the Governor, Sir Anthony Ughtred, was a stickler for protocol. He had received orders to admit no one who came from the other side of the Border, without a safe-conduct, not even his sovereign's sister. The Queen and her party, therefore, took sanctuary at Coldstream Priory.

The Regent immediately sent the French ambassador, Du Plains, with conciliatory offers – he had no wish to appear an inhuman monster in the eyes of all Europe – but a few hours before the unfortunate Frenchman arrived at the Priory gate, Lord Dacre came in person with the safe-conducts from Henry and escorted Margaret to the safety of his military headquarters, Harbottle Castle. Once she was under the Lord Warden's protection, the whole story tumbled out: how she had been surrounded by spies, forced to sign documents, her freedom curtailed and her letters opened, so that sometimes even those containing the secret passwords had never reached Dacre, or Henry. The truth of her statements was confirmed in the English view when Albany's messenger, Mathew de Villbresme, was apprehended outside Bedford and found to be carrying a huge packet of letters to the French King, including copies of letters Margaret had sent to

England and the Pope.[35] He made many excuses, saying that he was formerly a servant of Mary of France and that he had never wanted to work for the Duke of Albany. The Venetian ambassador in London neatly summarized things when he wrote to the Doge on 20 September to say that Wolsey had been made a cardinal:

> The disturbances in Scotland are raging more than ever. Albany laid siege to Stirling; the Queen fled leaving in his hands the royal infants; he overtook her, fleeing towards the kingdom with her royal wardrobe, seized her goods, leaving her nothing but the garments she had on and two attendants. The whole blame of this cruelty will be laid upon Francis.[36]

All Europe sympathized with Margaret. Wolsey was vehement against Albany, as he foresaw the wrecking of the French alliance. Leo X, who had made Gavin Douglas Bishop of Dunkeld in response to the many pleas to appoint him to the Archbishopric of St Andrews, now wrote to Albany demanding that he should release Douglas from captivity at once.[37] It was as though the shocking act of taking the children jerked everyone into a new awareness. De Bapaume, the French ambassador in London, felt so uncomfortable that he wrote to Louise of Savoy asking to be recalled.

Henry and Katherine lost no time in sending everything Margaret might need for her confinement. Dresses fit for a queen, bed-hangings, baby clothes were all sent to Lord Dacre's home, Morpeth Castle, in the care of the sensitive and gentlemanly courtier Sir Christopher Garnyshe. Unfortunately, Margaret had arrived at Harbottle on the verge of collapse and was too ill to be moved. When on 7 October, after a prolonged and painful labour she gave birth to a daughter, Lord Dacre was in a fearful predicament.[38] He had no means of providing a royal layette. The child, Lady Margaret Douglas, as Henry's niece, was often styled Princess of Scotland and was later to become Countess of Lennox, the mother of Lord Darnley, who was to marry Mary Queen of Scots. She was thus destined, as James VI's grandmother, to fulfil the prophecy Henry VII had made that if his male progeny should die out, Margaret's descendants would be heirs to both kingdoms. At the time of her birth, however, circumstances were not propitious. The countryside around Harbottle was infested by rough riders, outlaws and brigands. There was no way Lord Dacre could have taken delivery of the delicacies Sir Christopher had brought to Morpeth. It was even difficult to find a wet nurse, let alone the medicines and skilled doctors demanded by Margaret's dangerous state of health. However, by 18 October she was well enough to sit up and read the letters sent by her brother and sister-in-law. Dacre wrote immediately to Henry to say how comforted she had been to receive them, but he was not allowing her to leave the sickroom: 'The Queen lieth yet in childbed and shall keep her chamber these three weeks at least.'[39]

It was November before they could move her. Even then she was in such pain that she could not bear the jolting of a horse litter, so Lord Dacre ordered his servants to carry her daybed on their shoulders. They took her by slow stages to Morpeth Castle. From Harbottle she went to Sir Edward Ratcliffe's house at Cartington, a distance of only four miles, after which she rested for five days. On 21 November she travelled a further five miles to Brinkburne Priory, where she was met by Lord Ogle and the Abbot of Newminster, so that at least her journey began to have some semblance of a royal progress. Eventually they got her to Morpeth, where Lady Dacre welcomed her and began to prepare the household for Christmas. Lord Home came from Scotland with Archibald Douglas and a number of other Scottish gentlemen to bring news and pay her their respects. Sir Christopher Garnyshe listened to Home's grievances and his tales of adventure, and wrote to London to say that he thought the King 'would like him well' if he met him. He was willing to venture his life and his lands in Henry's service. The arrival of the Chamberlain must have caused Margaret to rally. Sir Christopher chose that day to show her the wonderful gifts her brother had sent. She was carried in a chair from her bedchamber to the great hall of Morpeth Castle, where all the beautiful dresses Henry and Katherine had chosen were laid out in a show of regal magnificence. Her self-esteem restored, she cried out exultantly to Home, 'So, my lord, here ye may see the King my brother hath not forgotten me, and that he would not that I should die for lack of clothes.'[40]

By early November there was a general feeling in London that Henry should go to war with France to avenge his sister. On 6 November the French ambassador, Robert de Bapaume, wrote to Louise of Savoy, who was acting as Regent of France while Francis was fighting in Italy. He had just had an audience with Henry, who was eager for news of Francis's campaign, but the King of England had been far from friendly. Later Bapaume met Suffolk, who received him 'very civilly' and explained that Henry was making a show of warlike preparations to please his subjects, who wished him to make war, but that the King himself wanted peace. The ambassador then visited Wolsey, who had laid his hand on his heart, swearing that Henry wanted peace. The talk turned to the King's new ship, the *Princess Mary*, which Bapaume believed to be bristling with armaments. Wolsey explained that Henry had simply wanted to please the two Queens, his sister and his wife. The great galley had been launched the previous Thursday with impressive ceremony. Henry had gone aboard dressed in a sailor's suit of cloth of gold and piloted her down the Thames himself, to the great delight of Katherine and Mary. Round his neck the King had worn a gold chain to which was attached a whistle, which, said Wolsey, 'he blew nearly as loud as a trumpet'. The Queen had performed the naming ceremony and the Bishop of Durham celebrated Mass on board. Everyone had then sat down to dinner. Although Henry's intentions were peaceful, Wolsey pointed out that the new ship was equipped with seventy brass cannon (207 pieces of artillery in all) and that she carried between 4,000 and 5,000 bullets and between 400 and 500 barrels of gunpowder. The Cardinal put it like this: 'If the Duke of Albany did not abstain from, and make reparation for, his injuries to Margaret and her children, Henry would make him do so.'[41]

De Bapaume told Louise that in his opinion there would be no Scotch war for six months. Albany, meanwhile, had sent the unfortunate Du Plains to Morpeth to try to reach some form of agreement with Margaret. Sir Christopher Garnyshe mentioned that Du Plains arrived on 8 December, but he was more concerned to give the King an account of the wonderful

Christmas festivities arranged by Lord and Lady Dacre. 'Here is a great house kept,' he wrote. Angus and Home were there, together with Home's wife, Lady Bothwell, Lord Ogle and Lady Musgrave, who were all staying as guests, and many more who had come to see Margaret. Lord Dacre had decorated his castle superbly. Sir Christopher 'never saw a baron's house better trimmed in all his life'. New tapestries hung in all the chambers; there was a cupboard of gold plate and a great golden standing cup; the table was filled with silver dishes, the food was good and the game the best 'that can be gotten for money'.[42]

The only thing amiss was Margaret's health. 'Her grace hath such pain in her right leg that this three weeks she may not endure to sit up while her bed is a-making, and when her grace is removed it would pity any man's heart to hear the shrieks and cries that her grace giveth,' wrote Sir Christopher. 'Nevertheless she has a wonderful love of apparel.'

Although Margaret could not get out of bed, her leg being swollen by what was later diagnosed as sciatica, she had found a way to cure her depression. Once or twice a day, she made her ladies bring the fine gowns Henry had sent her and she had them held up so that she could look at them. She loved especially a cloth of gold gown and a 'cloth of tinsel' one which had been sent from London. She had managed in the weeks she had been at Morpeth to accumulate twenty-two gowns of cloth of gold and fine silk, and she was having one made up in purple velvet lined with cloth of gold, one of crimson velvet furred with ermine and 'three gowns more and three kirtles of satin'. In the past few days she had done nothing but look at her wardrobe. There was one great sorrow, however. Sir Christopher believed Lord Dacre had already written to Henry to tell of the death of the little Duke of Ross. He had died while in Albany's care. No one had dared to tell Margaret. Her attendants feared the shock might kill her, and in the last four or five days she had been talking of Prince Alexander, praising him 'even more than she doth her elder son the King'. As Sir Christopher wrote sadly, 'I think her one of the lowest-brought ladies.'[43]

Chapter 10
Done Like a Scot

Margaret's convalescence was slow. After the Christmas festivities were over on Twelfth Night 1516, Lord Dacre wrote anxiously to Henry VIII to ask for a special doctor to be sent from London to Morpeth. He spoke of the 'intolerable pain' in the Queen's right leg. He thought her general health would be better 'if the pain were abated', for she would then be strong enough to get up and walk about. In Dacre's opinion, the 'great joint, the seat of sciatica' was the part affected. The patient also had a poor appetite. In the three months Margaret had been at Morpeth, Lady Dacre's cooks had prepared all the correct foods for an invalid, 'almond milk, good broths, pottages and boiled meats', but the Queen would touch none of them. She preferred to pick at a little roast meat, or toy with some jellies and then push them aside.[1]

At some point in January or February they must have told her of her youngest son's death. According to one account, he died at Stirling Castle on 18 December.[2] News of the tragedy probably reached Morpeth around Christmas Eve, or when Home and Angus arrived, since Sir Christopher Garnyshe certainly knew of it by 28 December, when he wrote to say that it had been decided not to tell Margaret until she was stronger. By her own admission this was in March, when she gradually responded to the Dacres' careful nursing and began to dictate coherent notes to her brother to be relayed to the Scottish ambassador in London. As her strength returned, her grief and anger were channelled into a vehement catalogue of the injuries done to her by the Duke of Albany. Lady Margaret Douglas's birth had been premature, hastened on, Margaret Tudor claimed, because 'being great with child and nigh my deliverance [I] was enforced for fear and jeopardy of my life to go and enter into the realm of England, where eight days after, I was delivered of [a] child fourteen days afore my time to my great spoil* and extreme danger'.[3]

Margaret maintained that her labour had been brought on by 'the great dread and affray' she had 'of the said Duke and of his cruel intentions'. She had fallen into 'such extreme disease and sickness,' she said, that from the day of her daughter's birth, on 8 October, 'till this month of March' all who surrounded her had expected her to die.[4] The list of Albany's infamies was endless. He had driven her out of her castle at Stirling, her own enfeoffment paid for by her father. He had kidnapped her sons, forcing her to write letters to her brother and the Pope professing that she agreed to this. He had paraded about Edinburgh 'wearing the robe royal, bearing the cap of maintenance and having the sceptre [carried] afore him'. He had deprived her dearest husband, the Earl of Angus, of his estates, illegally seizing the castles of Tantallon and Borthwick. He had ignored the Pope's order to set Gavin Douglas free, even though bulls from Rome had been delivered to Holyroodhouse, expressly demanding the poet-bishop's liberation. He had stolen Margaret's jewels and clothing (although she had, more accurately, fled leaving these behind). He had passed an act of attainder against Lord Home and when, wretched and heavily pregnant, the Queen had taken sanctuary at Coldstream Priory, where she had been visited by Home's mother, who wished to comfort her, Albany had exacted a most ungentlemanly revenge. After Margaret had crossed into England, his men had taken the Dowager Lady Home hostage. On the Duke's orders, the Sieur de la Bastie, with no regard for her age or fragility, 'took her suddenly from out of her home in a furious and cruel manner'. He set the old lady on a 'trotting horse to her extreme peril and pain', instead of placing her on an ambling palfrey, as might have been expected, and, related Margaret, he 'conveyed her to the Castle of Dunbar', where she

---

* The usual sixteenth-century term for damage to the womb making further childbearing unlikely.

was kept prisoner for six weeks and fed upon dry crusts and water, without being allowed to have any attendants.[5]

The Queen did not mention that Lord Home, having been placed under the supervision of the Earl of Arran for planning to abduct the King, had broken parole, caused his captor to change sides and instigated a bond signed by Angus, Arran and himself to restore Margaret to the regency. He had also plotted continuously with Dacre to foment local rebellion in the Border regions. When Lord Arran's mother had begged pardon of the Duke at Hamilton for her son's behaviour, it had been granted. Old Lady Home was obviously made of sterner stuff. Her incarceration had clearly been an attempt to put pressure on the obstreperous Earl. Deeply aware of the damage to his reputation, the Regent sent several emissaries to Morpeth asking Margaret to return to Scotland. He promised her the guardianship of her son if she would only agree to keep him in the kingdom. It was of no avail. Albany became the villain of all Europe.

The Queen's plight excited much sympathy, and since Henry genuinely wished to preserve the peace with France, it was in the English interests that Albany, not Francis, should be the scapegoat. In the autumn of 1515 Giustinian, the Venetian ambassador had reported that Wolsey 'spoke with great vehemence' against the Scottish Regent. Such a thing had never been done as offer violence to a queen and her children.[6] On 24 December the Venetian newsletter announced (wrongly as it happened) that Henry would definitely go to war with France the following year. By January the Doge and council were assured that the King of England still had 'the affairs of Scotland very much at heart'. The ambassador had got hold of a rumour that Margaret's daughter had died at birth. He had an audience with Henry in which the King passionately laid the blame for Margaret's troubles on Francis for having allowed Albany to leave France to accept the regency. She was expelled from Scotland by the Duke, 'who had exiled some of her friends and put others to death; one of her children was dead, and if the other died the kingdom would fall to Albany'.[7] Clearly the memory of Richard III and his nephews, the two murdered Princes, remained in Englishmen's minds. On 6 February Giustinian wrote to say that the French ambassador had insisted that day that Francis desired peace as much as Henry did. The French King had suggested that Margaret should be restored to her throne, her dower rents secured and her children committed to the guardianship of the nobles, or the point referred to arbitration. Henry had replied scornfully that it was beneath his dignity 'to refer these matters to arbitration'. He would judge the affairs of Scotland himself. 'There will evidently be war between England and Scotland,' wrote Giustinian.[8]

Albany was at that very moment frantically negotiating for an agreement with Henry. He wished to send a spokesman to London at the earliest possible opportunity. Jean Du Plains wrote to Wolsey from Edinburgh on 3 February to congratulate him on becoming a cardinal. He had been trying to explain since the previous summer, he ventured, that the Duke wished above all to maintain peace between the two realms. Albany had done every-thing to behave respectfully towards the Queen of Scots. There had been a misunderstanding. He was greatly relieved that Henry was allowing him to come to London with the Scottish ambassadors, who hoped to negotiate a treaty. Perhaps he could give his own account of the Duke's position.[9] As Du Plains was Francis's personal representative, being French ambassador to Scotland, Henry could scarcely have refused to receive him.

It was proposed that Margaret and Angus should go to London to visit Henry and give their own account of affairs. Margaret wrote to Albany to acknowledge his various letters to her. She hoped, she said frostily, that he would reform his ways. She would have had more confidence in him if only he had released her trusty friend Gavin Douglas, whom the Pope had made Bishop of Dunkeld. She was fully determined 'to repair southwards to the King her brother'. She wished Albany would liberate Gavin Douglas to conduct her to London, release Lord Drummond from prison and send the jewels that she had left behind at Tantallon. If he wished his peace overtures to be taken seriously, he should also restore the castles of Tantallon and Bothwell to her husband.[10] While Margaret was in this resolute frame of mind, Dacre and Thomas Magnus, the Archdeacon of the East Riding and one of Henry's private chaplains, had composed a businesslike docu-ment by the King's command. It was 'a book' listing all the injuries done or attempted by Albany against Margaret. The first half consisted of her own eight-page statement of grievances and is signed in her own hand. The second part listed all the violations and breaches of the laws which were supposed to be observed in the borderlands, as laid down in Henry VII's Treaty of Perpetual Peace, since Albany's arrival in Scotland. Dacre wrote on 15 March to announce the book's completion.[11] He also advised that Margaret should be sent south as soon as possible. She had been corresponding with Albany since she got stronger and this had encouraged some of her friends to support her, but the 'daily messages from Scotland' troubled her mind, putting her into a state of indecision. Dacre and Magnus had censored her letter, which had grown very demanding, so that she could not damage the peace proposed by the Duke.[12] Although the long-suffering Warden of the Marches described the King's sister as 'a great and wise woman' who would do nothing without her brother's consent, he clearly foresaw that Margaret, eager to see her son, might go back to Scotland and cause just as much trouble as before. Meanwhile, no letters had arrived from London authorizing Du Plains to travel south with the Scottish ambassadors, whom Albany would soon be sending to England.

Sir Christopher Garnyshe, the much-harassed equerry who had been back and forth between Morpeth and the English court, was put in charge of the Queen's travelling arrangements. He was sent north with a litter and horses, arriving at Morpeth on 5 April, but the equipage must have been held up by the March weather and bad roads, as it reached the castle the day before Margaret was due to set out. The unfortunate horses had to make the long trek back to London with only one overnight stay to refresh them. Angus and Home, meanwhile, had gone back to Scotland to see what could be done about salvaging their estates, for without the income they drew from their great feudal holdings they would have been penniless outlaws. It had confidently been assumed that Angus, as Margaret's husband, would accept his brother-in-law's invitation to go to England with his wife and baby daughter. At the end of March, Dacre rode to meet the Earl at Etall Castle. He spent two days, 2 and 3 April, remonstrating with Angus and Home, for the Scots lords had agreed to accept

Albany's terms rather than forfeit everything they owned. They had decided not to venture to London. The news came as a shock to Dacre, although Angus's defection must have taken place early in the New Year, since Clarencieux Herald had written to Wolsey on 18 February, reporting a conversation with Home and his kinsman George Home of Wedderburn. On being asked what they intended to do 'now that Angus had entered with Albany', George Home had said that 'so long as they had meat and drink they could continue in their houses, but if they should chance to be driven out, what hope might they have, as they had not a groat'.[13]

'The Queen,' wrote Dacre to Henry, 'is in much heaviness.'[14] She naturally saw Angus's refusal to accompany her as an act of betrayal and was understandably dejected. Over the years the sixth Earl's decision has earned him a bad press. Nineteenth-century historians were particularly censorious. 'To be deserted at her utmost need by a husband for whom she had sacrificed her royal pomp and power was an ungrateful return for her love,' wrote Tytler in his *History of Scotland*. This stern view was echoed by Margaret's biographer, Agnes Strickland.[15] A Scottish laird's first duty, however, was to his king and clansmen. Angus was only twenty-three years old when his father, George, Master of Douglas, eldest son of Bell-the-Cat, had been killed at Flodden. Six months later, when his grandfather died, he succeeded to the most powerful earldom in Scotland. His first wife, Margaret Hepburn (a kinswoman of the prelate who later besieged his uncle, Gavin Douglas, in the Castle of St Andrews) died childless in 1513. Before his maternal grandfather, Lord Drummond, pushed him into marrying the Queen, Angus had been betrothed briefly to Lady Jane Stewart of Traquair. Little is known of this shadowy beauty, but it has always been presumed that the young couple loved each other. In the first eighteen months of his marriage to Margaret Tudor, the young Earl had struggled both to serve the interests of his family and to protect his wife and his newly acquired stepson, the infant King. It had been Angus's idea, when Margaret was besieged at Stirling, that if Albany's men should really attack, the Queen would need only to show James V on the battlements in full regalia to make the Regent's henchmen desist and drop on bended knee in midfield. Clearly the sixth Earl retained some notion of chivalry.

Angus was lord in his own right of the mighty fortresses of Tantallon and Borthwick. He owned vast tracts of the Lowlands and had the allegiance of Scotland's fiercest and most indefatigable clan. By paying lip service to Albany in 1516, he was able to hang on to his own powerbase and to have control over his revenues, even though Albany had already executed summary justice by burning the Earl's manors and laying waste his forests. If he had gone south to seek the help of his wife's brother, Angus would have risked the possibility of permanent exile, or at best return as a mercenary in the pay of the King of England, who to the other lords remained the hated victor of Flodden. By staying in Scotland, Angus at least retained an independent stance and was in a position to side, as his grandfather had before him, with the English or his peers as necessity dictated. Lord Dacre saw the Earl's decision as a breach of a gentleman's word, but the Warden was far too pragmatic to sever all contact with Angus and continued to intrigue with him for years to come.[16] When Henry learned of his brother-in-law's refusal to accompany Margaret to London, he said contemptuously, 'Done like a Scot.'[17]

Neither Margaret nor Dacre had much time for reflection on the matter. Punctually on 8 April the royal procession set out. As Lord Warden of the Marches, Dacre rode with the Queen to Newcastle, where she was welcomed by Katherine of Aragon's equerry Sir Thomas Parr and the Mayor. On the 9 April the party went to Durham to be met by Lord Lumley and Sir Ralph Bowes, the Sheriff. Then Dacre returned to Morpeth to be ready for the Scottish ambassadors, headed by the Bishop of Galloway and the Abbot of Dryburgh, with Monsieur du Plains for added credibility. Gavin Douglas had at last been released. The Pope had first written to Albany in August 1515, but by November letters of protest were still being dispatched from Rome. The Regent had sent Balthazar Stewart to the Holy See to argue against Douglas's release, but having already appointed him Bishop of Dunkeld (partly because of the recommendations of Margaret and Henry VIII), the Pope and cardinals were incensed that Albany should argue against the brief which had already been sent by the Bishop of Worcester. A copy had gone to Henry and, believing that Angus would go to England with Margaret, Thomas Allen, an agent at Rome, had sent a further copy to the Earl with a letter stating that the Pope had 'too good an opinion' of his uncle's 'nobility, science, and other good qualities to desert him'.[18] Knowing how much moral support Margaret would derive from the company of the urbane poet-bishop, Lord Dacre tactfully detained the ambassadors at Morpeth to allow Douglas to catch up with the Queen's party, which by then was riding towards York.[19]

Du Plains and the Scottish ambassadors reached London before Margaret. Giustinian told the Venetian council that they entered the city on 24 April, but Henry refused point blank to receive them until he had first heard his sister's side of the story. On 27 April she arrived at Stony Stratford in Buckinghamshire, which was about fifty-five miles from London by the route she travelled. She wrote a note to Henry to thank him for all the creature comforts he had arranged to make her progress more agreeable. She was 'in right good health and as joyous of my said journey towards you, as any woman may be in coming to her brother'. She had not seen him since he was twelve years old. 'I am most desirous now to come to your presence and to have a sight of your person,' she wrote.[20] The party rode on to Enfield, where she arrived on Ascension Day. She rested at a house belonging to Sir Thomas Lovell, the Lord Treasurer, until 3 May, when she continued on her journey and was met by Henry at Tottenham Cross, which was still some eight miles for the company to travel. That afternoon she made a triumphal entry into London, riding a white palfrey sent by Queen Katherine and followed by a great procession of lords and ladies, whom Henry had brought along to welcome her. It was six in the evening before she reached Baynard's Castle, where she was to be lodged, and where fifteen years earlier she and Henry had danced as children at Arthur's wedding feast.[21]

May 1516 was a time of family reunion. On 18 February Katherine had at last borne Henry a child who lived. Princess Mary had been baptized at Greenwich in the Church of the Friars Observant, where Henry himself had been christened. Wolsey stood godfather and the baby's great-aunt, Lady Katherine

Courtenay, and the Duchess of Norfolk were godmothers. Suffolk and Mary had produced a son, Lord Henry Brandon, who was born at Bath Place, the house they used in London, on 11 March. The King had been present at the christening and had given his nephew the name Henry in a very grand ceremony. To show Mary's enduring connection with the royal line of York, the child also had Lady Katherine for a godmother, while Wolsey and the King were his godfathers. All the proud parents assembled at Greenwich to greet Margaret, only the Earl of Angus, father of the six-month-old Lady Margaret Douglas, being absent.

If the Queen of Scots felt inwardly desolate, she at least had the solace of family affection. Katherine and Mary greeted her joyfully. Henry had made lavish preparations in honour of his sister's visit. The Brandons, who were to fall further and further behind in their attempts to repay Mary's vast debt to the King, were worrying as early as February about how to keep up appearances at court, for they had established a pattern of household economy by which Mary remained on Charles's East Anglian estates when her husband was in attendance on the King. This must at least have reduced her dressmaker's bills and the number of paid attendants required for the occasions when she was 'the French Queen'. Shortly after the Brandons' wedding at Greenwich, Henry had granted Suffolk the lands and manors formerly belonging to Edmund de la Pole, the last Yorkist Earl of Suffolk, who had been attainted before his execution in 1513. The Manor of Donnington in Berkshire was probably the largest country house the couple owned in the first twelve months of their marriage. Suffolk consolidated his East Anglian properties by buying lands and manors from the Earl of Surrey, but at exorbitant interest rates, so that his income and Mary's fluctuating French pension were never enough for the couple to keep abreast of their financial commitments. It was not until Suffolk built Westhorpe in 1527 that Mary enjoyed any proper country palace befitting her status. In 1516 the Brandons were regular visitors at Butley Priory, the rich Augustinian house near Ipswich, where the canons were flattered to be visited by the King's sister. From Butley at the end of February, Brandon wrote to Wolsey about his debts, and to Henry he sent a present of a fine hawk, mentioning that he would bring Mary to London for her confinement in March. He understood that the King was planning 'some pastime' in May, but he pointed out that he was 'ill furnished' to cut a dashing figure at such an entertainment.[22]

Suffolk need not have worried. The birth of Princess Mary had put the King in good humour. The entire month of May was given over to feasting and 'pastime'. Jousts were to be held on 19 and 20 May, with Henry, Suffolk, the Earl of Essex and Nicholas Carew as the star performers. Apparel was provided from the Great Wardrobe. The challengers and their horses were attired in black velvet 'covered all over with branches of honeysuckle' appliquéd in 'fine flat gold'.[23] The embroidery was cunningly contrived so that the leaves and branches appeared to move and shimmer in the May sunshine. Henry's attendants included the Marquis of Dorset and the Earl of Surrey, Lord Abergavenny, Lord Hastings and Sir John Peche, Lord Ferrers and Sir William Fitzwilliam plus twelve other knights all clad in blue velvet fringed with gold.

'On that day,' wrote chronicler Hall, 'every man did well, but the King did best.' On the second day of the tournament, 20 May, Henry and his men were in purple velvet embroidered with golden roses and rose leaves. The noblemen's mottoes were picked out in pure gold on the borders of their accoutrements. The King's team consisted of five lords and fourteen knights dressed in yellow velvet, stunningly bordered with cloth of gold, and thirty gentlemen on foot, similarly attired. The officers of the tiltyard wore yellow satin, also edged with cloth of gold. The opponents were in white and gold. Hall recorded that many a great blow was struck, and the King tilted against Sir William Kingston, a very strong, tall knight whom Henry succeeded in unhorsing. At the end of the official programme, Suffolk and Henry ran 'volant at all comers', which means they delighted the spectators with a virtuoso display of freestyle jousting. That evening a magnificent banquet was held in Queen Katherine's apartments in honour of Margaret's visit.[24]

She stayed in England for a little over a year. As a political gesture she was moved from Baynard's Castle to Scotland Yard, the ancient palace of the Kings of Scots. Her separation from Angus created a great deal of speculation. Giustinian picked up a rumour that 'the authorities here, pretending Scotland was under the ban of excommunication' at the time of her wedding to Angus, 'maintain the marriage was null. The report is it has been dissolved and the Queen betrothed to the Emperor.'[25] A correspondent of Louise of Savoy, writing on the same topic, swore he had overheard Wolsey say that he would willingly renounce his cardinal's hat, 'or lose a finger of his right hand, if he could effect a marriage' between Margaret and the Emperor. The Queen herself rejected this idea. She did not wish to repeat Mary's experience of marriage to an ageing foreign sovereign and she still felt loyalty towards Angus. Divorce was very much easier to obtain in the sixteenth century than is sometimes supposed, but the natural outcome of dissolving a marriage because of some canonical fault or alleged consanguinity was that any children of the union were automatically declared bastards. Henry had taken a great liking to his niece, Lady Margaret Douglas, who had lived at his court since her childhood.

Negotiations with the Scottish ambassadors dragged on throughout the twelve months of Margaret's stay. Henry's main bargaining point was that, as Albany would obviously wish to visit his wife and to see to his estates in France, it was assumed he would require a safe-conduct to travel through England. This disregarded the fact that the Duke could have returned as he had come, by sea, but the advantage of such a plan was that if he went to France via London, Albany would be able to visit the English court for a summit meeting with Henry. The outcome of any negotiations between them, however, would be dependent on the balance of power in Europe. Through 1516 this was in France's favour. Francis had won the Battle of Marignano, which made him master of Milan. He planned a further Italian campaign, but Henry, who had never ceded Tournai, became more determined than ever to hang on to his conquests in France. In May 1515 he sent 1,200 carpenters and masons and 300 common labourers to build a castle there 'to chastise the city' if its people rebelled.[26] Tournai was, as far as Henry was concerned, English territory and English it would remain, whatever the cost of garrisoning it. As though to underline the old connections of the English with the

Angevin empire, Henry Benolte, Clarencieux King of Arms, was sent to communicate with Albany.

One result of the discussions with the Scottish ambassadors was that Margaret's wardrobe and jewels were returned. Everything she had left at Tantallon was meticulously inventoried and sent to England. Far from having been pillaged, her goods were all intact. Her beautiful cheverons, or hoods, were still trimmed with gold and precious stones. One of crimson velvet was decorated with sixty-one pearls, another with twenty-one rubies and thirty-three pearls. Her jewels included heavy gold collars, enamelled with red and white roses; a great diamond sent by the King of France and set upon a red silk hat; and a balas ruby set on a black hat with three pendant pearls. They were all quite safe, as were her cloth of gold sleeves, her exquisite partlet strips, or neck pieces, one of crimson satin set with diamonds, one of cloth of gold, one of white taffeta sewn with pearls and one of fine gold mesh with precious stones at the interstices. Intact also, though perhaps no longer of value, was a bond for 2,000 marks from the Laird of Bass, made out to the Bishop of Caithness, who had been Margaret's treasurer at the time it was signed. There were ten links of a gold chain weighing forty-two ounces, which had belonged to the same laird and had obviously represented an effort to repay some of his debt, for jewels were often used as pledges or in lieu of money payments.

A number of the items listed give us an insight into Margaret's habits of personal devotion. Like her grandmother, the Countess of Richmond, she must have prayed often in the quiet of her closet or private chapel. Four rosaries were included in the inventory: 'your Grace's testament', which may well have been the beautiful James IV Book of Hours she was later to give to her sister, Mary, and two 'beasts of silver with Holy wax', which were probably candleholders or Agnus Dei. There was also a golden roundel of Our Lady, which must have been a bas-relief. These things were Margaret's personal treasures. Her chapel furniture, consisting of altar cloths, vestments for her priests, chalices and silver sacring bell were sent to England separately in October with her chaplain, William Husband, who was one of her commissioners. The luxurious furs to which she had grown accustomed ever since her first winter in Scotland, when as James IV's bride she had been swathed in gowns lined and trimmed with ermine, had been left at Stirling in the care of the Bishop of Galloway. As he was away in the north, the lords of the council promised the 'furrings' would be delivered to Margaret's procurators, factors and commissioners with all speed as soon as he returned, for presumably only the bishop had the key to the place where they were stored. The council declared themselves her 'humble servitours', but the inventory of 22 September was a carefully drafted legal document, making clear in its first paragraphs that the Queen had left her goods in the realm and that they had not been seized indiscriminately by Albany.[27]

The lords of the council also promised to assist Margaret's commissioners with 'the raising and uptaking of the rents and duties' of her dower lands, which they swore under the Great Signet of Scotland they had 'thankfully received'. Instructions had been specifically sent to Clarencieux King at Arms on 9 August, so the commissioners had a period of seven weeks to negotiate for the dower rents.[28] The herald had written to Wolsey to say James V was 'a fair young Prince', but no money seemed to change hands. By 23 August Dacre wrote to Wolsey to say the Master of Graystock had been sent to Scotland to levy Margaret's feoffment.[29] No money was sent to London, nor were there any reasonable letters of explanation. It has been reckoned that of £14,334 due to her for the period from her leaving Scotland, her commissioners collected only £114.[30] Despite repeated promises from the Regent and the Scottish ambassadors in London, the dower rents never arrived. Margaret was completely dependent on her brother during the whole of her stay in England.

By Christmas 1516 Margaret was seriously embarrassed. She wrote to Wolsey to say she needed money for New Year's Day as she must give 'rewards and other things', both for her brother's honour and for her own, to her servants and attendants. Margaret's concept of her honour was becoming something of a burden to her brother, but it was certainly necessary amid the general opulence of the Tudor court for her to give New Year's gifts which accorded with her queenly status. When the Cardinal was slow to reply she sent him a handwritten note begging him to advance her £200. She needed money for herself and her servants. She had expectations that her income would come from Scotland. 'They promise to pay it,' she wrote naïvely and if they did not, she added, she hoped Henry 'would see reason done' to her. She would give Wolsey a promissory note for the loan, so that Lord Dacre could 'take as much from the first sums that come to me from Scotland. I pray you heartily, my Lord, to put me off no longer for the time is short and if you will do so much for me this time, I pray you send word.'[31]

Margaret still hoped to regain everything she had lost. The arrival of her jewels, the grandeur of Scotland Yard, with its view of the Thames and proximity to Westminster where her father and mother lay magnificently entombed, and the deference of her brother's courtiers all combined to restore her self-esteem. She deluded herself that the powerful King of England had simply to say the word and her throne, her son and the status she had enjoyed as James IV's wife would all be miraculously restored.

After a short stay at Westminster, where he transacted the last business of the old year, Henry went to spend Christmas at Greenwich. On the Feast of the Epiphany 1517 there was a lavish entertainment. When the King, accompanied by Katherine and Margaret, had come into the hall and the royal party were seated, a great pageant was wheeled in called 'the Garden of Esperance'. This garden, wrote Hall 'was towered at every corner and railed with rails of gilt'. It was decorated with banks of artificial flowers with leaves of green satin and silken petals, glittering with gold, but so exquisitely made that they seemed like real summer flowers. In the middle of the garden stood an antique pillar, set with gold and pearls. We should more probably have called it a wide plinth, for according to the chronicler, it was six foot square and on top of it was an arch within which stood a bush of red and white roses for England and a pomegranate tree for Spain. Katherine's father, Ferdinand of Aragon, had died and the young Prince Charles had at last come into his Spanish possessions. If the French ambassador was present, the heraldic symbolism was loud and clear. The nine-month-old Princess Mary, sleeping in the royal nursery, was the living proof of an enduring union.

In the garden of silken flowers six knights and six ladies walked about in rich clothes. They descended from the pageant, danced before the King and the two Queens, returned to the garden and were wheeled out of the chamber. Then, well satisfied with life, Henry VIII 'was served a great banquet'.[32]

The King spent a good deal of time hawking during the early months of 1517, but in the city of London there was growing unrest. Foreign craftsmen and labourers were thriving; English workmen could not make a decent living. The French and Genoese were particularly arrogant and disregarded the trading rules set by the Mayor and aldermen. Some of the strangers 'were so proud that they disdained, mocked and oppressed the Englishmen', which, wrote Hall, 'was the beginning of the grudge'. A particularly unpleasant incident happened in Cheapside Market when a carpenter called Williamson bought two birds, which were snatched from his hand by a Frenchman, who said they were not meat for a carpenter. The Englishman pointed out that he had paid for them and the matter was referred to the French ambassador, who complained against the carpenter, who ended up in prison. A number of respectable citizens, headed by Sir John Baker, objected, but the ambassador never apologized. An Italian also enticed a man's wife and stole his plate, and when the case was tried at Guildhall, the Italian won and demanded that the Englishman should pay for his wife's board and lodging. This piece of cruel mockery received much publicity and, according to Hall, 'there increased such a malice in the English men's hearts, that at last it burst out'.[33]

Matters came to a head in Easter week when Dr Beal, a Canon of St Mary's Spitalfields, preached a sermon on the miseries of the common artificers, who could get no work to feed their wives and children on account of the large number of foreigners 'that took away all the living'. Mob violence followed and on 1 May 1517, known ever after as 'Evil May Day', several hundred Londoners rioted. Many were apprentices who roamed the streets attacking foreigners' houses. They insulted the Spanish and Portuguese ambassadors and shouted abuse against the Mayor and aldermen, and also the Cardinal, who had recently set up a new court to protect the interests of poorer citizens against oppression.

The King was at Richmond for Easter. Informed by the Venetian ambassador that the Londoners were up in arms, Henry promised to take all precautions. He got up at midnight, rode out into the fields with a company of soldiers and sent messengers ahead to London announcing that he was coming with a large army, 'though in reality,' Giustinian explained, 'he never quit Richmond'.[34] Wolsey and the Earl of Surrey rode to London, where they found the apprentices had locked the city gates. Surrey forced an entry and his father, the Duke of Norfolk, brought reinforcements. The disturbances were swiftly quelled. Forty of the rioters were hanged, drawn and quartered. Their grisly remains were displayed on scaffolds at the city gates. More than 400 offenders had been herded into the city prisons, most of them youths of thirteen or fourteen. They were brought to trial in Westminster Hall on 7 May. Wolsey, as Lord Chancellor of England, opened the proceedings with a long speech reproving the miscreants and castigating the city authorities for not keeping the peace. The King himself was present and the hall was hung with banners and arras of cloth of gold. In a spectacular piece of theatre, more reminiscent of a court masque than the daily routine of an English law court, first Wolsey and the peers, and later Queen Katherine, with tears in her eyes, begged Henry to show mercy. The prisoners, in their shirts and with halters about their necks, were paraded past the King. Eleven were women. They all fell upon their knees shouting, 'Mercy.' Finally, amid much emotion, the great Cardinal knelt and pleaded a second time for their lives and Henry ordered them to be released. The apprentices jumped for joy and threw their halters in the air. According to an Italian account, almost everyone present wept tears of relief.[35] 'Then were all the gallows within the city taken down,' wrote Hall, 'and many a good prayer said for the King.'[36]

On 16 May, Margaret set out for Scotland. Henry rode with her for four days and he was then conducted to Doncaster by the Earl of Shrewsbury. Her brother had worked out her itinerary and for the most part she kept to schedule, reaching York at the beginning of June. She was met at the Border by Angus, the Earl of Morton, and De la Bastie, who had been appointed Deputy-Governor while Albany was in France. In November 1516 the Duke had formally requested permission from the council and the Scottish Parliament to visit his wife for four months. It had been granted on condition that he did not travel through England. The Regent sailed on 7 June, taking with him the eldest sons of various noble families to act as hostages for their fathers' good behaviour while he was away.

The five-year-old King had been entrusted to the care of the Archbishops of Glasgow and St Andrews, and to the Earls of Huntley, Arran, Angus and Argyll. Margaret had not seen her son for over a year, but the terms of the treaty, which had finally been hammered out by Henry and Wolsey with Albany, provided for her to keep Stirling Castle and to have unlimited access to her child. It was to last, if both sides behaved properly, until St Andrews Day with options for renewal. James was at Edinburgh when Margaret arrived in Scotland. She went immediately to see him, but was refused entry to Edinburgh Castle. The reason given was that plague had broken out in the city and the boy was to be removed to Craigmillar. Here she was allowed limited access, but it soon became clear that many of the lords viewed her with suspicion, fearing that she would again become involved in schemes to carry off the King. In the Regent's absence, De la Bastie was carrying out his duties as Deputy-Governor and Warden of the East Marches with great diligence. He soon gained a reputation for arriving swiftly at trouble spots and in person.

The previous October, while Margaret had been in England, Albany had executed Lord Home and his brother for treason. George Home of Wedderburn, a kinsman of the late Earl, considered revenge a family obligation. He laid an ambush for De la Bastie by pretending to besiege the Tower of Langton. The Deputy-Governor rode out to apprehend Home and his brothers on 19 September 1517. They promptly murdered him. At 'Battie's Bog', as it afterwards became known, the Frenchman's horse plunged into a marsh and the Homes took advantage while the animal floundered in the quagmire. George Home cut off De la Bastie's head and tied it by the hair to his saddle bow, galloping off to the nearby town of Dune, where he fixed his trophy to the market cross. The crime caused much repugnance. De la Bastie had first come to the Scottish court as a contestant in tournaments arranged by James IV. He was extremely handsome and, due to the frequent mispronunciation of his surname, many Scots thought it was 'Sieur de la Beautie'. Francis demanded that the Homes should be punished, but they went into hiding and although even Margaret herself assumed they had sought the protection of Lord Dacre, the English Warden disclaimed all knowledge of their whereabouts.[37]

The Earl of Arran was appointed the next Deputy-Governor and Warden of the East Marches. As the grandson of James II, he was next in line to the throne after Albany. His mother, the Princess Mary, had married James, Lord Hamilton, who died in 1479, leaving a two-year-old son as his only heir. The young man was created Earl of Arran by James IV, ironically after defeating De la Bastie in the tournament held to celebrate Margaret's wedding. He was proficient in all knightly accomplishments, but had displeased the King in 1513, when he had been sent to France with the *Great Michael* and had attacked Carrickfergus, which he stormed and plundered. During a short period of open piracy, when, according to Pitscottie, he 'pulled up his sails and passed wherever he pleased', believing he would get to France in due course, he managed to miss the Battle of Flodden. Taking temporary refuge at the French court, he also sold the *Great Michael* to Louis XII. Known to be a supporter of the French alliance, he was trusted by Albany until Lord Home caused him to defect to Margaret's party in the autumn of 1515. Arran suspected Angus of being behind the murder of De la Bastie, because of his earlier association with the Homes. He arrested Angus's brother, Sir George Douglas. Bitter rivalry broke out between the two Earls and their supporters the Hamiltons and the Douglases. It was to culminate three years later in the brutal street-fighting in Edinburgh known as 'Cleanse the Causeway'. Seventy-two corpses of the leading members of both houses lay piled in the narrow alleys and Angus perpetrated a blood feud by killing Arran's brother, Sir Patrick Hamilton. It was said that when Gavin Douglas tried to get Archbishop Beaton to mediate between the two parties, the venerable cleric struck his hand on his breast to emphasize his ignorance of the matter. This caused his armour to rattle loudly beneath his cassock. 'My lord,' observed Douglas, 'I perceive your conscience clatters.'

Albany was in no hurry to return to Scotland. He wrote to Margaret suggesting that she should ask the lords of the council to allow her to resume the regency. Reconciled briefly with her husband, she proposed that Angus should rule with her as co-Regent. This idea was opposed by the whole council. She was soon to discover why. While she had been away in England, Angus had been living with his former sweetheart, Lady Jane Stewart of Traquair. They had been cohabiting in Margaret's home and on Margaret's money. The Earl had seized his wife's rents from Methven and Ettrick Forest. Even with the support of the lords of the council, the Queen was able to recover only £2,000 of the £9,000 Angus had appropriated.

Bitterly Margaret wrote to Henry, remembering perhaps how Wolsey had spoken of marrying her to the Emperor. She did not use the word divorce, but she begged to be allowed to return to England and to live separately from her husband. By September 1517 Margaret was plotting to take control and on 30 October Dacre had confided to Wolsey, 'The Queen of Scots is badly treated and no promise kept to her.'[38] Henry's answer was not to send an army or a subsidy. Caught up himself in what Hall so aptly described as 'the chains of love', the King of England was enjoying an affair with one of Katherine's ladies, Bessie Blount, a cousin of Lord Mountjoy, who was eventually to bear him a healthy son, Henry Fitzroy, Duke of Richmond, but his sister's suggestion of leaving Angus shocked Henry to the core. He sent Friar Chadworth to Scotland to lecture her on moral values.

By the spring of 1519 Margaret was pawning her jewellery and dismissing her household servants, whom she could not pay. Robin Barton, her comptroller, had given her £500 from his own pocket. She could get nothing from Ettrick Forest or the Earldom of March. The lords themselves confessed she was being ill-treated, but, as she complained to Dacre, 'they do not mend'. She had come back to Scotland for her son's sake and was kept from him like a stranger. Her only hope lay in Henry. The Scots lords gave her 'nothing but fair words', she complained. 'I had rather be dead than live among them.'[39]

Chapter 11

The Divine Ordinance of Inseparable Matrimony

Feuding between the Scottish nobility continued intermittently until Albany's return. The Regent did not spend the four months agreed by the Scottish Parliament in France but remained there until the winter of 1521. Privately he had told Clarencieux Herald that he 'had so much trouble he wished he had broken both his legs before he set foot in Scotland'.[1] Albany, as James II's grandson by direct male descent, was heir apparent to the Scottish throne from the moment the little Duke of Ross had died. After Albany came the Earl of Arran, son of James's daughter Princess Mary. Third in line of succession was John Stewart, Earl of Lennox, son of James III's niece, Elizabeth. Before he left Scotland, Albany had taken the precaution of having his own half-brother declared illegitimate by the Parliament and also of having his own right to the throne formally ratified. As soon as he arrived in France he negotiated the Treaty of Rouen, which consolidated the 'auld alliance' between France and Scotland.

After the blood-letting of Cleanse the Causeway, Margaret sided with Arran and the Hamiltons. Angus still held power in Edinburgh, even though Arran had been appointed Provost of the city and remained Lord President of the Council. The discovery of Angus's unfaithfulness with Lady Jane of Traquair, by whom he had a daughter, Janet Douglas, bred an implacable hatred in Margaret which even Friar Chadworth could not restrain. Angus had signed a bond agreeing to let Lord Dacre deal with the collection of Margaret's rents. When she asked for a separation, he opposed her, demanding as her lawful husband full rights to share her income. The whole of the Earl's family supported him; even Gavin Douglas, who owed both his bishopric and his survival to the Queen, became her bitter enemy. Angus seized Margaret's estate at Newark and lived there openly with Lady Jane and her daughter.[2] Arran took up the Queen's cause and the council summoned Angus to appear before them. He ignored their orders to vacate Newark and continued to collect, and spend, Margaret's rents. Desperately she suggested surrendering her dower lands in return for a fixed income to be paid to her through the council. Henry objected.

In October 1518, after nine months of sordid domestic squabbling carried on through intermediaries, Margaret wrote to Henry, 'I am sore troubled with my Lord of Angus since my last coming into Scotland, and every day more and more, so that we have not been together this half year.' After her brother's kindness she had been loath to trouble him with further complaints, but she now admitted her abject poverty, told how she had been forced to pawn her plate and jewels and described Angus's seizure of her estates. She forbore to name Lady Jane, but told Henry that her husband had done her 'more evil, that I shall cause a servant of mine to shew your grace, which is too long to write', but she added, 'I am so minded that, an I may by law of God and to my honour, to part with him, for I wit well he loves me not, as he shows me daily.' Remembering again perhaps Wolsey's plan to marry her to the Emperor, she wrote humbly that she would never marry again but where Henry would 'bid' her.[3]

Henry and Katherine were horrified. The usual pleas entered at Rome for divorce in the sixteenth century were failure to bear children or precontractual obligations on the part of one of the partners. Archbishop Warham had expressed doubts about Henry's own marriage on this score, which had been raised again in 1514, when Anglo–Spanish relations were poor, but Francis I's accession and the birth of Princess Mary in 1516 had put an end to all such speculation. The indispensable Friar Bonaventure, who had been sent to console Margaret after Flodden, was again dispatched to Scotland to reason with the Queen. As divorce rendered the children of an existing marriage illegitimate, Henry was appalled by his sister's plan to leave Angus, which would bastardize his niece, Lady Margaret Douglas, thus making her devalued currency in any marriage negotiations which the King, who still clung to the concept of his suzerainty over Scotland, might enter into on her behalf. Margaret was forced into an intolerable position as it became clear that she could expect English support only if she remained on good terms with Angus. This view was endorsed by Lord Dacre, who saw the Douglases and their friends the Homes as England's surest allies. Since Arran's sympathies were pro-French, Margaret was in the curious position of being forced back into reliance upon Albany, while Angus and his family remained on amicable terms with Henry VIII.

The quarrel between husband and wife was to dominate Scottish politics for the next three years. Ultimately, the birth of Angus's illegitimate daughter rankled less with Margaret than his behaviour over Ettrick Forest. When Henry himself became the father of a royal bastard, shortly after Katherine's miscarriage of 1518, he was delighted; his ability to father male progeny was no longer in doubt. Mistress Blount was married off into the Tallboys family and awarded a grant of lands in Yorkshire by Act of Parliament.[4] Henry later made the child Duke of Richmond, the title associated with Henry VII before he came to the throne. To her credit, Margaret never publicly attacked Angus for having a mistress. She always accepted full responsibility for having married a second time according to her own desires, simply repeating as her personal plea, 'he loves me not'.[5] Angus's seizure of her rents and the other lords' inability to procure her 'conjunct enfeoffment' was her main grievance. The Douglases had come out of the Cleanse the Causeway fight rather better than the Hamiltons, and Angus used the breakdown of law and order in Scotland as a pretext to exploit his own claim to Ettrick Forest, which Robert the Bruce had granted to his ancestor Lord James Douglas.[6] Margaret never wavered from her belief that 'the forest of Ettrick should be worth 4,000 marks and the Earldom of March £500 a year'. She complained continuously that she never received a penny of this income and that the rest of her dower lands brought in less than £1,000 (Scots) a year, which was not enough for her to maintain even her household as Queen Mother.

Henry's energies were now absorbed by preparations for his grand summit conference with Francis I. The death of the Emperor Maximilian meant that Charles, who had been King of Spain since his grandfather Ferdinand died, now came into the full inheritance of his Habsburg dominions. As the Emperor Charles V, he was to enter a lifelong rivalry with Francis I, as the French and Imperial armies fought for domination of Europe, mostly on the battlefields of Italy. This gave England a new and more powerful diplomatic role than ever before, as Henry VIII pursued his policy of shifting alliances, usually keeping himself in league with whichever of his fellow sovereigns seemed most likely to win.

In 1518 Henry's daughter, Princess Mary, was betrothed to Francis and Claude's infant son, the Dauphin of France. Prince Francis was still in his cradle when the French ambassadors arrived in London to negotiate the marriage in the last week of September. On 3 October a general peace was proclaimed between England and France at St Paul's. The French were to retain Tournai, paying Henry compensation; the remainder of Mary's dowry, 323,000 crowns, was to be settled and proper arrangements made for her income as Queen Dowager to be sent to her. The Duke of Albany's stay in France was to be tacitly extended, though nothing was set down on paper about this last condition. Writing to Francis next day, the French Admiral, Lord Bonnivet, who was to stand proxy for the Dauphin, told how 'the King of England with a great train of gentlemen, richly dressed' and with Wolsey, and the Spanish and Venetian ambassadors, went in procession to a Mass, 'celebrated by all the Bishops and Abbots of the kingdom'. Henry swore to observe the peace. 'The solemnity,' wrote Bonnivet, 'was too magnificent for description.'[7]

The King and his company then went to dinner at the Bishop of London's palace, after which Henry went over the river to Durham House in the Strand, where he spent the afternoon. That evening Wolsey gave a banquet at York Place. Giustinian, the Venetian ambassador, had never seen its equal. 'We sat down to a most sumptuous supper, the like of which, I fancy, was never given either by Cleopatra or Caligula: the whole banqueting hall being so decorated with huge vases of gold and silver that I fancied myself in the tower of Croesus.'[8] After supper twelve gentlemen and twelve ladies in masks, very richly dressed, began to dance. When they took off their visors the two principals were Henry and his sister Mary, a pretty piece of allegory, as the King of England partnered the Dowager of France. 'All the others,' Giustinian told the Doge, 'were lords and ladies who seated themselves apart from the tables and were served countless dishes of confections and delicacies.' After the feasting great bowls were placed on the tables, filled, according to the Venetian, 'with ducats and dice' for those who wished to gamble. Then the supper tables were removed and the dancing began again and continued until midnight.

Two days later in the Queen's Great Chamber at Greenwich, the French Admiral stood proxy for the Dauphin, placing a ring set with a great diamond on the hand of the two-year-old Princess Mary. The Venetian ambassador was again present as Henry 'stood in front of his throne' with the two Queens, Katherine and Mary, on either side. 'The princess was in front of her mother, dressed in cloth of gold with a cap of black velvet on her head, adorned with many jewels.' Opposite were the two legates, Wolsey and the Pope's representative, Cardinal Campeggio, who had come to England in the summer in the hope of discussing a new crusade which Leo X wished to initiate against the Turks. Dr Cuthbert Tunstall made an elegant Latin oration in praise of marriage. Then the little Princess was lifted up while Wolsey put the ring on her finger and Bonnivet solemnly pressed it into place. The infant bride was blessed by both cardinals, 'every possible ceremony being observed'. In the royal chapel Henry swore another oath and Wolsey celebrated Mass. Giustinian was again impressed by the breathtaking magnificence: 'The whole of the choir being decorated with cloth of gold, and all the court in such rich array that I never saw the like.' At the subsequent banquet, when Henry washed his hands before eating, he was served by three dukes, Norfolk, Suffolk and Buckingham, and a marquis.[9] Nor were the celebrations over. The King invited the company to Richmond to hunt and suggested that Wolsey should organize a further entertainment to show off Hampton Court, which the Cardinal had been steadily embellishing ever since he acquired it in 1514. George Cavendish, as Wolsey's gentleman usher, never forgot the feverish preparations made to impress the French visitors. While Henry and Bonnivet set off for Richmond, Wolsey called for his steward, his comptroller and the clerks of his kitchen, 'whom he commanded to prepare for this banquet at Hampton Court'. They were ordered 'to spare neither expense nor labour, to make the French such triumphant cheer that they might not only wonder at it here, but make a glorious report in their country to the King's honour and that of this realm'.[10]

Cavendish later recalled that 'the purveyors brought and sent in such plenty of costly provision as you would wonder at the same. The cooks wrought both night and day in diverse subtleties and many crafty devices.' The Frenchmen were to spend the night at Wolsey's palace before going on to Windsor Castle. Their rooms were 'hung with costly hangings' and furnished with 'beds of silk'. Cavendish was sent from York Place to oversee the arrangements:

> Our pains were not small or light, toiling daily from chamber to chamber. Then the carpenters, the joiners, the masons, the painters and all other artificers necessary to glorify the house and feast were set to work. There was carriage and re-carriage of plate and stuff . . . nothing lacking . . . fourteen score beds provided, and furnished with all manner of furniture . . . too long here to rehearse, but to all wise men who know what belongs to the preparations for such a triumphant feast or banquet, imagination will suffice.

The end result was sumptuous perfection in every detail. No one knew how to give a party as brilliantly as Wolsey, and at each entertainment there was some element of surprise. When the Frenchmen arrived each guest was taken to his chamber, 'where were great fires and wine ready to refresh them'. They remained there until supper time and were then taken to the various banqueting rooms, all hung with fine tapestries. The first dining chamber was lit by an ingenious new method of placing cande-

labra on polished silver salvers so that the light was reflected
about the room. The tables were covered with fine white cloths,
some of linen, some of damask, while the sideboards or
cupboards were laden with silver and gold plate. In the Presence
Chamber, where the most important guests would sit, the table-
cloths were sweetened with perfume and there was a display of
gold plate so precious that it was 'barred round that no man
might come near it'. This plate was purely for show. In his meteoric career as Henry's chief minister and Europe's leading diplomat, the Cardinal had acquired such a superabundance of treasures that there were plenty of other silver and gold dishes to
serve the company. Trumpets announced the beginning of the
feast, and the guests sat down to the sound of such beautiful
music that Cavendish thought the Frenchmen seemed 'rapt into a
heavenly paradise', but still the Cardinal had not arrived. At the
second course he suddenly burst in, 'booted and spurred', bade
them welcome and sat down still in his riding clothes, 'laughing
and being as merry as ever I saw him in all my life'. Cavendish
never explained whether his master had ridden from London, but
if so, since the full legal term was still in course and he was
Chancellor of England, Wolsey's arrival must have impressed on
the French the full efficiency of the English system. Everything
about Henry's court implied carefree magnificence. The cornu-
copia, it seemed, would never run out.

The second course of the banquet was even more exotic than
the first. A model of St Paul's Church, complete with steeple, was
brought in, a triumph of the pastrycook's art. There were dishes
in the shape of birds and beasts, there were edible models of
English soldiers fighting with swords and crossbows and, most
impressive of all, a chessboard made of 'spiced sweetmeat'.
Wolsey gave it to a French gentleman, who apparently considered
it too beautiful to eat, so a case was made for it to be transported
back to France as a souvenir. The climax of the banquet came
when the Cardinal raised a golden bowl filled with spiced wine
and, taking off his hat, said, 'I drink to the King my sovereign lord
and master and the King your master.' Then, handing the bowl to
the Duc de Montmorency, he asked him to pledge likewise, 'and
so caused all the other lords and gentlemen' to take up their cups

and drink 'to these two royal princes'.[11] In London the hard bargaining had continued. The Duke of Norfolk, the Bishop of Durham and the Earl of Worcester had signed a solemn document planning a personal meeting which was to take place between Henry and Francis before 31 July 1519.[12]

The Treaty of London, as the negotiations of 1518 were known, has been viewed from various perspectives. It was also called the Treaty of Universal Peace, since Wolsey's grand design was to involve all the lesser European states in the agreement between England and France, so that to some historians it represented an early 'non-aggression pact'.[13] The two royal Princes had announced that they were so keen to meet each other they had jokingly vowed not to shave until the encounter took place. In fact Katherine objected so much to the length of Henry's beard that she soon obliged him to break his word. Maximilian's death in January 1519 and the subsequent Imperial elections interrupted all political business. Although it was a foregone conclusion that, as the late Emperor's grandson, the eighteen-year-old King of Spain would be the most suitable candidate, the formal process by which he was officially chosen had to be observed before he was proclaimed Charles V. Traditionally the electors, those German princes with power to vote for the Holy Roman Emperor, met in Frankfurt. Henry even put himself forward as a candidate, sending Richard Pace to Cologne to plead his cause. Ignominiously, he did not receive a single vote. Charles was chosen on 28 June 1519. All this meant that the summit between Henry and Francis was postponed until 1520. Preparations for their meeting, which was to go down in history as 'the Field of the Cloth of Gold', began in March. Six thousand workmen set off to prepare the English quarters. At least 2,000 including bricklayers, carpenters, masons, glaziers and scene painters, worked on the wood and canvas structure which was to be Henry's temporary palace. Designed on the principles of a banqueting house, or one of the theatre sets so frequently erected for Henry and his gentlemen to storm during court masques, it was much praised by the French, who were astonished by its brick foundations and glass windows. Fleuranges thought them the finest and clearest he had ever seen.

The area chosen for the meeting was the wide plain between the English citadel of Guisnes and the French town of Ardres. Each King was to be encamped in his own territory. Coincidentally, the plain was known as the Val d'Or, although the meeting took its name not so much from the location as from the legendary quantities of dazzling fabric in which both Kings and their courtiers were arrayed. Some French nobles had mortgaged their estates to pay for their clothes.[14] Francis built a small city of golden tents. The pavilion in which he proposed to welcome Henry was sixty feet long and made of gold brocade lined with blue velvet, embroidered with fleurs-de-lis. A gilded statue of St Michael stood at its entrance to distinguish it from the other tents, which were of cloth of silver and purple velvet, embroidered with lilies.[15]

As Guisnes Castle was not large enough to house all the personnel Henry and Wolsey envisaged taking with them, preliminary sketches were commissioned of some glorious tents for the English. Three are perfectly preserved in the Cotton Manuscript. Striped in the Tudor livery colours of green and white, a plain canvas pavilion was probably intended as a field kitchen and for domestic officers. A grander one of blue and gold probably doubled as a dormitory and hospitality tent, while a scarlet and gold one, its poles fluttering with pennants displaying the royal arms, was obviously intended for the King. Carvings of heraldic beasts, the lions of England, the Welsh dragons, the white harts of the Angevin rulers and the yales (deer popularly supposed to have swivelling antlers) which supported the Beaufort arms, held the flagstaffs in place.[16] Royal mottoes were emblazoned in gold on the outside of the tent, but in the end the plan for a *trompe-l'œil* palace, painted to look like a fairy-tale castle, was adopted instead. The wood and canvas structure built round a courtyard included chambers for the King and Queen, a rich chapel, a special suite for Mary as Dowager of France and Wolsey's apartments, which formed the administrative hub from which the whole operation was directed. Early in the proceedings, Garter King of Arms drew up a book filled with devices suitable for interior and exterior decoration. Heraldic painters worked swiftly and expertly under the direction of John Rastell, Sir Thomas More's brother-in-law. A

Venetian observer reckoned their work equalled that of Leonardo da Vinci, who had died the previous year.[17] In the panorama commissioned some twenty-five years later to commemorate the event, huge Tudor roses combining the red of Lancaster with the white petals of York dominate the central entrance, while outside a fountain fit to grace any Italian piazza runs with wine.

Tents were imported in their hundreds. Richard Gibson, Master of the King's Halls, Tents and Pavilions, erected nearly 400 in the neighbouring fields to house an army of purveyors, cooks, servants, knights, squires and armourers, who would all be required to attend upon the King, the two Queens and the major courtiers, many of whom were lodged in Guisnes Castle. In general, the English tents followed the superior designs which had been mooted earlier: green and white stripes, the colours of the Tudor livery, denoted field kitchens and dormitories; sumptuously painted or embroidered tents housed courtiers; and a cloth of gold one was provided for the King, curtained with blue arras. The English camp was surrounded by a nine-foot circular rampart.

In addition to the golden pavilion in which Francis and Henry were to hold their discussions, the French had built a spectacular tiltyard 900 feet long and 320 feet wide on the eastern side of the field, where the tournament, scheduled to last from 11 to 22 June, was to be held. Suffolk and Bonnivet were jointly responsible for organizing the programme of jousts and feats of arms which were to be the principal entertainment. A tree of honour, composed of the English emblem of hawthorn and the French raspberry leaves intertwined, was erected on a mound at the end of the lists, upon which the challengers could hang their emblazoned shields. All kinds of excitements arose during the hectic weeks before the meeting, and when later a French tent was blown down by the high winds it elicited much pleasure among the English as it proved their superior workmanship. Many tourists were lured to Picardy by the promise of royal spectacle and free drink. Space was at a premium and visitors from West Flanders took up all the spare accommodation in local inns; Hall noted that the small farms did a thriving trade in bed and breakfast, and some ladies and gentlemen were grateful to lay themselves down in hayricks.

When the jousting began in earnest, so much free wine was dispensed that vagabonds, ploughmen and labourers lay in drunken heaps and Francis had to issue a royal proclamation limiting access to the city of Ardres.[18] It was reckoned he turned away 10,000 would-be spectators.

Henry arrived at Canterbury on 25 May. While he was preparing to cross the Channel with a train of over 5,000 persons, including the Dukes of Suffolk and Buckingham, ten earls, five bishops, the Cardinal and the Archbishop of Canterbury, to say nothing of the two Queens, their ladies and very nearly 3,000 horses, the Emperor's ships were sighted at Hythe. Charles was on his way from Spain to his coronation, which was to take place at Aachen. Originally Henry had hoped to meet him on English territory in France. He had proposed Calais as a suitable location, but Charles announced that he would land at Sandwich some time in the middle of May, breaking his journey from Spain to his northern dominions. He wished to meet Henry before the Anglo–French alliance became irrevocable, but contrary winds held him up at Corunna, so that he did not arrive in England until 26 May, which was the deadline Henry had given for postponing his own departure. Despite the incredible inconvenience and expense of detaining for a further five days the flotilla designed to carry the entire English court to France, the King rode to meet Charles at Dover Castle. When Henry galloped into the courtyard, his guest, according to one version of the story, had already retired for the night, but the King of England insisted upon waking the Emperor to bid him welcome. In another account Henry arrived early in the morning and Charles, descending to greet him, bumped into him on the staircase.[19] The following day they left for Canterbury, where Queen Katherine was waiting. She wept with joy to see her nephew.

They said that Charles also wept, though not on account of meeting his aunt. When the young man beheld the exquisite beauty of Mary Tudor, the Princess to whom he had been betrothed in his boyhood, they said he shed tears of bitterness to see the prize of which he had been robbed by the cruel and arbitrary decision of his advisers. To enhance the pageantry with which he proposed to dazzle the French, Henry had given the royal ladies permission to order all the finery they might need. In the procession to Canterbury Cathedral for a Mass of Thanksgiving, Mary walked immediately behind the Emperor in cloth of silver, decorated with costly pearls. In his train Charles had brought another great beauty, Germaine de Foix, Dowager Queen of Spain, the second wife of Ferdinand of Aragon, whom he had married after Queen Isabella's death. Widowed in 1516, she had taken the Margrave of Brandenburg as her third husband and was travelling in the imperial entourage to join him in Germany. She was as famed for her appearance as Mary and must have excited the curiosity of her stepdaughter, the rapidly ageing Queen of England.

After the birth of Princess Mary in 1516, Katherine had made a pilgrimage of thanksgiving to Walsingham. Her prayers for the male heir Henry longed for seemed to have been answered when she conceived her sixth child in 1518. It was delivered stillborn in November. To those close to Henry this must surely have increased the poignancy of his fathering a healthy bastard by Bessie Blount the following year. Although specialists were brought over from Spain, it was generally agreed by 1520 that the Queen of England's childbearing days were over. To Henry, therefore, arranging the right dynastic alliance for his daughter, Mary, was of paramount importance as were the health and safety of his nephew, the young King of Scotland, who as Margaret's son, was second in the English line of succession. The Duchess of Suffolk, meanwhile, had given Brandon two daughters, Lady Frances in 1517 and Lady Eleanor in 1518. Their brother, Lord Henry Brandon, died when he was six, but Mary gave birth to another son, also christened Henry, to whom the King gave the title Earl of Lincoln. After Lady Eleanor was born, Mary was ill and absent from court during the terrible sweating sickness which raged through England that summer, but by 1520 she was restored to health and in dazzlingly good spirits, so that shortly she was to prove one of Henry's greatest diplomatic assets.

Having entertained the Emperor and arranged to meet him for further talks after the French expedition, the King set sail from Dover on 31 May. At eleven o'clock Henry, Katherine, Mary and the glittering train of dukes, earls, bishops and their retainers landed at Calais. Four days later they set off for Guisnes. There had been the usual jostling for place among the staff of the various households and once again French speakers were accorded precedence. As Papal legate, Wolsey generously entitled himself to twelve chaplains, fifty gentlemen and 237 servants. The two dukes were allowed 140 each, while the Archbishop of Canterbury was reduced to a skeleton staff of seventy. When the mighty procession arrived at Guisnes, where the finishing touches had been put to the painted palace and an underground passage built, linking it to the castle, a freshly gilded statue of Bacchus glinted above the fountain, which was already running with red wine, white wine and claret.[20] Carved into its stonework was an invitation to *'Fait bonne chere qui voudra'*. On the opposite side of the entrance, mounted on an antique pillar, a gilded Cupid reminded spectators that the whole event was supposed to be a feast of love and amity. It took three days for everyone to settle into their lodgings.

On 7 June, the Feast of Corpus Christi, the two Kings faced each other across the plain of Ardres. The English footguard marched with such precision that it almost seemed as though they were drawn up for battle, as they had been in the past, for many present had fought each other within living memory. Then a cannon was fired from Guisnes Castle and an answering shot came from Ardres. To the sound of trumpets and sackbuts, Francis and Henry spurred their horses, rode to the centre of the field and embraced as brothers in arms.[21] In the feasting and jousting which followed both seemed to be trying to outdo each other in chivalrous behaviour. On the great tree of honour which dominated the tiltyard, so that neither King should be seen to be placing his shield higher than the other, Henry tactfully insisted they should be placed side by side. During the tournament both Kings ran an equal number of courses and broke an equal number of spears. Francis rose very early one morning, stole into Henry's bedchamber and helped him to put on his shirt.[22] Henry gave him a golden collar and Francis produced a costly bracelet. At the open-air Mass held to mark the end of the meeting there was a long pause, while each King tried to let the other be first to kiss the Gospel. Later their wives went through the same pantomime when the Cardinal of Bourbon offered them the Pax to kiss. In the end, 'after many mutual respects', the two Queens moved forward at the same moment 'and kissed each other instead'.[23] During the Mass a firework in the shape of a magnificent dragon shot across the sky from Ardres. It was meant to be a memorable finale after the Mass, but was slightly mistimed, so that many were frightened, thinking it a comet or monster.

Suffolk did not perform as brilliantly in the tournament as expected. Some thought he held back for modesty, not wishing to outshine the two Kings. In fact, the Duke had hurt his hand.[24] On this occasion, however, he was not expected to steal the limelight; he was present as Mary's consort and she was the star. In the procession to the tiltyard on 11 June, the Dowager Queen of France was carried in a litter of cloth of gold embroidered with lilies and monograms of the initials L and M, supported by the late king's emblem of the porcupine.[25] The French went wild. She was so very beautiful, their own Reine Blanche, Louis XII's Queen, widowed so tragically young. Three carriages followed her, draped with cloth of gold, crimson and azure, and crowded with beautiful ladies. Hall said it would have taxed ten men's wits to describe their attire. Then came Queen Claude, dressed all in cloth of silver, and last Louise of Savoy, miraculously elegant in black velvet, 'with an infinte number of ladies' in crimson velvet, the sleeves lined with cloth of gold.[26]

It was said that the French King's mother had purchased 'a whole emporium' of cloth of gold. The ladies competed in the fashion stakes as seriously as their husbands in the tournament. On one occasion Katherine excited everyone's admiration by wearing a Spanish headdress with her hair hanging down over one shoulder, but for sheer beauty and charisma no one could outdo Mary. She and Henry led a party of masquers into the French camp one morning while Francis went to dine with Katherine. The King was followed by nineteen gentlemen in elaborate disguise, while Mary and her ladies rode identical palfreys all in white and yellow velvet. Outside the English headquarters, the fountain continued to splash forth an unlimited supply of fine wines, some days claret, some days malmsey. Silver drinking cups were constantly to hand for whomsoever chose to refresh themselves. Apparently no one tried to pilfer them, which the French thought *'une chose singulière'*.[27] One food and drink bill for the King and Queen of England and their nobles with ordinary wine at 12s, French and Gascon at 110s the tun, sweet wine £27 a barrel and Ippocras at £80 a pipe came to £7,409 13s 4d.[28] In commenting that the English chapel was positively stuffed with holy relics, Fleuranges mentioned that the King's cellars must have been similarly well stocked, for he said that 'both princes kept open house throughout the proceedings'.[29] On 25 June, after appropriate farewells and the exchange of many splendid gifts, the English made their way back to Calais. Henry thanked all his gentlemen for their support. He realized that in putting on such a display of wealth and conspicuous consumption, many courtiers had strained their reserves to the limit. He therefore gave them permission to dismiss half their suites and bade them live carefully to the end of the summer. This was interpreted 'frugally' and some demurred, for the Field of the Cloth of Gold had been a time of genuine enjoyment.[30] The competitive spirit which had led their ancestors to fight the French for generations had been channelled in a novel way and among those who actually accompanied the King there seems to have been little resentment over the cost.

Henry waited at Calais until 10 July. He then went to Gravelines to meet the Emperor. This time Margaret of Austria came with her nephew, so that Mary met face to face the *'chère tante'* to whom she had written in her girlhood as Princess of Castile. Henry has been accused of duplicity for making one treaty with Francis and starting a separate set of talks with Charles immediately afterwards, but Professor Scarisbrick's view that 'at neither meeting did Henry do anything that was contrary to the treaty of 1518 or secretly engage to disown one whom he had just met', is valid.[31] With Francis, Henry ratified the marriage treaty between his daughter and the Dauphin. With Charles, he discussed separate matters and arranged for new ambassadors to be appointed following Maximilian's death.

In the first days at Guisnes before the tournament began, Wolsey had ridden to the French camp for serious political discussions. It was decided that as Francis would undoubtedly be returning to Italy, Wolsey and Louise of Savoy should be jointly responsible for supervising affairs between England, France and Scotland. The immediate outcome was that the Field of the Cloth of Gold had so raised Henry's international prestige that Margaret's status was greatly enhanced. Francis had promised to stop intriguing with the Scots and for the first time since Flodden the Queen seemed in a position to establish a relatively stable powerbase for herself.

Albany, meanwhile, had acquired considerable influence at Rome by the marriage of his sister in-law, Madeleine de La Tour, to the Pope's nephew, Lorenzo de Medici, Duke of Urbino. Margaret began a friendly correspondence with Albany, guessing that he might be able to further her plans for a divorce from Angus. The Papacy itself had recently been under attack. The German reformer Martin Luther had written a number of critical pamphlets, the latest of which, *De Captivitate Babylonica*, had been printed in 1520, roundly attacking the nepotism and simony in the Roman Catholic Church which were regular abuses of the time. Henry, who prided himself on his theological knowledge, was deeply absorbed in the spring of 1521 in composing a reply. The King's book, *Assertio Septem Sacramentorum*, was published in the summer of 1521. It was not only to become a best-seller but also to earn Henry the coveted title Defender of the Faith. That his sister the Queen of Scotland should be actively seeking divorce at the same moment that the King of England was expounding the sanctity of marriage was an unwelcome embarrassment. A further royal confessor was dispatched to Scotland to back up the arguments which had already been put forward by Father Bonaventure and Friar Chadworth. Unfortunately, the discreet man did not sign the draft of the arguments he had prepared entreating Margaret to be reasonable, to remember how deeply her brother loved her and how important it was for her to follow 'the vyvely doctrine of Jesu Christ, the only ground of salvation'.[32]

Whoever the unknown friar was, he couched his appeals in the most courteous language. He was also obviously a most learned man and in the habit of tempering his arguments with scriptural quotations. I Corinthians 3 and Matthew 7 were invoked to remind Margaret that Jesus alone was the rock 'whereupon any building immoveably abideth and unto this foundation behoveth your Grace to fashion the state of your life, advertising the divine ordinance of inseparable matrimony first instituted in paradise between man and woman, now for no cause to be sundered'. The writer tactfully absolved Margaret herself, blaming her actions upon those of her councillors who had 'synystrally seduced' her to damnable self-destruction by persuading her to seek 'an unlawful divorce from lawful matrimony directly against the ordinance of God and utterly repugnant to man's law'. Some of her council had turned her against 'the right noble Earl of Angus', the friar conceded, but 'they were impelled by malice'. If Margaret would only remember her duties as a mother, he implored, she should then have 'natural love and tender pity' towards the fruit of her body, her 'most dear child and natural daughter', Margaret Douglas. Finally the writer tried an appeal to her family pride, recalling her 'noble lineage' and 'most excellent honour'.[33]

Lord Dacre had also written to Margaret remonstrating. He was convinced that the Douglases and the Homes were better allies for the English than the Hamiltons. On 11 March 1521 Margaret bluntly replied:

> My lord,
> As to my lord of Angus if he had desired my company or my love, he would have shown him more kindly than he hath done. For now of late, when I came to Edinburgh to him, he took my house without my consent and witholding my ferms [rents] from me which he should not do.

A new self-assurance seemed to determine both Margaret's words and her actions.

> I had no help of his Grace my brother, nor no love of my lord of Angus and he to take my living at his pleasure and despoil. Methink[s] my lord, ye should not think this reasonable, if ye be my friend.

Since her return from England, Dacre was supposed to have been responsible, she pointed out, for seeing that the Scots lords paid her income, but she had been reduced to pawning her jewels and her plate, and would have lost them all had it not been for Albany's intervention. Since the talks at the Field of the Cloth of Gold, he had written to the lords of the council, securing some of her rents, and her money from France had also been sent. The Douglases, she guessed, had been spreading scandalous stories about her, but, 'My lord Dacre,' she wrote, 'ye should not give so lightly credence to evil tales of me as ye do when ye know the truth.'

All previous correspondence between Margaret and Dacre had been obsequiously polite. She never before mentioned Henry in any but the humblest terms, and she always wrote as an Englishwoman, putting her own country's interests first. The tone of this letter, written with her own hand, is completely different. Obviously, feeling that she would get no help from Dacre or Henry, Margaret identified with the Scots: 'I must cause me to please *this* realm, when I have my life here,' she ended.[34]

It would seem that reports of Henry's magnificence at the Field of the Cloth of Gold had brought Margaret to a painful new state of self-realization. Her brother would spend thousands on his own wardrobe and accoutrements, but he was not going to pay for the armies, fortifications and comparatively modest dress bills which she considered a prerequisite to her 'honour'.

The Scottish estates now entreated Albany to return. They had had enough of the anarchy which had prevailed throughout James V's minority. Charles had paid a second visit to England, and as Henry consolidated his pact with the Emperor, the alliance between England and France, celebrated the previous year with such panoply, crumbled into hostilities. Francis gave his permission for the Duke to go back to Scotland. He arrived on 18 November 1521 and was warmly welcomed by Margaret. He wrote immediately to Henry and Katherine of his wish to prolong the peace between England and Scotland.[35] His first act as Governor was to remove the Douglases from the offices they had seized. Angus went into exile in France and Gavin fled to the court of Henry VIII. He was summoned to Rome and, failing to reply to the Pope's letter, was deprived of his see of Dunkeld. He lost no opportunity to spread scandalous stories about Margaret and she immediately ascribed to his malice the amazing rumour which was soon circulating through all the courts of Europe: Margaret Tudor was supposed to be in the midst of an adulterous affair with the Duke of Albany.

When he had reached Edinburgh and the Constable handed him the keys of the castle, the Duke as a gesture of courtesy gave them back to Margaret. Jointly as Regent and Queen Mother they began to apply themselves to the day-to-day business of restoring the factious country to order. It followed that they were often closeted together, although almost certainly with other counsellors present. Since it was known that the Duke was backing Margaret's application for a divorce at Rome, the Douglases fuelled the rumour that the pair were lovers. Even Lord Dacre believed it and wrote a panic-stricken letter to Wolsey, predicting that James V would be murdered and that Albany would make himself King and marry Margaret.[36]

Wild reports reached Henry, who sent Clarencieux King of Arms to Scotland to reproach Margaret and fired off an aggressive letter to Albany, refusing to prolong the truce, which was to end at Candlemas. Even the collaboration between Wolsey and Louise of Savoy at the Field of the Cloth of Gold had not produced a permanent peace between the island kingdoms. In London Francis's ambassador swore to Henry that Albany had returned to Scotland without the French King's 'knowledge, consent or goodwill'. Testily, Henry accused the Duke of 'pretending to be next in succession' to the Scottish crown, of having unlawfully gained custody of the King and of 'the dishonourable and damnable abusing of our sister, inciting and stirring her to be divorced from her lawful husband for what corrupt intent God knoweth'. The King of England declared grandly, 'We cannot be contented with your said arrival nor yet take your being there in good part.'[37] It was tantamount to a declaration of war. Stoutly supported by the Scottish Estates, Margaret and Albany protested their innocence. Lord Dacre, meanwhile, disillusioned by years of garrisoning Border castles without ever achieving permanent peace, predicted trouble and advised Henry to spend £1,000 on creating better roads.[38]

Gavin Douglas, having arrived in London, wrote out a fifteen-point memorandum against Albany. He dredged up the old fiction that the Frenchman had poisoned the little Duke of Ross. He accused him of taking away James V's rich clothes to dress his own pages while the boy King was clad in badly made doublet and hose. The Duke, he said, had sold off ecclesiastical benefices, wardships and the remnants of James IV's great navy. He had misappropriated 50,000 French francs from the Scottish treasury, urged Margaret to divorce the Earl of Angus and, in short, was a corrupt usurper likely to follow the example of Richard III by murdering the King and seizing the throne.[39] Margaret wrote immediately to Wolsey, maintaining that Gavin Douglas was 'the cause of all the dissension in the realm'. She gave short shrift to the rumours about herself and the Duke, suggesting that Henry should have more sense than to believe such 'false reports'. She welcomed the sending of Clarencieux, she said, for he knew Scotland well, and she informed Wolsey that she was writing with her own hand, which was 'muckle labour', stressing that Henry was not to believe she had been coerced.[40] Instantly Wolsey advised Dacre that Albany was playing false; he had 'suborned the Queen' to write such letters.[41]

Speculative correspondence flew back and forth until, despite Lord Dacre's lack of faith in the roads, Clarencieux arrived in Edinburgh to deliver Henry's broadside. Margaret thought it 'sharp and unkind'. She had never contemplated divorcing Angus, she wrote to Henry; it had all been made up by 'yon wicked Bishop of Dunkeld'. But, she added darkly, 'His purpose will fail.' She insisted the King was well treated and under the care of 'as good and true lords as any in the realm'. Scotland, she said, desired 'peace with honour'.[42] On the same day that Margaret wrote to her brother, 11 February, the Estates of Scotland replied formally to Clarencieux's accusations, declaring Albany the lawful Governor and tutor of their King. 'He does not meddle with the King's person,' they said; he had arranged for the boy to be looked after by some of 'the most aged and honourable lords' in the land, all with the Queen's approbation.

Albany was able to command enough support to lead an expedition against England in July 1522. His army reached the gates of

Carlisle, but the memory of Flodden dampened the spirits of the Scottish commanders, who refused to lead their men over the Border. Dacre, who believed Albany had a larger force than was the case, offered a truce, even though he had no authority to do so. Albany then returned to France to make it clear to Francis that if he hoped for effective military action from the Scots, he must send both men and munitions. Prompted by Margaret, Henry offered a five-year peace to the Scots, hinting to his sister that a marriage could be arranged between the six-year-old Princess Mary and James V. That Mary was betrothed to the Emperor seemed a minor consideration. Margaret, for the first time since she had left England at the age of thirteen, found herself fulfilling the role for which she had originally been destined, that of peace-maker between the island kingdoms, but having committed themselves to a renewal of the 'auld alliance' with France the Scottish Estates rejected the proposal. Border incidents continued to flare and in June 1523 the English raided Kelso, burning most of the houses. Henry had sent the Earl of Surrey, the son of the victor of Flodden, north to assist Lord Dacre. Margaret spent much of the summer trying to persuade the English commanders to attack Edinburgh itself. Border warfare of the type they were waging, she pointed out, injured only the peasants, while the nobles were left unscathed.

Surrey believed that as James was nearly of an age to end his minority, Margaret should bring him from Stirling to sue person-ally for peace. The English would then cease their devastation and the Scots lords and people would understand what authority Margaret herself could wield, backed by Henry's might. Such a move, it was argued, could only increase the Queen's popularity. She told the English commanders, what Dacre already knew, that the only thing which would influence the Scots was money. Many already received French pensions and although Henry promised to offer bribes these were never forthcoming. On 31 August, when the Scots Parliament met, Margaret went to the Tolbooth, where a speech which the young King had written out with his own hand was read aloud, passionately entreating the lords to grant him freedom to make peace with his uncle, the King of England. The Abbot of Kelso was present and sent a wonderfully graphic account to Dacre. The French ambassadors had protested, saying 'the Governor would be there in six days'. The Queen replied that this was mere gossip 'from the Canongate'. The lords ('whether seduced or not by French gold' the Abbot did not know) appointed new guardians for the King, but arranged for him to have freedom to hunt and hawk within a four-mile radius of Stirling, where Albany had kept him under strict guard. The Scottish Commons 'murmured' for their King to be set at liberty, and it was the Abbot's opinion that Albany had 'without doubt lost the hearts' of the common people, but, he told Dacre, 'Our daft unnatural lords and misadvised council, seduced with France [ie French gold]' had deferred James's 'coming forth' until fourteen days after Michaelmas, when they believed Albany might return.[43]

On 20 September Surrey, who was being pestered by Wolsey to make a show of force, burnt the town of Jedburgh, blowing up the Abbey with barrels of gunpowder. On the same day Albany landed on the west coast with reinforcements sent by Francis of 4,000 infantrymen and 600 horse. As reports of the cruelty of the English spread across the country, Margaret's popularity waned. She was seen as the sister of the infamous tyrant Henry VIII and even the Prioress of Coldstream, the venerable nun who had given her shelter when, pursued by Albany, she had fled with Angus from Tantallon, wrote of the Queen, 'She is right fickle.'[44] Accounts of the numbers of French soldiers whom Albany had brought with him differed wildly, but it seems certain that it would have been too expensive for him to have maintained them in Scotland throughout the winter, so the Duke began his campaign to invade England in October, when the weather was already stormy.

Undeterred, he commandeered teams of oxen to haul the artillery Francis had sent through mud and torrential rain. Surrey was hoping he would attack Wark Castle, which was the best fortified of the Border strongholds. Dacre had been reinforcing it since 1518, and Surrey ordered new bulwarks to be built, which he thought could withstand a ten-day siege.[45] Margaret, who was constantly in touch with the English, informed them that Albany had twenty-eight cannon, four double cannon, greater than any that had been seen at Flodden, and other ingenious machinery for siege-breaking. The French had also sent much small artillery, ample ammunition and twelve shiploads of provisions. She reported that 3,000 German mercenaries were expected to join them. Albany's men were armed, she said, with crossbows, small hand-guns, pikes and halberds.[46] With these forces the Duke hoped eventually to take Berwick and then to advance down the country. In addition, Richard de la Pole, the last Yorkist pretender, had set sail with thirty ships to invade England from the south.

Once again the Duke marched his men to the very walls of an English stronghold. This time he put Frenchmen in the front ranks, not trusting the perfidious Scots. Wark held out. As the weather grew worse, it was learned that Surrey and his men were approaching. The Scots began to retreat. The rain fell steadily and the Tweed seemed about to burst its banks. Albany was forced into an ignominious withdrawal. As his men marched back to Edinburgh, the rain turned to sleet and the sleet to a violent snowstorm. Since the cost of maintaining the French infantrymen through the winter would have been too heavy, they took ship from Dumbarton. Albany himself left Scotland on 31 May 1524, never to return.

Chapter 12

A Shame and a Disgrace to All Her Family

Encouraged by the gentle ministrations of Friar Chadworth, Margaret and Angus had been reconciled in the spring of 1519. They had ridden in triumph, and apparently in concord, into Edinburgh together, Angus with a train of 400 horses, Margaret wildly cheered by the populace, but the Earl soon succumbed again to the superior charms of Lady Jane Stewart of Traquair. This, together with his blatant refusal to pay Margaret the rents from Ettrick Forest, despite many promises to Lord Dacre that he would do so, resulted in the irretrievable breakdown of the Queen's marriage.

During Albany's second regency, Angus had fled to France, where by 1524 he was living in restless exile. When the Duke's reputation in Scotland was at its lowest ebb, after his inglorious retreat from Wark Castle, Angus lost no opportunity to spread bad tidings. He informed Henry VIII that Albany was in disfavour with the French King and Louise of Savoy. The Duke had promised the Scottish Parliament that he would return from France by the end of August, but Francis I needed him to serve in his Italian campaigns, for France was by then engaged in full-scale war with the Emperor.

After Albany's departure a new determination seemed to inform Margaret's actions. She seized power in a *coup d'état* which had the full backing of Arran and the Hamiltons. Albany's wife had died, leaving the Duke without any children to follow him in the Scottish succession. This meant Arran's own chances had improved, and it seemed to him that he should take a lead in deciding Scottish policy as the young King reached the end of his minority. The Kings of England could not rule until they were eighteen, but in Scotland the sovereign could assume power at fourteen. James V was only twelve in 1524. To Henry VIII, who at seventeen had been obliged to accept his grandmother's regency, it seemed natural for James to submit to a similar dynastic arrangement. The impetus for ending Albany's regency, however, came from Margaret.

On 19 June she wrote to her brother that she believed it was time for James V 'to have his proper position of authority and throw off the governance usurped by Albany'.[1] At least that was how Henry interpreted her letter, although the Queen and the Duke had parted three weeks earlier on perfectly friendly terms. Before he took his leave of Margaret and James at Stirling, Albany had insisted that the lords of the council must understand 'that the Queen should be obeyed in all her rights'.[2] James was still in the care of his faithful tutor, Sir David Lindsay, but the household at Stirling was closely guarded by Albany's henchmen. On 11 June Lord Dacre had written to Wolsey to say that at the time of the Duke's departure, the lords and Albany 'did not agree very well'.[3] The fiasco at Wark Castle had greatly harmed the Governor's standing and at the last session of the Scots Parliament the lords spiritual had pointed out that they had paid over £40,000 for his support 'with small return'.[4] In short, the bishops wanted value for money. It did not help matters when the Duke asked for a loan to subsidize his journey back to France.

On hearing that Albany was on his way, Angus managed to escape to England. The exiled Earl made immediately for the court of Henry VIII. He was welcomed warmly by his brother-in-law, who was now in league with the Emperor against France. Lord Dacre had never wavered from his view that the Douglases were England's strongest potential allies in Scotland. Henry liked Angus and he accepted the Warden's opinion unconditionally, as did Wolsey. The King and the Cardinal thought the best way to retain English suzerainty over Scotland was to have James V, backed by his mother, as nominal ruler, with Angus, who could command more clansmen than any other overlord, supplying the power behind the throne. Henry was prepared to spend good money to further this arrangement, regardless of realities. Margaret, with her deeper understanding of Scottish politics, believed restoration of the Douglases was the least desirable option. She poured out letter after letter to Henry, to Wolsey and to Dacre, stating that if Angus were sent to Scotland, she would be forced to seek help elsewhere; that is, she would turn again to Albany and the French alliance. Dacre did not trust her judgement, especially after the Earl of Arran professed himself willing to settle his differences with Angus and ready to submit to arbitration.[5] In the summer of 1524, however, all parties agreed that what was most urgent was to secure a formal declaration that the young King's minority was at an end and to publicize it by his investiture.

As the whole plan hinged on James escaping from his French guards at Stirling Castle, Margaret's cooperation was essential, so Henry at first agreed to her demands to keep the Earl of Angus out of Scotland. He offered her the support of Thomas Howard, the former Earl of Surrey, who had been Duke of Norfolk since his father's death in May. To send the son of the victor of Flodden to back a *coup d'état* which would begin with the investiture of the Scottish King was scarcely a tactful gesture, but it served as a powerful reminder of England's might. Margaret welcomed the idea. Norfolk was a person of sufficient standing to negotiate with Chancellor Beaton, the recalcitrant Archbishop of St Andrews, but she warned her brother that if Angus came north, he would create 'great jealousies' and destroy the affinities she had built up.[6] Henry solemnly promised that Angus would remain at the Border.

On 26 July James was brought from Stirling Castle to Edinburgh. He was formally invested with the crown, sceptre and sword of state. Five days later he presided over his first council, where it was proposed that Albany's regency should be officially terminated. Beaton objected on the grounds that the Duke's term of office was not due to expire before 1 September. Margaret threw him into prison.

Henry made a great fuss of his nephew. He sent him a jewelled

sword, calculated to delight a boy of twelve, and made him a
member of the Order of the Garter. He also sent Archdeacon
Magnus to Scotland with five cartloads of treasure, a quantity of
cloth of gold and a brief to discuss a possible marriage between
James and his eight-year-old cousin, Princess Mary.[7] Margaret,
who sincerely desired a perpetual peace rather than the unsatis-
factory truces which had been arranged up to that date, was
delighted. She still feared Albany might return and she sent
Henry a very businesslike proposal, pointing out that a marriage
between James and Mary would be a 'great barrier' to any future
French alliance. She stressed that she and Arran had 'exposed
themselves to great danger and destruction' by terminating
Albany's regency. She demanded a trained bodyguard of 200 men
to protect the King and again insisted that if Angus were sent to
Scotland it would be 'a great impediment to peace'. She ended by
grandly demanding that he should be kept in prison.[8] Henry was
baffled. Angus, homesick for Scotland and his estates, appeared
to wish wholeheartedly for a loving reconciliation with his wife.

Letters flew between London and Edinburgh, largely intercepted by Lord Dacre. Having established to his own satisfaction
that Arran was willing to patch up his quarrel with Angus, Dacre
hinted to Henry and Wolsey that Margaret was wilfully scheming
to prolong the feud with her husband. Subsequently Henry,
Wolsey and the Warden began to use Angus as a threat, Dacre
pointing out that if Margaret did not fall in with their plans,
Henry would almost certainly cause the Earl to come to Scotland.
No one fully trusted Margaret. On 1 August Wolsey wrote chau-
vinistically to Norfolk, 'It is right to use the Queen of Scots as an
instrument in this matter, but not so as all shall depend upon her.
A good archer should have two strings to his bow, especially
when one is made of threads wrought by [a] woman's fingers.'[9]
That James's investiture took place at all in this climate of intrigue
and suspicion was something of a miracle.

Henry sent the bodyguard of 200 men which Margaret had
requested. He gave his nephew a gift of 1,000 golden nobles and
sent Arran £100 and the Queen 200 marks to cover ceremonial
expenses. He also authorized Norfolk to spend between £1,000
and £2,000 on bribes to build up the Queen's party. The English

Duke had by this time reached Newcastle with enough troops to make his presence felt. He made no move to cross the Border, leaving Dacre to communicate amicably with the Scots, among whom he had so many spies, informants and pensioners. What Margaret wanted most was approbation. She pointed out to Norfolk that since bringing James from Stirling she had performed 'right great acts' and, she claimed, 'not very expensive to the King'.[10] Unfortunately Wolsey, Norfolk and Dacre knew that she would soon need more funds. She told them naïvely that owing to the misrule of Albany, her son the King 'was not well furnished with money'. She also thanked Henry so effusively for the bodyguard that Norfolk and Dacre devised a scheme to manipulate her by withholding the men's pay, or sending it very slowly. Margaret genuinely feared that Albany might return. She begged Norfolk not to move far from the Border. She was terrified of her letters being intercepted and longed for clear directions from Henry and Wolsey.[11] Norfolk, meanwhile, proposed a meeting between himself and Arran at Berwick. He disliked dealing with a woman and wrote to Margaret with some hauteur, appealing to her sense of queenly duty. Her reconciliation with Angus, he said, would be for the good of the realm; she should put personal feelings aside. He implied that the tone of her previous letters sounded like blackmail and pointed out that Henry could not detain Angus indefinitely.[12] On 4 October Angus swore an oath, along with his brother Sir George Douglas, promising to do all he could to support James V. If the Duke tried to return, he was to oppose him; he was to encourage James to remain friendly with England; he was not to pursue his hereditary feud with Arran; and he was 'to endeavour to recover the Queen's favour and forbear to visit the Court until he had done so'.[13]

The following day the Earl left for Scotland. Henry and Wolsey sensed that they had gone too far and that nothing was likely to induce Margaret to take her husband back. Wolsey wrote to Norfolk at once, suggesting that he should detain Angus for as long as possible at Newcastle. It was a deliberate piece of buck-passing. The Duke was to 'entertain and watch' the Earl and work out whether it would be 'expedient' for him to return to Scotland if the Queen were not appeased. They sent Norfolk copies of all the letters Margaret and Arran had written, accusing Angus of double-dealing, authorizing the Duke to show them to the Earl on his arrival so that he would not take his detention at Newcastle 'unkindly'.[14] It was not a move calculated to promote matrimonial reconciliation, but Norfolk complied. On 1 November Angus wrote a short, gentlemanly note to Margaret. He had come to Scotland, he said, 'to do service to the King his master' and to her. If his enemies had spread 'sinister reports', perhaps they could discuss the matter in private.[15] The note was an archetype among divorce letters. Predictably, the Queen returned it unread. Magnus was with her when she received it and immediately reported this illogical piece of feminine behaviour back to Wolsey. Three days later, Magnus and his fellow envoy, Roger Radcliff, a gentleman of Henry's Privy Chamber, wrote to Angus to congratulate him on having crossed the Border.[16]

The Scottish Parliament was due to meet in ten days' time. Margaret was preparing to send her ambassadors to England. She had chosen the Earl of Cassilis, the Bishop of Dunkeld and the Abbot of Cambuskenneth, but she had to wait for the Parliament to ratify her appointments. When it opened on 14 November, the atmosphere was charged with tension. The first business was an act formally depriving Albany of the regency.[17] Everyone was waiting to see whether there would be another skirmish between the Douglases and the Hamiltons. Furious with Henry for allowing Angus to cross the Border, Margaret vented her wrath upon Magnus and Radcliff. Magnus pointed out nervously in a letter to Norfolk that few people of his rank (he was still a mere archdeacon) could have dared go so far 'in remonstrating with the Queen'.[18] She had in fact flown at him in such a towering rage that the unfortunate envoy had forgotten to reply to Norfolk's dispatches.

Shortly after the opening of Parliament, together with the Earl of Lennox, the Master of Kilmorris and the Earl of Buccleuch, Angus scaled the walls of Edinburgh with about 400 followers. They opened the city gates, proceeded to the Market Cross and proclaimed that they came in peace, as faithful subjects of the King. They simply desired, as barons of the realm, to sit in Parliament as their ancestors had always done. James and

Margaret were at Holyroodhouse. A force of between 400 and 500 foot soldiers was hastily assembled outside, but because the palace was the King's private residence there were very few of the great guns which James IV had collected at the castle. Margaret ordered four or five light cannon to be trained on the Earl and his men. Magnus and Radcliff protested helplessly that she really must not attack her lawful husband. The Queen rounded furiously upon them, telling them to 'go home and not meddle with Scottish matters'.[19] One of the great cannon was then fired from the castle, killing two merchants, a priest and a woman. The Earls had control of the town until four in the afternoon, but then at the King's command they left and went to Dalkeith. James and Margaret went by torchlight in a huge procession to the castle, where they remained in safety. Shaken but resolute, the Queen sent her own version of events in Scotland to her brother. Angus had assembled 'broken men and rebels and brought them into the King's presence,' she wrote. When the three ambassadors finally set out for England, Cassilis carried firm instructions 'given by me, Margaret Queen of Scots to the King's grace my brother', requiring Henry VIII not 'to assist any Scotch subject, except at the King of Scots' desire'.[20]

The Parliament confirmed Margaret's regency. This meant that for the first time since Flodden, she ruled from a secure powerbase. She was Queen not because she was James IV's widow, not because of any leading faction in the council and not even because her brother was the all-powerful King of England, but because she had taken the reins of government into her own hands, earning the respect of both peers and people. All Europe was shocked by the spectacle of a woman ordering guns to be fired against her own husband. Angus retreated to Tantallon. Henry fulminated over his sister's scandalous behaviour and the Emperor, having won the Battle of Pavia on 14 February, took the French King prisoner in Italy. Margaret was openly in love. The attack upon Angus seemed to unleash extraordinary energies in a woman who had previously conformed to the submissive pattern of the age. She promoted Henry Stewart, the handsome young courtier who held the office of King's Carver, to Captain of the Guard. She renewed her plea for divorce at Rome, using the grounds that at the time of her marriage to Angus it was reported that James IV was still alive after Flodden. Albany used his influence with the Pope to further her suit.

Henry wrote severely to his sister. Magnus gave her his letter at the end of March 1525, reporting that after she had read the contents 'it was an hour before she could stop weeping. Such a letter, she said, 'had never been written to a noble woman'.[21] No perpetual peace came of Cassilis's embassy, but very soon Margaret was receiving offers to renew the 'auld alliance' with France. Louise of Savoy, Regent in her son's captivity, refused to accept defeat. 'The affairs of France are in good order,' she assured her ambassador in Scotland, adding proudly that Francis 'would soon return in freedom and honour having been unsurpassed in personal bravery' at the Battle of Pavia.[22] She ordered the ambassador to offer Margaret a pension of 4,000 livres, advising him to flatter the Queen by suggesting that she was 'too wise to give up an ancient friend for an enemy, who wishes to become reconciled with Scotland in order to separate it from France'. Louise cruelly pointed out that Henry's promises to marry his daughter to James V would not come to fruition. 'As to the Princess Mary, she has already been promised to the Dauphin and the Emperor, and in like manner,' she wrote scornfully, Henry would 'break promises made to the Scots'.[23] James V should marry a French Princess, one of her own granddaughters.

While Louise offered pensions and protection to Margaret, Mary Brandon's income as Dowager of France ceased after the outbreak of war between Henry and Francis. In 1523 the French King seized his stepmother's revenues of 60,250 livres. This greatly affected the Brandons' ability to pay off their huge debt to Henry, which was renegotiated at regular intervals after 1516. Technically the Duke was supposed to pay 2,000 marks a year, but by February 1521 only a fraction of the total debt of £25,234 6s 9d had been settled.[24] In 1522, when the Emperor met Henry at Canterbury, Brandon had courted his patronage. Both he and his followers received Imperial pensions, but these were not large enough to compensate for the loss of Mary's income. The Brandons, nevertheless, managed to entertain the Emperor lavishly with a banquet at Suffolk Place, followed by hunting in the park. Their second daughter, Eleanor, may well have been named after the Emperor's sister. When the French war began, Suffolk set off at the head of one of the largest armies Henry had ever assembled. Illness broke out among the troops and premature frost caused Margaret of Austria's general, Count van Buren, to disband his men early, so that the Anglo-Flemish campaign of 1523 was a failure. Suffolk returned with his men in a pitiful condition, but as he had implicitly obeyed the King's orders, his military reputation remained untarnished.

Henry lost men and money in the French war, but, eighteen months later, the disaster of Suffolk's expedition was quickly forgotten amid the euphoria with which the English greeted Francis's defeat at Pavia. It was said that the French had lost 6,000 men. When the news reached Henry VIII, he leapt out of bed, put on his shirt and asked after Richard de la Pole, the last Yorkist pretender, who was among Francis's officers. 'The White Rose is dead in battle,' replied the messenger. Henry is supposed to have said,'God have mercy on his soul. All the enemies of England are gone,' and called for the man to be given more wine.[25] Briefly Henry saw himself again in the mould of Henry V, heroically subduing the might of France, and patriotically reclaiming England's lost possessions. Charles V, however, did not share his desire to restructure the map of Europe with Normandy, Picardy and Brittany going to the English, and the Treaty of the More, signed at Wolsey's house at Rickmansworth on 30 August 1525, settled things more modestly. Despite his promise to Margaret that Princess Mary should marry James V, Henry had continued to offer his daughter to the Emperor. He was surprised and pained when Charles rejected her in favour of a grown-up Portuguese Princess whom he had been courting for some months. Mary was nine that summer and the Emperor twenty-five. Anglo–Imperial relations cooled and Wolsey was therefore able to resume his *entente* with Louise of Savoy, who continued as Regent of France, for it was not until January 1526 that Francis was finally released from captivity.

The Treaty of the More provided for both Henry's sisters. The arrears of Mary's dower rents, amounting to about £2,000 a year in English money, were paid for the three years when they had been interrupted by the war. Wolsey also negotiated a better rate by having the remainder farmed to Jean Joachim de Passano, an agent of Louise's, who took a smaller cut than Bonnivet, who had been the previous agent. Mary Brandon became the richer by approximately 22,000 livres a year. By another clause in the treaty, the French were solemnly bound not to allow the Duke of Albany to enter Scotland during the remainder of James's minority.[26] Margaret's *coup d'état* had successfully brought about the end of French domination over Scotland. She received no thanks from Henry, who continued to rely upon Angus and the powerful faction of his clan, the Red Douglases. Margaret turned down a French bribe of 30,000 crowns, but continued to correspond amicably with Albany, who supported her through his connections at Rome in seeking a divorce. Despite her love for Henry Stewart, she accepted another formal reconciliation with Angus for appearances' sake. At the state opening of the next Scots Parliament, full ceremony was observed. James and his mother headed the procession, warmly cheered by the people. Angus carried the crown, Arran the sceptre and the Earl of Argyll the sword of state. The family tensions must have been unbearable.

Angus had gathered a huge band of supporters. Magnus estimated that the Earl rode into Edinburgh that day with 600 or 700 men. Margaret held the castle, which was bristling with artillery. Outside the city walls were gathered 2,000 clansmen who had ridden with Angus from Dalkeith. To the ordinary folk of Edinburgh, it must have seemed that the Douglases were about to start a siege. It was made clear to the gunners in the castle that if they fired, there would be appalling reprisals, but the opening of Parliament went smoothly. Magnus offered to mediate between the two parties, although in the end there was no need. The Douglas supporters stayed out of range of the castle guns. The Archdeacon later told Wolsey that he thought Angus's party was more peacefully inclined than Margaret and Arran's. The Queen was by now so anxious to get a divorce, he wrote, that she would be 'glad to give Angus 1,000 marks out of her lands for it'.[27]

There was a certain feminine logic about her reasoning. She had married Angus for love and been badly let down. Made

Regent originally by James IV's will, she had lost her position and the respect of the other lords by marrying a Douglas. Clearly, as James's widow and mother of the King, she still had a place in the hearts of the Scottish people. Angus, therefore, was the cause of all her miseries and, as she had reiterated many times, 'he loved her not'. Her marriage to him must be declared invalid. James IV's stature had risen to mythical proportions since his death, and his people looked back to a golden age when their strong, popular King controlled the factious Earls. Stories abounded that he had survived Flodden. He was supposed to have been seen staggering wounded about Kelso three nights after the carnage. He had been sighted in the Holy Land, where he had gone to do penance for bringing about his own father's death. All these folk tales fitted exquisitely into the framework of Margaret's perceptions. Her conscience told her, particularly as she had just found 'true love' with Henry Stewart, that she had erred by marrying Angus while her first husband was still alive. This was her consistent plea at Rome. It was to the great credit of the Pope and the Roman curia that when Clement VII finally granted her divorce in February 1527, the decree was on the grounds of Angus's precontract with Lady Jane of Traquair. As Margaret had been ignorant of this at the time of her marriage, the Pope added a special clause allowing legitimacy to Lady Margaret Douglas, who became yet another archetype in the story – the innocent child of wicked parents.

By the time Clement granted the divorce, the fighting in Europe was so heavy that it took nine months for the papal messenger to reach Scotland. Margaret was not aware of her freedom until December 1527, but in the two years before the Pope granted the decree, she tried all possible stratagems to gain her divorce. She was thwarted by Angus at every turn in a classic tale of matrimonial acrimony. The Earl may not have loved the Queen but she was his wife, and when she began openly to cohabit with Henry Stewart, the chief of the Douglases reacted accordingly. A regency council, similar to the one which had operated under Albany, provided for the Earls of Arran, Angus, Lennox and Argyll to have charge of the King by rota. When it came to Angus's turn to relinquish custody, he refused to do so. The

Queen and Arran immediately accused him of treason. The Earl
made the boy write a letter to his mother saying that he was
happy to be in his stepfather's care, but James wrote secretly to
Margaret, begging her to rescue him. Supported by Arran, Argyll,
the Earl of Moray and Archbishop Beaton, who had again
changed sides, the Queen gathered an army and rode to
Edinburgh. Angus came out to meet her, so that once again
husband and wife faced each other in battle array, but Margaret's
army dared not fire, because the Earl forced the King to ride
beside him so that the Queen's men feared to attack 'the person
of their Prince'.

According to Margaret, James was kept in thraldom. He
detested his stepfather but was powerless to resist being
completely surrounded by Angus's relatives. Sir David Lindsay,
the tutor who had brought him up since childhood, was replaced
by the Earl's brother Sir George Douglas, who became Master of
the Household. Angus's uncle, Archibald Douglas of Kilspindie,
became Treasurer; James Douglas of Drumlanrig was made
Master of the Larder. On 14 June 1526 the King was declared
legally of age, but he had less independence than before. Angus's
view of sovereignty differed radically from Margaret's. He took
James with him to preside at the Justice Ayres, so that the boy
began to acquire a thorough knowledge of Scottish law. He also
encouraged him in the masculine pursuits of the day: hawking,
hunting, gambling and wenching. Davy Lindsay saw his protégé
turned into an adolescent debauchee and recorded it sorrowfully
in his poem 'The Complaint'.[28]

The Earl of Lennox was the next to attempt a rescue. Angus
had deprived Beaton of the Great Seal and made himself
Chancellor of Scotland. Backed by Margaret, Beaton and the Earls
of Argyll, Moray and Cassilis, Lennox marched to Linlithgow,
where there was a short, decisive battle. Angus was victorious
and Lennox, who eventually surrendered, was murdered in the
field. Arran called him 'the hardiest, stoutest and wisest man that
ever Scotland saw'. James now hated the Douglases even more
bitterly for killing his friend and kinsman.

Angus heaped further humiliation on the boy by compelling
him to attend the siege of Stirling Castle, which Margaret and

Harry Stewart had seized.[29] Outraged by his wife's behaviour, Angus made James give orders for Stewart to leave forthwith. Certain highlights of this episode must have impressed themselves deeply on the mind of the adolescent King. At one point during the Battle of Linlithgow he had tried to go to Lennox's aid. Sir George Douglas is supposed to have said, 'Bide where you are, Sir, for if they get hold of one of your arms, we will seize you and pull you in pieces, rather than part with you.' After the fighting was over, Archbishop Beaton escaped in the disguise of a shepherd. Three rescue attempts had failed and the King, shortly after his sixteenth birthday, decided to take his fate into his own hands. In an episode worthy of the novels of Sir Walter Scott, James, who was staying at Falkland Palace, told his captors that he wished to go hunting.[30] He was in the care of James Douglas of Parkhead, whom he ordered to send for the Laird of Fernie, the Forester of Falkland. The King announced a deer hunt which was to start at seven in the morning. He told Parkhead they should go to bed early and proposed a toast. Parkhead drank deeply and slept soundly. The King rose. He dressed in the clothes of a yeoman of the stable and slipped out of the palace with two trusted servants. They rode to Stirling, where Margaret and Henry Stewart had lowered the drawbridge. The King entered the castle and the drawbridge clanged safely down. In Pitscottie's rousing version of this story, Sir George Douglas, who had been to St Andrews, came back to Falkland at midnight. He asked where the King was and was told he was sleeping. Sir George went to bed, but was wakened at dawn by the Baillie of Abernethy, who told him the King was 'past the Bridge of Stirling'.[31]

Angus, Sir George Douglas, Archibald Douglas of Kilspindie and James Douglas of Parkhead rode immediately to Stirling, but as they approached the town they met a herald bearing a proclamation forbidding them to go within six miles of the King's person. The Earls of Moray, Argyll, Arran, Eglinton, Bothwell, Montrose and Rothes, and the Lords Maxwell and Home had joined Margaret and Henry Stewart, who since the divorce from Angus was made public had married the Queen. Faced by such a formidable array, the Douglases retreated to Tantallon. Less than two months after his sixteenth birthday, James V was master of his own destiny. He created Henry Stewart Earl of Methven and made Sir David Lindsay Snowdon Herald, while his old school-master, Gavin Dunbar, Archbishop of Glasgow, became Chancellor of Scotland.

Shocked at first by his sister's attempts to obtain a divorce, Henry VIII began to revise his opinions as early as February 1526 when he wrote to Archdeacon Magnus to say that privately he thought Margaret had 'sufficient reason to be divorced'.[32] He continued, however, to support Angus, always preferring the Earl's version of events in Scotland to that offered by Margaret. Lord Dacre had died in the autumn of 1525. He had been succeeded as Warden of the Northern Marches by his son, Lord William Dacre. Just before James escaped from Angus, Lord William wrote to Wolsey to tell him of Margaret's marriage to Henry Stewart. Dacre's letter reported the matter succinctly: 'Harry Stewart hath married the Queen of Scots, as she hath confessed herself and for that cause the King her son caused the Lord Erskine and a certain company to lie about the Castle of Stirling and attack him ... he is put in ward by the King's commandment.'[33] Lord William's letter is dated 2 April 1528, seven weeks before Angus lost control. Henry Stewart was obviously imprisoned by the Earl's orders, not those of the King. Henry VIII did not know this. He may not even have been aware that Clement's decree had arrived in Scotland. He assumed that James V was as shocked by his mother's behaviour as he was himself. Margaret had outraged Henry's sense of decency by cohabiting with Stewart before either party was divorced. The spectacle of a Dowager Queen living openly with her paramour was wholly against the conventions of the age. The King of England felt she had disgraced her whole family. In the spring of 1527 he had told Turenne, the French ambassador in London, that it was 'impossible for anyone to live a more shameful life than she did'.[34] When he heard Dacre's story of James ordering Henry Stewart to leave Stirling Castle he had Wolsey fire off a scorching epistle, warning Margaret of the dangers of damnation to her soul.

News of James's *coup d'état* reached London slowly. He had

escaped from Angus between 27 and 31 May. Three weeks later the King of Scots wrote to the Earl of Northumberland, the Warden of the East Marches, to say that 'disturbances had occurred in the inland of our realm'. Henry Percy, who had inherited his title the previous May, when his father, the formidable fifth Earl, died, sent a spy to Scotland to find out what was going on. By 2 July he was able to tell Wolsey of the proclamation issued against Angus and the Douglases and that the King of Scots was calling a council at Stirling and a Parliament in Edinburgh. James had asked him to keep order on the Borders but Scotland was again in turmoil.[35]

On 18 July Lord William Dacre supplied further details. The King and the lords had met at the Tolbooth, he reported, adding that James was 'ruled by the Queen, Henry Stewart, now her husband, Lord Maxwell and the Lord of Buccleuch'. He described the last two as 'chief maintainers of all misguided men on the borders' and added that James's bedfellow was the 'Sheriff of Ayr, who slew the Earl of Cassilis'. James and his people were keeping nightly watch at Edinburgh Castle, he said, 'for fear of Angus's party'.[36] Early in September the Scottish Parliament passed a death sentence on Angus, Sir George Douglas and Douglas of Kilspindie. They were accused of treason and of holding the King for two years against his will. Angus fled to Tantallon. James pursued him. Borrowing cannon from the nearby Castle of Dunbar, he besieged the Douglas stronghold with all the vehemence of his sixteen years, but Tantallon held out and the King had to retire rather ingloriously, leaving the action to be concluded by the Earl of Argyll, who had more military experience.

Angus surrendered in November. He and his kinsmen fled to England, taking Lady Margaret Douglas with them. She was just thirteen. Her father left her at first in the household of Sir Thomas Strangeways at Berwick, where she certainly remained until the following summer. Queen Margaret must have attempted to get her daughter back. Probably she made several attempts, for on 29 July 1529 Sir Thomas wrote to Wolsey to say that he was watching over Lady Margaret carefully, but dared not allow her too much freedom, 'fearing she would be stolen into Scotland'.[37] Later her uncle the King and her godfather the Cardinal arranged for her to travel south to be brought up with the Princess Mary. Of marriageable age and royal blood, Margaret Douglas was a useful asset in Henry's network of diplomatic alliances. She was frequently referred to in dispatches as 'the Princess of Scotland', particularly by the Imperial ambassador, Messire Eustace Chapuys, who arrived in England at the end of 1529. Henry kept a strict check on his niece, fearing she may have inherited a streak of Margaret's wantonness. Although the bull authorizing her mother's divorce clearly granted Margaret Douglas legitimacy, Henry continued to fume against his sister's behaviour. He was by this time in love with Anne Boleyn and shortly after the conversation with Turenne, when he had called the Queen of Scotland 'a shame and a disgrace to all her family', he began actively seeking his own divorce. He made a great point, however, of behaving correctly. Although there is evidence that the King was a vigorous wooer, all the authorities concur that the couple did not actually sleep together. Nor at first did they openly cohabit. Anne did not have apartments in the royal palace until December 1528, when the arrival of the papal legate made the King certain his divorce would go through. This naturally increased his feeling of self-righteous indignation against Margaret, who had made no such concession to public decency.

Obsessed by his own problems, the King of England may not even have realized that the Pope had exempted his niece from bastardy. Questions of legitimacy troubled Henry deeply at this time. His only son, the Duke of Richmond, had been given a household impressive enough for some people to believe the King might try to change the law to make the boy his heir. This would have been very difficult, especially in canon law, as Henry had never married Richmond's mother, but the young Duke was given precedence over all the nobility of England, except for the legitimate members of the royal family, and he was being brought up in a manner befitting a King's son. Richmond's establishment was at Sheriff Hutton in Yorkshire, a few miles north of York. He had been sent to learn the art of good government, just as Prince Arthur had once been trained in the Welsh Marches. Magnus was transferred from his ambassadorial duties in Scotland to a post which combined mastery of the Duke's household with presidency of the Council of the North. Richmond's titles included Lieutenant of the North and his retainers in their blue and yellow livery made the King's presence felt in the northern counties. Henry Fitzroy himself flourished in the wholesome atmosphere, dutifully writing to his father of his progress in his studies, asking for the paternal daily blessing and proving a gentleman in every way, particularly in field sports. There existed at Sheriff Hutton a pack of small bloodhounds, specially bred to ride pillion on the huntsman's saddle. Their fame reached Scotland and James V asked his cousin to send him some.

The advancement of Richmond was offensive to Katherine. Since England had no salic law, she saw no reason why her daughter should not remain legal heiress to the throne. When Henry had gone to fight the French at the beginning of the reign, he had no prejudices against petticoat government. The Queen had been made Regent of England and she had harangued the army before they marched north just as her mother, Isabella, had once addressed Spanish troops before battle, proud of her title as 'King' of Castile. It seems highly unlikely that Henry would have tried to legitimize Richmond and much more probable that Wolsey sent the King's children north as part of his regional policy, to enhance the King's authority in the Marches, but to placate Katherine, Mary was given a household as grand as her illegitimate half-brother's. She was sent to Thornbury in Herefordshire with her Lady Mistress, the Countess of Salisbury, her schoolmaster, Dr Richard Fetherstone, and a retinue of some 304 persons.[38] Her servants and henchmen were clothed in distinctive liveries of blue and green. Mary, however, was never given the title 'Princess of Wales' and Richmond, in Henry's eyes, remained living proof that he could father healthy male children.

Why then, the King asked himself, had Katherine's sons been stillborn or died in infancy? Why did God deny him an heir? Henry sought an answer in the Scriptures. He worried desperately over a passage in Leviticus: 'If a man shall take his brother's wife, it is an impurity; he hath uncovered his brother's nakedness, they shall be childless.' When it became clear that Katherine could conceive no more children, this text struck Henry with shattering force. He became convinced that as he had married his brother's wife, God was punishing him and through him the people of England. So began the great scruple in his conscience. There had been clerical discussion about the validity of the King's marriage since the beginning of the reign, but in the summer of 1527, according to Grafton, there 'began a fame in London that the King's Confessor', Dr Longland, Bishop of Lincoln, 'and diverse great clerks had told the King that the marriage between him and the Lady Katherine, late wife to his brother Prince Arthur, was not good but damnable and the King hereupon should marry the Duchess of Alençon, sister to the French King'. When Henry heard of this tavern talk, he sent for Sir Thomas Seymour, the Mayor of London, 'and charged him to see people should cease this rumour upon pain of the King's high displeasure'.[39]

Later in the summer Wolsey set out for France amid great pomp. This fuelled the rumour, and tempers rose when his men were seen loading great chests at Dover said to contain £240,000 of the King's money which was going to succour the Pope. Officially Wolsey was on his way to convene a congress of cardinals at Avignon, but he also intended to hold secret discussions with Francis about a possible marriage for Henry with the French King's sister-in-law, Madame Renée. As a preliminary to divorce, Wolsey and Archbishop Warham held a secret court at Greenwich in May. They formally cited Henry for living in sin with his brother's widow in order that the original bull of 1503 allowing Katherine's second marriage could be further examined by experts in canon law. This procedure was confidential and Henry was angry that those outside the court circle should have caught the whiff of scandal, but the first step had been taken. In June he informed Katherine that he planned to seek a divorce after eighteen years of marriage. He had every expectation of a speedy and straightforward settlement. The Pope would pronounce his marriage invalid and he would receive absolution for committing adultery through ignorance. Katherine could go to a nunnery. Henry would marry Anne, who would produce a legitimate boy, and in the meantime, the plan to make James V his heir having been discarded, Mary Brandon's son, the Earl of Lincoln, could take second place to Anne's putative boy.

As the theological debate which was later to rage through the universities of Europe would prove, there was genuine doubt about Henry's marriage and, as a preliminary measure, the Pope issued a bull in 1527 granting the King a dispensation to remarry, when he was free to do so. Anne Boleyn's matrimonial status also needed clarification, and some paperwork which had not been completed when Suffolk married Mary Tudor had to be cleared up. The bull providing for Henry's remarriage was carefully worded. It allowed union with a woman who had precontracted marriage with another person, as long as such a marriage had not been consummated.[40] According to Wolsey's biographer George Cavendish, Anne had entered a discreet understanding with Lord Percy, when she was one of the Queen's maids of honour and he a junior member of Wolsey's household. The couple had met whenever the Cardinal went to court. Percy would 'fall in dalliance among the Queen's maidens, being at the last more conversant with Mistress Anne Boleyn than any other'. A secret love grew between them, but Wolsey, knowing the King was attracted to Anne, warned Percy not to 'tangle' with her. Apart from anything else, his father, the Earl of Northumberland, intended to match him with Mary Talbot, a daughter of the Earl of Shrewsbury. Wolsey reminded the young lord that God had called him to a high estate, and that after his father's death he would 'inherit and possess one of the worthiest earldoms of this realm'.[41] Ignorant of the King's attachment, Harry Percy assumed the Cardinal meant that Anne, the daughter of Sir Thomas Boleyn, a mere knight, was an unsuitable match for one of his rank. He continued to plead his suit, pointing out that her uncle was the powerful Duke of Norfolk. Wolsey sent for Percy's father, the redoubtable fifth Earl, advising him of what half the court was already whispering, that Anne was expected to become the King's mistress. Northumberland told his son he was 'a proud, presumptuous, disdainful and very unthrift waster' and married him to Mary Talbot without more ado.[42] The fifth Earl died soon after this confrontation and Percy was conveniently packed off to attend to his hereditary duties in the Marches. By December 1527 he was Warden of the East Marches, exchanging the frivolities of the Tudor court for the harsh realities of Border warfare.

Although he was the foremost diplomat in Europe, the Ipswich butcher's son was hated for his meteoric rise by the older nobility. A magnificent host, who gave lavish parties, he was reviled by Katherine of Aragon as one who lived 'a voluptuous life' in 'abominable lechery'. She accused him of hating her nephew, the Emperor, 'worse than a scorpion'. *(By courtesy of the National Portrait Gallery, London)*

Hampton Court Palace from the river. The magnificence of Wolsey's palace led people to accuse him of setting up a rival court to the King. After the Cardinal's fall in 1529, Henry made the palace his own. *(Ashmolean Museum, Oxford)*

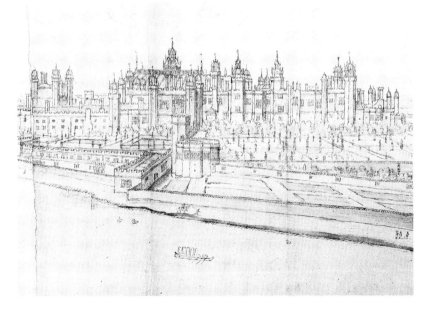

Lucas Hornebolte was a court painter to Henry VIII for two decades. This miniature shows Katherine of Aragon in her early forties. She was past childbearing age, but had not completely lost her looks. *(In the collection of the Duke of Buccleuch and Queensberry KT)*

The Battle of Pavia, 1525. Francis I was defeated and held prisoner by Charles V. The Emperor's troops later sacked Rome, driving Clement VII into exile. With the Pope in his power, the Emperor, being Katherine's nephew, was able to block Henry's divorce. *(The Royal Collection © Her Majesty The Queen)*

Francis I, surrounded by his family. His sons, Dauphin Francis and Henri d'Orléans, were held hostage by the Emperor after Francis's defeat at the Battle of Pavia. Henry VIII, Katherine and Mary campaigned for the French princes' release. *(Lauros-Giraudon)*

In this letter, Henry VIII's illegitimate son, the nine-year-old Duke of Richmond, asks his father for a jousting harness, arguing that Julius Caesar would have approved. Lady Margaret Beaufort had paid for Henry's own first jousting harness when he was fifteen. *(Crown copyright material in the Public Record Office is reproduced by permission of the Controller of Her Majesty's Stationery Office SP1/46)*

Anne Boleyn. Chosen to accompany Mary to Paris because of her excellent French, she was later called 'The King of England's whore' by Francis I's sister, Marguerite d'Angoulême. *(By courtesy of the National Portrait Gallery, London)*

Sir Thomas More, Chancellor of England from 1529-1534. Executed in 1535 for refusing to swear to the Act of Supremacy, he is revered by Catholics as a saint and martyr. *(By courtesy of the National Portrait Gallery, London)*

William Warham, Archbishop of Canterbury for over forty years. After Henry and Thomas Cromwell pushed the Act for the Submission of the Clergy through parliament, the 82-year-old Archbishop was ready to risk martyrdom and defy his sovereign as Thomas à Beckett had done before him. *(The Royal Collection © Her Majesty The Queen)*

Henry VIII at prayer. His last speech to the House of Commons in 1545 showed that Henry took religion seriously. He could not bear to hear the word of God 'jangled in every alehouse and tavern' by unlearned clergy. *(Reproduced by permission of the Dean and Canons of Windsor)*

never been married to Bessie Blount. Apart from enabling Mary's son, the six-year-old Earl of Lincoln, to take his place in the line of succession, the Brandons' case was parallel to Henry's own, for the King wished to claim that Katherine's marriage to Prince Arthur had been valid and the dispensation granted for his own rested upon an error. In May 1528, therefore, the successful conclusion of Suffolk's affairs served both to encourage the King's hopes and to exacerbate his frustration.

Throughout that summer the sweating sickness raged in England. The court dispersed to places where there was least fear of contagion. The Suffolks visited the monasteries of Ely, Butley and Eye, picnicking and hunting. Henry and Katherine went on progress together, calling at a number of religious houses, but in rather less of a holiday mood than the Brandons. In London it was reckoned that 40,000 people had been infected, although only 2,000 had died. Anne Boleyn was in Surrey. Henry wrote nervously recommending her to move. She went to Hever Castle, her parents' home in Kent, and succumbed to the disease shortly after the King had written reassuringly, 'another thing may comfort you – few women have this illness and moreover, none of our court have died of it'.[44]

Anne's brother, Lord Rochford, who was with the King's household, fell ill and then recovered, but her brother-in-law, William Carey, the husband of Mary Boleyn, died. When Anne herself fell sick, Henry was consumed with anxiety. His best physician was away, so he sent his second best, Dr Butts, 'praying God he may soon make you well' and sternly admonishing her to follow his advice. The King prided himself on his up-to-date medical knowledge and wrote also to Wolsey, who was terrified of catching the sweat, advising him to drink less, to be sure to keep his pores clear and to take Rasis pills.[45] When Anne was convalescing, he sent her some tender venison and one of his most memorable love letters:

> The cause of my writing at this time, good sweetheart, is only to understand of your good health and prosperity, whereof to know I would be as glad as in manner mine own; praying God (that it be his pleasure) to send us shortly

together for I promise you I long for it, howbeit trust it shall not be long . . . and seeing my darling is absent, I can no less do than to send her some flesh representing my name, which is hart's flesh for Henry, prognosticating that hereafter, God willing you must enjoy some of mine which, [if] He pleased, I would were now.

No more to you at this time, mine own darling, but that a while I would we were together of an evening.

H R[46]

By the end of the summer, Jean du Bellay, Bishop of Bayonne, the worldly-wise French ambassador, reported, 'Mademoiselle Boulan has returned to court'. He noted that Henry's passion for her had not abated. From private conversations with Wolsey, he understood that the Cardinal hoped Henry might tire of her as he had of others. Then if the divorce went through, the King might be induced to marry the French Princess, Madame Renée. Wolsey still cherished his impossible dreams of a permanent peace between England and France. Du Bellay, like many others, shook his head over Henry's infatuation. He felt the King had committed himself so far over Anne Boleyn 'that none but God can get him out of it'. The Cardinal had confided a good deal in Du Bellay. He had told him while walking in the gardens of Hampton Court that he wanted to retire from politics and 'serve God to the end of his days', but first he saw it as his duty to sort out the English succession. Shrewdly the ambassador guessed that the Cardinal's own fate hung in the balance; that there were those in the Council who wished to bring him down; that his influence over Henry would be at an end if the Pope should refuse divorce. The ambassador had been present when the King had used 'terrible language' to Wolsey for even hinting that Clement might make difficulties.[47]

In September the papal legate, Cardinal Campeggio, arrived in London. Anne was whisked off once more to Hever Castle. The King of England wanted no breath of scandal before the case opened. In his view, his sister Margaret's open adultery with Henry Stewart had already tainted the Tudor name through all the courts of Europe. Ostensibly, from the moment of his arrival the Cardinal worked hand in glove with Wolsey to further 'the King's Great Matter', as the dispute had become known. The Pope, however, still wretchedly sheltering with the remnants of the Roman curia in the dilapidated episcopal palace at Orvieto, was wholly dominated by the Emperor. He had no wish to clash further with Charles V by ruling against his aunt. Clement, therefore, had given secret instructions to Campeggio to make use of every kind of delay. The Londoners planned to give the legate a triumphal welcome. Many simple, good-hearted folk believed that his coming would put an end to the terrible troubles between their King and Queen, which were now discussed openly throughout the town – much to the annoyance of the King, who had a fastidious dislike of alehouse gossip. Campeggio disembarked, pleaded gout and asked to be taken quietly to the Bishop of Bath's house outside Temple Bar, where he was to stay. When he eventually met the King at Bridewell, the newest of Henry's London palaces, the Cardinal Legate arrived in a crimson velvet litter, ostentatiously carried by four attendants, professing to be in such pain that he could not stand.[48] By the time he recovered, the court had moved to Greenwich for the Christmas holidays.

Chapter 13

Never Cardinal or Legate Did Good in England

When news of the Cardinal Legate's arrival reached Henry, the Duke and Duchess of Suffolk had been staying at Butley Priory. They were enjoying a picnic in the autumn sunshine under the oaks of Sholgrove Wood, after a satisfactory morning's hunting. So satisfactory, according to the local chronicler, that the whole party was in a state of 'jocundity and cheerfulness of heart'. Suddenly a messenger burst upon them, summoning Brandon to court to welcome the papal envoy. A sense of foreboding must have come over Mary. The prospect of a royal divorce filled her with horror. She had been Katherine's confidante through the traumatic summer of 1527 and she broke out in bitter lamentations 'that a legate should ever come into England'.[1] Suffolk held his tongue and obeyed his master. Many of the duties he was to perform in the coming months were to prove distasteful. Mary found it difficult to conceal her feelings, but the view that the couple ended up 'taking sides', Charles supporting the King and Mary the Queen, is an over-simplification.[2] Mary had known and loved Katherine since her childhood. The Queen had stayed with the Suffolks when making a pilgrimage to Walsingham after the birth of Princess Mary. The Duchess knew of her sister-in-law's difficulties in childbirth and of her disappointments. She stood godmother to Princess Mary and she understood how slighted Katherine had felt over the elevation of Richmond in 1525, but the fact remained that Margaret and Mary had both borne healthy boys; there seemed to be no reason why Henry, too, should not beget sons. In a letter written after she had been ill, apologizing for not accompanying Brandon to London, Mary assured her brother that a sight of him would be the best cure in the world, ending, 'I pray God send you your heart's desire.'[3] In 1528 this can only have been a reference to his longing for a legitimate heir.

The Suffolks played a leading part in the merrymaking and feasting at Greenwich that Christmas. Katherine strove to preside with serenity, but Hall says she rarely smiled 'and made no joy of nothing, her mind was so troubled'.[4] During the season of misrule Anne had acquired a suite of rooms in the royal palace. Katherine had gone to Richmond at the beginning of December. When she returned to London, her rival's presence was a *fait accompli*.

A bizarre situation developed. More than one biographer has ascribed to this time Katherine's acid remark made while playing cards: 'My lady Anne,' she is supposed to have said, 'you have good hap to stop at a King, but you are not like others, you will have all or none.'[5] It has been interpreted in various ways, but the simplest explanation is that Katherine meant that, unlike her sister Mary, Anne refused to part with her virtue. A great deal of amorous dalliance must have gone on between the King and his sweetheart, but she remained a virgin and took care to advertise the fact, so that the whole court marvelled at her ability to keep Henry in a state of white-hot desire without apparently giving in. These were daring tactics, but since the couple did not actually sleep together, the incongruity of keeping a wife and a mistress under one roof did not seem to occur to Henry. During the New Year festivities he made a great fuss of Cardinal Campeggio, giving him a golden chain of office, and knighting his son, for before he entered the Church the legate himself had been a married man. Clement had selected him as one well versed in understanding matrimonial disputes. Campeggio, meanwhile, had been dreading Christmas at Greenwich. The English councillors kept impressing upon him the urgency of the King's situation. He had been told that during the twelve days of feasting 'all the barons and prelates of the kingdom would come to court'.

Musing on such a formidable assembly, he begged his friend Cardinal Salviati, the Pope's nephew, to send him some definite instructions so 'that I may be able to breathe freely'.[6]

From the moment he set foot on English soil, the legate had been under pressure from all parties. In the autumn Katherine called on him at nine one morning (an hour late by the standards of Tudor London, but abhorrently early for Campeggio) to make her confession. She asked him to dispense with the customary secrecy. She wished the details to be made known to the Pope. From 14 November 1501, when she married Arthur, to 2 April 1502, when he died, Katherine insisted, she had slept only seven times with the Prince. She had emerged from his bed as intact a virgin as the day she was born. In canon law this should have been the end of the matter, an unconsummated marriage was a marriage which had simply not taken place, and no amount of papal bulls could possibly therefore invalidate her marriage to Henry, which had been blessed with legitimate issue in the person of the Princess Mary. This was not what the Cardinal Legate expected or wanted to know. He pleaded with her to stop making difficulties. Why could she not accept the traditional and aristocratic solution open to queens who failed to produce male heirs and enter a convent? Failing that, she could take a vow of chastity, as Lady Margaret Beaufort had done, and live as a virtuous matron, but Katherine assured him 'she would never do so'.[7]

The Queen intended 'to live and die in the estate of matrimony into which God had called her' and nothing would alter her opinion, not even if they sentenced her to a martyr's death and tore her limb from limb. In the face of such determination, Campeggio was nonplussed. 'I have always judged her to be a prudent lady,' he wrote to Salviati, but 'her obstinacy in not accepting this sound council does not please me.' Queen Katherine was nearly fifty, he reflected, and it seemed obvious that for her to retire into a religious house would be 'less scandalous and more secure'.[8]

Scandal was the one thing Henry could not avoid. Whatever the truth of his self-restraint, the London fishwives had nicknamed Anne Boleyn the 'goggle eyed whore'. There was a great deal of sympathy in the country for Katherine and in November, while Campeggio was still languishing with his gout, the King and Queen had passed through an open gallery at Bridewell Palace. A large crowd spontaneously cheered the Queen. Henry, sensing the public mood, summoned a group of nobles, judges and privy councillors to a conference the following Sunday. He spoke seriously and eloquently of his record as King. His rule had been prosperous. No enemy had oppressed them. He had invaded no realm without bringing back 'victory with honour', but, 'when we remember our mortality and that we must die,' the King went on, 'if our true heir be not known at the time of our death, see what mischief and trouble shall succeed to you and your children'. He reminded them of the Wars of the Roses, a time of 'mischief and manslaughter'. It was stirring stuff. Henry then turned to the matter in hand. God had sent him a fair daughter. She brought 'comfort and joy' to him and Katherine. Yet 'diverse great clerics' had said 'neither she is our lawful daughter, nor her mother our lawful wife'. When he had tried to marry Mary to the Duke of Orléans, even the French King's councillors had questioned her legitimacy.

Henry spoke movingly of his affection for Katherine: 'She is a woman of most gentleness, most humility . . . yea, and of all good qualities appertaining to nobility. She is without comparison, as I this twenty years almost have made true experiment.' If he were to marry again, he assured them, he would 'surely choose her above all other women'. If, however, it should be proven that his marriage was against God's law, then he would be 'sorrowful to leave such a good lady and loving companion', but he would be sorrier still to think how he had cheated them all of an heir to rule the kingdom through having 'lived in adultery to God's great displeasure'. These, said the King, 'be the sores that vex my mind, these be the pangs that trouble my conscience', and he appealed to them all to pray for him.[9]

There was a mixed reaction. Some sighed and were silent, some were sorry for the King and others favoured the Queen, but the Bridewell speech, coming as it did after the dreadful sweating sickness, made men ponder on the succession. Campeggio continued his delaying tactics. The legatine court did not open until 31 May 1529. Mary Brandon slipped quietly back to her country estates as soon as the Christmas festivities at Greenwich were over. She loved London and the court, but for once in her life must have gone gratefully away to the shelter of Westhorpe and the care of her children and stepdaughter. Suffolk was sent on an embassy to France. He was to canvas support for Henry's marriage to Anne from Francis I. This meant he was not among those who testified against Katherine in June 1529, even though he had been among Prince Arthur's attendants the morning after his wedding. Katherine made another visit to the legate before the trial opened. She would have preferred the case to be heard at Rome. Patiently Campeggio explained that it would be a procedural error, a discourtesy to his Holiness, who had personally appointed *two* legates, himself and Wolsey, to try the matter in England. He exhorted her to have courage and trust her counsel, assuring her, he wrote to Salviati, that 'nothing inconsistent with justice and reason would be done by us legates'.[10] He made a last attempt to persuade her to climb down gracefully by entering a nunnery. It would have vindicated the honour of Castile, freed the Emperor and the Pope from a tricky situation and afforded a great deal of relief to his own gout, but, he told Salviati, 'she does not accede in the least to these hints of taking vows'.

And so began the most famous divorce case in the history of Western Europe. The King and Queen of England fought each other in open court, each clinging obstinately to their own version of the truth. Henry aired his celebrated scruple, using Katherine's aborted pregnancies and stillborn children as incontrovertible evidence that God was displeased with him and had denied him a legitimate heir, because he had known his brother's wife. Katherine repeated that Arthur had never 'carnally known' her, which in brutal modern English meant no act of penetration ever took place, either on the wedding night or subsequently when they slept together at Ludlow. In short, Doña Elvira had been right, her Infanta had emerged each morning a virgin, but it did not seem like that to half the nobility of England, who had watched their beloved Prince go formally off to bed with her after the wedding feast. Nor did it seem like that to the gentlemen, now middle-aged but in 1501 lusty young squires of the bedchamber, who had heard Arthur call for a drink next morning, because he had been 'in the midst of Spain' and it had been thirsty work.[11]

Limited by the scope of Tudor medicine, they understood little of the illness from which their Prince had died. It was commonly agreed that the sweating sickness had hastened his end, but in the sixteenth century the term was used generically to cover anything which caused a persistent high fever from pneumonia to tuberculosis. Tuberculosis is characterized by night sweats. Several nineteenth-century writers assume the Prince died of consumption, which was the contemporary term for tubercular diseases in Victorian times. The fullest account of Arthur's death however, was left us by the herald chronicler, who wrote the official record of the royal funeral in the spring of 1502.

> The most pitiful disease and sickness that with so sore and great violence had battled and driven in the singular parts of him inward, that cruel and fervent enemy of nature the deadly corruption did utterly vanquish and overcome the pure and frendfull [healthy] blood without all manner of physicall help and remedy.[12]

The description, written probably about the time when Arthur's body was prepared for embalming, suggests he may have died of a malignant disease, which had taken hold before the pneumonia or some transient chest infection dealt the final blow. Two explanations fit the jigsaw of historical evidence volunteered so passionately and so positively before the legatine court at Blackfriars during the tense summer of 1529. One is that the deadly organism which blocked Arthur's lungs was indeed tuberculosis, and that he had suffered from it long enough for it to have spread through to other parts of his body including the testicles. In the early stages testicular tuberculosis is popularly believed to increase libido, but in its early stages testicular tuberculosis would have been compatible with erection, ejaculation even, but not with the sustained sexual performance which Katherine, looking back after twenty years of marriage to the more vigorous Henry, would have recognized as being 'carnally known'. The second possibility is that the deadly corruption noted by the herald chronicler was a cancerous growth. If this had affected the 'singular parts', no amount of youthful bravado could have enabled Arthur to conceal his disability from his beautiful young wife, which may explain why Katherine never reported back to the vigilant Doña Elvira that she had enjoyed full conjugal bliss. Cancer of the testicles frequently spreads later to the lungs, where its growth is often the cause of death. It is one of the tumours which are notorious for attacking in the patient's youth.

Henry did not attend the opening of the trial, but Katherine did. She made her entry, in the scene later immortalized by Shakespeare, flanked by four bishops and lodged a formal appeal for the case to be heard at Rome. Three days later both the King and the Queen appeared in person. It was a magnificent spectacle. The two legates in their scarlet robes sat upon chairs of cloth of gold with a long table before them. On the right was a canopy of estate for the King with a chair beneath it filled with rich cushions. On the left of the court was another chair, equally richly upholstered, for the Queen. She had been allowed to choose her own counsel, Archbishop Warham, John Fisher, Bishop of Rochester, Dr Nicholas West, Bishop of Ely, and the Bishop of St Asaph's in Wales.[13] There are three eyewitness accounts of the proceedings, Campeggio's, Du Bellay's and Cavendish's, and also Hall's version, which he had first hand from Campeggio's secretary. In addition there is the official court record, a bundle of documents in the British Library, half in English, half in Latin.[14] Cavendish's version is irresistible. It circulated in manuscript long before it was printed. Just as in Shakespeare, the crier began the proceedings, calling: 'King Henry of England come into the court.'

The King replied, 'Here my Lords.'

Then the crier called, 'Katherine, Queen of England come into the court.'

She made no answer, but rose from her chair to sweep past her counsel to the King's side of the court. Then, kneeling before him in a gesture of complete obedience, 'in the sight of all the court and assembly', she spoke in her heavily accented English:

> Sir, I beseech you for all the love that hath been between us and for the love of God let me have justice and right, take of me some pity and compassion for I am a poor woman and

a stranger born out of your dominion. I have here no
assured friends, and much less impartial counsel. I flee to
you as the head of justice in this realm. Alas Sir, wherein
have I offended you or what occasion of displeasure have I
deserved against your will . . . I take God and all the world
to witness that I have been to you a true humble and obedi-
ent wife, ever conformable to your will and pleasure.

I loved all those whom ye loved, only for your sake,
whether I had cause or no and whether they were my
friends or my enemies. This twenty years or more I have
been your true wife, and by me ye have had diverse children, although it hath pleased God to call them out of this
world, which hath been no default in me.

And when ye had me at the first, I take God to be my
judge I was true maid without touch of man. And whether
it be true or no, I put it to your conscience. If there be any
just cause by the law that ye can allege against me, either of
dishonesty or any other impediment to banish and put me
from you.

There was a good deal more. She did not only appeal to Henry's
memory of their wedding night, she called upon the whole
court's recollections of his father, 'accounted by all men the
Second Solomon', and her father, the highly intelligent
Ferdinand. 'They were both wise and excellent Kings', she
reminded him. They had been surrounded by 'men of as good
judgement as there are at this present time in both realms who
thought then the marriage between you and me good and
lawful'.

Katherine, from the moment she had been told she could
choose her own counsel, had been awaiting the arrival of Luis
Vives, the Spanish advocate expert in canon law whom she felt
most capable of putting her case before Campeggio. He would
have grasped the complexities of Julius II's bull, which had stated
tactfully in Latin that she had 'perhaps' been carnally known by
Prince Arthur. Much of the case was to turn on that 'perhaps',
which had been omitted from a letter which accompanied the
bull. The Emperor held the original letter, but a notarially attested

copy had been procured for the legates. Its arrival had dumb-founded Henry and Wolsey, since Wolsey's agents had tried to intercept the messenger sent to fetch it from Spain. Katherine went on:

> It is a wonder to me what new inventions are now invented
> against me . . . therefore I most humbly require you, in the
> way of charity and for the love of God, who is the just judge
> to spare me the extremity of this new court . . . And if ye will
> not extend to me so much impartial favour, your pleasure
> then be fulfilled, and to God I commit my cause.[15]

She rose from her knees and, making a low curtsy to the King, left the room, leaning upon the arm of her Receiver General, Master Griffith. The crier called her again, 'Katherine Queen of England come into the court', but she replied contemptuously, 'It makes no matter for it is no impartial court for me, therefore I will not tarry.'

'And,' recorded Cavendish, 'she departed out of that court without any further answer at that time or any other. Nor would she ever appear in any court afterwards.'[16]

Henry was visibly moved. 'She hath been to me as true, obedi-ent and as conformable wife as I could in my fancy wish or desire,' he admitted. Wolsey was also shaken. He had known since the summer of 1528 that Katherine urgently desired Spanish counsel, which he considered 'frivolous', but he seemed shattered that Katherine thought him the chief instigator of the divorce. 'Sir,' he appealed to Henry, 'I most humbly beseech your Highness to declare before all this audience whether I have been the chief inventor or first mover of this matter, for I am greatly suspected by all men.' The King simply repeated what he had said earlier at Bridewell, that during negotiations for a French marriage for Princess Mary the Duke of Orléans had questioned the girl's legitimacy; that this had bred a doubt which 'pricked, vexed and troubled' his mind; that he had first brought the matter up in confession with the Bishop of Lincoln, and he appealed to Archbishop Warham for corroboration.[17]

Cavendish makes no mention of Katherine's attack on Wolsey,

though he describes the occasion. After the formal citations, which took place on 18 June, the court held daily sessions. Because of her refusal to appear again, Katherine had been accused of contempt of court, but the trial had proceeded without her. Gossip and scandal abounded. What would now be called 'tabloid' versions were evidently circulating in London. Henry sent for Wolsey and spent an hour closeted with him at Bridewell, trying to persuade him to get Katherine to drop the case. Wolsey must have received a horrible dressing-down, for afterwards, when he took his barge to Westminster, his companion, the Bishop of Carlisle, on seeing the Cardinal wipe the sweat from his face, observed that it was a hot day and Wolsey replied wryly, 'If ye had been as well chafed as I have been within this hour, ye would say it were very hot.' As soon as he reached his own house he lay on his bed without any sheets, apparently utterly exhausted. Two hours later he was disturbed by Lord Rochford,* Anne Boleyn's father, who told him that Henry wished him to go at once with Campeggio and speak to Katherine at Bridewell. It would be 'much better for her honour than to stand the trial of the law and to be condemned'.[18] By this time popular support was mainly for the Queen. On 22 June Du Bellay sent off a magnificent dispatch to Francis describing some of the scenes outside the court. 'If this matter was to be decided by women,' he said, Henry would certainly 'lose the battle, for they did not fail to encourage the Queen at her entrance and departure by their cries telling her to care for nothing, and other such words, while she recommended herself to their good prayers and used other Spanish tricks'.[19]

In an earlier dispatch Du Bellay had confided his suspicions that Anne must be pregnant. This would explain Henry's incredible sense of urgency. 'I much fear that for some time past the King has come very near Mademoiselle Anne, therefore you need not be surprised if they want to hasten it, if her womb swells everything will be ruined,' he wrote.[20] Nothing could have been further from the truth, but the fact that all sorts of rumours were flying about the court and the town increased Henry's annoyance. The two

* Sir Thomas Boleyn did not owe all his advancement to Anne. He had been created Viscount Rochford in 1525.

legates set out to make another attempt to persuade the Queen to settle things privately. Cavendish recalled that when they arrived she was sitting sewing with her ladies. She came out of her privy chamber 'with a skein of white thread about her neck'. When she heard the Cardinals' errand, she told them 'to speak it openly before all these folks. For I fear nothing that ye can say or allege against me, but I would that all the world should both hear and see it.' Profoundly embarrassed, Wolsey spoke to her in his best diplomatic Latin.

'Speak to me in English,' she commanded. They again begged her to hear them in private. She again told them she distrusted her counsel. Did they really think, she asked cynically, any Englishmen would be

> friendly unto me against the King's pleasure, they being his Grace's subjects? Nay, forsooth my lords! And for my counsel those in whom I do intend to put my trust, be not here they are in Spain . . . I am a poor woman lacking both wit and understanding, sufficiently to answer such approved wise men as ye be both.

She took Wolsey by the hand and went into her privy chamber. Cavendish and the rest of Wolsey's attendants heard her voice raised, but they could not make out what she said.[21]

In Hall's account the language used by Katherine is a great deal stronger. Her meeting with the two legates takes place before the trial and her scorn rings down the ages. 'Is it now a question whether I be the King's lawful wife or no?' she asks. 'When I have been married to him almost twenty years and in the mean season question was never made before . . .' Then follows the speech which Cavendish reports she made kneeling in the courtroom before Henry. She points out the legal niceties of the Pope's dispensation, observes that neither Henry VIII nor Ferdinand of Aragon was such a fool that he would have allowed a marriage between herself and Henry without the proper legal formalities and then launches into a virulent attack on Wolsey. The content is similar to the speech Shakespeare gives her when she accuses the Cardinal of having a heart, 'so crammed with arrogancy, spleen and pride'.[22]

Hall's version is even more theatrical. It is tempting to dismiss it as a deliberate piece of invention, to assume the chronicler is indulging in a melodramatic propaganda exercise. For 'this trouble,' Katherine says, 'I only may thank you my Lord Cardinal of York, for because I have wondered at your high pride and vainglory and abhor your voluptuous life, and abominable lechery . . . of malice you have kindled this fire'. She accuses him of hating the Emperor 'Worse than a Scorpion, because he would not satisfy your ambition and make you Pope . . . therefore you have said, more than once, that you would trouble him and his friends and you have kept him true promise'. According to Hall, 'these words were spoken in French and written by Cardinal Campeggio's secretary, which was present, and by me translated as near as I could'.[23]

Hall, however, follows almost exactly the text of what seems to be an official copy of the court records. Lumped in with the depositions of those who swore Katherine and Arthur had lived as man and wife is a document in the Cotton Manuscript which differs so little from the King's Bridewell speech and the Queen's attack on Wolsey that it is certainly either another English copy of Campeggio's secretary's version or a draft of Hall's own translation.[24] The document also sets the scene at Bridewell, not in the courtroom, but the Queen's language is as virulent as in Hall's version. Since a strong case has been put for Anne Boleyn 'bringing down' Wolsey, it is intriguing to find Katherine attacking him with such venom. The Manuscript version seems to have been overlooked because of the more sensational material bound in the same volume, the scribbled depositions made by the clerks of the court, half in Latin, half in English, as one by one the nobility of England testified against their Queen.

The witnesses were interrogated in English and gave their answers in plain language. In the first drafts the clerks alternated giddily between the vernacular and the euphemisms of legal jargon, copying everything out later in neat script and faultless Latin for the records. The Earl of Shrewsbury, who had fought beside Henry VII at Bosworth and was nearly sixty, remembered how he and the Earl of Oxford, Arthur's godfather, had conducted the Prince to Katherine's bedchamber on their wedding night. He thought Arthur was fifteen, so must have consummated the marriage. He had consummated his own marriage, the Earl recalled, 'when he was not fifteen years of age and without knowledge of woman'. Shrewsbury recounted his own virility in the misty days of his adolescence in frank detail. *'In somnis pollutiones'*, wet dreams, scribbled the clerk.

'And,' continued the old soldier gallantly, he supposed Prince Arthur, being of the same age and 'lying with so fair a lady did carnally know her'. The Prince was 'a gentleman of a good and sanguine complexion and able he supposed for that purpose'. The Marquis of Dorset, who had also been present at Arthur's christening, spoke of the 'great multitude of noblemen and women' at his marriage, and of how among the merry, half-tipsy throng Arthur got into the bed where 'Lady Katherine lay covered under the coverlet, as the manner is of Queens in that behalf'. Sir Anthony Willoughby, who had been five years in Arthur's service by the time of the wedding, was most circumstantial. When the Prince had woken on the morning after the ceremonial bedding, four other gentlemen had been in attendance, Maurice St John, Mr Cromer, William Woodall and Griffith Rice, but it was to Willoughby that Arthur turned first, crying gaily, 'Bring me a cup of ale.' Flushed with his manly exertions, he had added, 'Masters, it is good pastime to have a wife.'[25] Like Shrewsbury, he supposed the Prince 'carnally knew the said Lady Katherine'. Wolsey's staff had scoured the length and breadth of the land for witnesses who had been present at the wedding, or who had served Arthur at Ludlow. Anthony Poynes, who had been a squire of the bedchamber, had retired to the Isle of Wight and Gloucestershire, but he corroborated Dorset's testimony. Elderly Sir William Thomas was brought down from Carmarthen. As one of the Prince's Privy Chamber, he had often conducted Arthur in his nightgown to the Princess's bedchamber door, received him in the morning and conducted him to his own room. 'They called each other Prince and Princess, man and wife,' swore the old Welshman, 'and were always so reputed.'

Two witnesses stuck up for Katherine. They were her own counsel, so from the start their testimony was not impartial. Nicholas West, the Bishop of Ely, on being cross-examined on oath, broke the seal of the confessional and vowed Katherine had told him on the testimony of her conscience (and again the clerk broke into Latin) that she had 'never been carnally known by the aforesaid Arthur'.[26] Perhaps the prurient sniggered in the alehouses. Perhaps the royal virility and the royal morality were secretly mocked. Perhaps Henry was filled with real distaste that so much scandal flew about the town, but there was an even greater sensation in store. On 28 June John Fisher, the venerable Bishop of Rochester, stood up in open court and thundered the very words Henry had used to his sister Margaret of Scotland: 'This marriage of the King and Queen can be dissolved by no power, human or divine.' For this opinion, reported Campeggio to Salviati, 'he would even lay down his life'. Dr Standish, the Bishop of St Asaph's, expressed the same view 'but with less polished eloquence'.[27]

In a secular and more cynical age it is difficult to rate the impact of Fisher's objection. He stood for all that was old and true and tried and holy. He had been confessor to Lady Margaret Beaufort. His 'Month Mind' sermon, delivered as her memorial, and his funeral sermon for Henry VII had both been printed in two editions. His sermon against Martin Luther circulated in five editions. His version of the *Penitential Psalms* soared into eight editions.[28] Here was the voice of reason and orthodoxy. The Bishop caused further excitement when Henry and Warham produced a paper with the signatures and seals of all the bishops in England. Rochester's reaction had the force of a headline-making sleaze allegation in our own time. Once again Cavendish's account is too lively to be omitted. Henry showed the paper to the two legates to prove that when his scruple first surfaced he had asked all the bishops whether he should seek further counsel.

'Ye have all agreed by writing,' said the King, and the Archbishop backed him up, saying, 'All my brethren here present will affirm the same.'

'No Sir, not I,' said Fisher. 'Ye have not my consent hereto.'

'Have I not?' snapped Henry. 'Look here upon this. Is not this your hand and seal?' and he showed him the document.

'No forsooth, Sire,' said the Bishop, 'it is not my hand nor seal,' and in open court he reminded Warham: 'I said to you that I would never consent to any such act, for it were against my conscience.'

The Archbishop argued that Fisher had allowed his name to be added after discussion, but the old prelate stood his ground.

'All which words and matter, under your correction my lord, and support of this noble audience, there is nothing more untrue.'

According to Cavendish, Henry swiftly tried to gloss things over. 'Well, well,' he said, 'it shall make no matter. We will not stand in arguement with you herein, for you are but one man.'[29] The court was swiftly adjourned until the next day.

Fisher probably swayed Campeggio more than the legate dared admit. He confessed his misgivings and his feelings of total inadequacy to Salviati, wished again that the English would not be in such a hurry over this matter and noted that Suffolk had been recalled from France. The Duke had left England on 17 May. He reported on his conversations with Francis directly to Henry, not to Wolsey. Louise of Savoy and the Archduchess Margaret were planning an elaborate summit at Cambrai to bring about peace between the Pope and the Emperor, France and the Habsburgs. Louise hoped Wolsey, with his vast knowledge of international affairs, would attend, but Henry refused to take the 'Ladies' Peace' seriously. He was too caught up in the events at Blackfriars and was absolutely determined the divorce should be brought to a swift conclusion.

Preliminary talks were already in progress at Cambrai. As Suffolk was already in France, it was rumoured that he might go to the conference as the English delegate, but the King finally settled for Sir Thomas More, the Bishop of London, and Sir John Hacket. Meanwhile, in Italy the French, who were clinging tenuously to Milan, were defeated by the Emperor's troops at the Battle of Landriano. This put an end to any serious expectation that Clement would rule against Katherine, whose appeal for the case to be heard at Rome reached the curia on 5 July. The Pope burst into histrionic tears and 'weeping, prayed for death'. He gave orders for the proceedings in London to be stopped. News reached Campeggio and Wolsey at the end of July. On the last day of the month the court was packed. The King's proctor had demanded that sentence should be passed. Henry himself was in the gallery. The legate rose and in elegant Latin adjourned the case on the grounds that the Roman ecclesiastical courts had started their summer recess. Nerves were strained to breaking point and Suffolk, who by this time had returned from France, is said to have banged the table, shouting, 'By the Mass, now I see that the old said saw is true, that never cardinal or legate did good in England.'[30]

With great dignity Wolsey is supposed to have reproached the Duke after the table-banging, reminding him that 'of all men in this realm, ye have least cause to dispraise or be offended with cardinals. For if I, simple Cardinal, had not been, you should have at this present no head upon your shoulders.'[31] He referred to the time he had saved Suffolk and Mary from the King's displeasure over their secret marriage in Paris. As cardinals, he pointed out, he and Campeggio could not proceed to judgement without 'the knowledge and consent of the chief head of our authority, who is the Pope'. For as long as there was a glimmer of hope that he could still perform some miracle of foreign policy which would outwit the coalition of Pope, Emperor and the Queen of England, Wolsey was safe. No one moved against him through August and September, though Henry declined his invitation to stay at the Moor, on the plausible grounds that there had been another outbreak of sweating sickness. After the defeat at Blackfriars Henry had gone to Greenwich and thereafter on his summer progress to Woodstock and Grafton. Stephen Gardiner became the King's principal secretary, while the Cardinal laboured to get the Queen to withdraw her demand for the case to be heard at Rome. He hoped John Clerk, the Bishop of Bath might persuade her to take matters no further, for the nobility of England found the idea of Henry being cited in an Italian court very distasteful. There was no ostensible break between the King and his chief minister, but when the new Imperial ambassador, Chapuys, arrived at the end of August he quickly sensed the winds of change. 'The affairs of the Cardinal are getting worse and worse every day,' he wrote.[32]

Suffolk was ill shortly after his return from France, so he was able to spend part of the summer in East Anglia with Mary and their family. With daughters of marriageable age and legitimacy a contentious issue, the couple took care to have Suffolk's own divorce papers notarially attested. The bull Clement had signed the previous year at Orvieto was formally exhibited to the Bishop of Norwich on 20 August. When the Duke returned to court to join the King in the autumn, the hue and cry against Wolsey had already begun. Inexorably, because of his position at court and in the council, Suffolk became drawn into the circle of Boleyn supporters. Anti-clerical feeling was high in England. Thomas, Lord Darcy, had prepared a book of articles against the Cardinal, listing all the evils which were supposed to have flourished in the realm since he came to power. He was accused of abusing his authority as Chancellor and his 'faculties legatine'. The 'wrongs, exactions and extortions' he had sanctioned were said to have impoverished 'all the nobles, and others the King's servants'. They were set out in detail. He was accused of 'wrongfully seizing the goods of Bishop Smith of Lincoln, Archbishop Savage, Bainbridge and other clergy'. Darcy's book outlined plans for overthrowing Wolsey's authority, creating legislation to see that 'never legate nor cardinal should ever be in England again'. Wolsey's palaces and possessions would be forfeit to the King.[33]

Campeggio went to say goodbye to Henry before returning to Italy. Wolsey accompanied him. The King was with Anne at Grafton, a small hunting lodge in Buckinghamshire. The only available lodgings were given to Campeggio, while Wolsey was obliged to borrow a room from Henry Norris, the chief gentleman of the Privy Chamber. In Cavendish's version of the story, this was humiliating for the Cardinal, who was accustomed to having his own suite of rooms when he visited the King. When the two legates entered the Presence Chamber, Wolsey knelt before Henry, who raised him up, took him to a window embrasure, where the others could not hear what was said, and spent a long time in private conversation with him. He told Wolsey to return next day, but when the Cardinal came back to Grafton, Anne had already whisked Henry away on a hunting expedition.[34] An account by Thomas Alward, written five days after the meeting at Grafton, tells a different story. Unlike Cavendish, who wrote with dramatic hindsight, Alward saw nothing unusual in the lack of accommodation. He noted 'as much observance and humility to my Lord's grace' from Suffolk, Rochford, Gardiner and Brian Tuke as was usual. He saw no evidence of a cabal, nor did he record the meeting at Grafton as a triumphant victory for Anne and her supporters.[35]

In Cavendish's version, after the King has lovingly raised Wolsey from his knees and spoken with him in the window embrasure, the Cardinal dines with the rest of the court, including his enemies, those very lords who had been laying bets that the King would bring him down. Anne and Henry eat in her chamber, where, says Cavendish disapprovingly, she already 'kept state more like a Queen than a simple maid'. With serpentine cleverness, Anne leads the conversation round to Wolsey, because she is piqued that Henry treated him so gently.

'Sir, is it not a marvellous thing to consider what debts and danger the Cardinal hath brought you in with all your subjects?'

'How so sweetheart?' asks the King.

'Forsooth there is not a man within your realm worth five pounds, but the Cardinal indebted you unto him by his means.'

After this subtle reminder of Wolsey's most unpopular tax, the Amicable Grant, a forced loan, which had caused widespread grumbling, Anne twists the knife further.

'There is never a nobleman within this realm that if he had done but half so much as the Cardinal hath done, he were well worthy to lose his head. If my lord of Norfolk, my Lord of Suffolk, my Lord my father or any other noble person within your realm had done much less than he, they should have lost their heads by now.'

To which Henry replies with magnificent understatement, 'Why then I perceive ye are not the Cardinal's friend.'[36]

All this was table talk, repeated to Cavendish by the waiters and written down several years after Anne had lost her own head, when it was fashionable to represent her as playing Delilah to Henry's Samson.

The Grafton meeting took place between 19 and 20 September 1529, but Wolsey remained in office until 6 October, when he chaired the council meeting in the normal way. When the end came, it was swift, sudden and deadly. On 9 October, the day the

Michaelmas law term began, he was charged in the Court of King's Bench with the offence of *praemunire*, which meant that in allowing the legatine court to be set up, he had broken the law of England by introducing an illegal foreign authority into the land.[37] Wolsey did not fight the charge. On 19 October he was deprived of the office of Chancellor. Norfolk and Suffolk paid a formal visit to take away the seals.

Three days later Du Bellay was writing his regular dispatch when news reached him that Wolsey had been 'put out of his house and all his goods taken into the King's hands'. The ambassador was so shocked that he stopped using diplomatic cipher and went on in ordinary French: 'Besides the robberies of which they charge him, and the troubles occasioned by him between Christian Princes,' he wrote, 'they accuse him of so many other things that he is quite undone. The Duke of Norfolk is made chief of the Council, Suffolk acting in his absence, and at the head of all, Mademoiselle Anne.'[38]

The Cardinal was sent to a modest dwelling in Esher, which belonged to the bishopric of Winchester, which he had recently acquired by exchanging it for Durham. He called together all the officers of his household to inventory his goods at York Place. Cavendish was present at the stripping of the Gilt Chamber, when long trestles were set up to hold all the gold plate and jewelled standing cups. The adjoining Council Chamber was piled with silver, and in the Long Gallery all the hangings, arras, cloth-of-gold curtains and canopies of estate were laid out, together with the richly embroidered copes, which had been specially designed for Wolsey to wear at his two colleges of Ipswich and Oxford.[39] Campeggio by this time had reached Dover, where an over-zealous customs official searched his baggage, expecting to find that the legate was smuggling money or plate out of the country for Wolsey to use if he fled abroad. When he reached Paris, Campeggio wrote to Salviati:

> Immediately after my departure from London, the design against the Cardinal of York began to develop with great violence, so that before I had crossed the sea, they had deprived him of the Seal and of the management of all

affairs ... He has done nothing in the past so far as ecclesiastical matters are concerned to merit such disgrace, and
therefore it may be thought his Majesty will not go to
extremes, but act considerately in this matter.[40]

Soon after Wolsey left for Esher, Henry and Anne went to York
Place to gaze in wonder at the spoils they had acquired. It was
rumoured throughout London that the Cardinal would be sent to
the Tower. Cavendish reported that all the citizens took to the
river to view his arrest. 'There were no less than a thousand boats
full of men and women waffeting [sic] up and down the Thames,'
but Wolsey boarded his barge at his private stairs surrounded by
his own gentlemen and sailed to Putney, where horses were waiting to take him to Surrey.[41]

Parliament met in November. Sir Thomas More became the
new Chancellor and Thomas Cromwell, who had been trained by
Wolsey, was made the King's chief secretary. Forty-four separate
offences were listed against Wolsey, ranging from obtaining legatine authority, which injured the King's prerogative, to the buying
of beef at the same favourable rate as the King's purveyors. The
Cardinal was accused of using the expression 'the King and I', as
though he had been Henry's equal, and of falsifying accounts. His
illegitimate son, Thomas Wynter, was set down for maintenance
of £2,700 a year, but Wolsey's accusers said he was only given
£200. Wynter was the son of a Mistress Lark, the daughter of a
Thetford innkeeper. He was rector of a church in Ipswich and also
drew revenues from Wells, Salisbury and York, while still in his
early teens. Wolsey was also charged with imprisoning Sir John
Stanley, a Cheshire gentleman, and of taking his farm to give to a
member of the Leigh family who had married another woman
who was supposed to have been Wolsey's mistress. Sir John,
broken-hearted, became a monk at Westminster Abbey. The
suppressing of small religious houses to finance the colleges at
Ipswich and Oxford was another grievance, as was failure to
prevent the spread of Lutheran heresies at Cambridge. The document listing the charges was signed by all the members of the
council, including Norfolk and Suffolk on 1 December.[42]

A week later Anne's father was made Earl of Wiltshire. Henry

by this time was lavishing jewels upon his sweetheart, whom
Chapuys in dispatches to the Emperor referred to sometimes as
'the Lady' but more often as 'the Concubine'. From 1 August, the
day after the legatine court adjourned, causing so much disappointment, the King sent almost weekly to Cornelius Hayes, the
royal jeweller. It was as though he was deluging Anne with love
tokens to compensate for the delays. 'A ring set with emeralds
delivered to Mistress Anne at Beaulieu 3 Aug. with numerous
other presents of jewellery,' runs the account. 'A crown of gold 27
August, a brooch 20 Oct.' Towards Christmas the gifts were
grander: 'For Mistress Anne, a diamond in a brooch of Our Lady
of Boulogne, a red riband with the same . . . 19 diamonds for her
head 29 December. Two bracelets for her set with 10 diamonds
and 8 pearls.' And by January: 'A ring with a table diamond, 19
diamonds set in the form of lovers' knots and 21 rubies set in
roses of crown gold.'[43] At the banquet held on 9 December to celebrate her father's promotion to his earldom, therefore, we must
picture Anne blazing with beautiful jewels and sitting beside
Henry in the place normally occupied by the Queen. She took
precedence not only over the two Duchesses of Norfolk, the leading noblewomen of the land, but also over the Duchess of Suffolk,
who as Dowager of France, had the right to be served as a Queen.
There is no record of Mary's outward demeanour on this occasion, but it is reasonable to assume that inwardly she was
outraged.

Wolsey spent the early part of 1530 at Esher, but in the autumn
he travelled north to visit the diocese of York. Although he had
held the see since 1514, he had never been formally enthroned as
Archbishop. He made a slow progress through Yorkshire, visiting
churches and confirming children. By 2 October he reached the
episcopal palace of Cawood, about ten miles outside York. The
dean and canons rode out to meet him, explaining that by the
statutes of the cathedral no archbishop could enter its precincts
until he had been enthroned. Preparations for the ancient ceremony were accordingly made to the delight of the local people.
Alarming reports reached London meanwhile that Wolsey was
living with all his customary pomp. They coincided with the
arrival in England of a papal nuncio, and Norfolk managed to

persuade the King that the Cardinal was involved in an Imperial plot to prevent him from remarrying, on pain of excommunication. Henry, who had had to shoulder a great deal more business than he ever expected, lost his temper in council one day, sweeping out of the room, shouting that 'the Cardinal was a better man than any of them for managing matters'. Since then, wrote Chapuys to the Emperor, the Duke of Norfolk, the Lady Anne and the Earl of Wiltshire had 'not ceased to plot against the Cardinal, especially the Lady.'[44]

Wolsey was arrested by the Earl of Northumberland, who was ordered to bring him back to London for trial. He was taken to Pontefract Castle under guard and then to Sheffield Park, the home of the Earl of Shrewsbury. The people of York wept with grief, for the Archbishop had achieved great popularity in the short time he had been in the north. On 26 November Sir William Kingston, the Keeper of the Tower of London, arrived with twenty-four men at arms. They escorted Wolsey to Leicester Abbey, but the Cardinal was so ill that he nearly fell off his mule. When the Abbot went forward to greet him, the Cardinal said, 'Father Abbot I am come hither to leave my bones among you.'[45] Three days later he died.

His last words were faithfully recorded by Cavendish, and included the famous epitaph, 'If I had served God so diligently as I have served my King, He would not have given me over in my grey hairs.'[46] When news of the Cardinal's death reached London, a company of actors sponsored by Anne's father played a distasteful comedy called *Of the descent of the Cardinal into Hell*. Norfolk ordered the text to be published, but Henry is said to have sighed, 'Every day I miss the Cardinal of York.' Suffolk's reaction to Wolsey's death is not recorded.

Ascendancy of the Boleyn party now came about as a matter of course. As Anne's influence increased, Mary Brandon spent more and more time in the country. She had plenty to occupy her. Until Anne should actually produce for Henry the longed-for male heir, the little Earl of Lincoln remained in the line of succession. There were also two daughters to be matched and married, a household to be run and charities to be patronized. Suffolk had built a grand new wing at Westhorpe, surmounted by battlements and decorated with terracotta figures. The total cost was £12,000, which came mostly from Mary's French revenues. In East Anglia she was still very much 'the French Queen', keeping state in a cloth-of-gold pavilion at the summer fair at Butley Abbey. She who had been equal in rank to Queen Katherine was not going to expose herself to situations where she took second place to 'the Concubine'. In 1532, when Anne was created Marquis of Pembroke, Mary was not present. She pleaded ill-health and she refused absolutely to accompany Henry when he took his mistress to Calais to meet Francis I. Marguerite d'Angoulême, the French King's sister, and his second wife, Eleanor, who was the Emperor's sister and Katherine's niece, followed Mary's lead, so that in the end no royal ladies were present.

Suffolk's daughters by his first wife, Anne Browne, were well matched. Anne Brandon married Lord Powis and somehow, despite her father's huge debt to the King, a respectable dowry was found for her. Her younger sister, who was called Mary, eventually married Thomas Stanley, Lord Mounteagle. During his minority the young man had been raised in Wolsey's household, where he had developed expensive tastes. He was heir to a large fortune and his wardship was bought by Lord Darcy and Sir John Hussey. It was expected that he would marry Hussey's daughter, but Brandon had managed to buy the young lord's wardship some time before the summer of 1527. Later that year or early in 1528, Lord Mounteagle married Suffolk's younger daughter. It seemed a sparkling match, but he was to cause his father-in-law considerable financial embarrassment. The Stanleys quickly produced an heir, which must have delighted the Brandons, but Mounteagle came into his inheritance in the summer of 1528. Apparently he could not restrain his delight. Suffolk was later obliged to pay his son-in-law's debts to thirty-one different creditors, including the King's goldsmith and the royal shoemaker.[47] Meanwhile, the bull confirming the legitimacy of Brandon's children by his second marriage had finally arrived in England. It was firmly exhibited to the Bishop of Norwich. He was old and blind, but Suffolk's chief steward, Sir Humphrey Wingfield, had it read aloud to him and notarially attested before several witnesses.[48]

This immediately made Mary's daughters, the Ladies Frances and Eleanor, much more attractive prizes in the aristocratic marriage market. In 1530 a match was discussed between Norfolk's eldest son, Henry Howard, Earl of Surrey, and the Brandons's eldest daughter. As Norfolk and Suffolk were at this point working amicably together in the council and considering the proximity of the two families' estates, it seemed a natural arrangement. In spite of the fact that Frances was the King's niece, however, Norfolk turned her down on account of her slender dowry. This is some indication of the Brandons' precarious finances. Lady Frances, who was thirteen at the time, seems to have survived the disappointment. An alternative match was soon arranged for her with Henry Grey, heir to the Marquis of Dorset. The Marquis had died in October 1530. Suffolk gained the approval of Henry Grey's mother, the Dowager Marchioness, for a marriage with Frances, and 4,000 marks was paid to the King as the first instalment to buy the young man's wardship.[49] He had previously been betrothed to the Earl of Arundel's daughter, whom he did not wish to marry. When she was sixteen, Frances married the young Marquis in a spectacular ceremony at Suffolk Place, arranged by her parents and attended by her uncle the King. Mary's younger daughter, Eleanor Brandon, was betrothed to the Earl of Cumberland's son, Henry, Lord Clifford.

Although Suffolk was outwardly pleasant to Anne Boleyn, Chapuys was in no doubt that the Duke secretly shared his wife's opinion of her, suppressing his real feelings only out of loyalty to the King. When the two Dukes and an impressive delegation of thirty councillors held a conference with the Queen at Greenwich on 31 May 1531, Katherine still insisted that she was Henry's lawful wife and that the case must be heard at Rome. Norfolk and Suffolk reported the proceedings to the King, who by this time had opened the question to debate through all the universities of Europe. Norfolk apparently gave a biased version of what had passed, but Suffolk told Henry that although the Queen was ready to obey him in all things, she recognized two higher authorities. Assuming these to be the Pope and the Emperor, Henry asked Suffolk whom he meant. The Duke replied bluntly, God and her conscience. Chapuys told Charles V that Henry made no answer to this. 'Suffolk and his wife,' added the ambassador, 'if they dared, would offer all possible resistance to this marriage.' Two days previously he had heard Brandon talking with the treasurer. They had said 'the time was come when all the world should strive to dismount the King from his folly'.[50] Chapuys believed that if the Pope could disabuse Henry of his scruple by declaring Katherine's marriage valid, instead of suspending sentence, then as a good son of the Church Henry would drop his plan for marriage with Anne Boleyn and opt, more reasonably, to keep her as his mistress.

As the 1530s progressed, the two Dukes became increasingly hostile towards each other. There were clashes in the council and conflict between their followers over a number of issues in East Anglia. In London the henchmen of the two magnates soon began to form bands. In time of war or national emergency, this meant that each Duke had a body of loyal retainers whom he could call upon, but bands were always a source of anxiety to Tudor governments as they aroused memories of the violent feuding between the great noblemen in the Wars of the Roses. Things reached a climax in April 1532. The Duchess of Suffolk may have been in London at the time, or she may have been in East Anglia. Anne by this time was wholly dominant at court, flaunting her beautiful dresses and flashing jewels. Katherine had been banished to Wolsey's old house, the Moor, in Hertfordshire and the King, full of plans for the visit he and Anne were to make to see Francis I, had asked the Queen to give up her jewels. Although Mary probably avoided the court, she had a clear idea of what was going on, and she was free to come and go to Suffolk Place, when her health permitted. She made one such visit in 1531, when Chapuys noted that she had come to London on business concerning her dowry. This was one of the areas in which Suffolk must have missed Wolsey's brilliant managerial talents, for he now had to see to the French payments himself, in addition to a great many other affairs.[51] Wherever Mary was, she had evidently made sarcastic remarks about Anne Boleyn. These had been repeated, eventually reaching the level of tavern talk, bandied about by the two Dukes' followers. When the Venetian ambassador, Carlo Capello, went to discuss business with

Norfolk, he found 'the whole court was in an uproar'. There had been a murder in Westminster Abbey. One of Norfolk's chief gentlemen, with a band of twenty henchmen, had goaded a group of Suffolk's men until violent fighting broke out. Sir William Pennington, one of Suffolk's gentlemen, tried to take sanctuary by the traditional method of throwing himself before the high altar, but he was pursued and brutally killed by Norfolk's men inside the Abbey.

Some said the affair was a private quarrel between the Southwell brothers, two of Norfolk's retainers, and Pennington, but Capello dismissed this theory. When he arrived at court, he was told that Brandon had gone off to 'remove the assailants by force from the sanctuary'. The King sent Cromwell after Suffolk, for 'the turmoil displeased him'. After making his own inquiries, Capello sent a report to the Doge and Signory. 'I am assured,' he wrote, 'it was owing to opprobrious language uttered against Madam Anne by his Majesty's sister, the Duchess of Suffolk, Queen Dowager of France. The affair of the divorce becomes daily more difficult.'[52]

Chapter 14
The King of England's Whore

As in all good divorces one of the children chose the summer of the Blackfriars trial to go through an educational crisis. The Duke of Richmond, by the time he was ten years old, was passionately devoted to manly sports and country pursuits. Although very bright, he was easily distracted and seemed to be losing interest in his studies. The northern gentry had little respect for learning. Delighted to have their King's son in the neighbourhood, they called on him almost every day, besieging him with invitations, 'some to hear cry at a hare, some to kill a buck with his bow, sometimes with greyhounds, and sometimes with buckhounds'. He was regularly asked to go hawking, or to try out a new horse, or tempted by 'many other devices found within the house, when he cannot go abroad'.[1] A humane solution was swiftly sought. John Palsgrave, Mary's old tutor, who had later been her secretary, was sent to take charge. A friend of Sir Thomas More, an admirer of Erasmus and one who had proved capable of instructing the King's giddy younger sister to speak passable French, he had something of a reputation as a remedial teacher. Henry had spoken earnestly to him in the gallery at Hampton Court: 'Palsgrave,' he said, 'I deliver unto you my worldly jewel – bring him up in virtue and learning.'[2]

The tutor quickly got to the core of the matter. His letters to the King and to More give us a lively glimpse of humanist education at its best. A Yorkshire monk had obviously taught Henry Fitzroy his elementary Latin. The boy simply did not pronounce the language like a gentleman, let alone like a King's son. Having just lost his front teeth, he was also inclined to lisp. To Palsgrave's fastidious ear, the child's vowels were horrible. 'The barbarous tongue of him that taught him his matins,' he wrote to More, 'is, and hath been, a great hindrance to me', but, he explained, he had found material to capture the little boy's interest, weaning him on to Greek with a hilarious comedy by Plautus. The tutor never let him go on working until he was weary and he tried to make his studies pleasant, 'in so much that many times his officers wot not whether I learn him or play with him'.[3] 'I do my uttermost best to cause him to love learning and be merry at it,' he wrote to Henry. He also asked the King to find an illustrator, reminding him that, 'It is a great furtherance in learning to know the names of things by their pictures.'[4]

Henry's reference to Richmond as his 'worldly jewel' spoke volumes. The poets, painters and philosophers of the Renaissance made a clear distinction between the spheres of the earthly and the heavenly Venus. In its purest form, heavenly love was supposed to elevate a man's soul to the contemplation of higher truth, while the earthly Venus inflamed a man's physical passions to the point where he pursued sensual pleasures to the exclusion of all else. The Church made an equally clear distinction between children conceived in a fit of joyous abandon with a mistress and those lawfully and carefully conceived in the marriage bed. Heavenly treasure to Henry would be the son he confidently expected Anne Boleyn to bear him, if only the Pope would proceed to sentence and declare his marriage to Katherine invalid.

In the summer of 1530, when the King of England was still canvassing the major universities of Europe for opinions in favour of his divorce and fulminating helplessly against Clement's decision to revoke the case to Rome, an ambassador from the Vatican arrived in Scotland. He joined James V and Margaret on a summer progress to the Highlands. They were magnificently entertained by the Earl of Atholl in a banqueting house made of green timber and woven birches. Its windows were glazed and the walls were hung with fine tapestries. The floor was laid with turf and covered with sweet-smelling herbs and flowers. For the King, his mother and their guest, every kind of local delicacy had been provided – white almond bread, gingerbread, beef, mutton, lamb, rabbits, swans, wild geese, partridges, plovers, duck, turkey, peacocks, blackcock, moorfowl and delicious capercaillie. The best wines were served, and fish ponds were specially dug and stocked with fresh salmon and trout. The King and his party stayed for three days hunting and feasting. Atholl spent £3,000 on their entertainment. When the guests were leaving, the papal nuncio was amazed to see the whole banqueting hall go up in flames. James coolly explained to him that it was the custom of the Highlanders to burn their lodgings when they departed.[5]

The King of Scotland was by this time seventeen. He had five illegitimate children by five different mistresses. Elizabeth Shaw, Lady Margaret Erskine, Euphemia, the daughter of Lord Elphinstone, and Lady Elizabeth Stewart all bore him sons; Elizabeth Beaton probably gave him a daughter. Sexual morality in pre-Reformation Scotland was very different from the standards set by the English court. While Anne Boleyn clung proudly to her virginity and would not give in to Henry until marriage was an absolute certainty, the Scottish noblewomen were proud to bear children of the royal half-blood.

Henry was shocked by his nephew's lifestyle, while Queen Margaret's dearest wish was to see her son settle down, preferably by marrying his cousin, Princess Mary, to cement the Anglo–Scottish alliance. That Henry's impending divorce would bastardize his daughter did not seem to trouble the Dowager Queen of Scots, though James himself was more astute. From childhood he had been brought up to assume he would marry the French King's daughter, Princess Madeleine, to whom he had been betrothed by the Treaty of Rouen. By 1524–5, when the marriage to Mary Tudor was being seriously discussed, Francis's fortunes had been at their nadir after the Battle of Pavia. With his sons held hostage, the French King wished to maintain his alliance with England. He was therefore not eager to honour the Treaty of Rouen, or revive the 'auld alliance' in any way that might offend Henry VIII. By that time the Duke of Albany was back in France and proposed a match for James with his wife's niece, Catherine de Medici, one of the richest heiresses in Europe. She was the Pope's ward, however, and Clement considered that Scotland was too remote and climactically unsuitable for one of her refined Mediterranean blood. The Emperor, meanwhile, offered his sister, Mary, the widowed Queen of Hungary, to

James. The young King tried to enlist Albany's help. He wrote a splendid letter to the former Regent, who was still technically his heir. It was a masterpiece of understatement. The King of Scots explained that he was under pressure to marry from his Parliament, principally to 'avoid the procreation of bastards, who in former times have caused great trouble in this Kingdom'.[6]

Like his father, James V was a gallant and adventurous lover. He would ride alone at night to visit his mistresses, and there are many tales of his exploits under the pseudonym of the Gudeman of Ballengeich. He often assumed disguises and delighted in surprising his countrymen by suddenly revealing himself as their King. James deeply shocked his mother by contemplating the possibility of marrying one of his mistresses, Margaret Erskine, later famed in Scottish ballads as 'the Lady of Lochleven'. As she was a noblewoman, there was no reason why the King should not have married her at the time she bore his son, James Stewart, who as Earl of Moray eventually became Regent of Scotland, but Margaret's child was born in 1533. By 1536, when the King realized how deeply he loved Margaret Erskine, she had already become the wife of Lord Lochleven. The Pope would not grant Lady Lochleven a divorce, and since James's council preferred the idea of a foreign princess who could bring a dowry with her, the King surrendered gracefully. He made various efforts to renew the pledges of the Treaty of Rouen with Francis, but the French King was still extremely protective of Princess Madeleine, a beautiful but fragile fourteen-year-old, and he replied that she was still too young.

Francis offered James the choice of three high-born French ladies instead: Marie de Bourbon, the daughter of the Duke of Vendôme; Marie de Guise, the Duke of Guise's daughter; and Princess Isabelle of Navarre. The Emperor, who had sent James the coveted Order of the Golden Fleece, continued to offer Mary of Hungary or Mary of Portugal and, since her own father seemed intent on bastardizing her, he gallantly defended the honour of his unhappy young cousin Mary of England. Later, when Henry's divorce became a reality, the English Parliament stripped Mary of her title and she was demoted to plain 'Lady Mary'.

During the summer of 1531, Mario Savorgnano, a Venetian visitor to England, went to see the Princess at Richmond. After he had presented his credentials, for he seems to have been in the diplomatic service, he was asked to wait in a large chamber, where there were some grand elderly gentlemen. Mary came down to them accompanied by her lady governess, the old Countess of Salisbury, and six maids of honour. Savorgnano described Mary as '15 years old, not very tall and with a pretty face'. She is 'well proportioned, with a very beautiful complexion,' he wrote. 'She speaks Spanish, French and Latin, besides her own mother-English tongue, is well grounded in Greek and under-stands Italian, but does not venture to speak it.' The visitors were then taken to a sumptuous banquet. When they returned to their lodgings they found that, after the custom of the country, they had been sent 'bouche of court', consisting of wine, ale and fine white bread. Savorgnano was enchanted by England. He espe-cially admired the great parks of the nobility, the custom of giving flowers to ladies, which the ladies then wore, and the fine malm-sey wines. He also commented on Henry's civilized treatment of Katherine: 'The King is of the opinion that the Pope [Julius II] was not authorized to grant the dispensation for his marriage to the present Queen, she being his brother's widow', adding, 'The Princess is much beloved by her father, who does not make any demonstrations against the Queen – always treats her with respect and occasionally dines with her.'

After visiting Hampton Court, the Venetian met Henry himself at a hunting lodge some thirty miles from London. He said he never saw 'a prince better disposed than this one. He is also learned and accomplished and most generous and kind', but even as a casual observer Savorgnano could not help deploring the divorce.

Seeking to repudiate a wife with whom he had lived for twenty-two years was a thing which detracted from Henry's merits, wrote the diplomat.

There is now living with him a young woman of noble birth, though many say of bad character, whose will is law to him, and he is expected to marry her, should the divorce take place, which it is supposed will not be effected as the peers of the realm, both spiritual and temporal, and the people are opposed to it; nor during the present Queen's life will they have any other Queen in the kingdom.[7]

Savorgnano's dispatch, which is among the Venetian diplomatic archives, was obviously considered 'informed comment', since he was clearly a visitor of some status. He also went to see Katherine at Wolsey's old Palace of the Moor in Hertfordshire, recording:

Her Majesty is prudent and good. In the morning we saw her dine: she had some 30 maids of honour standing round the table and about 50 who performed its service. Her Court consists of about 200 persons but she is not so much visited as heretofore, on account of the King. Her Majesty is not of tall stature, rather small. If not handsome, she is not ugly; she is somewhat stout and has always a smile on her face.[8]

This was the situation as it stood in the late summer of 1531, with Henry still longing to marry Anne for the sake of the legitimate boy child she was young enough to bear; with the Queen banished to a relatively remote country manor, steadfastly refusing to give up her status and attended by servants adamant that they would not call her 'Princess Dowager', the title she might expect if the divorce went through and she was declared 'Arthur's widow'; with the King's closest counsellors Suffolk and Norfolk reduced to a state of perplexity; and with the Pope still refusing to pronounce sentence, although he had already issued a bull forbidding Henry to remarry on pain of excommunication. Christmas at Greenwich that year was a dismal affair. 'There was no mirth because the Queen and the ladies were absent,' wrote Hall.[9] Anne, meanwhile, had been given Wolsey's old house, York Place. She was also allowed to occupy the Queen's lodgings at Greenwich, but Henry did not, dared not, allow her to preside at the Feast of Christ's birth, with its twelve days of attendant misrule and merriment. For the first time in his life, the King did not send New Year's gifts to Katherine and her ladies. Mary and Suffolk do not seem to have been present at Greenwich either, although they sent particularly elegant gifts, Mary some writing tablets and a gold whistle for the King to use hunting, or on board ship, and Suffolk a golden pomander.[10] Henry was deeply embarrassed by the Queen's present of a golden standing cup of such rarity, beauty and fine workmanship that it could not be omitted from the customary display on one of the sideboards, where it obviously attracted much attention.[11] The Queen henceforth was forbidden to send gifts to the King, and this ban also extended to the Princess Mary, although it was never enforced.

What Margaret of Scotland heard about the bizarre court her brother kept that Christmas is not recorded. Border disturbances had increased and Henry, wishing to prolong the peace established by the Treaty of Berwick, renewed his offer of a marriage between James and Princess Mary. He sent Lord William Howard to Edinburgh to discuss the matter, thereby delighting Margaret. Henry's energies were completely absorbed by the divorce and, in the spring of 1532, by the surge of anti-clericalism which led Parliament to demand reform in matters of religion. The King left Scottish policy mainly to the Earl of Northumberland, who was Warden of the East and Middle Marches. Archdeacon Magnus had long since been relieved of his post as English ambassador and sent from Edinburgh to preside over the Duke of Richmond's Council of the North, but as an expert on Border affairs, he went often to Berwick to confer with James's agents.[12] He was regarded as an authority on almost everything from cattle stealing to the price of Scotch salmon, though a little before his sixty-sixth birthday, wearied by the bad weather and appalling roads, he grumbled that he was 'feeblished and made weak with [so] many winter journeys'.[13]

After he had expelled the Douglases and confiscated Tantallon, the young King of Scots had set about restoring law and order. He reclaimed his mother's territory of Ettrick Forest and returned Newark Castle to her, dismissing its governor, the Laird of Buccleuch, and giving the office to Margaret's husband, Lord Methven. The King captured and hanged the notorious outlaw Johnny Armstrong, who for years had terrorized villagers on both sides of the Border, swearing he recognized neither the King of England nor the King of Scotland. The Douglases, meanwhile, remained outlawed. James hated them to the end of his life because of the indignities heaped upon him during his minority.

He continued to persecute the whole family with great violence and in 1537 had Angus's sister, Lady Glamis, burned as a witch. Henry, who never understood the Scots' temperament, as Margaret did, continued to support Angus. This enraged James, who announced that if his uncle went on aiding such a scoundrel, he would go to war with England. Henry probably did not take him seriously, but on 25 August 1532 he stipulated in a letter to Angus that 'in case we should move to actual war to the King of Scotland', the Earl should back him with his 'servants adherents and friends'.[14] Angus swore to recognize Henry's suzerainty over Scotland and Henry paid him an annual pension of £1,000. Horrified by the prospect of her son overthrowing everything she had striven to achieve for thirty years, Margaret offered her services as a mediator, but Henry's affairs became so complex and fast-moving during 1532–3 that the threats came to nothing.

Ecclesiastical matters now took precedence over all else for the King of England. Cynics and vulgarians are sometimes inclined to judge Henry at this point as either totally blinded by his passion for Anne Boleyn, or led greedily astray by the vistas of unlimited wealth and power which could be his if he threw off the shackles of papal domination. The unshakeable belief that it was his duty to produce a male heir to carry on the peaceful rule established by his father after the Wars of the Roses, however, was certainly one of the demons which drove him through the summer of 1532. The death of Archbishop Warham in August was an unexpected bonus for Anne and Henry. It opened the way for the King to nominate Dr Cranmer, the bright young cleric, formerly chaplain to the Boleyn family, who had first come up with the idea that Henry should consult the universities of Europe for opinions about the lawfulness of his marriage. Henry could not afford, and probably did not wish to provoke, any open breach with the papacy. He believed implicitly in the apostolic succession and was conservative enough to seek the Pope's confirmation of his new appointment. Warham had held the see of Canterbury for nearly thirty years. Despite his avowed intention to retire from politics, he had spent the last two years of his life trying to protect the traditional rights and privileges of the clergy against the onslaught of the secular powers.

When Parliament assembled in the spring of 1532, the Commons presented a list of small complaints to the King, the Supplication against the Ordinaries. This brought the lower house into direct conflict with the higher clergy, who drew up a document strongly defending their ancient franchises. Henry, having read it, handed it to the Speaker of the House of Commons with the remark, 'I think it will smally please you.'[15] On 10 May the grumblings of the Commons were replaced by a formal document demanding that future clerical legislation should be subject to the royal assent, and that a committee of thirty-two persons should examine all the franchises and liberties exercised by the Church courts. It was a bid to get rid of quirky and outdated clerical rights which sometimes interfered with the ordinary course of justice. Henry himself had gone down to the House of Lords one evening in March and, according to Chapuys, spent one and a half hours urging them to reform certain immunities, including the ancient right of sanctuary, which notorious criminals could claim as a means of evading the law.[16]

That an abuse of the sanctuary laws should take place just a few weeks after this harangue, in the precincts of the Abbey and while Parliament was still in session, was an irony. To Henry, Pennington's murder must have seemed a complete justification of his own views, although in the case of the famous affray said to have been caused by his sister's 'opprobrious words', the abuse had been the opposite of the type cited by the King. By killing Pennington on holy ground, the Southwell brothers had broken the ancient right, not by claiming it to evade justice but by blatantly ignoring its existence. There was widespread horror at such a sacrilege. It lent fuel to the fire with which Convocation, the assembly of bishops and higher clergy, rounded on those who were attacking their privileges. In May they quoted Henry's own words from his book against Luther as reason to resist the changes he now pressed upon them. The King retaliated by scrutinizing the oath to obey the Pope which bishops took at the time of their election. Its wording, he insinuated, infringed the royal prerogative and was tantamount to treason. Warham and Fisher fought like lions, but on 15 May the bishops surrendered, but not until Henry had been down to Parliament three times to address them. In pushing through the laws eventually embodied in the Act for the Submission of the Clergy, the King had 'bludgeoned his way to victory'.[17] The next day Sir Thomas More resigned the Chancellorship, while Warham, his imagination undoubtedly fired by the murder in the Abbey, reminded himself that he was the successor to the martyred Thomas à Becket and prepared, at the age of eighty-two, to resist his sovereign, as St Thomas had, if things came to such a pass.[18]

It followed that by June Henry VIII was in the mood for recreation. When the court moved to Eltham, detailed preparations for his visit to Calais claimed his attention. The King had developed a passion for bowls. A new bowling alley was built at Eltham at a cost of £4 4s 8d. Here Henry amused himself with the Duke of Norfolk, while Anne ordered her wardrobe for the summer progress. Twelve yards of black satin went into the making of a cloak to ward off light breezes and a further thirteen yards of black satin were ordered for a magnificent dressing gown lined with taffeta and stiffened with buckram. Perhaps these sensational outfits earned her the name of Henry's 'night crow', which was another of the popular insults heaped upon her. She also had a wonderful dress made up in green damask to set off her creamy complexion and dark hair. Henry had jewels brought to Eltham to the value of 1,600 crowns that month. Several messengers must also have gone between the French and English courts. On 18 June a Frenchman arrived with two beautiful sleek greyhounds, as a present from Francis.[19] Speculation must have run high as to whether Mary Brandon would relent at the last minute and join her brother's expedition.

Some courtiers believed Henry and Anne might follow the example set by Mary and Suffolk sixteen years earlier and marry secretly in France. They would then return to present Katherine, the Pope and the more recalcitrant members of the English clergy with a *fait accompli*. Certainly the couple set out for Calais in a holiday mood, which even the deliberate snubbing of Anne Boleyn by the Duchess of Suffolk, Marguerite d'Angoulême and Queen Eleanor could not dampen. Marguerite had been forthright enough in her objections to use the word that English courtiers dared not even think. Like the London fishwives, the French King's sister described Anne as 'the King of England's whore'.[20]

Henry, meantime, demanded that Katherine should surrender

some of the crown jewels. Predictably, she refused, pointing out that at Christmas she had been forbidden to send the King gifts. Privately she said she would not give up what was rightfully hers to adorn 'the scandal of Christendom'.[21] Mary's point-blank refusal to attend the meeting was widely interpreted by the French to reflect a similar view. To avoid her brother's wrath she pleaded ill-health, but Suffolk joined the party, as did the Duke of Richmond, very proudly and publicly accompanying his father the King, even though he had not quite reached his thirteenth birthday.[22] This allowed the stuffier element at court to deplore the spectacle of the King going to France with his mistress and his bastard in tow.

Anne's final recognition as future Queen came on 1 September, when she was made Marchioness of Pembroke in an elaborate ceremony at Windsor Castle. Much has been made of the wording of the patent conferring on her and her heirs the title 'Marquis'. This was to ensure that any future male child of hers would inherit the lands worth £1,000 a year which went with the new honour, but contemporary references do not dwell on the nicety, and certainly to most European observers she was now a 'Marquise'. As no royal ladies could be found to attend the ceremony, her cousin Mary Howard, Norfolk's daughter and Richmond's prospective bride, carried her crimson velvet train. Gilles de la Pomeroye, the French ambassador, was a guest of honour at the state banquet which followed. In the absence of an archbishop, Stephen Gardiner officiated, as the *Te Deum* was sung in St George's Chapel to celebrate the forthcoming meeting between the Kings of England and France. Ostensibly they were to discuss the possibility of setting out together on a crusade to expel the Turks from Constantinople.

On 11 October Henry and Anne left Dover aboard the *Swallow*. They sailed in record time to Calais. There followed ten days of pure holiday. In the English town which was part of mainland Europe, the couple were at last able to relax. They feasted on carp and porpoise, an unusual delicacy found more often in northern France than on English shores. They ate pasties of red deer and enjoyed the delightful gift of pears and grapes sent by M. de Montmorency, the Grand Master of France, to 'Madame la Marquise'. Henry lost heavily at dice, playing with Norfolk and

Señor Domingo, a rich London merchant whose name appears often in the King's Privy Purse Expenses.[23] Henry and Anne did not stay at the castle but at the Exchequer, a large house with new extensions including a tennis court, a gallery, two privy gardens and, for Anne, a suite of seven rooms with a bedchamber joined to Henry's by interconnecting doors. It was the perfect setting for the dissolution of the King's great scruple and the Marchioness's last great fear. If all the learned men who have asserted that Anne clung tenaciously to her virginity through Henry's six years of passionate wooing are correct in their assumptions that the title and patent with which she was invested on 1 September represented some final security to Anne Boleyn, then feminine intuition dictates that it was very probably in the Exchequer House at Calais that smoothly, delicately, luxuriantly she gave in. The point cannot be proved, but when he reached France proper the King of England bought a new hat with a feather in it and made an offering at the efficacious shrine of Our Lady of Boulogne.[24]

It had been agreed that each King should pay the expenses of entertaining the other. On 16 October the Duke of Norfolk met Montmorency to arrange the rendezvous with Francis which was to take place at Sandingfield on the Anglo–French border. Meanwhile, magnificent lodgings were prepared for the French King by the Calais merchants at the Staple Hall. On 21 October Henry went to meet Francis with an escort of 140 lords and gentlemen in velvet coats, forty guards and a train of about 600 horse. The two Kings made a great show of embracing and managed to ride for a mile alongside each other holding hands. They stopped to drink wine at a little thicket near the French border. As they approached Boulogne, the Dauphin, with his younger brothers, Henri d'Orléans and the Comte d'Angoulême, four cardinals and 1,000 horsemen rode out to meet them. It was an emotional moment. Twelve years had elapsed since Francis had been defeated at the Battle of Pavia and his sons held hostage by Charles V. At that time the whole English royal family had campaigned compassionately for their release, writing to both the Pope and the Emperor to exercise clemency. The Venetian ambassador noted that Henry kissed both the Dauphin and Prince Henri on the mouth, embracing them tenderly.[25]

Before the procession entered Boulogne, there was a magnificent gun salute. The French account records that more than 1,000 cannon were fired; the printed English version mentions that the sound could be heard twenty miles away. Henry rushed a semi-official report of the meeting *The Manner of the Triumph at Calais & Boulogne* over to Wynkyn de Worde, the royal publishing house, to be sold by John Gough in Cheapside.[26] According to the pamphlet, Boulogne was a very masculine gathering. 'There were no ladies or gentlewomen there.' In order that no one could complain of conspicuous consumption so soon after Parliament's proposals to divert clerical income to the royal exchequer, the pamphlet stressed the extravagance of the French King's appearance, his doublet 'overset all with stones and rich diamonds valued by discreet men at £100,000'. Francis's company, claimed the writer virtuously, 'far surpassed the English in apparel'.[27] When Henry returned the hospitality on English soil at Calais, the ladies, led by the lady Marquesse of Pembroke, appeared masked and danced before the French at supper. Anne was accompanied by Mary Howard, Lady Derby, Lady Fitzwater, her sister-in-law Lady Rochford, Lady Lilly and the wife of the English ambassador to France, Lady Wallop. Emphasis is laid on the official content of the meeting, with both Kings solemnly attending Mass, and a joint session of their councils, where the proposals put forward at Windsor Castle for an Anglo–French crusade against the Turk were discussed. For Henry, the most important achievement of the expedition was that Francis promised to use his influence to persuade the Pope of the English King's real need for remarriage. Two French cardinals were to be sent to plead Henry's cause at Rome forthwith.[28]

In the French account of the meeting, which is much lighter, Henry gaily sports a crimson satin doublet set with pearls and a robe of white velvet richly embroidered with gold thread, which was a gift from Francis. The Kings hear Mass in separate oratories and listen to sacred motets together. Henry entertains the French lords to a lavish dinner and nonchalantly remits 300,000 crowns of the previous French debt as a present to Francis's sons. Suffolk and Norfolk are invested with the Order of St Michael. When the party ride back to Calais, Henry wears cloth of gold over a slashed doublet fastened with diamonds and rubies. He lays on another magnificent banquet, playing host in violet cloth of gold with a jewel as big as a goose's egg about his neck. There is no effort to conceal conspicuous consumption. Francis, lodged at the Staple Hall, sends Anne a gift of a diamond worth 15,000 or 16,000 crowns. Henry cohabits openly with 'La Marquise de Boulan' and proudly presents his son of the half-blood, the Duke of Richmond, to the King of France. To the French chronicler, all these things seem very natural in the courts of princes.[29]

At some point between Christmas 1532 and New Year 1533, Anne Boleyn became pregnant. The King did not doubt for an instant that she was bearing his heir. On 25 January Cranmer performed a secret marriage to ensure that the child would be born legitimate. According to tradition, the ceremony took place before first light in a room over the gatehouse at Whitehall. Although the bulls from Rome had not yet arrived confirming that Dr Cranmer would be the new Archbishop, it was widely assumed that his appointment would go through. Chapuys wrote frantically to the Emperor to warn of the prospective primate's radical leanings. 'If the Pope knew the reputation Cranmer has here of being devoted heart and soul to the Lutheran sect, he would not be hasty in granting the bulls,' he scribbled.[30] Yet Clement assented, and by March letters appointing the King's nominee to the ancient see of Canterbury arrived in England. At the opening of Parliament, Andrea del Borgho, the papal nuncio, had appeared enthroned beside the King. He was warmly received at court. There was not the slightest sign of any breach with orthodoxy. Two weeks after his appointment, however, Cranmer summoned Henry to a private hearing to ask him why he had lived for twenty years in sin with his brother's widow. As Archbishop, he explained to Henry, he must now look into 'the great cause of matrimony' which was causing so much disturbance among the common people. After a brief hearing at Dunstable, he pronounced the marriage between Henry and Katherine void.

Anne and Henry could not keep their secret much longer. Anne apparently did not wish to do so. One day she shocked Chapuys by telling Sir Thomas Wyatt that she felt a craving for apples. The King, she said, had told her that she must be pregnant and she had replied that this was not true, but she had then burst into hysterical laughter before returning to her room.[31] Whether the King's sister knew the couple's secret is unrecorded. The Duchess of Suffolk's last glittering social appearance in London was as hostess at Suffolk Place for the wedding of her daughter Lady Frances to the young Marquis of Dorset. If the Venetian ambassador's assumption is correct, and there was blatant enmity between Anne and Mary, it is to be hoped that the King's new wife had the tact to keep away. It was one of those tricky pieces of etiquette which Charles and Mary Brandon had grown accustomed to facing with aplomb. Sixteen years earlier at Lady Frances's christening at Bishop's Hatfield, when the godmothers had been Queen Katherine and Princess Mary, neither of whom could be present, Lady Anne Boleyn had sponsored the new-born child at the font.[32] To exclude her from a family gathering would have been offensive to Henry, but there is no record of her attendance, or of anything untoward ruining Frances's wedding day.

After the celebrations at Suffolk Place, Mary travelled back to Westhorpe, taking her younger daughter, Lady Eleanor, with her. The Duchess must have drawn on her last reserves of energy for Frances's marriage. She was ill as soon as she got home. Suffolk remained at court, making a hurried trip to Westhorpe in May to see his wife, but even though it must have been apparent that Mary's illness was serious, he quickly returned to London to supervise the arrangements for Anne Boleyn's coronation, which was scheduled for 1 June. On 25 June Mary died at Westhorpe. Some said the shock of learning her brother had secretly married Anne and that she was carrying his child, killed her. The problems of arranging a state funeral for the Dowager Queen of France, which would require the presence of French heralds and mourners from over the Channel, must have been immediately apparent to Henry and Suffolk, who as part of his duties as Lord High Steward had organized all the details of Anne's great triumph. In a doublet dripping with pearls, riding a charger trapped with crimson velvet, Suffolk had directed the whole show, from the new Queen's entry into the Tower on the eve of her procession through London, to the great banquet in

Westminster Hall, where 800 persons had sat down to dine off courses which included twenty-eight to thirty-two separate dishes.[33]

There was no court mourning for Mary. Drained of all energy, Suffolk hurried back to Westhorpe, where her body was embalmed and placed in a lead coffin. It was not the custom for a husband to attend his wife's funeral, so whatever his private grief, after paying his last respects, he returned to London to join the King. For three weeks Mary lay in state in the chapel at Westhorpe. Her coffin was covered by a pall of richly embroidered blue velvet. Wax tapers burned day and night, while her family and attendants kept constant vigil. On 10 July Henry ordered a Requiem Mass to be sung at Westminster Abbey.[34] In East Anglia arrangements were still being made for the funeral. Francis sent a French pursuivant to help the English heralds work out the correct ceremonial. The first official mourners arrived at Westhorpe on 20 July. Daily Masses had been offered in the chapel, but now, led by the young Marchioness of Dorset, who was chief mourner, with her brother, the eleven-year-old Earl of Lincoln, the family assembled for the solemn funeral. Lady Eleanor came after her brother and sister, accompanied by Lady Catherine Willoughby, Suffolk's ward. Mary's stepdaughters, Lady Powis and Lady Mounteagle, came next. The family attended the first Mass of the day, then took breakfast together in the house which had once been so filled with Mary's laughing presence.

The procession formed up in the courtyard. Six gentlemen lifted the coffin from the chapel, placing it on a carriage draped with black velvet and drawn by six horses trapped in black. A pall of black cloth of gold was placed over the coffin, upon which rested a beautiful funeral effigy of the late Queen in her robes of state, a golden crown on her head and a sceptre brought specially from France in her hand. In front of the coffin 100 poor men in black carried wax tapers. Immediately behind the young Marchioness, escorted by her husband, rode a palfrey accoutred in black velvet. Lord Clifford, who was to marry Lady Eleanor, rode beside them, while ten noblewomen who had served Mary at various times rode single file behind them. Next came two carriages with the Queen's gentlewomen and lastly the yeomen and servants. As the cortège passed through the Suffolk villages, deputations came from each parish to pay their respects and offer condolences. It was two o'clock before the procession reached Bury St Edmunds, where the abbot and monks received the mourners and the Bishop of London waited in full pontificals. A hearse had been prepared for the coffin, all hung with black drapes, fringed and embroidered in gold with Mary's arms and her gentle motto, '*La volonte de Dieu me suffit.*' Banners embroidered with the symbols of Lancaster and York, the Tudor portcullis and the fleur-de-lis, adorned the church from the gate of the monastery right up to the high altar. The monks began to chant the solemn dirge and the French herald cried out at proper intervals, 'Pray for the soul of the right high and excellent Princess and right Christian Queen Mary, late French Queen, and for all Christian souls.'[35]

While the monks of Bury St Edmunds continued to offer Masses for the repose of Mary's soul, Thomas Cromwell was pushing through Parliament the acts which were to sever the English Church from Rome. The Act of Appeals, with its vague and famous preamble starting 'This realm of England is an Empire', was a device to prevent Katherine attempting to get the Pope to overturn Cranmer's annulment of her marriage. The King of England, it declared, had 'whole and entire power' to decide matters temporal and spiritual. The Act of Dispensations forbade the issuing of special licences and the Act in Conditional Restraint of Annates proposed to annex episcopal taxes which had previously been paid to the Holy See for the use of the crown. The Act for the Submission of the Clergy also made law the changes discussed in 1532 which had caused Sir Thomas More to resign as Chancellor. Meanwhile, the Duke of Norfolk, who had been absent from his niece's coronation, was in Lyons, where he hoped to join Francis, who was due to meet the Pope in Marseilles. News reached Norfolk that on 11 July Clement had condemned Henry's marriage to Anne and ordered him to take back Katherine on pain of excommunication. It is said that on learning of this development the Duke nearly fainted.

Chapter 15
I Am Weary of Scotland

To godfearing Englishmen, excommunication of the King was a terrible sanction. It could bring in its wake excommunication of the whole realm, insurrection, rebellion, civil war. Clement's sentence was suspended until September, the month in which Anne gave birth, not to the boy child predicted by the astrologers, but on Sunday 7th at three o'clock in the afternoon, to a girl. She was christened Elizabeth after the King's mother in the Church of the Observant Friars at Greenwich, where Henry himself had been baptized. A *Te Deum* was sung at St Paul's, but the jousts planned to herald a new prince into the world were cancelled. Chapuys crowed over the King's discomfiture. For this, Henry had quarrelled with the Pope and the Emperor. He had alienated his people by his treatment of Katherine, who, recently removed to the Manor of Buckden in Huntingdonshire, still stubbornly refused to accept the title of Princess Dowager. He had bastardized his true daughter, the Princess Mary, and allowed legislation to go through Parliament which Chapuys thought so outrageous that it would surely have to be repealed at the next session.

Lord Mountjoy had been chosen to head the first deputation sent to Katherine to inform her that Anne was Queen of England and that she henceforth should be referred to as the Princess Dowager, or as Arthur's wife 'the King's dearest sister'. When shown the document which Mountjoy brought with him she struck out the words 'Princess Dowager' wherever they occurred. 'Should I agree to your persuasions,' said Katherine, 'I should be a slanderer of myself and confess to have been the King's harlot these four and twenty years.'[1] Princess Mary rebelled with equal force. Suffolk was chosen to make the next attempt and, complaining that he would rather have broken his leg than go on such an errand, he reached Buckden on 18 December. He was to explain to Katherine that her servants should no longer address her as Queen, and that Henry proposed to send her to Fotheringhay. She announced she would not go. Brandon lost his temper and began to shout. Katherine slammed the door of her bedchamber in his face, and left the Duke raging and blustering at a piece of solid oak. She resisted him for five days, during which his men took down all the furniture and hangings from the great hall, but when the Queen said that if he wished to remove her from the premises, he must first break down the door, the Duke's courage failed him. Watched by the people of Buckden he made a few arrests and returned to London.

Anne conceived again early in 1534. Henry excitedly ordered a new cradle from Master Cornelius Hayes, his jeweller and silversmith, but by July the Queen miscarried. This meant the only legitimate male heir in line of succession to the English throne that summer was James V, for in March 1534 Charles Brandon lost his only son, Henry, Earl of Lincoln, who died nine months after his mother's funeral. In 1532 James had issued an ultimatum that if his uncle did not stop befriending the Earl of Angus, he would be prepared to go to war with England. Margaret had offered to mediate between her son and her brother. She was certainly influential in bringing about the renewal of the Treaty of Berwick, which was signed on 12 May 1534. Both sovereigns promised to observe peace between England and Scotland for as long as they lived. James also formally recognized Henry's marriage to Anne Boleyn.

Early in 1536 Margaret persuaded her son to agree to a meeting with Henry. The English King wanted it to take place at York, but James refused to go further south than Newcastle. His council was not enthusiastic about the idea. The bishops feared Henry might infect his nephew with his own zeal for the reformed religion, and Scottish relations with the Holy See were amicable. Characteristically Margaret prepared for the meeting between her son and her brother by buying new clothes. Carried away by accounts of the Field of Cloth of Gold and the more recent Anglo-French summit at Calais, she spent a staggering total of £20,000 Scots on equipping herself. When it became clear that the meeting would not take place, she wrote to Thomas Cromwell, who though technically still 'Master Secretary' had effectively replaced Wolsey as the King's chief minister. Margaret asked Henry to reimburse her for the sum she had spent on her wardrobe, because her rents from Ettrick Forest had been reduced by Border fighting. She wrote on 18 July 1536 and her timing could not have been worse. On 19 May Anne Boleyn had been executed, accused of adultery with six men, one of them her own brother. That the charges were trumped up, that it has since been amply proven that the Queen was not even under the same roof as her supposed lovers on the nights when some of the offences were alleged to have occurred is not important to our story.[2] Henry was in no mood to respond to his thrice-married sister. Ever the optimist in matters of the heart, he had at last found a creature who matched up to his expectations of womanhood, the virtuous and docile Lady Jane Seymour, a paragon of gentleness and submission.

His reply to Margaret was severe. He reminded her that their father had provided her with an ample dowry and that her son, the King of Scotland had a duty to support her. 'You must not ask me to disburse notable sums,' he wrote, 'merely because you are my sister.'[3]

Anne Boleyn's death threw the succession into further confusion. The Act of Supremacy declaring Princess Elizabeth heiress to the English throne, had ruined Princess Mary's prospects in the European marriage market. Chapuys thought she would be lucky even to marry a Duke. Throughout 1533–4 he had quixotic plans to rescue her by spiriting her out of the country. He even dreamed of a Catholic movement for her restoration, led by the gallant young King of Scots, but by the summer of 1536 the position had changed. Anne's divorce was announced before her execution and Elizabeth joined the line of royal bastards. The fortunes of Mary and Richmond were in the ascendant, particularly after Henry got hold of a rumour that Anne Boleyn had tried to poison them. According to Chapuys 'when the Duke of Richmond went to say good night to his father and ask for his blessing, after the English custom, the King began to weep.' Henry said that Mary and Richmond were 'greatly bound to God for their deliverance'.[4]

A savagely worded Act of Succession of July 1536 formally barred the two-and-a-half-year-old Elizabeth from inheriting the crown and deprived her, like her sister, of the title of Princess. It was an act of treason to refer to Henry's daughters in any other way than as 'the Lady Mary' and 'the Lady Elizabeth'. Nevertheless Jane Seymour strove to get Mary reinstated in her father's favour, and Elizabeth was certainly back at court by the autumn, when the royal family were at Windsor Castle, during the rising in the north known as the Pilgrimage of Grace. Cromwell's religious reforms had not been popular. Wild rumours circulated that the King's chief minister, a layman, was trying to gain direct control over the Church. It was even believed that he intended to marry the Princess Mary, abolish parish churches and introduce a tax on the eating of white bread.[5] Suffolk was sent to quell the rising in Lincolnshire, but the men of Yorkshire, Lancashire, Cumberland, Westmoreland and Durham crossed the River Don intent on marching to London. They faced the forces of Norfolk and the Earl of Shrewsbury, but they did not give in until December, when Norfolk promised there would be a free Parliament at York to discuss their grievances.

Against this background of political unrest, there was a further domestic imbroglio to upset relations between Henry VIII and his sister. Margaret's daughter by Angus, Lady Margaret Douglas had been brought up at the English court. She had been one of Anne Boleyn's ladies and, as the King's niece, was automatically his ward. She had managed to fall in love with Thomas Howard, a younger brother of the Duke of Norfolk. There had been an exchange of gifts. She had given him her miniature and he had given her a cramp-ring. When this indiscretion came to light, Henry was furious. Lord Thomas was sentenced to be executed and, technically, Lady Margaret was liable for the same punishment. A clause was added to the Act of Succession, stressing that it was a capital offence to 'espouse, marry or deflower being unmarried' any of the King's female relations. Commenting to the Emperor on the severity of the measures, Chapuys observed that Margaret Douglas was blameless, since in her case 'copulation had not taken place'. Even if it had, he went on drily, the Princess of Scotland could scarcely be blamed, 'seeing the number of domestic examples she has seen and sees daily'.[6]

Henry wrote thunderously to his sister about her daughter's misdemeanour. 'She hath behaved herself so lightly as was greatly to our dishonour,' he fumed.[7] Margaret had scant sympathy with her daughter. She threatened to disown the child she had scarcely seen, if she did not obey her uncle in a more fitting manner. After a short spell under the surveillance of the Abbess of Sion, Margaret Douglas returned to court, quite undeflowered, but penitent enough to have written several abject letters to Cromwell, promising that she had erased all feelings for Thomas Howard from her heart. She remained at the English court for a further eight years, a pawn, like her cousin Mary, to be shifted about in her uncle's diplomatic alliances, until he finally married her to the Earl of Lennox a little before her twenty-eighth birthday. The whole episode served to reinforce Henry's conviction that Margaret's surviving children were hopelessly tainted by their mother's passionate and sensual nature. Queen Margaret meanwhile had striven relentlessly throughout 1536 to promote the meeting between her son and her brother, scheduled to take place in York at Michaelmas. She had faced the opposition of the Scottish bishops, who were trying to postpone or prevent the meeting. She had also fallen out with James by speaking home truths over his plan to marry Lady Lochleven.[8] His mother's interference had made the young King very angry. Margaret, however, was determined to further the English alliance. She had even offered to go to York herself to meet Henry. In a private interview with his ambassador, Lord William Howard, she confessed her longing to retire to her homeland in one heartfelt phrase, 'I am weary of Scotland.'[9]

James V meanwhile had his own matrimonial plans, which did not include any kind of mesalliance with his cousin, the unfortunate Lady Mary. Having established a further truce with England, he evaded the meeting with his uncle and set sail on a private visit to France to see the bride King Francis now offered him,

Marie de Bourbon. In July his first expedition had been curtailed by storms. The King fell asleep and woke to find his ship heading back to Scotland. Sir James Hamilton, having deemed it too dangerous to continue, had steered the vessel to safety. Margaret in a fit of motherly anxiety wrote to Henry to say her son had almost lost his life on the high seas. Undeterred the King of Scots set out again in September, this time with seven ships and a proper retinue of lords spiritual and temporal. He prayed to Our Lady of Loretto for a happy voyage and ten days later reached Dieppe.

When James arrived the whole French court was in mourning for the King's eldest son, Dauphin François, who had died in August. The loss must have brought back memories to Francis of the deaths of his two older daughters, Louise and Charlotte. Although he had been constantly unfaithful to her, the French King missed Queen Claude. His marriage to the Emperor's sister, Eleanor, had not been a sparkling success and he was deeply depressed by the death of François. The new Dauphin, Prince Henri, welcomed James and conducted him to his father's bedchamber. When Henri knocked, Francis asked who had come to disturb him. The Prince replied James V, whereupon the French King bounded out of bed, embraced the King of Scots and showed him 'love and favour so fervently, as he had been his own natural son'.[10] The King asked the Parlement of Paris to welcome James as 'a son of France' and to wear scarlet robes for the occasion. The Parlement grumbled that scarlet was only worn for Princes of French blood. Black was the customary garb for receiving foreign dignitaries. Francis ordered them to put on scarlet and enthusiastically set about organizing a round of festivities, but when James set eyes on Marie de Bourbon, the lady he had come to meet, he was unimpressed.

The radiantly beautiful Princess Madeleine was by this time sixteen. The young couple, who had been destined for each other since childhood, fell in love. Reluctantly Francis gave them his blessing, for both Kings wished sincerely to renew the 'auld alliance', which they confirmed in November by the Treaty of Blois, but Francis had misgivings about his daughter's health. With magnificent ceremony James and Madeleine were married at Notre Dame de Paris on New Year's Day 1537. The King of France, the King of Navarre and seven cardinals were present. The Duke of Vendôme's brother, the Cardinal of Bourbon, officiated. Some time later his unfortunate niece, the jilted Marie de Bourbon, became a nun.

After the wedding James and Madeleine remained at the French court until the spring. The people of Paris took a great liking to 'le beau Roi d'Ecosse' and the couple were fêted extravagantly. They arrived at Leith on 19 May 1538. Madeleine gathered up two handfuls of Scottish earth, as a public gesture that she was Queen. The French historian Brantôme, describing her 'high and lofty nature', said she had dreamed of being a Queen all her life. It was not to be. Queen Margaret welcomed her new daughter-in-law; Henry VIII congratulated his nephew formally and Sir David Lindsay, who had been created Lyon King of Arms, made extensive preparations for Madeleine's coronation. She was to have ridden in triumph into Edinburgh, as Margaret had done with James IV thirty-four years earlier, but by 7 July Francis's fears for his daughter's health proved correct. She died at Holyroodhouse. Davy Lindsay wrote a tragic lament, *The Deploration of the Death of Queen Magdalene,* describing all the fine preparations made for her state entry into the capital. Instead of riding into Edinburgh under a golden canopy of estate she lay under a funeral pall, while the Provost of the city and all his dignitaries were dressed in purple, black or brown. Death, the untimely reaper, had turned the cloth-of-gold gowns which the Scottish nobility had ordered for her coronation 'all to sable'.[11]

During James's absence in France, Margaret had been made Regent of Scotland. Her third husband, Lord Methven, however, had proved worse than Angus. He had stolen her rents and become the lover of Lord Atholl's daughter, Janet, by whom he had a son. Margaret lost no time in seeking another divorce. Inspired by her brother's example in consulting the universities of Europe about the validity of his marriage, she had her case researched and supported by forty famous provers. As wild and scandalous rumours were once more flying about Scotland, Henry sent Sir Ralph Sadler to Edinburgh to investigate. When James returned with his bride, he stopped his mother's divorce proceedings. Margaret believed

Methven had bribed her son, and had persuaded him that she intended to return to Angus. She stole across the Border into England, but was brought back by Lord Maxwell.

Margaret was forty-nine. She begged Henry, since she was now 'his only sister' to protect her. She wished only to 'live like a Princess' as the King their father intended. She complained that she was not allowed the use of any of her dower palaces, that she was obliged 'to follow her son about like a poor gentlewoman' instead of being treated with respect and honour.[12] The following summer James re-married. Margaret pulled herself together to welcome her new daughter-in-law, Marie of Guise. She wrote again to Henry to ask for money for clothes, so that she might welcome her son's second bride in style. This letter was pointedly ignored. Marie of Guise was a devout Catholic, and she was also intelligent, warm-hearted and supremely tactful. She managed to make Margaret regain her self-esteem. She saw to it that the 'old Queen' as the Scots unflatteringly called their Dowager, was often at court. Marie's first child was born in May 1539. By July the Queen of Scotland was starting her second pregnancy. Margaret fell into the role of grandmother joyfully and gracefully. She became reconciled with Methven, although in her later years she became deeply attached to the memory of Angus, whom she had loved so much, and who had treated her so badly.

Margaret and Methven lived mostly at Stirling, but James, impressed by the beautiful chateaux and fairy-tale palaces he had seen in France, restored Linlithgow and built Falkland Palace, where he and Queen Marie spent much of their time. Henry wrote hardly at all to Margaret, though he made various efforts to interest James in the reformed religion. If the King of Scotland would follow his example and seize the property of the greedy prelates and monks, ran one such letter, he would be able to give up keeping sheep. James, much influenced by his Queen and Cardinal Beaton, continued to burn heretics, but an extreme form of Protestantism was spreading in Scotland. The King began to realize that he was not in a strong position to declare war upon England, or lead as Chapuys had suggested, a Catholic counter-attack. He agreed to meet Henry at York, but once again enraged his uncle by failing to turn up.

In April 1541 the two baby Scottish Princes died within a week of each other. Their sorrowing parents turned to Margaret for support. She wrote to Henry explaining she had 'done great diligence to put my dearest son and the Queen his wife in comfort'. She was constantly with them and apologized to Henry for the shortness of her note, 'I pray your Grace to hold me excused that I write not at length ... I can get no leisure.'[13] James became deeply depressed. He followed the pattern of his father James IV, blaming himself for past mistakes.

He grew obsessed with the belief that he had treated Angus's sister, Lady Glamis, unjustly. When he had her burned at the stake, James had believed she was trying to poison him. Fresh evidence which came to light after her death suggested she had been innocent of the charges of treason and heresy brought against her. Some said the King of Scots was haunted by her ghost. Marie became pregnant again, but even this joyful news gave the King no pleasure.

Margaret was nearing her fifty-third birthday. She had been staying with the King and Queen in Edinburgh, but had left in the autumn for her Castle of Methven. There she had a stroke. It was not at first realized that her illness was serious. The doctors diagnosed it as a palsy, which in the sixteenth century covered anything from stiffness after a hunting accident to total paralysis. When she realized she was dying, Margaret sent for James, who was at Falkland Palace. Her last words were to her confessors and brought tears to the eyes of all who heard them. 'I desire you,' she said to the friars, 'to beseech the King to be gracious to the Earl of Angus. I beg God for mercy that I have so offended the Earl.' She asked that her daughter, Lady Margaret Douglas, should have her jewels.[14]

Margaret died on Tuesday 18 October, before James reached Methven Castle. Despite his mood of penitential sorrow, the King ignored his mother's last requests. She had died almost a pauper, leaving only 2,500 marks. Her jewels reverted to the crown, but she was given an elaborate funeral and was laid to rest in the vault of the Carthusian Abbey at Perth, among the Kings of Scotland.

Although James V strove to keep his country Catholic, the

floodtide of the Reformation overwhelmed his pious intentions. Twenty years after Margaret's death a group of Calvinists desecrated the royal tombs. They burned Margaret's skeleton and scattered her ashes about the Abbey so that now only a blue slab marks the spot where she was buried. Neither she nor her son lived to see James's daughter Mary, born a week after the Battle of Solway Moss, when Henry VIII's forces once again routed the Scots armies. James survived the holocaust until the first week of December 1542. As he lay dying at Falkland Palace in a state of dreadful despair, a messenger came to tell him Queen Marie had given birth to a girl. Referring to Margery, the daughter of Robert the Bruce, who had married Walter the High Steward, founder of his ill-fated dynasty, James V is supposed to have said, 'It came with a lass, it will pass with a lass,' but the baby Princess who lay in her cradle at Linlithgow, and who was to be known to history as Mary Queen of Scots, was to bear another Stewart Prince, when she married her cousin Henry Stewart, Lord Darnley.

Epilogue

Henry VII's prophecy that, if his sons should die without heirs male, Margaret's descendants would inherit the crowns of both the island kingdoms came true in 1603, when Queen Elizabeth I signified on her deathbed that James VI of Scotland was her chosen heir. Over a century had elapsed since her grandfather's prediction. As the son of Margaret's grandchildren, Mary Stuart and Lord Darnley, James was doubly descended from Henry VII's eldest daughter.

Despite the early deaths of Prince Arthur and Prince Edmund, the male line seemed destined to succeed, when at Hampton Court Palace on 12 October 1537 Jane Seymour gave Henry VIII the son he so much desired. As Edward VI, this child reigned from 1547 until his death in 1553. Henry VIII's will directed that his own body should be buried beside Jane Seymour's in St George's Chapel, Windsor. He clearly saw his third Queen as his true wife, although he was to find great domestic happiness with his sixth wife, Katherine Parr. Henry's will declared the succession of the crown was to go 'to Prince Edward and the heirs of his body', and in default to any children the King might get by Katherine Parr. After that came Princess Mary and her heirs, or in default Princess Elizabeth. Neither Princess was to marry without the consent of the council. Magaret's descendants, apart from a vague clause about 'right heirs', which seemed too remote for anyone to take seriously, were passed over. If his daughter Elizabeth died childless, Henry directed that the crown of England should pass 'to the heirs of the body of Lady Frances, daughter of his late sister the French Queen' and after that to Lady Eleanor and her heirs.

In his own estimation Henry died a Catholic. His will shows he fully expected the Virgin Mary and all the saints to pray for him, but as a reformed Catholic he wanted no chantry chapels or Masses for the dead. Edward VI, aged nine when he succeeded his father, became a zealous Protestant. He tried to prevent his sister Mary from restoring the old religion by bequeathing the crown to his cousin Lady Jane Grey. The daughter of Frances Brandon and Henry Grey, Marquis of Dorset, 'the nine days Queen' was beheaded in 1553. All England rose to support Mary, the rightful heiress.

She reigned five and a half years with her consort Philip of Spain. Together they restored the Catholic religion. When Mary died without issue, Henry VIII's third child, Elizabeth, became Queen. Although her people, her peers and her parliaments urged her to marry, she died a spinster. Some say she feared losing her virginity, because she associated sexual consummation with her mother's death on the executioner's block. During her lifetime Elizabeth adamantly refused to name her successor, but she kept a wary eye on her cousins in whose veins there flowed the dangerous blood royal. At one point she imprisoned the heiress to the throne, Frances Brandon's daughter, Lady Katherine, in the Tower for marrying the Duke of Somerset's son, Lord Hertford without seeking royal permission. Like her grandmother, the Mary Tudor of our story, young Lady Hertford married for love and managed to get pregnant before completing the paperwork. Elizabeth had Mathew Parker, her Archbishop of Canterbury, declare the Hertfords' marriage null and void.

Margaret's granddaughter, Mary Stuart, also married for love. Elizabeth was outraged when the widowed Queen of Scots sought a dispensation to wed Darnley, whom she considered an English subject. As a child of ten Elizabeth had been present when his mother, Lady Margaret Douglas married the Earl of Lennox. Although they were cousins, the Pope allowed the match between Mary and Darnley. When their son, Margaret Tudor's great-grandchild inherited the crowns of England and Scotland, he took the title James the First and Sixth.

Notes

List of Abbreviations

Acts Parl Scot	*The Acts of the Parliaments of Scotland* (Edinburgh, 1814)
Acts Lords Scot	*Acts of the Lords of the Council in Public Affairs, 1501-44* (Edinburgh, 1932)
BL	British Library
Bodl	Bodleian Library, Oxford
Cal Docs Scot	*Calendar of Documents Relating to Scotland* (Edinburgh, 1881–88), ed J Bain
Cal Pat Rolls	*Calendar of Patent Rolls*
Cal Scot	*Calendar of State Papers Relating to Scotland* (London, 1858)
Cal Span	*Calendar of State Papers Spanish*
Cal Span Supp	*Supplement to the Calendar of State Papers Spanish*
Cal Ven	*Calendar of State Papers Venetian*
Cavendish	George Cavendish, *The Life and Death of Cardinal Wolsey* (Folio Society edn, London, 1962)
Chapman	Hester Chapman, *The Sisters of Henry VIII* (London, 1969)
CWE	*The Complete Works of Erasmus* (Toronto, 1974), trans R A B Mynors and D F S Thomson
DNB	*The Dictionary of National Biography*
Du Bellay	*Les Memoires de Martin et Guillaume du Bellay et les Memoires du Marechal de Fleuranges et le Journal de Louise de Savoye* (Paris, 1753) 7 vols
Exch Rolls	*Exchequer Rolls of Scotland, 1264–1600*
Green	M A E Green, *Lives of the Princesses of England* (London, 1849)
Gunn	S J Gunn, *Charles Brandon, Duke of Suffolk* (Oxford, 1988)
Hall	E Hall *The Union of the Two Noble and Illustre Famelies of York & Lancaster* (London, 1809) ed H Ellis
Hughes and Larkin	P L Hughes and J F Larkin, *Tudor Royal*

	Proclamations (New Haven and London, 1964–9)
Ives	E W Ives, *Anne Boleyn* (Oxford, 1986)
Jones and Underwood	M Jones and M G Underwood, *The King's Mother* (Cambridge, 1992)
L & P Hen VII	*Letters and Papers, Illustrative of the Reigns of Richard III and Henry VII* Rolls Series (1861–3)
L & P Hen VIII	*Letters and Papers, Foreign and Domestic of the Reign of Henry VIII 1509–47* (1862–1932), ed J S Brewer *et al*
Leland	John Leland, *De Rebus Britannicis Collectanea* (London, 1770), 2nd edn, ed T Hearne
Leslie	J Leslie, (Bishop of Ross) *The Historie of Scotland* (Edinburgh, 1830)
Loades	D Loades, *Mary Tudor* (Oxford, 1989)
McDougall	N McDougall, *James IV* (Edinburgh, 1989)
Mattingly	Garrett Mattingly, *Catherine of Aragon* (London, 1961)
Op Epist	*Opus Epistolarum Des. Erasmi Roterodami* (Oxford, 1906) ed P S Allen
Pitscottie	R Lindsay of Pitscottie, *History and Chronicles of Scotland* (Edinburgh, 1814)
PRO	Public Record Office
Richardson	W Richardson, *Mary Tudor: The White Queen* (London, 1970)
Scarisbrick	J J Scarisbrick, *Henry VIII* (London, 1968)
SHR	*Scottish Historical Review*
Strickland	Agnes Strickland, *Lives of the Queens of Scotland* (Edinburgh and London, 1852–6, 2nd edn)
STC	*Short Title Catalogue of Books Printed in English 1475–1640,* A W Pollard and G R Redgrave

Chapter 1: Dramatis Personae

1 *CWE*, vol 1, p 198.
2 Ibid, n 105. Mountjoy married the daughter of Sir William Say in 1497, the year in which he also fought against Perkin Warbeck. He was eighteen but had not finished his studies; she was probably considered too young to cohabit with him and so continued to live with her father in Bedfordshire until Mountjoy came into his inheritance. See also G E Cokayne, *The Complete Peerage*, vol 9 (London, 1910), p 338; *DNB*, vol 2, p 721; and F M Nichols, *The Hall at Lawford Hall* (London, 1891), pp 198–204.
3 *Cal Pat Rolls, Henry VII*, vol 2, p 192. Mountjoy, who had held the title since he was seven, came into his inheritance on 31 January 1500

(ibid, vol 1, p 198). His wardship was granted to his uncle, Sir James Blount, who sold it to Mountjoy's stepfather (Nichols, *The Hall at Lawford Hall*, pp 194–5), who left it in his will to Mountjoy's mother, Dame Laura. She remarried the powerful Earl of Ormond and was responsible for calling Mountjoy back from Paris.

4   *Op Epist,* vol 1, p xxviii. CWE refers to Mountjoy as Henry's 'tutor' but no formal appointment was made. Erasmus referred to Mountjoy as Prince Henry's *'socius studiorum'*, ie a friend and mentor rather than a paid schoolmaster.

5   Ibid, vol 1, p 193. Fausto Andrelini was poet laureate to Louis XII, King of France.

6   BL, MS Egerton 616, ff 14, 16.

7   Ibid, f 17.

8   *Op Epist,* vol 1, p 6. Erasmus's letter to Botzheim was written in 1523: *'Ubi ventum esset in aulam convenit tota pompa non solum domus illius verum etiam Montioiae.'*

9   Ibid. Erasmus made a mistake of one year in the children's ages. I have used the true ages. Prince Edmund died in 1501.

10 CWE, vol 1, p 195, which refers to the 1500 edition printed by Jo. Philippi. I had access only to Erasmus, *Adagiorum* (Paris, 1508), but clearly the work became an approved textbook of the times.

11 *Op Epist,* vol 1, p 6. In the letter to Botzheim, Erasmus congratulates himself on having written something light and easy for a boy of Henry's age (*'Id scriptum est simplicissimo'*). He discussed teaching theory many times over the years with Colet, who was the founder of St Paul's School.

12 CWE, vol 1, p 195.

13 Ibid, lines 17–22.

14 BL, MS Cotton Julius BXII, ff 88–103, printed in *L & P Hen VII*, Appendix A. Cf Julius BXII, ff 58–66, for Arthur's creation as Prince of Wales, which is reported in less detail.

15 *L & P Hen VII*, vol 1, Appendix A, p 389; and BL, MS Cotton Julius BXII, f 89.

16 *Cal Pat Rolls, Edward IV*, vol III, p 322. At the beginning of his reign Henry VII had granted the house and land at Coldharbour, which had previously been given in perpetuity to the Officers of Arms by Richard III, to his mother for life. She remained on good terms with the heralds. See also C L Kingsford, 'On Some London Houses of the Early Tudor Period', *Archaeologia*, vol LXXI, pp 17–54; and Jones and Underwood, pp 66–7.

17 *The English Works of John Fisher* (Early English Text Society, series no 27, 1876), p 293, 'Mornynge Remembrance at the moneth mynde of the noble Princess Margaret, Countess of Richmond and Derby' (hereafter cited as 'Month Mind'). She traced her ancestry back to thirty kings and queens and was proud of it.

18 *L & P Hen VII*, vol 1, p 390; and BL, MS Cotton Julius BXII, f 90: 'The

parlement chambre where were XX baynes and beddes which hadden sparvers', ie canopies over them.

19   *L & P Hen VII*, vol 1, p 391; and BL, MS Cotton Julius BXII, f 92.

20   *L & P Hen VII*, vol 1, p 392; and BL, MS Cotton Julius BXII, f 92.

21   *L & P Hen VII*, vol 1, p 394; and BL, MS Cotton Julius BXII, f 94.

22   Leland, vol IV, p 209.

23   I Arthurson, *The Perkin Warbeck Conspiracy* (London, 1994), p 56, n 14; and L Homme, *Marguerite d'York* (Brussels, 1959), p 415.

24   Hall, p 462.

25   Homme, *Marguerite d'York*, pp 268–9.

26   Ibid.

27   BL, MS Royal 2 AXVIII, f 29 (The Beaufort Hours).

28   Leland, vol IV, p 179. Leland describes them as 'Ordinances by Margaret, Countess of Richmond, as to what Preparation is to be made against the deliverance of a Queen, as also for the Christening of the Child of which she shall be delivered'. Hearne states he copied them from BL, MS Harley 6079. In 'Royal entry into the World'. *England in the Fifteenth Century* (*Proceedings of the Harlaxton Symposium*, 1986), p 299, n 8, Kay Staniland accuses Leland of 'a spurious attribution', since MS Harley 6079 makes no mention of Lady Margaret. Written in a sixteenth-century hand, this MS belonged to the herald-painter Henry Lilly, Rouge Rose (*sic*, f 1). It seems to be a copy of an older order of proceeding, probably dating back to the fifteenth century. There is no reason to suppose, however, that Lady Margaret did not have access to the older document. As Coldharbour, her London house, had previously been granted to the heralds by Richard III, she had close contact with the Officers at Arms and even allowed them to retain a room there. Ms Staniland merely throws doubt upon the idea that Lady Margaret drew up the ordinances in the form printed by Leland.

29   Leland, vol IV, p 181; and BL, MS Cotton Julius BXII, f 61v–63.

30   Leland, vol IV, p 207; and BL, MS Cotton Julius BXII, v 23v.

31   Richardson, p 3.

32   *Cal Span*, vol I, 198, De Puebla to Ferdinand and Isabella, 14 June.

33   Ibid, 210, De Ayala to Ferdinand and Isabella, p 170.

34   Ibid, p 176.

35   Ibid.

36   BL, MS Royal 2 AXVIII, f 32v.

37   Leland, vol V, pp 353ff.

38   H M Colvin, *The History of the King's Works* (London, 1975), vol III, pt 1, p 34.

39   College of Arms MS, 1 M 13, f 47; Hall, p 493; and 'Month Mind', p 306.

40   College of Arms MS, 1 M 13, f 47v.

41   Leland, vol V, p 355.

42   Ibid, p 358. Buckingham was related to Lady Margaret through her

second marriage. He had only recently come into his inheritance and was revelling in showing off his wealth and status (Jones and Underwood, p 67).

43 Gunn, p 4.
44 Leland, vol V, p 361.
45 Ibid, p 372.
46 College of Arms MS, 1 M 13, f 66r & v.
47 *The Register of the Great Seal of Scotland*, ed J Balfour Paul (Edinburgh, 1882), 2602, p 553.
48 Leland, vol IV, pp 262ff. The Fyancells of Margaret, eldest daughter of King Henry VII to James, King of Scotland by John Yonge, Somerset Herald.

Chapter 2: The Thistle and the Rose

1   Hall, p 494.
2   H M Colvin, *The History of the King's Works* (London, 1975), vol IV, pt 2, p 25.
3   Leland, vol IV, p 263.
4   Ibid, p 263.
5   Green, vol IV, p 61, n 2.
6   Colvin, *The History of the King's Works*, vol IV, pt 2, p 223.
7   Leslie, p 208.
8   Leland, vol V, p 373.
9   PRO, LC2/1, f 21.
10 Leland, vol V, p 373.
11 C A J Skeel, *The Council of the Marches of Wales* London, 1904), p 202.
12 Leland, vol V, p 381.
13 PRO, LC2/1, ff 10v–35.
14 *Cal Span*, vol I, p 319.
15 N H Nicholas, *Privy Purse Expenses of Elizabeth of York* (London, 1830), p 103.
16 Ibid, p 22.
17 Ibid, p 5. The Queen paid off £32 6s in April, a further £10 in June (p 19) and £42 6s on 4 November (p 55), but continued to buy other items from Bryan, paying up immediately. She realized the advantages of ongoing patronage.
18 Ibid, pp 33, 34.
19 Ibid, pp 36, 37, 56.
20 Hall, p 497.
21 Nicholas, *Privy Purse Expenses of Elizabeth of York*, p 86.
22 Ibid, p 89.
23 BL, MS Royal 2 AXVIII, f 31.
24 C L Kingsford, 'On Some London Houses of the Early Tudor Period', *Archaeologia*, vol LXXI, no 1, p 47.

25   Jones and Underwood, p 84.
26   Leland, vol IV, p 265.
27   Ibid, pp 267, 278.
28   Ibid, p 268.
29   Pamela Tudor-Craig, 'Margaret Queen of Scotland in Grantham',
     Proceedings of the Harlaxton Symposium, 1993 (Stamford, 1995),
     pp 276–9. The author argues convincingly that Margaret *needed* this
     period of withdrawal to rest and compose herself after the excite-
     ments of Collyweston and the trauma of bidding farewell to her
     father and grandmother. Recent restoration has revealed that the
     chapel of Mr Hall's house had been decorated with the thistle and
     rose emblems in honour of her visit.
30   Leland, vol IV, p 271.
31   Ibid, p 273.
32   Ibid, p 276.
33   Ibid, p 281.
34   Ibid, p 283.
35   Ibid, p 286.
36   Ibid, p 287.
37   Ibid, p 290.
38   'The Thrissil and the Rois', *The Poems of William Dunbar*, ed W
     Mackay-Mackenzie (London, 1932), p 111, lines 141–4.
39   Leland, vol IV, p 294.
40   Ibid, p 296. The following morning, it being the custom of the Kings
     of Scotland to present their brides with a gift the morning after
     deflowering them, James gave Margaret Kilmarnock (*Acts Parl Scot*,
     vol 2, p 239).
41   BL, MS Cotton Vespasian FXIII, f 134.
42   *Original Letters Illustrative of English History*, ed H Ellis (London,
     1824), vol 1, pp 41, 42.
43   Green, vol IV, p 100, suggests she was jealous of Surrey's friendship
     with the King, while Chapman, p 43, calls it a 'staggering dismissal
     of everything that had been done for her'. Although both these writ-
     ers quote BL, MS Cotton Vespasian FXIII, f 61 (old foliation; now f
     134) as their source, neither appears to have consulted the original
     MS.
44   BL, MS Cotton Vespasian FXIII, f 134.

Chapter 3: Princess of Castile

1   Louis XII's claim rested on his grandfather's marriage to Valentina
     Visconti, whose family ruled Milan until 1450, when the condottiere
     Francesco Sforza captured the city. The people elected him Duke.
2   Lady Margaret was a patron of William Caxton and Wynkyn de
     Worde. Richard Pynson printed her 'Englyshing' of the French poem

'The Mirrour of Golde for the Synfulle Soule' in 1506. It was reprinted four times before the end of Henry VIII's reign.

3   *Cal Span*, vol I, p 156.
4   Ibid, 294, p 255.
5   S J Gunn, p 5.
6   F Bacon, *Historie of the Raigne of King Henry VII* (London, 1622), p 243. The book was 'full of notes and memorialls in his own hand'. Bacon believes a member of the Privy Chamber egged on the monkey to its act of destruction because the courtiers hated Henry's habit of 'spying' on them.
7   As Prince of Wales, Arthur's household expenses were £660 a year. Later Prince Henry's, as Duke of York, were £1,000 a year. Mary's £1,200 in 1504 kept pace with her brothers' expenditure of the 1490s.
8   *Cal Span*, vol I, 319, p 268.
9   Ibid, pp 191–2, 205.
10 Ibid, p 253.
11 This had been promised since 1488, when she was three years old (*Cal Span*, vol I, pp 13, 263). Arthur made the endowment at Westminster on 20 November 1501, six days after the wedding, and Henry ratified it.
12 Ibid, 321, p 268.
13 *Cal Span Supp Vols I and II*, pp 1–12, holograph letter from Don Pedro de Ayala to Queen Isabella.
14 *Cal Span*, vol I, pp 278–9.
15 N H Nicholas, *Privy Purse Expenses of Elizabeth of York* (London, 1830), p 12.
16 *Cal Span*, vol I, p 271.
17 *Cal Span Supp Vols I and II*, p 10.
18 *Cal Span*, vol I, 313, p 265.
19 Hall, p 494.
20 Scarisbrick, p 189.
21 Ibid, p188.
22 Ibid, pp 186–9.
23 *Cal Span*, vol I, p 265.
24 Mattingly suggests that Isabella regarded such a match as unprofitable for Spain (see *Catherine of Aragon*, p 53: 'it was simply that the bargain was not good enough …'), but there was also a text in Leviticus forbidding marriage between father-in-law and daughter-in-law. Isabella described such a marriage to Dr De Puebla as 'a very evil thing, one never before seen and the mere mention of which offends the ears' (*Cal Span*, vol I, p 295).
25 *Cal Span Supp Vols I and II*, introduction, p xxxiv, letter of Almazam to Cardinal Cisneros, dated 7 June 1506 (in the archives at Simancas).
26 Mattingly, p 57.
27 *Memorials of King Henry VII*, ed J Gairdner (London, 1858), pp 288–9.
28 Jones and Underwood, p 79.

29 *Memorials of King Henry VII*, p 303.
30 *Cal Span*, vol I, pp 358–9.
31 *The Solempnities & Triumphies doon & made at the Spouselles and Mariage of the Kynges doughter, the Ladye Marye to the Prince of Castile, Archduke of Austrige* (London, 1509). See Camden Society reprint (*Camden Miscellany*, vol 9), p 4, n (a).
32 *STC*, 4659: *Petrus Carmelianus Honorificia gesta solemnes cerimonii & triumphi habiti in suscipienda legatione pro sposalibus et matrimonio inter princepem Karolum & dominam Mariam* (London, 1508); *STC*, 17558: *The Solempnities & Triumphies doon & made at the Spouselles and Mariage of the Kynges doughter, the Ladye Marye to the Prince of Castile, Archduke of Austrige* (London, 1509).

Chapter 4: God us Defend

1 *Cal Docs Scot*, vol 4, 1735, 1737, ed Bain. When seisin of the castle was given to Margaret's attorney, Edward Benstead, who was also her treasurer.
2 *Accounts of the Lord High Treasurer* (series *Chronicles and Memorials of Scotland*) (Edinburgh, 1902), vol 2, pp 397-9.
3 Ibid, p 399.
4 Ibid, p 394.
5 Green, vol IV, p 119.
6 McDougall, pp 162-3.
7 Ibid, p 163; D Hume of Godscroft, *The History of the House of Douglas & Angus* (Edinburgh, 1644), p 232; Strickland, vol 1, p 70.
8 *The Register of the Great Seal of Scotland*, ed J Balfour Paul (Edinburgh, 1882), 2585.
9 *Exch Rolls*, vol 13, pp 203, 463.
10 Green, vol IV, p 108.
11 Leslie, p 96.
12 *Accounts of the Lord High Treasurer*, vol 2, p 419.
13 *History of Galloway*, vol 1, p 422.
14 *History of Scotland*, vol 2, *Scotland, the Later Middle Ages*, R Nicholson (Edinburgh, 1974), pp 529–30; Leslie, p 57 and Pitscottie, p 208.
15 McDougall, p 196.
16 The original is now at Chatsworth in the collection of the Duke of Devonshire. For many years it was thought that the lavishly illustrated MS referred to as 'Margaret Tudor's Book of Hours', now in the collection of the Duke of Northumberland at Alnwick Castle, was the book given to Margaret by her father when she said goodbye to him at Collyweston. The mistake was a natural one, as Margaret stayed at Alnwick on her wedding journey and the Alnwick MS was purchased in Scotland during the eighteenth century. Recent research by Miss Janet Backhouse, a curator of

illuminated manuscripts at the British Library, has shown that the Alnwick MS belonged not to Margaret Tudor but to Lady Margaret Beaufort. Unfortunately, Patricia Buchanan, Professor Emeritus of History at Clemston University, South Carolina, used an illustration from the Alnwick MS before the new provenance was known, so that her *Margaret Tudor* (Edinburgh, 1985) shows the kneeling figure not of Queen Margaret but of her grandmother. The arms on the Alnwick MS are clearly those of Lady Margaret, and the Beaufort portcullises lavishly adorn the borders. Lady Margaret wears a coronal, to which she was entitled by virtue of her marriage to Henry VI's half-brother, and her gown is embroidered with royal insignia, which was obviously the source of the original confusions. Ms Backhouse's findings will be published in the forthcoming *Proceedings of the 1996 Harlaxton Symposium.*

17   The original is in the National Library of Austria, Vienna, but excellent facsimiles are kept by the British Library and the National Library of Scotland. My own observations are drawn from BL, MS Facs 581/8585.

18   *The Poems of William Dunbar*, ed W Mackay-Mackenzie (London, 1932), pp 66–7.

19   McDougall, pp 155–6.

20   *Exch Rolls*, vol 13, preface, pp liii–vii.

21   BL, MS Cotton Caligula BVIII, ff 150–54; printed *Letters of James IV*, Scottish History Society (3rd series), vol XLV, ed Robert Kerr Hannay, R L Mackie and Ann Spilman (Edinburgh, 1953), pp 108–9.

22   Ibid, f 150. This phrase has caused difficulties. Strickland, p 73, says James was busy with 'the very incomprehensible occupation of "scotting hewmyss"', and *Letters of James IV*, 'shooting howmys'. In *L & P Richard III and Henry VII*, preface, pp 61–2, Gairdner attributes the hand to Wolsey. A swift glance at other holograph material shows that Wolsey formed his 'g' and 'h' similarly; 'shooting guns' is the correct reading, but the mistakes give some indication of the speed at which the young diplomat scribbled his dispatches.

23   BL, MS Cotton Caligula BVIII, f 151v.

24   Ibid, f 152v.

25   *Exch Rolls*, vol 13, preface, p lv.

26   *Cal Span*, vol I, 604. Katherine wrote to Ferdinand saying that she would 'not believe he looks on her as his daughter unless he punishes the ambassador'. Mattingly, p 90, goes further: Fuensalida had simply written to Ferdinand suggesting that it would be more seemly for the Princess to have an older friar than the handsome 'Fray Diego' as her confessor. Don Gutierre considered it a scandal that he should come and go so familiarly. Mattingly says that she wrote to Ferdinand, 'Your ambassador here is a traitor. Recall him immediately and punish him as he deserves.'

Chapter 5: Ye Are to Fight a Mighty People

1 BL, MS Cotton Tiberius EVIII, f 10v. The original 'Devise' for Henry's coronation followed the order used for Richard III and Henry VII.
2 Jones and Underwood, p 236.
3 *The English Works of John Fisher* (Early English Text Society, s no 27, 1876), p 306.
4 BL, MS Cotton Tiberius EVIII, f 102.
5 *L & P Hen VIII*, vol 1, pt 1, p 38.
6 Hall, p 507.
7 BL, MS Tiberius EVIII, f 102.
8 Hall, p 507.
9 BL, MS Cotton Vespasian FIII, f 36.
10 *Letters of James IV*, Scottish History Society (3rd series), vol XLV, ed Robert Kerr Hannay, R L Mackie and Ann Spilman (Edinburgh, 1953), p 263.
11 Jones and Underwood, p 241.
12 *L & P Hen VIII*, vol 1, pt 1, p 5.
13 *Letters of James IV*, 429, p 236.
14 Ibid, 494, p 273, n 1, James to John of Denmark.
15 Ibid.
16 *Letters of James IV*, p 277; and BL, MS Cotton Caligula BIII, ff 28–30.
17 *Letters of James IV*, p 276, Louis XII to Councillors of Finance, Blois, 8 December 1512.
18 Hughes and Larkin,vol I, 65, p 94.
19 *Letters of James IV*, 506, p 281, James to John of Denmark, 12 January 1513.
20 Green, vol IV, pp 164–5.
21 *L & P Hen VIII*, vol 1, pt 1, 1735, p 791.
22 Ibid.
23 Green, vol IV, p 81.
24 *L & P Hen VIII*, vol 1, pt 1, 1735, p 791.
25 Ibid, p 794.
26 Ibid, 1775, p 810.
27 BL, MS Cotton Caligula BVI, f 67.
28 Green, vol IV, p 81.
29 Flodden Papers, Scottish History Society (3rd series), vol XX, ed Marguerite Wood (Edinburgh, 1933), p 79, instructions from Louis XII given at Blois to Master James Ogilvy. Louis considered that James had a historic claim to the English crown, just as Henry VIII felt that he had a claim to the Scottish and French titles. The wording is 'to invade in great force' so that he may 'more easily attain to the *recovery* of the crown of England'.
30 Hughes and Larkin, 73, p 107. As opposed to the more merciful eighteenth-century practice of 'hanging, drawing and quartering', in Tudor times the disembowelling was performed before the strangulation.

31 Ibid, pp 106–15.
32 Hall, pp 544–5.
33 Ibid, p 545.
34 Ibid.
35 Ibid, pp 545–7.
36 Chapman, p 70; also cited in Green, vol IV, who quotes William Drummond of Hawthornden, *A History of Scotland from the Year 1423 Until the Year 1542* (London, 1655).
37 *L & P Hen VIII*, vol 1, pt 2, 2283. The Bishop of Durham, writing to Wolsey on 20 September, 'would not have believed that their [ie the Scots'] beer was so good had it not been tasted and viewed by our folks to their great refreshing, who had nothing to drink but water for three days'. The health hazards to an army on the march from drinking water in sixteenth-century England were unspeakable.
38 Ibid. Ruthal's letter to Wolsey reports the Scots dead as 10,000. In Dacre's dispatch (ibid, p 1007) the figure swells to 11,000. Thomas Spinelly, writing from Lille to Cardinal Bainbridge on 20 September, estimated (ibid, 2286) that there were 12,000 Scots dead. Henry himself had the last word. The King wrote to Leo X numbering the Scots dead as 13,000.

Chapter 6: The Person of the King

1 Strickland, vol 1, pp 85–6.
2 *L & P Hen VIII*, vol 1, pt 2, 2283, p 1021.
3 *Exch Rolls*, vol 13, preface, pp 53–4.
4 Pitscottie, vol 1, pp 268–9.
5 *SHR*, vol V, 1908, p 449.
6 *Acts Lords Scot*, p 1.
7 Ibid, pp 1, 4.
8 Ibid, p 2.
9 *Accounts of the Lord High Treasurer* (Edinburgh, 1902), vol 4, pp 434, 424.
10 *Acts Lords Scot*, p 11.
11 Ibid, p 7.
12 BL, MS Cotton Caligula BVI, ff 37, 42; printed in *L & P Hen VIII*, vol 1, pt 2, Dacre's letters of 22 October and 13 November, 2386 and 2443.
13 *L & P Hen VIII*, vol 1, pt 2, 2299, letter of Peter Martyr to Lud. Furtado.
14 Ibid, 2268; and BL, MS Cotton Vespasian FIII, f 15.
15 Strickland, pp 97–8.
16 *L & P Hen VIII*, vol 1, pt 2, 2355, 2469.
17 *Acts Lords Scot*, p 2.
18 Ibid, p 3.
19 Ibid, p 5.
20 Ibid, p 17.

21 Ibid, p 7.
22 P J Murray, *Scottish Historical Society*, vol LXXIV, April 1995, pp 26–44.
23 R K Hannay, *Letters of James V* (Edinburgh, 1954), pp 1, 2.
24 *L & P Hen VIII*, vol 1, pt 2, 2443.
25 Ibid, 2461.
26 Ibid, 2323.
27 Ibid, 2445.
28 Ibid, 2302.
29 Ibid, 2355.
30 Ibid, 2465.
31 *Cal Ven*, vol II, 371.
32 *Acts Lords Scot*, p 13. Margaret did not attend the session in person but she sent a speech from Stirling, which was to be delivered by the treasurer.
33 BL, MS Cotton Caligula BIII, f 26v.
34 *L & P Hen VIII*, vol 1, pt 2, 3333. Katherine was pregnant again by the summer of 1514, but her child did not live. A pathetic entry in the State Papers is the warrant for 4 October to the Great Wardrobe to deliver a cradle covered with scarlet 'for the use of our nursery, God willing'.
35 Pitscottie, vol 2, p 208.
36 *Acts Lords Scot*, p 18.
37 Ibid, p 20.
38 Ibid.
39 McDougall, p 285.
40 Hannay, *Letters of James V*, p 12.
41 Ibid, pp 15, 18, 19.
42 Ibid, p 17.
43 Ibid, pp 15, 16, 17.
44 Strickland, p 106.

Chapter 7: A Nymph from Heaven

1   *L & P Hen VIII*, vol 1, pt 2, 2656.
2   *CWE*, vol 2, p 216.
3   *L & P Hen VIII*, vol 1, pt 2, 2656.
4   BL, MS Cotton Vitellius CXI, f152.
5   *L & P Hen VIII*, vol 1, pt 2, 2656, p 1160.
6   BL, MS Cotton Galba BIII, f 109.
7   Scarisbrick, p 40.
8   BL, MS Cotton Vitellius CXI, f 150.
9   Scarisbrick, p 54.
10 Ibid.
11 N J Williams, *The Cardinal and the Secretary* (London, 1975), p 146.
12 Cavendish, p 39.

13 Hall, p 568.
14 *CWE*, p 287.
15 Gunn, p 26.
16 Ibid, p 28.
17 *L & P Hen VIII*, vol 1, pt 2, 2760, 2701.
18 Gunn, p 28.
19 *L & P Hen VIII*, vol 1, pt 2, 2779.
20 Ibid, 2768.
21 Hall, p 568.
22 *L & P Hen VIII*, vol 1, pt 2, 3101; Richardson, p 78.
23 *L & P Hen VIII*, vol 1, pt 2, 3139.
24 *Cal Ven*, vol II, p 505.
25 Ibid, p 201.
26 Ibid, p 198.
27 Hall, p 569.
28 *Cal Ven*, vol II, p 200.
29 BL, MS Harleian, 3462, f 142.
30 Richardson, pp 79–80.
31 *Cal Ven*, vol II, 482, p 190.
32 *L & P Hen VIII*, vol 2, pt 1, 227.
33 Hall, p 569.
34 *L & P Hen VIII*, vol 1, pt 2, 3334.
35 Ibid, 3155, 3156.
36 *Cal Ven*, vol II, 500. Various attempts have been made to locate 'the
    Row'. Middle Row near Staple Inn, a series of houses shown on the
    Agas Map, seems most probable, being very near the present Hatton
    Garden, which is the centre of the London diamond market.
37 Ibid.
38 *L & P Hen VIII*, vol 1, pt 2, 3252.
39 Ibid, 3344.
40 BL, MS Cotton Vitellius CXI, ff 158–61.
41 *L & P Hen VIII*, vol 1, pt 2, 3262.
42 Ibid, 3272.
43 *Cal Ven*, vol II, 500.
44 PRO, LC/21, f 73.
45 *Cal Ven*, vol II, 500.
46 Ibid, p 196.
47 Hall, p 570.
48 Ibid.

Chapter 8: La Reine Blanche

1 *L & P Hen VIII*, vol 1, pt 2, 3332, 3333.
2 D M Mayer, *The Great Regent* (London, 1966), p 70; Du Bellay, vol VI,
   p 183.

3   *Cal Ven*, vol II, 505, p 202.
4   Ibid, 511, unsigned report sent to the Bishop of Asti.
5   Ibid, p 207.
6   Ibid.
7   Du Bellay, vol VII, p 184.
8   *Cal Ven*, vol II, p 207.
9   Du Bellay, vol VII, p 185.
10 Ibid, p 208.
11 Ives, p 33, n 25. Professor Ives argues that a payment for services to Mary Tudor between October and December 1514 was made to 'Marie Boulonne', not Anne. He deduces that Anne joined Mary's household in Paris, perhaps some time after the establishment lists were drawn up. The English lists, *L & P Hen VIII*, vol 1, pt 2, 3348, have 'M. Boleyne'. 'M' could stand equally for 'Mary' or 'Mistress'. Another list (BL, MS Cotton Vitellius CXI, f 155v, printed *L & P Hen VIII*, vol 1, pt 2, 3357) simply refers to 'Madamoyselle Boleyne', which could refer to Mary or to Anne. The list, signed by the King, is written in an endearing mixture of French and English.
12 H Paget, 'The Youth of Anne Boleyn', *Bulletin of the Institute of Historical Research*, vol 54, 1981, pp 163–4, printing of Cambridge, Corpus Christi Coll, MS 119, f 21.
13 *Cal Ven*, vol II, 511, p 208.
14 Ibid, 505, p 202.
15 Ibid, 511, p 209.
16 Ibid, p 210.
17 Ibid.
18 Du Bellay, vol VII, p 187.
19 *Cal Ven*, vol II, 511, p 211.
20 Mayer, *The Great Regent*, p 72.
21 *Cal Ven*, vol II, 511, p 211.
22 Du Bellay, vol VII, p 187.
23 Ibid.
24 *Cal Ven*, vol II, p 496, 507, 535.
25 BL, MS Cotton Vitellius CXI, f 155r & v; calendared in *L & P Hen VIII*, vol 1, pt 2, 3294, 3357. See also 3348, p 1409.
26 BL, MS Cotton Caligula DVI, f 257.
27 *Cal Ven*, vol II, p 211.
28 BL, MS Cotton Caligula DVI, f 146.
29 *L & P Hen VIII*, vol 1, pt 2, 3416.
30 Hall, p 571.
31 Gunn, p 32. Their disguise fooled no one, but was part of the romantic conventions of the era. Sir Henry Guildford followed with a detachment of Yeomen of the Guard.
32 *L & P Hen VIII*, vol 1, pt 2, 3376.
33 Ibid, 3387.
34 Ibid.

35 Ibid, 3331.
36 Ibid, 3336.
37 Hall, p 571.
38 Du Bellay, vol VI, p 184.
39 BL, MS Cotton Vespasian BII.
40 Hall, p 571.
41 BL, MS Cotton Vespasian BII, f 6.
42 Ibid, f 10. When the rose bud stopped moving, the maiden (an obvi-
    ous forerunner of the belle springing from the birthday cake) recited:
    Fleur odorant de saveur melliflue
    Rameau de paix ou toute grace afflue
    Rose vermeille en Cherico plantée
    Humble Marie dont tout bien sourt et flue
    En ce pays tu soies la bien venue.
43 Hall, p 573.
44 *L & P Hen VIII*, vol 1, pt 2, 3449.
45 Ibid, 3461; BL, MS Cotton Caligula DVI, f 196v.
46 *Cal Ven*, vol II, 553.
47 *L & P Hen VIII*, vol 2, pt 1, 15.
48 BL, MS Cotton Vespasian FXIII, f 281; *L & P Hen VIII*, vol 2, pt 1, 16.
49 *L & P Hen VIII*, vol 2, pt 1, 68. £1,470 was paid out for transportation
    from 30 September to 17 December 1514. This included a bill for
    'unshipping 232 of the Duke of Suffolk's horses'.
50 *L & P Hen VIII*, vol 2, pt 1, 133, 139, p 50.
51 BL, MS Cotton Caligula DVI, ff 163–265 (new foliation). Square
    brackets are used to supply words damaged in the Cotton fire and
    where I have modernized slightly for the convenience of the
    contemporary reader. Many of the items in BL, MS Cotton Caligula
    DVI are duplicated in the Public Record Office. Cotton, however,
    seems to include more 'holograph' material, ie the original drafts.
52 Richardson, pp 145–8, argues that there was no understanding
    between them. He defeats his own argument by mentioning that
    Henry made Brandon promise not to propose to her. He bases his
    information on the assumption that the Cotton MS is all undated,
    whereas much of the material cited is *clearly dated*, although the
    dates are not always included in the printed versions.
53 *L & P Hen VIII*, vol 2, pt 1, 224.
54 BL, MS Cotton Caligula DVI, ff 246–7.
55 *L & P Hen VIII*, vol 2, pt 1, 139, p 50.
56 Ibid, 80.
57 Ibid, 222.
58 Suffolk's account of the secret marriage, printed in *L & P Hen VIII*,
    vol 1, pt 2, 80, p 26. I am indebted to Dr Nigel Ramsey, former
    Curator of the Cotton Manuscripts, for pointing out that it was prob-
    ably *'per verba de praesenti'*.
59 Obviously a reference to Mary's 'dirty' behaviour in the sense of

    underhand or dishonest, not, as Richardson suggests (p 140), an allusion to her lack of personal hygiene.

60   *L & P Hen VIII*, vol 2, pt 1, 223.

61   Ibid, 224.

62   Ibid, 225.

63   Du Bellay, vol VI, p 185. Louise did not in this instance write, as Richardson asserts (p 173) that Suffolk was 'of low estate'.

64   *Cal Ven*, vol II, p 618.

65   Gunn, p 38.

66   *L & P Hen VIII*, vol 2, pt 1, 468.

67   Francis even offered to buy the piece back for 30,000 crowns.

Chapter 9: One of the Lowest-brought Ladies

1   'A Remembrance of any information by me, Margaret Queen of Scots to be recorded for my declaration to the Ambassador of Scotland': BL, MS Cotton Caligula BVI, f 117. This undated text is one of several statements of complaint made by Margaret for the benefit of Henry's lawyers. It has been dictated to a secretary, and in tone seems to predate a number of other statements she made. It is a brief two-page memorandum, less vehement than the formal accusations she made in March 1516: 'The great manifest and detestable injuries done and committed to me, Margaret Queen of Scots by John Duke of Albany.' My guess is that the 'Remembrance' was taken down at Morpeth, perhaps in December 1515, when Margaret's prevailing sentiment was relief that she was safe and alive. The language has great freshness and immediacy. The point Margaret wishes to make is that Lord Drummond was arrested purely for defending her honour.

2   *Acts Lords Scot*, p 20.

3   BL, MS Cotton Caligula BI, f 164; Strickland, vol 1, p 109.

4   Ibid, p 110.

5   Ibid, p 111.

6   *L & P Hen VIII*, vol 2, pt 1, 27, Adam Williamson to Gavin Douglas; ibid, 49, Margaret to Williamson, and 50, Sir James English to Williamson. English's letter mentions that the Bishop of Dunkeld is dead. Margaret later asked for this see for Gavin Douglas, as she had received no reply from the Pope to her letters recommending him to St Andrews.

7   *L & P Hen VIII*, vol 2, pt 1, 47. This phrase was a secret password known to Williamson, English, Dacre, Henry and Wolsey. It meant Margaret was in danger of being spied upon. She thus appeared to decline the escape project, but wanted Dacre to know she was ready to flee. So many letters were intercepted, opened and copied that it was difficult to know which reached whom.

8 Ibid, 62. Dacre had received her letter. This should mean he understood that she wished to escape but that it was too difficult for her
   to say so. He therefore wrote guardedly that he was pleased to hear
   she would 'consent to the instructions' which Sir James English
   would give her verbally.

9 Ibid, 1. Designs of Louis XII and Henry against Ferdinand of
   Aragon.

10 Ibid, 63.

11 Ibid, 65.

12 Ibid, 66. In an age when formal salaries were rare, it is sometimes
   difficult to establish who was in the pay of whom. It seems obvious
   that Gavin Douglas had paid Williamson a retainer to blacken
   Forman's reputation. Forman was also accused of bribing emissaries
   at Rome to run a smear campaign against Douglas.

13 Ibid, 67.

14 Ibid, 214.

15 Ibid, 296, p 94.

16 Ibid, 297.

17 BL, MS Cotton Caligula BVI, ff 136, 137v, 216v.

18 *L & P Hen VIII*, vol 2, pt 1, 705, Dacre to lords of the council, Carlisle,
   14 July: 'The Bishop of Moray has returned without having obtained
   the Archbishopric of St Andrews; he is in strict keeping at the Priory
   of Petween and not allowed to come to Court.'

19 BL, MS Cotton Caligula BVI, f 117v.

20 *L & P Hen VIII*, vol 2, pt 1, 779, pp 205–6.

21 Margaret's ancestress Joan Beaufort had been married to James I of
   Scotland. Chester Herald assures me that although the portcullis is
   associated nowadays (by purists) with the Beaufort arms, it was in
   general use during Margaret's lifetime as a device of the Tudors.

22 *L & P Hen VIII*, vol 2, pt 1, 850, p 232.

23 Ibid, 783.

24 Ibid, 788; BL, MS Cotton Caligula BII, f 369.

25 BL, MS Cotton Caligula BVI, f 87.

26 BL, MS Cotton Caligula BVI, f 224. This recollection is from 'The
   great manifest and detestable injuries done to me Margaret etc'
   (hereafter cited 'Injuries'). See note 1.

27 Ibid, f 22.

28 Ibid, f 91.

29 *L & P Hen VIII*, vol 2, pt 1, 840.

30 BL, MS Cotton Caligula BVI, f 196. Lord Home obviously wrote in
   great haste, for the manuscript is full of ink blots.

31 *L & P Hen VIII*, vol 2, pt 1, 850, p 232.

32 Ibid.

33 Ibid.

34 *L & P Hen VIII*, vol 2, pt 1, 861. Albany's men had taken Blackadder,
   but Home's brother William recovered it on 29 August.

35   Ibid, 819, 885, 913. Villbresme had been carrying a letter from
      Albany to Mary, who had written to him to intercede for her sister,
      but he was clearly a man of divided loyalties.
36   Ibid, 929.
37   Ibid, 1106.
38   Ibid, 1044, p 278.
39   Ibid.
40   Ibid, 1350, p 365.
41   Ibid, 1113, p 295.
42   Ibid, 1350, p 365.
43   Ibid, pp 365–6.

Chapter 10: Done Like a Scot

1   *L & P Hen VIII*, vol 2, pt 1, 1387.
2   Strickland, vol 1, p 129.
3   BL, MS Cotton Caligula BII, f 225v.
4   Ibid.
5   Ibid, f 227r & v.
6   *L & P Hen VIII*, vol 2, pt 1, 948.
7   Ibid.
8   Ibid, 1495.
9   Ibid, 1477.
10   Ibid, 1598, p 433.
11   BL, MS Cotton Caligula BVI, ff 110v–11.
12   Ibid. The printed version *L & P Hen VIII*, vol 2, pt 1, 1671, quotes the
      manuscript accurately. Margaret has 'of late sometimes written to
      the Duke of Albany, hoping to have part of her pleasure' [ie what she
      requests]. Dacre and Magnus state clearly that they have moderated
      her letters in such a way *'as the Duke would not consent to prevent any
      renewal of friendship between them'*. The double negative seems to
      have been misunderstood by a number of writers. Strickland (vol 1,
      p 130) paraphrases wildly: 'We have taken care that her letters to the
      Scottish Regent be so worded that no good understanding shall
      ensue between them.' Patricia Buchanan (*Margaret Tudor*, p 125) goes
      further: 'Lord Dacre doctored her letter so as to render it less appeal-
      ing to its recipient'. In fact Dacre and Magnus did exactly the oppo-
      site, they toned down Margaret's letters to prevent outright hostili-
      ties.
13   *L & P Hen VIII*, vol 2, pt 1, 1557.
14   Ibid, 1759.
15   Tytler, vol 4, p 112; Strickland, vol 1, p 130.
16   *L & P Hen VIII*, vol 2, pt 1, 1759.
17   Hall, p 584.
18   *L & P Hen VIII*, vol 2, pt 1, 1106.
19   Ibid, 1759.

20   BL, MS Cotton Caligula BI, f 220.
21   *L & P Hen VIII*, vol 2, pt 1, 1861.
22   Ibid, 1605, p 446.
23   Hall, p 584.
24   Ibid.
25   *L & P Hen VIII*, vol 2, pt 1, 1845.
26   Hall, p 585.
27   *L & P Hen VIII*, vol 2, pt 1, 2398.
28   Ibid, 2253.
29   Ibid, 2255.
30   Ibid.
31   BL, MS Cotton Caligula BII, f 283.
32   Hall, p 586.
33   Ibid.
34   *L & P Hen VIII*, vol 2, pt 2, 3204.
35   Ibid, 3259.
36   Hall, p 591.
37   *L & P Hen VIII*, vol 2, pt 2, 3712, 3713.
38   Ibid, 4541.
39   BL, MS Cotton Caligula BI, f 275; *L & P Hen VIII*, vol 3, pt 1, 1024.

Chapter 11: The Divine Ordinance of Inseparable Matrimony

1   Patricia Buchanan, *Margaret Tudor* (Edinburgh, 1985), p 148.
2   *L & P Hen VIII*, vol 2, pt 2, 4064, 4217.
3   Ibid, vol 3, pt 1, 166, 373.
4   Scarisbrick, p 147.
5   *L & P Hen VIII*, vol 3, pt 1, 166.
6   C Bingham, *James V* (London, 1971), p 43, n 7.
7   *L & P Hen VIII*, vol 2, pt 2, 4479.
8   Ibid, 4481.
9   Ibid, p 1377.
10   Cavendish, p 100.
11   Ibid, p 103.
12   *L & P Hen VIII*, vol 2, pt 2, 4483.
13   Scarisbrick, pp 71–2; G Mattingly, 'An Early Non-Aggression Pact', *Journal of Modern History* (1938), vol 10, p 8 ff.
14   Du Bellay, vol VI, p 132.
15   Ibid, vol VII, p 69.
16   BL, MS Cotton Augustus III, ff 11, 18, 19. Close study of F 18, the tent designed for Henry, reveals that it is decorated with two mottoes, 'Dieu et mon Droit' and 'Semper vivat in aeterno'. A crown surmounts one of the flagpoles. The royal beasts include the Beaufort yales, not antelopes as has sometimes been suggested, for the beasts have serrated horns, pointing in different directions. Medieval bestiaries

mostly attest that the yale's horns *swivelled* in their sockets. Lady Margaret was very proud of the yale badge. When an uninformed craftsman put an antelope into a pane of armorial glass at Collyweston, it was indignantly changed to a yale (Jones and Underwood, p 84).

17   *Cal Ven*, vol III, 88.
18   Hall, pp 611–20.
19   Ibid, p 604; Scarisbrick, p 76.
20   Hall, p 611, says the 'cellars' from which the fountain was replenished were within the rampart surrounding the English camp, 'well railed and barred'.
21   Ibid, p 610.
22   Du Bellay, vol VII, p 70.
23   *L & P Hen VIII*, vol 3, pt 1, 870, p 312.
24   Gunn, p 68; *L & P Hen VIII*, vol 3, pt 1, p 311.
25   *Cal Ven*, vol III, 84.
26   Ibid, p 67.
27   *L & P Hen VIII*, vol 3, pt 1, 869, p 305.
28   Ibid, 919, p 337.
29   Du Bellay, vol VI, p 69.
30   Hall, p 620.
31   Scarisbrick, p 80.
32   BL, MS Cotton Caligula BVI, f 225v.
33   Ibid, f 226v.
34   Ibid, f 270.
35   *L & P Hen VIII*, vol 3, pt 2, 1851, 1853.
36   Ibid, 1898.
37   M St Claire Byrne, *The Letters of King Henry VIII* (London, 1936), p 265.
38   *L & P Hen VIII*, vol 3, pt 2, 1897, p 810.
39   Ibid, 1898.
40   BL, MS Cotton Caligula BVI, f 243v.
41   *L & P Hen VIII*, vol 3, pt 2, 1950.
42   Ibid, 2038, p 875.
43   Ibid, 3313.
44   BL, MS Add. 24, 965, no 6, f 42.
45   *L & P Hen VIII*, vol 2, pt 2, 4217, p 1307; ibid, vol 3, pt 2, 3365. Surrey wishes Albany would come to Wark 'to try its strength', he had 'so trimmed it with ordnance'.
46   *L & P Hen VIII*, vol 3, pt 2, 3368.

Chapter 12: A Shame and Disgrace to All Her Family

1   *L & P Hen VIII*, vol 4, pt 1, 473.
2   Ibid, 382.

3 Ibid, 406.
4 Ibid, 346.
5 Ibid, 499.
6 Ibid, 491, 492.
7 Ibid, 694.
8 Ibid, 674.
9 BL, MS Cotton Caligula BVI, f 424.
10 *L & P Hen VIII*, vol 4, pt 1, 656.
11 BL, MS Cotton Caligula BVI, f 384.
12 *L & P Hen VIII*, vol 4, pt 1, 668.
13 Ibid, 707.
14 Ibid, 733.
15 BL, MS Cotton Caligula BVI, f 439. Angus couched his letter in courteous terms. He had acquired a good deal of sophistication at the French court and it is not surprising that Henry VIII trusted him. He knew well how to create an impression of dignity, civility and probity. The Queen knew otherwise. Magnus and his fellow envoy, Roger Radcliff, were present when she received the letter: 'The Queen opened and saw the same and sent it back again, saying she would not read it' (BL, MS Cotton Caligula BVI, f 436v).
16 BL, MS Cotton Caligula BVI, f 372.
17 *Acts Parl Scot*, vol II, 285.
18 *L & P Hen VIII*, vol 4, pt 1, 813.
19 Ibid, 854, p 382.
20 Ibid, 865, 870.
21 Ibid, 1224.
22 Ibid, 1461.
23 Ibid, 1462.
24 Gunn, p 61.
25 Scarisbrick, p 136.
26 *L & P Hen VIII*, vol 4, pt 1, 1600, 1601, 1602, 1603.
27 Ibid, 1088.
28 Sir David Lindsay of the Mount, *Works* (Early English Text Society, London 1865–83), pp 303–17.
29 Leslie, p 140, has Edinburgh, but Margaret and Stewart had fled to Stirling at this point. The castle was to be used by the King, but Margaret snatched it back as part of her enfeoffment.
30 *Exch Rolls*, vol XV, preface, pp 51–5, includes discussion of the romantic story which evolved around James's 'midnight ride'.
31 Pitscottie, vol 1, p 330.
32 *L & P Hen VIII*, vol 4, pt 1, 1968.
33 Ibid, pt 2, 4134.
34 Strickland, vol 2, p 231; Archives de la Royaume de France, Lettre de M Turenne.
35 *L & P Hen VIII*, vol 4, pt 2, 4397.
36 Ibid, 4531.

37   Ibid, pt 3, 5894, 6586.
38   Loades, pp 39–40.
39   R Grafton, *Chronicle* (London, 1569), p 393.
40   Ives, pp 101–2.
41   Cavendish, pp 59–60.
42   Ibid, p 62.
43   *L & P Hen VIII*, vol 4, pt 2, 4246, 4257.
44   Ibid, 4403.
45   Ibid, 4409.
46   Ibid, 4410.
47   Ibid, 4649, p 2021.
48   Hall, p 753.

Chapter 13: Never Cardinal or Legate Did Good in England

1   Green, vol V, pp 136–7; from Oxford, BODL, MS Tanner 90, ff 29–33.
2   Chapman, pp 203–9, devotes a chapter to the assumption that husband and wife were divided on this issue. Gunn argues that they were not. See also Ives, pp 172–3.
3   BL, MS Harleian, f 10. The official dating of this letter is 1528; there seems no reason to doubt it. Green, p 122, places it in 1520, but without explanation.
4   Hall, p 756.
5   Mattingly, p 190.
6   *L & P Hen VIII*, vol 4, pt 2, 4875.
7   Ibid.
8   Ibid, p 2108.
9   Hall, p 755.
10   *L & P Hen VIII*, vol 4, pt 3, 5681, p 2510.
11   Ibid.
12   College of Arms MS, 1 M 13, f 67v.
13   Cavendish, p 113; Hall, p 756–7.
14   BL, MS Cotton Vitellius BXII, ff 2–164.
15   Cavendish, pp 114–15.
16   Ibid, p 116.
17   Ibid, p 118.
18   Ibid, p 121.
19   *L & P Hen VIII*, vol 4, pt 3, 5702.
20   Ibid, 5679.
21   Cavendish, pp 122–3.
22   William Shakespeare, *King Henry VIII*, Act IV, Sc 2.
23   Hall, p 256.
24   BL, MS Cotton Vitellius BXII, ff 53–5.
25   Ibid, f 85v.
26   Ibid, ff 123–4.

27 *L & P Hen VIII*, vol 4, 5732.
28 *STC*, nos 10902–8 (inc 10903a).
29 Cavendish, p 119.
30 Hall, p 758; cf Cavendish, p 125.
31 Ibid.
32 *L & P Hen VIII*, vol 4, pt 3, 5859.
33 Ibid, 5749.
34 Ives, pp 149–50, discusses fully the nature of Wolsey's reception at Grafton. Alward's account suggests that the King had long discussions with the Cardinal.
35 Cavendish, p 113.
36 Ibid, pp 129–31.
37 *L & P Hen VIII*, vol 4, pt 3, 6035.
38 Ibid, 6019.
39 Cavendish, p 136.
40 *L & P Hen VIII*, vol 4, pt 3, 6738.
41 Cavendish, p 136.
42 *L & P Hen VIII*, vol 4, pt 3, 6075.
43 Ibid, vol 5, 276.
44 Ibid, vol 4, pt 3, 6738.
45 Cavendish, p 219.
46 Gunn, pp 131–2.
47 Ibid, p 131.
48 *L & P Hen VIII*, vol 4, pt 3, 5859.
49 Gunn, pp 131–2.
50 *L & P Hen VIII*, vol 4, pt 3, 6738.
51 Ibid, vol 5, 361.
52 *Cal Ven*, vol IV, p 761.

Chapter 14: The King of England's Whore

1 *L & P Hen VIII*, vol 4, pt 3, 5806, Palsgrave to More.
2 Ibid, 5807, Palsgrave to Lady Tallboys.
3 Ibid, 5806 (i) Palsgrave to More.
4 Ibid, 5806 (ii) Palsgrave to Henry VIII.
5 Pitscottie, vol 1, p 125.
6 R K Hannay, *Letters of James V* (Edinburgh, 1954), p 125.
7 *Cal Ven*, vol IV, 682.
8 Ibid, p 287.
9 Hall, p 784.
10 Richardson, p 253.
11 *L & P Hen VIII*, vol 5, 696.
12 *Cal Scot*, p 29.
13 *L & P Hen VIII*, vol 4, pt 3, 5070.
14 Ibid, vol 5, 1254.

15   Hall, p 788.
16   Scarisbrick, pp 297–8, n 4.
17   Ibid, p 300.
18   Mattingly, p 249; *L & P Hen VIII*, vol 5, 541.
19   *L & P Hen VIII*, vol 5, 'Privy Purse Expenses of Henry VIII', pp 758-9.
20   Mattingly, p 253.
21   *L & P Hen VIII*, vol 5, 1377; Ives, p 198.
22   *L & P Hen VIII*, vol 5, 1485.
23   Ibid, 'Privy Purse Expenses of Henry VIII', p 760.
24   Ibid, p 761.
25   *Cal Ven*, vol IV, 832, p 362.
26   John Gough, *The Manner of the Triumph at Calais & Boulogne* (London, 1532), printed by Wynkyn de Worde *cum priviligio*, p 2.
27   Ibid, p 3.
28   Scarisbrick, p 308.
29   *L & P Hen VIII*, vol 5, 1485.
30   *Cal Span*, vol IV, 585, 592, 597–9.
31   Ives, p 204; *L & P Hen VIII*, vol 4, pt 1, 212.
32   Green, vol V, p 119; BL, MS Add. 6113, f116; BL, MS Egerton 985, f 62v.
33   *L & P Hen VIII*, vol 4, 584; BL, MS Cotton Vespasian CXIV, f 139r 8v.
34   *L & P Hen VIII*, vol 4, 797.
35   MS College of Arms I, 15, f 124v; Green, vol V, p 140.

Chapter 15: I Am Weary of Scotland

1   Mattingly, p 264.
2   Ives, pp 389–91.
3   *L & P Hen VIII*, vol 11, 113.
4   Ibid, vol 10, 860.
5   *Rivals in Power* (London, 1990), ed D Starkey, p 82.
6   *L & P Hen VIII*, vol 11, 147.
7   *Hamilton Papers*, vol 1, 35, p 40, letter from Henry VIII to Margaret of Scotland, 27 December 1536.
8   *L & P Hen VIII*, vol 10, 728.
9   Ibid, 863.
10   Pitscottie, vol 1, pp 362–3; C Bingham, *James V, King of Scots* (London, 1971), p 122.
11   Sir David Lindsay of the Mount, *Works*, vol 1, pp 106–12 'The Deploration of the Deith of Quene Magdalene'.
12   *L & P Hen VIII*, vol 16, 573.
13   *L & P Hen VIII*, vol 16, p 829.
14   Ibid, 1307.

Bibliography

Calendars and Record Sources

Accounts of the Lord High Treasurer of Scotland 1473–1566 ed Thomas Dickson and Sir James Balfour Paul (11 vols 1877–1916)

Acts of the Lords of the Council in Public Affairs 1501–1544 ed Robert Kerr Hannay (Edinburgh, 1932)

The Acts of the Parliaments of Scotland ed T Thompson and C Innes (Edinburgh, 1814)

Calendar of Documents Relating to Scotland ed J Bain (Edinburgh, 1881–88)

Calendar of Patent Rolls Henry VII (London, 1914–16)

Calendar of State Papers, Milan, (1385–1618) ed Hinds (London, 1912)

Calendar of State Papers Relating to Scotland ed M J Thorpe (London, 1858)

Calendar of State Papers, Spanish ed Bergenroth, Gayganos and Hume (1862–1954)

Supplement to the Calendar of State Papers, Spanish, Vols 1 & 2 ed G A Bergenroth

Calendar of State Papers, Venetian ed Rawdon Brown (London, 1864)

Exchequer Rolls of Scotland 1264–1600 ed J Stuart and G Burnett (23 vols, Edinburgh, 1878–1908)

Letters and Papers Illustrative of the Reigns of Richard III and Henry VII ed J Gairdner, Rolls Series (2 vols London, 1861–3)

Letters and Papers Foreign and Domestic of the Reign of Henry VIII, 1509–47 ed Brewer, Gairdner and Brodie (London, 1862–1910, 1920)

Memorials of King Henry VII ed J Gairdner, Rolls Series (London, 1858)

Short Title Catalogue of Books Printed in English 1475–1640 ed A W Pollard and G R Redgrave, revised Ferguson, Jackson and Pantzer (1976–86)

State Papers of Henry VIII (11 vols London, 1830–52)

Tudor Royal Proclamations vol 1, The Early Tudors (1485–1553) (New Haven and London, 1964) ed P Hughes and J F Larkin

Early Printed Works

André, Bernard, *Historia Regis Henrici Sept.* (Printed in *Memorials of King Henry VII* ed J Gairdner, Rolls Series, London 1858)

Bacon Francis, *Historie of the Raigne of King Henry VII* (London, 1622)

Beaufort, Lady Margaret, *The Mirror of Golde for the Synfulle Soule* (London, 1506)

Carmelianus, Petrus, *Honorificia gesta solemnes cerimonii & triumphi habiti in suscipienda legatione pro sposalibus et matrimonio inter principem Karolum & Dominam Mariam* (London, 1508) translated into English (London, 1509) printed in Camden Miscellany vol 9 ed J Gairdner

Cavendish, George, *The Life and Death of Cardinal Wolsey* (Folio Society edn, London, 1962)

Dunbar, William, *The Poems of William Dunbar* ed W Mackay Mackenzie (London, 1932)

Erasmus, Desiderius, *Adagiorum* (Basel, 1508) *Moriae Encomium Opus Epistolarum*, ed P S and H M Allen (Oxford, 1906–58) [For English translations see *Complete Works of Erasmus*, Toronto edn]

Fisher, John, *The English Works of John Fisher* Part 1, ed J E B Mayor (Early English Text Society, London, 1876)

Fleuranges, Robert de la Marck, *Histoire des Choses Memorables en France*, printed in *Les Mémoires de Martin et Guillaume du Bellay avec les Mémoires du Marechal de Fleuranges et le Journal de Louise de Savoye* (7 vols, Paris, 1753)

Gough, John, *The Manner of the Triumph at Calais & Boulogne* (London, 1532)

Hall, Edward, *The Union of the Two Noble and Illustre Famelies of York & Lancaster* ed H Ellis (London, 1809)

Leland, John, *De Rebus Britannicus Collectanea* Vols IV and V ed Thomas Hearne (London, 1774)

Leslie John, Bishop of Ross, *The Historie of Scotland 1437–1561* (Bannatyne Club, Edinburgh, 1830)

Lindsay, Sir David, *The Works of the Famous and Worthie Knight Sir David Lindsay of the Mount* (Edinburgh, 1568, printed Early English Text Society London, 1865–83)

Lindsay, Robert of Pitscottie, *Historie and Chronicles of Scotland 1437–1561* ed J G Mackay (3 vols, Scottish Text Society, 1899–1911)

Palsgrave, John, *L'Eclaircissement de la langue Francoyse* (London, 1530)

Vergil, Polydore, *Anglica Historia, AD 1485–1537* ed and trans Denys Hay (Camden Series LXXIV Royal Historical Society, London, 1950)

(In most cases the earliest possible printed text has been consulted, but owing to disruption caused by the moving of the British Library, some texts cited are unavailable in London at the time of going to press, so that reliable modern editions have been used for page references.)

Secondary Sources

Anglo, S, *Spectacle, Pageantry and Early Tudor Policy* (Oxford, 1969)

Arthurson, I, *The Perkin Warbeck Conspiracy* (London, 1994)

Baumgarten, Frederick, *Louis XII* (London, 1994)

Bernard, G, (ed) *The Tudor Nobility* (Manchester, 1992)

Bingham, C, *James V, King of Scots* (London, 1971)

Buchanan, G, *The History of Scotland* ed J Aikman (Glasgow, 1827)

Buchanan, P H, *Margaret Tudor, Queen of Scots* (Edinburgh, 1985)

Chapman, H, *The Sisters of Henry VIII* (London, 1969)

Colvin, H M, *The History of the King's Works* (London, 1963–82)

Dickinson, W C, *Scotland from the Earliest Times to 1693* (London, 1961)

Drummond, William of Hawthornden, *History of Scotland* (Edinburgh, 1745)

Ellis, Sir Henry, *Original Letters Illustrative of English History* (London, 1824)

Elton, G R, *England Under the Tudors* (London, 1962)

Erasmus, Desiderius, *The Complete Works of Erasmus* trans R A B Mynors and D F S Thomson (Toronto, 1974)

Fraser, Antonia, *The Six Wives of Henry VIII* (London, 1992)

Gunn, S J, *Charles Brandon* (Oxford, 1988)

Green, M A E, *Lives of the Princesses of England*, (London, 1849)

Hannay, R K, *The Letters of James IV*, ed R L Mackie and Anne Spilman (Edinburgh, 1953)

Hannay, R K, and Denys Hay, *The Letters of James V* (Edinburgh, 1954)

Homme, L, *Marguerite d'York* (Brussels, 1959)

Ives, E W, *Anne Boleyn* (Oxford, 1986)

Jones M and Underwood M G, *The King's Mother* (Cambridge, 1992)

Kipling, G, *The Receyt of the Ladie Kateryne* (Early English Text Society, Oxford, 1990)

Loades, D M, *Mary Tudor: A Life* (Oxford, 1989)

Mackie, J D, *A History of Scotland* ed Bruce Leman and Geoffrey Parker (London, 1978)

MacDougall, Norman, *James IV* (Edinburgh, 1989)

Mattingly, G, *Catherine of Aragon* (The Bedford Historical Series, London, 1961)

Mayer, Dorothy, *The Great Regent* (London, 1966)

Nicolas, N H, *Privy Purse Expenses of Elizabeth of York* (London, 1830)

Nicolas, N H, *Privy Purse Expenses of King Henry VIII from November 1529 to December 1532* (London, 1827)

Nichols, F M, *The Hall of Lawford Hall* (London, 1891)

Paul, J E, *Catherine of Aragon and her Friends* (London, 1966)

Pinkerton, J, *The History of Scotland, from the Accession of the House of Stewart to that of Mary* (London, 1797)

Reid, R R, *The King's Council in the North*, (London, 1921)

Richardson, W, *The White Queen* (London, 1970)

Ridley, Jasper, *The Statesman and the Fanatic: Thomas Wolsey and Thomas More* (London, 1982)

Ridley, Jasper, (ed) *Love Letters of Henry VIII* (London, 1988)

Scarisbrick, J, *Henry VIII* (London, 1968)

Skeel, C A J, *The Council of the Marches of Wales* (London, 1904)

Starkey, D, *The Reign of Henry VIII* (London, 1985)

Starkey, D, (ed) *Rivals in Power* (London, 1990)

Starkey, D, (ed) *Henry VIII: A European Court in England* (London, 1991)

Strickland, A, *Lives of the Queens of Scotland* (second edn, Edinburgh and London, 1852–6)

Tytler, P, *History of Scotland, 1249–1603* (Edinburgh, 1841–3)

Wagner, Sir Anthony, and Anglo, S, (ed), *The Great Tournament Roll of Westminster* (Oxford, 1968)

Wickham-Legg, L G, *English Coronation Records* (London, 1901)

Williams, Neville, *The Cardinal and the Secretary* (London, 1975)

Index